Darkness Visible

Princeton Theological Monograph Series
K. C. Hanson, Charles M. Collier, D. Christopher Spinks,
and Robin A. Parry, Series Editors

Recent volumes in the series:

Steven C. van den Heuvel
*Bonhoeffer's Christocentric Theology and Fundamental
Debates in Environmental Ethics*

Andrew R. Hay
God's Shining Forth: A Trinitarian Theology of Divine Light

Peter Schmiechen
*Gift and Promise:
An Evangelical Theology of the Lord's Supper*

Hank Voss
*The Priesthood of All Believers and the Missio Dei:
A Canonical, Catholic, and Contextual Perspective*

Alexandra S. Radcliff
*The Claim of Humanity in Christ: Salvation and
Sanctification in the Theology of T. F. and J. B. Torrance*

Yaroslav Viazovski
*Image and Hope:
John Calvin and Karl Barth on Body, Soul, and Life Everlasting*

Anna C. Miller
*Corinthian Democracy:
Democratic Discourse in 1 Corinthians*

Thomas Christian Currie
*The Only Sacrament Left to Us: The Threefold
Word of God in the Theology and Ecclesiology of Karl Barth*

Darkness Visible
*A Study of Isaiah 14:3–23
as Christian Scripture*

KARLO V. BORDJADZE

FOREWORD BY
R. W. L. MOBERLY

☙PICKWICK *Publications* • Eugene, Oregon

DARKNESS VISIBLE
A Study of Isaiah 14:3–23 as Christian Scripture

Princeton Theological Monograph Series 228

Copyright © 2017 Karlo V. Bordjadze. All rights reserved. Except for brief quotations in critical publications or reviews, no part of this book may be reproduced in any manner without prior written permission from the publisher. Write: Permissions, Wipf and Stock Publishers, 199 W. 8th Ave., Suite 3, Eugene, OR 97401.

Pickwick Publications
An Imprint of Wipf and Stock Publishers
199 W. 8th Ave., Suite 3
Eugene, OR 97401

www.wipfandstock.com

PAPERBACK ISBN: 978-1-5326-1657-0
HARDCOVER ISBN: 978-1-4982-4043-7
EBOOK ISBN: 978-1-4982-4042-0

Cataloguing-in-Publication data:

Names: Bordjadze, Karlo V. | Moberly, R. W. L., foreword

Title: Darkness visible : a study of Isaiah 14:3–23 as Christian Scripture / Karlo V. Bordjadze, with a foreword by R. W. L. Moberly.

Description: Eugene, OR: Pickwick Publications, 2017 | Princeton Theological Monograph Series 228 | Includes bibliographical references and index.

Identifiers: ISBN 978-1-5326-1657-0 (paperback) | ISBN 978-1-4982-4043-7 (hardcover) | ISBN 978-1-4982-4042-0 (ebook)

Subjects: LCSH: Bible. Isaiah—Criticism, interpretations, etc. | Bible—Criticism, interpretations, etc.

Classification: BS1515.52 B672 2017 (print) | BS1515.52 (ebook)

Manufactured in the U.S.A.   10/06/17

"For the mountains may depart and the hills be removed, but my steadfast love shall not depart from you." (Isaiah 54:10)

For Laura,
whose steadfast love exegetes the meaning of this verse better than volumes of learned monographs.

Contents

Foreword by R. W. L. Moberly | ix
Acknowledgments | xi
List of Abbreviations | xiii

1. Introduction | 1
2. Text, Translation, and Philological Issues in Isaiah 14:3–23 | 9
3. The Meaning of משל | 39
4. Imaginative World of Isaiah 14:3–23 | 50
5. Myth and History in Isaiah 14:3–23 | 96
6. Isaiah 14:12–15 in Reception History | 130
7. Reading Isaiah 14:3–23 as Christian Scripture Today | 187
8. Conclusion | 249

Bibliography | 253
Index | 271

Foreword

ONE OF THE MOST significant developments in biblical studies in recent years has been an approach to the biblical text that is variously called "theological interpretation", a "canonical approach", "reading as Scripture", or sometimes a "postliberal approach". Whatever the nomenclature, a consistent concern is to take with full seriousness the fact that what motivates many to undertake study of the Bible in the first place—the desire to know God and grow in faith—should not be marginalized but rather be integral to their study.

Of course, the majority of biblical interpreters over the last two hundred years have been professing Christians, who have been concerned that their scholarly work should indeed be of value for faith. So the contemporary concern is not new. Yet the ways in which philological and historical study of the Bible had to fight to break free from ecclesial constraints in the nineteenth century led to many Christian scholars feeling that they had to bracket out their faith in their study, lest their work be skewed; moreover, the results of honest philological and historical study should be intrinsically valuable for a Christian faith that takes the Bible seriously. The gains and insights from such work have been many. Nonetheless, better understandings of the biblical text in its ancient contexts tended to stop there and not to be combined with better understandings of how the text should be used well in relation to the concerns of faith of those who are not professional scholars in a very different world some two to three millennia later.

The difference in recent work becomes apparent with regard to the way in which biblical study is undertaken: what questions are asked, and what goals are sought? Insights from the literary and hermeneutical turns in wider scholarship within the humanities, together with renewed confidence and finesse in the nature of theology proper, have led to some major shifts. These can be well seen in Bordjadze's present study of Isaiah 14, a passage which is best known for its depiction of the fall from heaven of the "daystar, son of dawn". Philological and ancient historical work is in no way neglected. But such work is seen to play a preparatory role to the asking of other questions which take seriously the enduring significance and use of ancient Israelite writings as Christian Scripture. There is thus discussion of how major Christian figures (Origen in antiquity, Calvin in the Renaissance/Reformation) read the material, and well as of what significant contemporary Christian scholars (Brueggemann, Seitz) do with it. Finally, Bordjadze offers his own reading, which both explores resonances of Isaiah 14 within the biblical canon and also probes its enduring mythic resonance through engagement with the work of J. R. R. Tolkien.

Bordjadze's work is an excellent contribution to this newer mode of biblical scholarship, and well displays its value and fruitfulness for Christian understanding and appropriation of the Old Testament.

Walter Moberly,

Abbey House,
Palace Green,
Durham, UK.

Acknowledgements

THIS BOOK GREW OUT of my doctoral thesis, undertaken for the PhD degree at Durham University. The completion of my PhD has allowed me time and space not only for significant reworking of that manuscript but also for reflecting on my graduate studies as a whole.

Looking back, I have often felt like a little kid trying to reach for a door-lock that was far too high, requiring the assistance from someone more mature and capable for the task. Three men have been instrumental in unlocking academic doors for me. Dr. David Baker fueled my initial passion for the Hebrew language and the Old Testament. He gently nudged me to get involved with SBL, write academic book reviews, and consider further graduate work. For those nudges I will be forever grateful. Ashland seminary classrooms came alive with Dr. L. Daniel Hawk's teaching. It was in his class "Hebrew Exegesis of Isaiah" that I first fell in love with that book. Having already developed a good relationship with him, I asked Dr. Hawk if he would honestly tell me if I had what it took to pursue a PhD degree. One day at the end of the class he pulled me aside and simply said, "You have what it takes. Go for it." Those words have sustained me in those moments of doubt that every PhD student is bound to face along the way. The impact of Dr. Walter Moberly on me is simply hard to describe. He is a superb doctoral supervisor, esteemed role-model, and treasured friend. His brilliant mind, encyclopedic mastery of the Old Testament field, and careful reading have been an inspiration for me. It was a rare treasure to experience the Moberly hospitality during my trips to Durham University. My memory still savors lovely dinners with Dr. Moberly and his family: Jenny, John-Paul, and Rachel. Late evenings drilling Dr. Moberly with questions about the Old Testament and the Christian faith over a cup of strong Lapsang have felt like getting another PhD on the subject called "life." The Moberly imprint is all over my work as well as my soul.

Special thanks are due to Drew Sylvester who spent countless hours putting this book into a publishable shape. Without his superb editorial skills this project would have faced seemingly insurmountable technological barriers.

How I feel about my family has been aptly summed up in *The Fellowship of the Ring* as Frodo discovers that his friends know about the Ring. Responding to Frodo's admission that he cannot trust anyone, Merry exclaims,

> You can trust us to stick to you through thick and thin—to the bitter end. And you can trust us to keep any secret of yours—closer than you keep it yourself. But you cannot trust us to let you face trouble alone, and go off without a word. We are your friends, Frodo. Anyway, there it is. We know most of what Gandalf has told you. We know a good deal about the Ring. We are horribly afraid—but we are going with you, or following you like hounds.[1]

My family—Laura, Jacqueleen, Paul, Daniel, and Greta—are my faithful companions in life. Jacqueleen and Paul cheerfully contributed their superb knowledge of Tolkien's works which not only saved hours of research, but also made writing the last chapter so much more enjoyable. Daniel and Greta faithfully greeted their dad with their "morning hugs" and frequently pulled him out of his cave with their fun projects. My wife, Laura, is the true companion in life. She is my confidant knowing my doubts and weaknesses. She is the source of encouragement and strength. She is the most wonderful gift of God. Every sentence in this book is undergirded by her love that she so generously lavishes on me, our family, and everyone around. It is only fitting to dedicate this work to her in gratitude and love.

---

1. Tolkien, *The Fellowship of the Ring*, 104.

Abbreviations

AB	Anchor Bible
ABD	*Anchor Bible Dictionary.* Edited by D. N. Freedman. 6 vols. New York, 1992
AJSL	*American Journal of Semitic Languages and Literature*
ANET	*Ancient Near Eastern Texts.* Edited by J. B. Pritchard. 3rd ed. Princeton, 1969
ANF	*Ante-Nicene Fathers*
AOAT	Alter Orient und Altes Testament
ARAB	*Ancient Records of Assyria and Babylonia.* Daniel David Luckenbill. 2 vols. Chicago, 1926–27
BASOR	*Bulletin of the American Schools of Oriental Research*
BDAG	F. W. Danker, W. Bauer, W. F. Arndt, and F. W. Gingrich. *Greek-English Lexicon of the New Testament and Other Early Christian Literature.* 3rd ed. Chicago, 2000. CD-ROM; release 4 for Macintosh with Accordance Bible Software 2009.
BDB	F. Brown, S. R. Driver, and C. A. Briggs. *A Hebrew and English Lexicon of the Old Testament.* Oxford, 1907). Electronic adaptation @ 2001 Oak Tree Software Inc. Version 3.5.
BHS	*Biblica Hebraica Stuttgartensia.* Edited by K. Elliger and W. Rudolph. Stuttgart, 1990
BJRL	*Bulletin of the John Rylands University Library of Manchester*
BZAW	Beihefte zur Zeitschrift für die alttestamentliche Wissenschaft
CBQ	*Catholic Biblical Quarterly*
CCSL	Corpus Christianorum: Series latina. Turnhout, 1953–
CEB	Common English Bible
CEV	Contemporary English Version

COS	*The Context of Scripture.* Edited by W. W. Hallo. 3 vols. Leiden, 1997–
DDD	*Dictionary of Deities and Demons in the Bible.* Edited by K. van der Toorn, B. Becking, and P. W. van der Horst. 2nd ed. Leiden, 1999
DJG	*Dictionary of Jesus and the Gospels.* Edited by J. B. Green, S. McKnight, and I. H. Marshall. Downers Grove, 1992
ESV	English Standard Version
ExpT	*Expository Times*
FOTL	Forms of the Old Testament Literature
GKC	*Gesenius' Hebrew Grammar.* Edited by E. Kautzsch. Translated by A. E. Cowley. 2nd ed. Oxford, 1910
HALOT	L. Koehler, Walter Baumgartner, and J. J. Stamm. *The Hebrew and Aramaic Lexicon of the Old Testament.* Translated and edited under he supervision of M. E. J. Richardson. 5 vols. Leiden, 1994–2000. CD-ROM; release 4 for Macintosh with Accordance Bible Software 2009
HAR	*Hebrew Annual Review*
HBT	*Horizons in Biblical Theology*
HTR	*Harvard Theological Review*
HUCA	*Hebrew Union College Annual*
IBHS	B. K. Waltke and M. P. O'Connor, *Introduction to Biblical Hebrew Syntax.* Winona Lake, 1990.
ICC	International Critical Commentary Series
IVP	InterVarsity Press
JAAS	*Journal of Assyrian Academic Studies*
JAOS	*Journal of American Oriental Society*
JBL	*Journal of Biblical Literature*
JES	*Journal on Ecumenical Studies*
JETS	*Journal of Evangelical Theological Society*
JNES	*Journal of Near Eastern Studies*
JNSL	*Journal of Northwest Semitic Studies*
JQR	*Jewish Quarterly Review*
JR	*Journal of Religion*

JSOTSup	Journal for the Study of the Old Testament Supplement
JSNT	*Journal for the Study of the New Testament*
JSS	*Journal of Semitic Studies*
KJV	King James Version
LCL	Library of Christian Classics
LW	*Luther's Works*. St. Louis, 1955–86
LXX	The Septuagint
MMJ	*Metropolitan Museum Journal*
NAB	The New American Bible
NAC	The New American Commentary
NASB	New American Standard Bible
NCV	New Century Version
NET	New English Translation
NIB	New Interpreters Bible
NIBC	New International Bible Commentary
NICOT	New International Commentary on the Old Testament
NIGTC	The New International Greek Testament Commentary
NIV	New International Version
NJB	New Jerusalem Bible
NJPS	The New Jewish Publication Society Translation
NPNF1	*Nicene and Post-Nicene Fathers* (series 1)
NPNF2	*Nicene and Post-Nicene Fathers* (series 2)
NTS	New Testament Studies
OTL	Old Testament Library
OTS	*Old Testament Studies*
PEQ	*Palestine Exploration Quarterly*
PSB	*Princeton Seminary Bulletin*
RBL	*Review of Biblical Literature*
SBL	Society of Biblical Literature
SBLABS	Society of Biblical Studies Archaeology and Biblical Studies
SHBC	Smyth & Helwys Bible Commentary
SJT	*Scottish Journal of Theology*

STU	Schweizerische Theologische Umschau
TB	Tyndale Bulletin
THAT	E. Jenni with C. Westermann (eds.), Theologisches Handwörterbuch zum Alten Testament. 2 vols. Stuttgart, 1971–76
ThZ	Theologische Zeitschrift
TWOT	Theological Wordbook of Old Testament (Electronic adaptation @ 2001 Oak Tree Software Inc. Version 3.5)
TZ	Theologische Zeitschrift
UBL	Ugaritisch-biblische Literatur
UF	Ugarit-Forschungen
VT	Vetus Testamentum
WMANT	Wissenschaftliche Untersuchungen zum Neuen Testament
WBC	Word Biblical Commentary
ZAW	Zeitschrift für die alttestamentliche Wissenschaft
ZBK	Zürcher Bibelkommentare
ZNW	Zeitschrift für die neutestamentliche Wissenschaft

Introduction

THE TITLE OF THIS book echoes the imagery found in the opening scene of Milton's *Paradise Lost*. Milton's imagination paints a tragic picture of Tartarus as a place devoid of hope:

> The dismal situation waste and wild,
> A dungeon horrible, on all sides round
> As one great furnace flamed, yet from those flames
> No light, but rather darkness visible
> Served only to discover sights of woe,
> Regions of sorrow, doleful shades, where peace
> And rest can never dwell, hope never comes
> That comes to all; but torture without end
> Still urges, and a fiery deluge, fed
> With ever-burning sulphur unconsumed.
> Such place eternal justice had prepared
> For those rebellious, here their prison ordained
> In utter darkness, and their portion set
> As far removed from God and light of heaven
> And from the center thrice to the utmost pole.[1]

My appropriation of the phrase "darkness visible" from these memorable lines seeks both to provocatively highlight the importance of Isaiah 14 for shaping Milton's understanding of the downfall of Satan, which has in turn played a significant role in how this text has been read in the church, and to expand the function of this metaphor beyond a location reserved for the ancient foe to an actual portrayal of creaturely hubris. This move itself might not be too far from Milton's own conception. Later in the poem, Satan exclaims, "Which way I fly is Hell; myself am Hell." Markos has argued convincingly that "though Milton's Hell is a real place of torment, the greater

---

1. Milton, *Paradise Lost*, 64–65.

Hell is the one that dwells in the twisted and perverse soul of Satan and his minions."[2] Thus, in a way congruent with Milton, the depiction of the downfall of the King of Babylon in Isaiah 14 may perhaps be read as a process of making the darkness of human hubris visible.

The Aim of the Book

Historical-critical study of the Old Testament that has dominated the scholarly field for the last hundred and fifty years has come to a major crossroads. Some twenty years ago Rendtorff summed up the situation:

> I think that, in the terminology of Thomas Kuhn, Old Testament scholarship at present is "in crisis." The Wellhausen paradigm no longer functions as a commonly accepted presupposition for Old Testament exegesis. And at present, no other concept is visible that could replace such a widely accepted position.[3]

On the one hand, Rendtorff was prepared to lay aside the dominant Wellhausen paradigm as something that has served the scholarship well, but has run its course. He wrote, "I do not see any new arguments that could turn back the wheel."[4] On the other hand, Rendtorff argued that the field was ready for new and exciting alternatives,

> The paradigm is changing. I believe it has changed already. But the field is open. Many new and fruitful approaches are visible that will lead Old Testament scholarship into the twenty-first century. At the moment there is no new model that could be expected to achieve common acceptance as a paradigm, and there will probably be none in the near future. This will give considerable freedom to those who are looking for new approaches and who are ready to move ahead. They are many, and therefore there will be hope.[5]

What Rendtorff said then still appears fully applicable today. One of the out workings of this search for fresh directions in biblical hermeneutics has been a renewed interest in theological interpretation.[6] As salutary as this renewed interest has been, theological interpretation has come with its own

---

2. Markos, *Heaven and Hell*, 134.
3. Rendtorff, "The Paradigm is Changing," 44.
4. Ibid.
5. "Paradigm," 52–53.
6. For a succinct reflection on the renewal of theological interpretation see R. W. L. Moberly, "What Is Theological Interpretation of Scripture?" 161–78.

set of questions and concerns. Hence, at the onset of a book that seeks to read a particular biblical text in that frame of reference, it is important to highlight briefly some of the issues surrounding theological interpretation.

It may be helpful to begin with outlining the notion of theological interpretation itself. A good entry point would be Hays' discussion on this topic which raises the question of what makes interpretation *theological*. He argues that when thinking about theological interpretation, we are not dealing with yet another distinct exegetical method like textual criticism or redaction criticism, rather, "a complex practice, a way of approaching Scripture with eyes of faith and seeking to understand it within the community of faith."[7] Similarly, Fowl has suggested that the idea of theological interpretation in a Christian context is inextricably linked with the *telos* of the Christian life which he defines as, "ever deeper communion with God and each other."[8] With that broad account of the *telos* of Christian life in mind, Fowl argues that theological interpretation involves, "those habits, dispositions, and practices that Christians bring to their varied engagements with Scripture so they can interpret, debate, and embody their proper end in God."[9] Finally, Levering has traced the current resurgence of interest in theological interpretation back to patristic-medieval exegesis, which read the biblical texts with a focus on the divine Teacher. In his mind, theological interpretation is inherently participatory. It is primarily a, "participation in the Teacher, Jesus Christ, in and through participation in the realities that Christ, by the Holy Spirit, communicates to his Church."[10] Levering goes on to quote approvingly Alister McGrath who states, "Scripture is read in order to encounter Christ."[11] These three examples of contemporary Christian interpreters who attempt to explain what they have in mind when describing theological interpretation shows that the commonality among them lies not in hermeneutical methodologies or preferred exegetical tools but rather in the broad frame of reference which seeks to read the biblical texts as Christian scripture.

Despite this common stance of reading the biblical texts as Christian scripture, proponents of theological interpretation have exhibited such an eclectic array of hermeneutical methods that some were led to wonder "what exactly is meant by the catchall term *theological exegesis*."[12] Others

7. R. B. Hays, "Reading the Bible," 161.
8. Fowl, *Theological Interpretation*, 13.
9. Ibid., 14.
10. Levering, *Biblical Exegesis*, 63.
11. Ibid. See Alister McGrath, "Reclaiming Our Roots and Vision," 67.
12. R. B. Hays, "Reading the Bible," 161.

have expressed their doubts about the whole enterprise of theological interpretation. Barton has been the most prominent dissenting voice who has labeled the proponents of theological interpretation as "a powerful lobby" whose starting position in reading biblical texts is seeing them as "the church's Scripture, not a playground for scholars."[13] His main line of objection seems to be that the proponents of theological interpretation attempt to collapse the two-stage operation involved in reading any text, including the Bible. In Barton's mind, reading begins with grasping the meaning of the text. This is then followed by an evaluation of that meaning in relation to what one already knows and believes. Barton argues, "This operation cannot be collapsed into a single process, in which meaning is perceived and evaluated at one and the same time and by the same operation."[14] According to Barton, the proponents of theological interpretation seem to be guilty of such collapsing of the two stage operation.[15] Even some of the seasoned practitioners of theological interpretation have expressed their apprehensions. For example, Moberly has confessed having difficulty writing an article that would introduce the topic of theological interpretation to the readers of the *Journal of Theological Interpretation*: "I got bogged down in attempts to do justice to the burgeoning and multifarious literature on the subject of theological interpretation."[16]

All of this amounts to a growing sense that the case for or against the renewed interest in theological interpretation is far from being settled. As Moberly's confession has indicated, the topic of biblical hermeneutics in general and theological interpretation in particular has generated a sizable scholarly discussion in recent years. The proliferation of volumes engaging in theoretical discussions regarding theological interpretation makes it hard to either map the growing field adequately or to respond to all of the objections. Moberly has, however, urged for the need to "get on with it" and offer readings of particular texts as "no amount of impressive-sounding discussion of hermeneutical theory or of particular approaches will make much impact until people can see how the proposals work in practice and how they genuinely enable a better grasp of particular biblical texts."[17] In light of this challenge, this book aims to work with Isaiah 14:3–23 and suggest what might this "getting on" look like in terms of taking this text with the

---

13. Barton, *Biblical Criticism*, 141.

14. Ibid., 159.

15. See Moberly's pointed and insightful response to Barton's charges in R. W. L. Moberly, "Biblical Criticism and Religious Belief," 71–100.

16. "Theological Interpretation," 163.

17. Moberly, *Old Testament Theology*, 4.

hermeneutical awareness and full imaginative seriousness that is appropriate to reading it as Christian scripture today.

The choice of Isaiah 14:3–23 is precipitated by a rich complexity of textual, historical-critical, theological, and history of reception issues surrounding this text. To highlight probably the most famous issue at the onset of our discussion, this text has had a long, albeit checkered, history of being a key text used in the church since the time of Origen to point to the downfall of Satan. Yet this classic theological reading has disappeared from view in recent years, as can be seen from its absence from the four full-length monographs written on this text in the last fifty years.

Erlandsson's work examines Isaiah 13:2—14:23 "The Oracle against Babylon." This close linguistic and thematic investigation probed the issue of the coherence of this material, its redaction history and related issues of date and authorship.[18] Gosse's monograph seeks to build a case for the post-exilic date of Isaiah 13–14 on the linguistic as well as historical grounds.[19] Keown focuses on the history of interpretation of this text from the early period of the Septuagint, the Targum of Isaiah, and the Rabbinic literature, through the centuries of readings of this text in the church (the early church fathers, the post-Nicene, and Reformation periods) to modern day interpretation.[20] Finally, Shipp's dissertation seeks to understand Isaiah 14:4b–21 as "mythological" poem. In concert with recent discoveries of Babylonian and Assyrian mythological texts, Shipp reads it as "a ritual text (albeit a parody one) which is a reflection of ancient Near Eastern cosmology tied to a myth of the primordium."[21]

As it will become apparent in the course of the discussion these monographs have a different focus than my book. Having learned much from them, I will seek to integrate and dialogue with them, but my focus on reading this text as Christian scripture will of necessity take the readers of this book down paths not taken by these interpreters.

The Shape of the Book

The book opens with a discussion of the major textual-critical issues related to Isaiah 14:3–23. In some ways chapter 2 is akin to ground clearing, to alert attentive readers to basic philological issues at play in this text. Fitzmyer has pointed out that the historical-critical method "applies to the Bible all

18. Erlandsson, *Babylon*.
19. Gosse, *Isaïe 13,1—14,23*.
20. Keown, "History of Isaiah 14:12–15."
21. Shipp, *Dead Kings and Dirges*, 31.

the techniques of classic philology."[22] A careful attention to the philological issues in Isaiah 14 bears witness to the fact that theological interpretation should have firm philological foundations. At the very least, as will be clear below, the fruit of careful philological inquiry in chapter 2 can be seen in chapter 3 where it is important for my approach to the reading of this text. Having said that, I must admit that some readers who stand at a distance from specialist academic discussions might find this chapter somewhat tedious. I would suggest that readers who are mainly interested in the fruit rather than process of theological interpretation of this text should feel free to skip this chapter and proceed to chapter 3.

In chapter 3 I discuss the major literary marker found at the onset of this section of Isaiah 14. How one understands the meaning and the function of the enigmatic word משל will substantially shape how one reads this poem as a whole. My analysis seeks to capture the breadth and semantic range of meaning found in this Hebrew word. While the basic meaning of משל is a *proverb* or a *saying*, scholars since the time of Budde in late nineteenth century have suggested a meaning of a *taunt*. My analysis here suggests that the issue cannot be settled by considering the word on its own, but rather of necessity takes us into a discussion of the text's genre. Leaning on the works of Polk, Yee, and Alter, I argue that the משל of Isaiah 14 is a powerful paradigmatic poem that seeks to impact its reader by taking a genre of funeral dirge and transforming it into an evocative taunt.

Chapter 4 offers a reading of the משל of Isaiah 14:3–23, focusing on the imaginative world that the reader of the text is invited to enter into. Ricoeur has suggested that the world of the text is the world "proper to *this* unique text."[23] It is a *proposed world* that I as a reader "could inhabit and wherein . . . could project one of my ownmost possibilities."[24] In the Ricoeurean sense, this chapter provides a guided tour around the משל of Isaiah 14:3–23 shedding light on various distinctive features that are characteristic for this text. At the same time, in line with our discussion regarding the nature and function of the Hebrew concept of משל, I seek to probe the types of moves the text invites from the seriously engaged reader who imaginatively seeks to inhabit this proposed world.

Having introduced the readers to the world of the משל of Isaiah 14:3–23, I proceed in chapter 5 to address several key questions that emerge in the process of that introduction. If one were to imagine chapter 4 being a guided museum tour around the משל of Isaiah 14:3–23, then chapter 5

---

22. Fitzmyer, *Scripture, the Soul of Theology*, 19.
23. Ricoeur, *Hermeneutics*, 104.
24. Ibid.

would be analogous to mid- or post-tour questions that curators of museums always get asked by the captive audience. Perceptive readers of Isaiah 14 have perennially voiced questions regarding certain issues of myth and history. The space and scope of this book limit my discussion to three significant issues that are often brought up in scholarly discussion of the מָשָׁל of Isaiah 14:3-23, namely the mythological background and function of the הֵילֵל בֶּן-שָׁחַר image in Isaiah 14:12-15; the historical referent of the king of Babylon; and the significance of the placement of Isaiah 14:3-23 in the larger corpus of the Oracles Against the Nations in Isaiah 13-23. My discussion of these issues of myth and history intends to help read the מָשָׁל of Isaiah 14:3-23 with much more hermeneutical precision and imaginative seriousness.

In chapter 6, I explore the history of reception of this text in the church by close analysis of how this text was read by two key Christian interpreters in the third century (Origen) and sixteenth century (Calvin). The importance of giving some sense of how the material has been handled by leading theological interpreters throughout centuries lies in a desire to underscore the enduring qualities of reading biblical texts in the community of faith. This desire is at the heart of theological interpretation as it was succinctly captured more recently by the nine theses formulated by the participants in the Princeton Scripture Project, which state that "faithful interpretation of Scripture invites and presupposes participation in the community brought into being by God's redemptive action—the church."[25] Similarly, Childs has insisted that theological interpretation should be able to identify "distinctive characteristic features that constitute and identify a family resemblance" among the interpreters who read biblical texts in the context of the community of faith.[26] He has argued that this likeness "arises from the serious encounter with the selfsame God who shapes obedient response into Christian likeness."[27] Likeness does not preclude difference. Situating both Origen and Calvin in their appropriate ecclesial and existential contexts I suggest hearing both notes that are predictably dissimilar but also, as a possible surprise for some readers, significantly in concert with one another.

Finally, before offering some concluding thoughts in chapter 8, I pause and in chapter 7, turn my attention to reading the מָשָׁל of Isaiah 14:3-23 as Christian scripture today. My discussion begins by analyzing how two contemporary Christian theological interpreters, Brueggemann and Seitz, have interpreted this text. The impulse is analogous to the rationale for

25. Davis and Hays, *Reading Scripture*, 3.
26. Childs, *Isaiah as Christian Scripture*, 299.
27. Childs, "The Bible Amid Cultural Change," 210-11.

discussing Origen and Calvin in the previous chapter. These two prominent Old Testament scholars have positioned their work firmly in the context of the twenty-first-century church and their writings have had a significant impact on the way the Bible has been read in that context as Christian scripture. Hence engagement with their discussions of the משל of Isaiah 14:3–23 provides, in my mind, a suitable starting point in attempting to position my own reading of this text. While their readings provide ample theological substance, two perhaps surprising omissions are to be detected. Despite the rich, albeit checkered, history of reading this text in relation to the fall of Satan in the ancient church neither Brueggemann not Seitz choose to engage with it. Similarly, the readings of both of these interpreters lack any engagement with the way this text has been used in the New Testament. At the very least, this indicates that theological interpretation is not practiced in any one agreed way and makes space for further exploration for what it might look like to read this text as Christian scripture today.

The aim of my own reading of the משל of Isaiah 14 that follows the discussion of Brueggemann and Seitz is to complement their work and to understand and appropriate the משל of Isaiah 14 in a perhaps more explicitly Christian framework of understanding God in light of the revelation of Jesus Christ.

In regards to the time-honored way of reading the משל of Isaiah 14 as referring to the downfall of Satan, my discussion turns to Tolkien's depiction of evil in his memorable characters of Morgoth and Sauron. Tolkien's imaginative portrayal of creaturely hubris provides an evocative way of resonating with the ancient reading of the text in relation to Satan, where symbolism and picture is often a better way of trying to get some purchase on intractable issues such as the nature of evil and resistance to the will of God.

2

Text, Translation, and Philological Issues in Isaiah 14:3–23

THIS CHAPTER WILL FOCUS on the major textual critical issues surrounding Isaiah 14:3-23. Before making an attempt to provide a reading of this text, I seek to highlight significant textual variants, philological peculiarities, and differences in ancient and modern translations. Though laying out the philological foundations of specific biblical text is significant for any serious academic study, those interested in the fruit of theological reading of Isaiah 14:3-23 could proceed directly to chapter 3.

While working from the Hebrew text in *Biblia Hebraica Stuttgartensia*, I will refer to the text of NRSV for citations. All of the pertinent textual issues to be discussed will be underlined in the NRSV text below. Where deemed significant, the following eleven English translations will be referred to as a way of displaying various linguistic and interpretive moves made by modern translators: CEB, CEV, ESV, KJV, NAB, NASB, NCV, NET, NIV, NJB, NJPS. The choice of these translations is not arbitrary, but rather seeks to represent a wide spectrum of modern readers of this text.

Text[1]

NRSV	BHS
3 When the LORD has given you rest from your pain and turmoil and the hard service with which you were made to serve,	וְהָיָה בְּיוֹם הָנִיחַ יְהוָה לְךָ מֵעָצְבְּךָ וּמֵרָגְזֶךָ וּמִן־הָעֲבֹדָה הַקָּשָׁה אֲשֶׁר עֻבַּד־בָּךְ׃

4 you will take up this <u>taunt</u> against the king of Babylon:
   How the oppressor has ceased!
   How his <u>insolence</u> has
     ceased!
	וְנָשָׂאתָ הַמָּשָׁל הַזֶּה עַל־מֶלֶךְ בָּבֶל וְאָמָרְתָּ אֵיךְ שָׁבַת נֹגֵשׂ שָׁבְתָה מַדְהֵבָה׃

---

1. Words underlined in the NRSV text highlight the key issues for discussions.

NRSV	BHS
5 The <u>LORD</u> has broken the staff of the wicked, 　the scepter of rulers,	שָׁבַר יְהוָה מַטֵּה רְשָׁעִים שֵׁבֶט מֹשְׁלִים׃
6 that <u>struck</u> down the peoples in wrath 　with unceasing blows, 　that <u>ruled</u> the nations in anger 　with unrelenting <u>persecution</u>.	מַכֶּה עַמִּים בְּעֶבְרָה מַכַּת בִּלְתִּי סָרָה רֹדֶה בָאַף גּוֹיִם מֻרְדָּף בְּלִי חָשָׂךְ׃
7 The <u>whole earth</u> is at rest and quiet; 　they break forth into singing.	נָחָה שָׁקְטָה כָּל־הָאָרֶץ פָּצְחוּ רִנָּה׃
8 The <u>cypresses</u> exult over you, 　the cedars of Lebanon, saying, 　"Since you were laid low, 　no one comes to cut us down."	גַּם־בְּרוֹשִׁים שָׂמְחוּ לְךָ אַרְזֵי לְבָנוֹן מֵאָז שָׁכַבְתָּ לֹא־יַעֲלֶה הַכֹּרֵת עָלֵינוּ׃
9 Sheol beneath is stirred up 　to meet you when you come; 　it <u>rouses</u> the <u>shades</u> to greet you, 　all who were leaders of the earth; 　it <u>raises</u> from their thrones 　all who were kings of the nations.	שְׁאוֹל מִתַּחַת רָגְזָה לְךָ לִקְרַאת בּוֹאֶךָ עוֹרֵר לְךָ רְפָאִים כָּל־עַתּוּדֵי אָרֶץ הֵקִים מִכִּסְאוֹתָם כֹּל מַלְכֵי גוֹיִם׃
10 All of them will speak 　and say to you: 　"You too have become as weak as we! 　You have become like us!"	כֻּלָּם יַעֲנוּ וְיֹאמְרוּ אֵלֶיךָ גַּם־אַתָּה חֻלֵּיתָ כָמוֹנוּ אֵלֵינוּ נִמְשָׁלְתָּ׃
11 Your <u>pomp</u> is brought down to Sheol, 　and the sound of your <u>harps</u>; 　maggots are the bed beneath you, 　and worms are your covering.	הוּרַד שְׁאוֹל גְּאוֹנֶךָ הֶמְיַת נְבָלֶיךָ תַּחְתֶּיךָ יֻצַּע רִמָּה וּמְכַסֶּיךָ תּוֹלֵעָה׃
12 How you are fallen from heaven, 　O <u>Day Star, son of Dawn</u>! 　<u>How</u> you are cut down to the ground, 　you who <u>laid the nations low</u>!	אֵיךְ נָפַלְתָּ מִשָּׁמַיִם הֵילֵל בֶּן־שָׁחַר נִגְדַּעְתָּ לָאָרֶץ חוֹלֵשׁ עַל־גּוֹיִם׃
13 You said in your heart, 　"I will ascend to heaven; 　I will raise my throne 　above <u>the stars of God</u>; 　I will sit on the mount of assembly 　on the heights of Zaphon;	וְאַתָּה אָמַרְתָּ בִלְבָבְךָ הַשָּׁמַיִם אֶעֱלֶה מִמַּעַל לְכוֹכְבֵי־אֵל אָרִים כִּסְאִי וְאֵשֵׁב בְּהַר־מוֹעֵד בְּיַרְכְּתֵי צָפוֹן׃

NRSV	BHS
14 I will ascend to the tops of the clouds, I will make myself like the Most High."	אֶעֱלֶה עַל־בָּמֳתֵי עָב אֶדַּמֶּה לְעֶלְיוֹן׃
15 But you are brought down to Sheol, to the depths of the Pit.	אַךְ אֶל־שְׁאוֹל תּוּרָד אֶל־יַרְכְּתֵי־בוֹר׃
16 Those who see you will stare at you, and ponder over you: "Is this the man who made the earth tremble, who shook kingdoms,	רֹאֶיךָ אֵלֶיךָ יַשְׁגִּיחוּ אֵלֶיךָ יִתְבּוֹנָנוּ הֲזֶה הָאִישׁ מַרְגִּיז הָאָרֶץ מַרְעִישׁ מַמְלָכוֹת׃
17 who made the world like a desert and overthrew <u>its cities</u>, who <u>would not let his prisoners go home</u>?"	שָׂם תֵּבֵל כַּמִּדְבָּר וְעָרָיו הָרָס אֲסִירָיו לֹא־פָתַח בָּיְתָה׃
18 All the kings of the nations lie in glory, each in his own <u>tomb</u>;	כָּל־מַלְכֵי גוֹיִם כֻּלָּם שָׁכְבוּ בְכָבוֹד אִישׁ בְּבֵיתוֹ׃
19 but you are cast out, away <u>from your grave</u>, like loathsome <u>carrion</u>, clothed with the dead, those pierced by the sword, who go down to <u>the stones of the Pit</u>, like a corpse trampled underfoot.	וְאַתָּה הָשְׁלַכְתָּ מִקִּבְרְךָ כְּנֵצֶר נִתְעָב לְבוּשׁ הֲרֻגִים מְטֹעֲנֵי חָרֶב יוֹרְדֵי אֶל־אַבְנֵי־בוֹר כְּפֶגֶר מוּבָס׃
20 You will not be joined with them in burial, because you have destroyed your land, you have killed your people. May the descendants of evildoers nevermore be named!	לֹא־תֵחַד אִתָּם בִּקְבוּרָה כִּי־אַרְצְךָ שִׁחַתָּ עַמְּךָ הָרָגְתָּ לֹא־יִקָּרֵא לְעוֹלָם זֶרַע מְרֵעִים׃
21 Prepare slaughter for his sons because of the guilt of <u>their father</u>. Let them never rise to possess the earth or cover the face of the world with <u>cities</u>.	הָכִינוּ לְבָנָיו מַטְבֵּחַ בַּעֲוֺן אֲבוֹתָם בַּל־יָקֻמוּ וְיָרְשׁוּ אָרֶץ וּמָלְאוּ פְנֵי־תֵבֵל עָרִים׃
22 I will rise up against them, says the LORD of hosts, and will cut off from Babylon name and remnant, offspring and posterity, says the LORD.	וְקַמְתִּי עֲלֵיהֶם נְאֻם יְהוָה צְבָאוֹת וְהִכְרַתִּי לְבָבֶל שֵׁם וּשְׁאָר וְנִין וָנֶכֶד נְאֻם־יְהוָה׃

NRSV	BHS
23 And I will make it a possession of the hedgehog, and pools of water, and I will sweep it with the broom of destruction, says the LORD of hosts.	וְשַׂמְתִּ֛יהָ לְמוֹרַ֥שׁ קִפֹּ֖ד וְאַגְמֵי־מָ֑יִם וְטֵאטֵאתִ֗יהָ בְּמַטְאֲטֵ֛א הַשְׁמֵ֖ד נְאֻ֥ם יְהוָ֥ה צְבָאֽוֹת׃

Discussion of the Philological Issues

4a The word "taunt" is rendering the Hebrew word משל. Polk has expressed well the conundrum surrounding this word, "The term *māšāl* is notable for its intractability to definition, having become something of an embarrassment to established critical methods, not least to form criticism."[2] This conundrum is displayed in the uncertainty regarding the actual meaning of the word משל and its rendering in the modern English translations of Isaiah 14.

According to *HALOT* this word could mean "to be like or be similar to." Yet it could also carry the meaning of "to rule or undertake something."[3] While the exact correlation between these two meanings has not been clear, McKane's words have been instructive, "It is perhaps better to be content with a simple review of the total field of usage and to say that 'to rule' is confined to Hebrew, whereas 'to be like' is distributed throughout the Semitic languages, and that there is no evidence either in Hebrew or the other Semitic languages that *māšāl* has any connection with the meaning 'to rule.'"[4] Hence, the majority of modern scholarship has focused on the meaning of "to be like" and the derivative use of this word as a "saying, proverb."[5] This, albeit tentative conclusion was anticipated by the work of Eissfeldt who early on suggested that the basic meaning of *māšāl* is "to be like."[6]

If the meaning of the word משל can be reasonably assumed to be a "saying, proverb" then one wonders about the way it has been rendered in translations of Isaiah 14. The idea that משל in Isaiah 14 is used enigmatically is not new. On the one hand, early on the LXX translated this word as

---

2. Polk, "Paradigms," 564.
3. "משל," n.p. *HALOT on CD-ROM*.
4. McKane, *Proverbs*, 25–26.
5. Interestingly Wildberger has raised an objection by pointing out that *māšāl* typically designates sayings that are very short such as the משלי שלמה, "proverbs of Solomon" (Prov 1:1). Hence he has wondered whether this term can adequately describe the whole of the poem in the Isaiah 14 text. See Wildberger, *Isaiah 13–27*, 50.
6. Eissfeldt, *Der Maschal im Alten Testament*, 2–4.

θρῆνος which means "lament for the dead, a dirge."[7] On the other hand, the idea that the word משל is to be rendered here as a *taunt* seems to be first suggested by Budde. Back in 1882 he wrote, "Gerade durch den Contrast zwischen der ironisch angewandten elegischen Form und dem höhnischen Triumphe des Inhalts erhält das Lied seine ätzende Schärfe."[8]

This conundrum is carried over into the modern English translations. Of our twelve target translations only KJV renders it as "proverb."[9] Additionally, NCV has a neutral translation of "song." All of the other translations imply that even if the word *māšāl* designates a proverb, it has a very specific use here. The majority of the translations render it as "taunt" (NRSV, NIV, ESV, NASB, CEB). NAB and NET offer a slight variation with NAB translating it as "taunt-song" and NET as a verb "taunt." NJB, CEV, and NJPS hint at the intended use this poem as well. CEV translates it as "make fun," NJB as "satire" and NJPS as "song of scorn."

As we see, the issues surrounding this enigmatic word are far from being settled. We will explore its meaning and use in Isaiah 14 at length in the following chapter as it frames the way this entire text could be read with more exegetical precision and nuanced appropriation.

4b "Insolence" translates a word מדהבה which does not occur anywhere else in the Old Testament. The matter is complicated because the context does not clarify its meaning. The degree of uncertainty can be seen in the range of early translations. LXX reads ἐπισπουδαστής (one who exhorts). Peshitta renders it as *mḥpṭn'* (one who incites). Targum settles on תקוף הייבא (the strength of the transgressor). The Vulgate translates it as *exactor* (vehement one). Older commentators such as Kimchi, Vitringa, Aurivillius, and Rosenmuller argued that this word was related to the Aramaic דהב (gold) and should be translated accordingly. Based on that reading KJV translates it as a reference to Babylon as the "golden city" that ceased to exist. Calvin translates it as "the city covetous of gold." He conjectures that this is the epithet by which the Babylonians distinguished their capital city. Calvin asserts that as this word is linked with the word "oppressor," it reflects the Babylonian hunger for more. He writes, "It is usually the case with great empires and states and wealthy nations, that the greater their abundance, the stronger is their greediness to possess more."[10] Martin Luther's translation

---

7. "θρῆνος," n.p. *BDAG on CD-ROM*.

8. Budde, "Das hebräische Klageleid," 14.

9. For a modern commentary that follows this translation of *māšāl* as a "proverb" see Young, *Isaiah: Volume 1*, 435.

10. Calvin, *Commentary on Isaiah*, 1:438.

of Isaiah 14 in his 1545 Bible reflects this as well, "so wirst du solch ein Lied anheben wider den König von Babel und sagen: Wie ist's mit dem Dränger so gar aus, und der Zins hat ein Ende!" Here the apparent "gold" implies the tribute (Zins) that has ceased to flow to Babylon. Most recently Erlandsson has postulated that based on the parallel with נגש which he takes to mean "exactor of tribute" מדהבה could be a word for the heavy tribute that was imposed on those conquered.[11] If the early translators were correct in linking it with an the Aramaic דהב (gold), then, Erlandsson argues, the literal meaning of מדהבה would be "gold tribute." While, with the notable exception of Erlandsson, scholarship has long abandoned this line of thinking, Mizrahi's recent article has provided two lines of reasoning for the rejection of the דהב (gold) alternative. First, while he does agree with Erlandsson that the context here requires a word that would stand in parallel with נגש (oppress), Mizrahi denies that the word דהב (gold) fits either structurally or semantically. Second, he wonders why such an obscure Aramaic word would be used when a common Hebrew word זהב (gold) was available and was used in a near context in Isaiah 13:17.[12]

As attractive and theologically suggestive as a זהב (gold) option might be, modern scholarship has assumed a dalet-resh (ר-ד) confusion based on the evidence of the Qumran scroll 1QIsa[a] and has emended מדהבה to מרהבה (fury)—a position already anticipated by Michaelis in the eighteenth

---

11. Erlandsson, *Babylon*, 30–31.

12. Mizrahi, "History" 435. Mizrahi's article is very thorough in its presentation of all of the pertinent issues surrounding the word מדהבה. His own suggestion that נגש and מדהבה are self descriptions of the Mesopotamian king who is portraying himself as an incarnation of deity Ninurta is not as convincing. He does admit that while the epithets of the warrior god Ninurta were indeed ascribed to Mesopotamian kings in the Neo-Assyrian royal inscriptions, no allusion to the passage of the Epic of Anzu he discusses ("seething with fury, he made his way towards his mountain") has been detected. While Mizrahi tries to get around it by pointing out that other parts of the epic have been alluded to in the inscriptions, his argument is weakened by this silence. For now it remains a conjecture at best. Furthermore, his appeal to Old Testament allusions to Ninurta tradition is based on research by van der Toorn and van der Horst research that links the references to Nimrod in Genesis 10:8–12 with Ninurta (see van der Toorn and van der Horst, "Nimrod," 1–29). They find resonances between Ninurta, a warrior god who is a renowned hunter and city-builder with Nimrod, son of Cush, the first mighty warrior and mighty hunter who also builds up cities. While suggestive, their argument has not been fully convincing. First, Ninurta and Nimrod are not connected philologically. Furthermore, the main biblical text referring to Nimrod (Genesis 10:8–12) does not say anything about his ultimate divine nature. Finally, according to the Genesis text Nimrod is the son of Cush, which makes him a human being of African descent which also conflicts with Ninurta's Mesopotamian origin. So based on these facts I remain unconvinced by Mizrahi's intriguing argument.

century.¹³ Thus, the elimination of the oppressor curbed the violence he imposed on the world around him.

Reflective of this emendation, the modern translations render it as "oppression" (NJPS), "fury" (NIV and NASB), "insolent fury" (ESV), "angry rule" (NCV), "hostility" (NET), and "turmoil" (NAB). The choice of NJB to translate it as "arrogance" seems peculiar as it stands at somewhat of an interpretive distance from the rest. Two looser translations to point out would be CEV which translates it as "he won't attack us again" and CEB which renders it as "the flood has receded."¹⁴

Orlinsky has been a rare voice of opposition to the dalet-resh (ר-ד) emendation.¹⁵ He argues that the early versions such as LXX, Peshitta, and Targum do not point to מרהבה but simply guessed at the meaning of the rare word מדהבה based on the general context of the passage and the parallel with נגש. Furthermore, he claims that 1QIsaᵃ supplies an easier reading which seeks to improve the more difficult reading of the Hebrew text and on that textual-critical basis ought to be set aside. Finally, he is dismissive of the text of 1QIsaᵃ on the basis of many secondhand and inferior readings which he attributes to the inadequacies of the scribe.¹⁶ In the absence of a clear alternative, Orlinsky tentatively suggests that מדהבה could contain the root דבה, "It may be that the ancients recognized in דבא, דאב, and דהב the common דב element, with the meaning "strong." Our word would then mean "might, power, oppression," or the like."¹⁷

The strength of Orlinky's argument lies in his appeal to the well-attested principle of textual criticism that prefers the more difficult readings of texts (*lectio difficilior*). According to Klein, "Grammatical, historical, theological, and lexical difficulties often were eliminated or modified by the scribes as they copied the manuscripts. The scribes would not knowingly insert a more difficult form for a common one or an archaic or rare word instead of one in everyday usage."¹⁸ Yet this principle has to be held

---

13. For insightful discussion of the development of Michaelis' thoughts and full bibliography, see Mizrahi, "History," 436-37.

14. CEB translation is reflected in Hays' recent suggestion that the emended word מרהבה should be translated as "the flood." He writes, "The reference here is quite likely to the king as the embodiment of the Assyrian military, which in turn is sometimes portrayed as a flood (Akk. *abūbu*) in Neo-Assyrian literature." See C. B. Hays, *Death*, 204. While this is an intriguing suggestion, Hays does not provide any suggestions as to how an Akkadian *abūbu* were to become a Hebrew מרהבה.

15. Orlinsky, "*MADHEBAH*," 202-3.

16. Orlinsky, "Studies," 329-40. Specifically § D (333-37).

17. Ibid., 203.

18. Klein, *Criticism*, 75.

in tension with the well-attested scribal propensity towards copying errors such as accidental omissions, confusion of letters, or haplography, which result in textual corruption.[19] Albrektson's classic work has issued a necessary warning against using the rule of difficult reading as a sure-proof tool to safeguard the Masoretic text and thus avoid emendations even when the text is either desperately corrupt or incoherent.[20] The dalet-resh (ד-ר) confusion was one of the most common causes of textual corruptions. Along with het-he (ח-ה) it was susceptible to confusion in both the archaic and the later square scripts.[21]

Furthermore, Mizrahi has pointed out that Orlinsky's argument that מדהבה could contain the root דבה is based on outdated linguistic approach. He writes, "It ignores the basic insight of modern semantics, that sense is not a pre-existing entity, but rather the outcome of relational interaction with other words that together form a system. The lost sense of an obsolete word cannot be recovered by assuming it is pristinely preserved in some sub-morphological element; it must rather be demonstrated on the basis of actual usages in clear comparable contexts."[22]

Thus, we lean towards the current scholarly trend and accept the dalet-resh (ד-ר) emendation as a reasonable one in the absence of other viable alternatives while waiting for possible new linguistic breakthroughs to shed more certain light on this textual conundrum.

5a The prevailing rhythm of the poem is the regular *Qina* meter (3:2) which is common for ancient funeral dirge.[23] Several scholars have early on suggested that the first colon in this verse is too long to fit this meter. The hypothesis has been that the word יהוה is a later scribal interpolation since it does not appear in the rest of the poem, 4b–21. Guthe seems to be the first one to propose that the word יהוה be eliminated and the first word be the augmented passive form of שבר, i.e. נִשְׁבַּר, (be broken).[24] In a similar vein, Staerk has proposed reading שֻׁבַּר (be shattered) as the first word here.[25]

---

19. For the classic statement of the causes of textual corruption see Würthwein, *Old Testament*, 107–12.

20. Albrektson, "Difficilior Lectio Probabilior," 3–18. This article is now published in Albrektson, *Text*, 73–86.

21. Roberts, *Text and Versions*, 93.

22. Mizrahi, "History," 439.

23. Budde was the first to highlight the peculiarity of the meter of a funeral lament song. See "Klagelied," 1–52. For the discussion of the *Qina* meter in Isaiah 14, see O'Connell, "Isaiah XIV 4B–23" 407; Sweeney, *Isaiah 1–39*, 517–19.

24. Guthe, *Das Zukunftsbild*, 41.

25. Staerk, *Das assyrische Weltreich*, 227.

While the *Qina* meter does run throughout this passage, there are other places where the text departs from this meter as in 14:10a (כֻּלָּם יַעֲנוּ וְיֹאמְרוּ אֵלֶיךָ) and 14:12b (נִגְדַּעְתָּ לָאָרֶץ חוֹלֵשׁ עַל־גּוֹיִם), where the first line appears to be short, thereby creating a 2:2 pattern. Furthermore, as will be discussed later, while the form of this section is that of a funeral dirge, it deviates from it both in augmenting the elements of the traditional lament and in its subversive use as a taunt. Hence, the text's own flexibility in its use of the *Qina* meter and the genre of dirge urges us to be reticent in our appeal to textual manipulation by scribes. Finally, the rationale for the interpolation seems less than compelling. The most prevalent idea of the reasons for interpolation has been expressed early on by Vanderburgh. He suggested that the "interest of clearness" was the reason for inserting the word יהוה (YHWH) here.[26] Supposedly, the scribal editors felt compelled to make clear that it was indeed YHWH who brought about the destruction of the tyrant. Hence, they inserted this word here and replaced the passive verb with an active one. Two objections must be registered against this line of thinking. First, while the poem proper in 14:4b–21 does not contain references to YHWH, the verses that bracket it do. YHWH's people will pick up this *māšāl* after he has given them rest from their pain and turmoil (14:3). At the other end, YHWH speaks directly in verses 22–23 stating clearly his intent to bring about the downfall of Babylon. Hence, even if one grants that this poem in 14:4b–21 had an independent history of composition and circulation, the canonical setting makes it clear that YHWH's actions are implied here. Furthermore, the text is comfortable with the divine passives (the verb ירד (bring down) in verses 11 and 15 is hofal and the verb גדע (cut down) in verse 12 is nifal. So it is unclear why scribes would choose to clarify the agency of action in verse 5, but leave it masked in verses 11, 12, and 15.

It is interesting to point out that even Wildberger, who is sympathetic to the idea of interpolation, seems apprehensive about it, "Since this does not deal with a misreading but would have been a conscious addition to the text, this name for God ought not, under any circumstances, be removed on the basis of text-critical considerations."[27] Since the presence of the divine name clarifies the sense of the text in its present context, we agree that the text ought not be emended.[28]

26. Vanderburgh, "King of Babylon," 112.

27. Wildberger, *Isaiah*, 43.

28. At the onset of this section on philological issues we must be transparent about our own apprehensions with the widespread use of emendation for handling textual problems. We are guided by the caution issued by Thomas, "It must be regarded as the first business of the Old Testament linguist to explain by comparative philology the forms he finds in Hebrew, and not, save in the last resort, to emend. Emendation

6a The participle forms of both נכה (strike) and רדה (rule) suggest the repeated or ongoing nature of the tyrant's evil reign.²⁹

6b מַרְדֵּף (persecution) is a *hapax legomenon* word, deriving from the root רדף (pursue, chase, persecute).³⁰ LXX appears to leave this word untranslated, παίων ἔθνος πληγὴν θυμοῦ, ἣ οὐκ ἐφείσατο (striking a nation angry blows without ceasing). While most of our target translations envision the king's tyrannical rule delivering the persecution, KJV renders it itself as an object of wrath, translating this verse as "He who smote the people in wrath with a continual stroke, he that ruled the nations in anger, is persecuted, and none hindereth."

Since the time of Döderlein, many scholars have detected here a scribal error. Some have argued that this word derives from the verbal root רדה (have dominion, rule) and should be rendered מִרְדַּת (dominion).³¹ This emendation would bring out clearer parallelism between two parts of this verse already signaled by מַכֶּה (struck down) and מַכַּת (blows) correlation. It would make מִרְדַּת (dominion) parallel with its cognate רֹדֶה (ruled). Recent scholarship has not followed the lead of these earlier commentators. Erlandsson has argued that while the Targum might be supportive of this emendation, 1QIsaᵃ, the Vulgate (persequentem) and Peshitta point to the presence of the root רדף.³² Gray has questioned whether רדה (have dominion, rule), which is used in the sense of a strict or hard rule, is strong enough to be used in this context.³³ Wildberger has also been doubtful about this emendation because the substantive מִרְדָּה does not occur anywhere else in the Old Testament.³⁴

While in the absence of compelling reasons the emendation for the sake of the clearer parallelism seems unnecessary, a more attractive alternative

---

is based upon the false assumption that all that can be known of Hebrew is known—it perpetuates the known as the norm by which language is gauged. Comparative philology, however, adventures into the unknown, and discovers new criteria by which language can be adjudged possible or impossible." See Thomas, "Language," 401. This does not mean that we are ready to close the door on any use of emendation (see note 4b), but rather to be cautious to turn to it as the last resort while holding the alternatives provided by emendation open to challenge.

29. *IBHS* §37.6d, 625.

30. "רדף" n.p. *BDB* Electronic adaptation.

31. Dillmann, *Der Prophet Jesaja*, 132; Duhm, *Das Buch Jesaia*, 118; Hitzig, *Der Prophet Jesaja*, 166; Marti, *Das Buch Jesaia*, 123.

32. Erlandsson, *Burden*, 33.

33. Gray, *Commentary on Isaiah*, 253.

34. Wildberger, *Isaiah*, 44.

has been suggested by the BHS editor of Isaiah D. Winton Thomas.³⁵ An active (piel) form מְרַדֵּף when combined with proposed repointing of חשׁךְ as infinitive construct (ceasing) seems to improve the sense of this phrase.

7 When this verse states that "the whole earth" is at rest, does the phrase כל־הארץ refer to the entire cosmos or to the whole land of Israel? If this is a song that Israel is invited to pick up, then it would make sense that the earth that they would be singing about is the one they care for most, namely the land of Israel. While, undoubtedly, the song implies the cherished homeland enjoying a much needed rest from the oppression, several details in the text point in the direction of the cosmic scope of reference to כל־הארץ (the whole earth). First, in the verse immediately following, the junipers of Phoenicia and cedars of Lebanon are depicted as jointly rejoicing over the downfall of this tyrant. As will be explained below, at least some of the trees mentioned in verse 7 are not native to Israel, hence the jubilant chorus invites the natural elements outside the land of Israel to join in. Furthermore, in verse 9 the word ארץ (earth) is used in parallel with גוים (nations) as כל־עתודי ארץ (all the leaders of the earth) and כל מלכי גוים (all the kings of the nations) are depicted as greeting the tyrant entering Sheol. Presumably, the entire cosmos is envisioned to be the scope of his operation. Finally, in verses 16–17 the word ארץ (earth) is used in parallel with ממלכות (kingdoms) and תבל (world). While describing the global impact of devastation, the tyrant is cast as a man who made the earth tremble, who shook the kingdoms, and who made the world like a desert. The majority of commentators agree that this verse has a period of worldwide peace in mind.³⁶

Few seem to suggest at least the scope of the lands under the control of Babylon. Dillmann links the use of the word ארץ (earth) here with its use in Isaiah 13:4 where he finds it referring to the entire Babylonian Empire.³⁷ This alternative could lead to a suggestive mediative position. The scope in mind could be all the earth as known to the author of the משל, which would, of course, be for the most part lands that had felt Babylonian power.

8 The word "cypress" (ברשׁ) has been variously translated as fir tree (KJV), juniper (NIV), pine (NCV, NJPS), or evergreen (NET). The majority of modern translations render it similarly to NRSV as "cypress" or "cypress trees" (CEB, CEV, NASB, ESV, NJB, NAB). According to *HALOT* this word

---

35. *BHS*, ii.

36. Brueggemann, *Isaiah 1–39*, 6; Calvin, *Isaiah*, 1:439; Childs, *Isaiah*, 126; Clements, *Isaiah 1–39*, 141; Duhm, *Das Buch*, 118; Goldingay, *Isaiah*, 102; Kissane, *Isaiah*, 172; Knobel, *Der Prophet Jesaja*, 96; Shipp, *Dirges*, 139; Wildberger, *Isaiah*, 57–58.

37. Dillman, *Der Prophet*, 127.

designates *Juniperus Phoenicea* and should be rendered as "Phoenician Juniper."[38] The correction makes not only a philological sense but also an exegetical one. This word is at times used to designate the building materials imported from Lebanon (1 Kgs 5.22). Cypresses were native to Israel and would not need to be imported.[39] Yet one can see the nature of the difficulty. Phoenician Juniper does closely resemble a cypress tree as they both belong to the broader *Cupressaceae* family of trees.[40]

Kalland has suggested that ברש could be referring to Aleppo pine (*Pinus halepensis*).[41] Yet while rare, the archeological data has indicated the presence of Aleppo pine trees in the Western Highlands as well in Transjordan region.[42] Hence, the suggestion of translating this word as "pine" could be dismissed on the same grounds as the option of "cypress" above.

9a In the MT the word "rouses" (עוֹרֵר) and "raises" (הֵקִים) are both masculine. This presents a problem as the word they modify is שְׁאוֹל (Sheol) which is feminine. Shipp sums up the problem succinctly, "In this instance either Sheol is depicted as masculine, or both verbs הֵקִים and עוֹרֵר, should be infinitives."[43] Two attempts have been made to resolve this issue. On one hand, GKC has suggested reading both "rouses" (עוֹרֵר) and "raises" (הֵקִים) as infinitive absolutes and towards that end reading הָקֵם for הֵקִים.[44] On the other hand, Shipp has pointed to Job 26:6 as an evidence that Sheol could be depicted as a masculine noun. Based on that evidence he has opted out to translate it as, "He rouses the Rephaim for you, all the great ones of the earth, he raises from their thrones all the kings of the nations."[45] Yet as suggestive as Shipp's alternative could be, it does not seem to offer much help in this context as the initial verb רגזה which clearly describes Sheol's state of being as feminine.

While both of these suggestions have their strengths, GKC's emendation resolves the issue in such a way that it provides a more coherent reading. If both הָקֵם and עוֹרֵר are taken as infinitive absolutes,[46] they further

---

38. "בְּרוֹשׁ" n.p. *HALOT on CD-ROM*.

39. Goldingay and Payne, *Commentary on Isaiah*, 1:184.

40. Hageneder, *Trees*, 116. See also Heilmeyer, *Ancient Herbs*, 62; Kitto, *The Cyclopedia of Biblical Literature*, 1:321.

41. "בְּרוֹשׁ," n.p. *TWOT* Electronic adaptation.

42. Cordova, *Landscape in Jordan*, 77; King and Stager, *Biblical Israel*, 111; Liphscitz, *Timber*, 118.

43. Shipp, *Dirges*, 130.

44. *GKC* §145t, 466.

45. Shipp, *Dirges*, 130. The emphasis added.

46. The repointed infinitive form for קום as suggested by the BHS marginal note

elaborate on Sheol's stirring up to meet the tyrant, to rouse the shades, and to raise them from their thrones.

9b The word רפאים (shades) has sparked an intense scholarly discussion especially since the publication of the Rephaim Texts in Ugaritic in 1941 by Charles Virolleaud. [47] Over time the scholarship has noticed an affinity between Ugaritic *rpum*, Phoenician *rp'm* and the Hebrew רפאים. Johnston aptly put it, "The term is well-attested in languages spoken in and around ancient Israel, but with a strange variety of meanings."[48]

The word רפאים (shades) has ambiguous etymology. In the past, scholarship thought that it derived from the root רפה (to be weak).[49] Following Schwally's lead,[50] *BDB* describes the רפאים as the powerless and shadowy thus leading to the translation of this word as "shades" in NRSV as well as in ESV, NJPS, and NAB. Yet in light of the Ugaritic parallels the current scholarly preference has shifted towards the root רפא (to heal). As the connection between the concept of healing and the departed is not straightforward many have been puzzled by the initial suggestion. Hence, Astour has argued, "those who are amazed by the etymology of Rephaim from *rāphá* "to heal," simply do not understand the organic association between the notions of the Nether World—the chthonic cycle—and healing, i.e., granting health, strength, fertility and fecundity."[51] According to Astour, the Ugaritic texts show that the realm of the underground was understood to have the power over the inhabitants of the earth and could at any point summon them out of the realm of the living.[52] Astour posits that the primitive mind in dread of death sought to appease the dead thus leading to the veneration of the inhabitants of the underground as givers and sustainers of life.

---

would be הָקֵם. The case of עור is more ambitious due to the fact ע roots and polel verbal forms are rare. An infinitive form could be עוֹרֵר.

47. Caquot, "Les Rephaim," 75–93; Gray, "The Rephaim," 127–39; Gray, "DTN and RPUM in Ancient Ugarit," 39–41; Horwitz, "The Significance of the Rephaim," 37–43. Jirku, "Rapa'u, der Fürst der Rapa'uma-Rephaim," 82–83; Johnston, *Shades of Sheol*, 128–42; Levine and de Tarragon, "Dead Kings and Rephaim," 649–59; Hays, *Death*, 167–68; L'Heureux, "The *yelîdê hārāpā'*, 83–85; de Moor, "Rapi'uma—Rephaim," 325–45; Parker, "The Ugaritic Deity Rap'iu," 103; Pope, "Notes on the Rephaim Texts from Ugarit," 163–81; Shipp, *Dirges*, 114–26; Suriano, *The Politics of Dead Kings*, 149–64; Talmon, "Biblical *repā'im* and Ugaritic *rpu/i(m),*" 235–49; Virolleaud, "Les Rephaîm," 1–30.

48. Johnston, *Shades*, 128.

49. "רפאים" n.p. *BDB* Electronic adaptation.

50. Schwally, "Ueber einige palästinische Völkernamen," 126–48 (esp. 127–35).

51. Astour, *Hellenosemitica*, 234.

52. On the power of the dead, see also Moor, "Rapi'uma—Rephaim," 341–42.

As significant as these Ugaritic parallels have been, the ambiguity remains. Keeping in mind Barr's definition of exegetical fallacy, that meaning is not simply determined by derivation, but by its use, we are wise to heed Johnston's reservation, "It is worth noting that no biblical text attributes a healing function to the dead in general or to the Rephaim in particular."[53] He commendably stays within the confines of the biblical text itself arguing that at least in Israel the רפאים were understood as "weak" based on Isaiah 14:10, where the dead king is greeted by them with these words, "You too have become as weak as we! You have become like us!"

While the questions regarding the etymology of רפאים, their precise identity, and interrelationship between the use of this word in different languages persist, we are still faced with the question of translating it in this verse into English. Of our target translations two options have dominated, "spirits" ("the spirits of the dead" in NASB, NCV, NET; "the spirits of the ancient rulers" in CEV; "the spirits of the departed" in NIV) and "shades" (ESV, NJPS, NAB). CEB and NJB translate it as "the ghosts." KJV opts out for translating it as "the dead."

Reading our text, two things are clear about the רפאים: they are dead and they reside in Sheol. In the face of yet-to-be-resolved issues surrounding this word, NRSV's choice to translate this word as "shades" seems to be as reasonable as any other alternative suggested so far.

11a The word "Pomp" (גאון) has been variously translated. Similarly to NRSV here, NJPS, NIV, ESV, KJV, NAB, and NASB translate it as "pomp" while NCV, NJB, and CEV opt out to translate it as "pride." NET interestingly translates this word as "splendor" while CEB renders it as "majesty." These two translations seem to follow the lead of the LXX which uses the word δόξα (glory). גאון could have a meaning of both "eminence" describing someone's majesty (Isaiah 24:14 describes the joyful celebration of YHWH's majesty) and of "pride" (Proverbs 16:18 describes the pride that precedes the destruction). This semantic range of meaning reveals the complexity of the translator's task. What precisely is being brought down to Sheol? Is it the royal majesty or pride? Each of these translations display the degree of interpretation inherently involved in the task of translation.

11b The phrase הֶמְיַת נְבָלֶיךָ is rendered by NRSV as "the sounds of your harps." All of our target translations understand this to be a reference to musical sound with most of them translating נבל as "harp" (CEV "music"; NJPS "lutes"; KJV "viols"; NET "string instruments"; NJB "lyres"). The

---

53. Johnston, *Shades*, 128. Similarly, Day, *Yahweh*, 220.

uniformity displayed by modern English translations differs from the early versions of this text. The variance is due to the fact that the root נבל could also mean "to wither, decay."[54] Even within the book of Isaiah it refers to the withering or decay of leaves (1:30; 34:4), flowers (28:1), and the earth (24:4). Furthermore הֶמְיַת (sounds of) is a *hapax legomenon* word which according to Carmignac was emended to המות (death) based on possible reading of 1QIsaᵃ, thus rendering הֶמְיַת נְבָלֶיךָ as "dans la mort ton cadavre."[55] This appears to be in line with the Vulgate and 1QIsaᵃ. The Vulgate reads נְבָלֶיךָ as *cadaver tuum* and 1QIsaᵃ as נבלתך both meaning "your corpse." Of modern commentators two notable supporters of this view would be Blenkinsopp and Watts. Blenkinsopp translates הֶמְיַת נְבָלֶיךָ as "together with throng of your dead,"[56] while Watts renders it as "a groan of your disgrace."[57]

Wildberger has suggested that for this reading to be plausible הֶמְיַת which usually carries the meaning of "roar, crowd, abundance" hence often translated as "sound" here, would have to mean "ostentatious display, pomp." Yet, he doubts that a display of a dead corpse could stand in parallel with the tyrant's pomp (גאון).[58] Furthermore, Shipp has insightfully pointed to Isaiah 5:11–14 as an "example of arrogant people engaging in feasts with musical instruments who are said to go down to Sheol."[59] In the face of these factors suggested by Wildberger and Shipp, the reading of the majority of the English translations should be upheld.

12a Isaiah 14:12–15 has been the focal point of scholarly discussion related to Isaiah 14. The impetus for the voluminous body of scholarly literature has centered around the discussion of the ambiguous *hapax legomenon* phrase הֵילֵל בֶּן-שָׁחַר (Day Star, Son of Dawn) in this verse. While the בֶּן-שָׁחַר portion of this phrase is both textually secure and straightforward in its meaning, the meaning of הלל has been enigmatic and hard to pin down. It has been postulated to be an intentional pun on the imperative form of *hêlîlû* or *hêlîlî* (to wail).[60] This seems to be in line with some of the early translations such as Aquila, Jerome, and Peshitta.[61] Aquila renders it as ὀλολύζων (crying out

---

54. "נבל" n.p. *HALOT on CD-ROM*.
55. Carmignac, "Six passages d'Isaïe éclairés par Qumran," 37–46.
56. Blenkinsopp, *Isaiah 1–39*, 283.
57. Watts, *Isaiah 1–33*, 205.
58. Wildberger, *Isaiah*, 44.
59. Shipp, *Dirges*, 130.
60. Sweeney, *Isaiah 1–39*, 229.
61. See Erlandsson, *Burden*, 35.

loud). Jerome reads it as *ulula, fili diluculi* (howl, son of morning). Peshitta renders it as הלל בשחר (wail at the dawn).

The LXX translates this word as ἑωσφόρος (bringer of the dawn). This rendering reflects a possible linking of this figure with the planet Venus, the brightest star of the morning as identified early on by König (Stern des Glanzes, der aufleuchten lässt Licht gleich dem Morgenstern)[62] and recently, on mythological grounds, by Grelot[63] and McKay.[64]

BDB[65] and HALOT[66] have suggested a link with an Arabic cognate *hilāl*. Arabic *halla* means "to appear on the horizon." Hence, *hilāl* has come to mean "new moon." On the basis of that identification, it has been suggested that הֵילֵל should be repointed to הִילֵל and שחר emended to שהר so this phrase could be translated as "new moon-god, son of the moon god."[67] Similarly, BHS proposes a marginal reading that emends הֵילֵל to הִילֵל and provides a translation of "luna crescens," albeit without a reference to the Arabic cognate. Koenig back in 1906 suggested a reference to the moon crescent on grounds other than the Arabic cognate. He argued that the author was making an appeal to a waning luminary about to disappear at the dawn. Hence he rejected the idea that this is a morning star which would have been known for its brightness. Instead he argued for the old moon which is barely seen and is about to vanish from the sky with the setting of the dawn.[68]

הלל has also been linked etymologically with Ugaritic *hll* found in the following phrases in KTU 1.24:41–42: *bnt hll snnt* (daughters of Brightness, swallows) and *bnt hll b'l gml* (daughters of Brightness, Lord of the Crescent Moon).[69]

While the meaning of the word הֵילֵל is not easy to pin down, it has been most often and most persuasively connected with the Hebrew verb הלל (to shine) which appears in Isaiah 13:10.[70] Grelot, who argues for a connection with the planet Venus, has linked the origin of הֵילֵל with an Akkadian cognate adjective *ellu* (shining) which entered the Hebrew language and be-

---

62. König, *Historisch-Kritisches Lehrgebäude der Hebräischen Sprache*, 106. See also König, *Das Buch Jesaja*, 181.
63. Grelot, "Isaïe 14," 18–48.
64. McKay, "Helel and Dawn-Goddess," 451–64.
65. "I הָלַל" n.p. BDB Electronic adaptation.
66. "I הלל," n.p. HALOT on CD-ROM.
67. Winckler, *Geschichte Israels in Einzeldarstellungen* II, 24.
68. Koenig, "Lucifer," 479.
69. See the discussion in Watson, "Helel," 393.
70. "I הלל," n.p. HALOT on CD-ROM.

came הֵילֵל through a long and complex phonological adaptation.[71] McKay has pointed out the strengths of this alternative, "The strength of this interpretation is that it does not require textual emendation, it recognizes the normal meaning of the word and it brings the myth within the context of known ancient mythology."[72]

Modern English translations have variously rendered this phrase. NAB translates it as "Morning Star, son of the dawn." CEB is close but opts to not use the capitalization, "morning star, son of dawn." NIV similarly avoids the capitalization but chooses to use the definite article, "morning star, son of the dawn." NASB opts to not capitalize and to use the definite article in both phrases "star of the morning, son of the dawn." NET and NJPS are similar to each other but have the same issues of capitalization and the use of the definite article, "shining one, son of the dawn" (NET) and "Shining One, son of Dawn" (NJPS). Two translations, NJB and ESV are identical, "Daystar, son of Dawn." Finally, two translations attempt to bring the issue of luminosity to the forefront, "the bright morning star" (CEV) and "morning star ... bright as the rising sun" (NCV).

12b NRSV follows the *BHS* marginal note and inserts a particle אִיךְ (how) which is a common feature of the ancient dirge.[73] The rationale appears to be the broken-down meter as the first line has only two accented syllables.[74] Of our target translations ESV, NJPS, KJV, and NAB similarly add the particle אִיךְ (how). Since the days of Budde this emendation has had wide scholarly support.[75] As observed above (note 5a) we are somewhat apprehensive about emendations to the MT purely based on the concerns for a consistent *Qina* meter without much textual support, especially when such emendations add very little to our understanding of the text at hand.

12c The phrase חוֹלֵשׁ עַל־גּוֹיִם (you who laid the nations low) has long puzzled interpreters. Van Leeuwen sums up well the reasons for the difficulty.[76] First, חלשׁ is a rare root. It only appears in the Old Testament five times—three times as a verb (Exod 17:13; Job 14:10; Isa 14:12) and twice as a substantive (Joel 4:10; Exod 32:18). While the substantive uses are contrasted by

---

71. Grelot, "Sur la vocalización de הילל (Is. XIV, 12)," 303.
72. McKay, "Helel," 454.
73. Sweeney, *Isaiah 1–39*, 228.
74. Wildberger, *Isaiah*, 45.
75. Duhm, *Das Buch*, 119; Cheyne, *The Prophecies of Isaiah*, 89; Hitzig, *Der Prophet*, 168; Marti, *Jesaja*, 124;
76. Van Leeuwen, "Isa 14:12," 173–84.

the explicit antithesis of גבר (strength) thus giving them the meaning of "weakness," the meaning of the verbal uses has not gathered a consensus. BDB supplies the meanings "to be weak," "prostrate," and "to disable."[77] Furthermore, the issue gets complicated by the uncertainty of whether to render חלש as transitive or non-transitive. If taken transitively, the translator must face the problematic particle עַל (on; upon) in עַל־גּוֹיִם. Since the time of Duhm, this problem has been understood by some as a scribal error which misread עַל (on; upon) for כָּל (all).[78] This would appear to be in line with LXX's use of πάντα (all) as in, ὁ ἀποστέλλων πρὸς πάντα τὰ ἔθνη (he who sent to all the nations).[79] If taken intransitively, the phrase עַל־גּוֹיִם (on/over the nations), as van Leeuwen puts it, "yields nonsense."[80]

Van Leeuwen's proposal is to take the reading of 1QIsa[a] as the starting place for solving this puzzle. He observes that the phrase חוֹלֵשׁ עַל־גּוֹיִם (you who laid the nations low) in 1QIsa[a] is missing a *mem* from *gwym*. Since the singular, "a nation," does not fit the context, Van Leeuwen suggests looking for another meaning. He follows the earlier lead of Gunkel who argued that גּוֹיִם (nations) should read גְּוִיּוֹת (corpses). Gunkel appealed to the use of this word in Daniel 10:6, but Van Leeuwen argues that the word גְּוִיָּה could also mean "torso." He then links it etymologically and semantically to the meaning of "back." Finally, the absence of the *mem* from *gwym* in 1QIsa[a] is explained as a result of the scribal failure to recognize an enclitic *mem* in the MT text and thus mistakenly removing it. Further comparison with Gilgamesh XI.6 yields a very close parallel where Gilgamesh, upon encountering the immortal yet aged existence exclaims, "My heart had imagined you as resolved to do battle, yet you lie indolent on your back." Thus, Van Leeuwen is led to conclude, "The crux *ḥōlēš ʾal gwym* is solved by reading *gĕwî(m)* (back) for MT *gôyim* (nations)."[81] His final proposal is to read the whole phrase as "helpless, on your back."[82]

Van Leeuwen's proposal is definitely suggestive. It has been gaining wider acceptance as seen in the CEB translation which renders this phrase

77. "חָלַשׁ" n.p. *BDB* Electronic adaptation.

78. Duhm, *Das Buch*, 119; See also Gray, *Isaiah I–XXVII*, 249, 257; Marti, *Jesaja*, 124; Wildberger, *Isaiah*, 45.

79. Though see van Leeuwen's explanation for this rendering by the LXX which, according to him confirms the soundness of the MT. His argument that the LXX reading here was influenced by the presence of כֹּל מַלְכֵי גוֹיִם and כֻּלָּם in verses 9–10 and 18 as well as עַל־כָּל־הַגּוֹיִם in verse 26, while suggestive, is simply a hypothesis awaiting further investigation. See Van Leeuwen, "Isa 14:12," 174.

80. Ibid.

81. Van Leeuwen, "Isa 14:12," 178.

82. Ibid., 177.

as "helpless, on your back" and several significant recent monographs.[83] Yet several issues might be raised to highlight problems with Van Leeuwen's proposal.

First, Van Leeuwen's appeal to an enclitic *mem* in the MT needs to be probed further. The discovery of the Ras Shamra tablets has shed a significant light both on the world of ancient Israel and its linguistic milieu. One of the illuminating, albeit controversial assertions that followed this discovery has been a theory that an enclitic *mem* could be found in the Hebrew Bible. While as early as 1936 Ginsberg argued that an enclitic *mem* could be found in Psalm 29:6, it was Hummel's article published in 1957 that really put this issue on the table for scholarly discussion. He furnished a list of thirty-one texts that have already been in scholarly circulation and suggested seventy-six other texts. His conclusion was bold, "It can now be considered as established beyond any reasonable doubt that an enclitic *mem* was once a prominent feature of literary Hebrew, especially in poetry, just as in Ugaritic."[84] Some have responded to this proposal with much enthusiasm. Moran, for example, says,

> After H. D. Hummel's completely convincing study on the subject, a skepticism which prefers to suspect the text rather than accept a linguistic feature attested in Amorite, Ugaritic and Amarna (Jerusalem!) should be virtually impossible.[85]

While Moran would claim that this theory "has cleared up scores of grammatical and logical inconsistencies of the Hebrew text,"[86] others have been either cautious or skeptical. Barr's caution is predicated on the large frequency with which enclitic men appears, if one grants the validity of this theory. He writes, "Very many Hebrew words end with ם; it is common as a plural ending and in pronoun suffixes. If in every such case it is likely to be suspected to be an enclitic of no meaning, a very large field of variability is laid open."[87] Driver's attitude towards this theory has been much more negative. A year prior to Hummel's article he argued that "all the examples cited can be otherwise explained or the text may be suspected."[88] Even after Hummel's arguments were made, Driver still remained unconvinced claiming that "all the supposed instances of this -*m* can be explained within the rules

---

83. C. B. Hays, *Death*, 205; Shipp, *Dirges*, 131; Watson, *Classical Hebrew Poetry*, 309.
84. Hummel, "Enclitic *Mem*," 106.
85. Moran, "The Hebrew Language," 60.
86. Ibid.
87. Barr, *Comparative Philology*, 33.
88. Driver, *Canaanite Myths and Legends*, 129–30.

of Semitic grammar or Hebrew paleography."[89] More recently Emerton has provided a thorough analysis of Hummel's theory. His compendious overview of textual examples furnished by Hummel leads him to suggest, "I do not claim to have proved that enclitic men can never have existed in Hebrew or that no relics of it can possibly lie in the present text of the Hebrew Bible. The question is whether there are enough convincing examples."[90] Emerton's cautious stance makes room for Hummel's prized example often cited in scholarship, namely the phrase כל־רבים עמים in Psalm 89:51 where the second word is suggested to be emended to רב(י) on the basis of the enclitic *mem* theory. Yet he argues,

> If Hummel had other examples as convincing as this one, his case would be much stronger. As it is, one example is not a sufficiently strong foundation for the theory in the evidence collected by Hummel to establish as probable the theory of its existence.... If scholars are to continue to maintain that enclitic *mem* has left traces in the Hebrew Bible, they need to advance a case based on a sufficient number of strong examples.[91]

Based on these observations, we should at least be wary of an argument that leans heavily on the validity of a theory that still has significant voices of dissent.

Second, since the crux of Van Leeuwen's argument revolves around the missing *mem* from *gwym* in the 1QIsaᵃ text of חוֹלֵשׁ עַל־גּוֹיִם an alternative might be suggested. Spronk writes, "According to Van Leeuwen this (i.e., omission of *mem*) was done because it was no longer recognized as enclitic. It is, however, more likely that this is another example of the tendency in 1QIsaᵃ to actualize the text, viz. reading "my nation.""[92]

Third, Day has argued that there is no need for emending עַל (on; upon) to כָּל (all) or for taking חלשׁ intransitively. His argument, in line with Barthélemy, is that there are a number of other verbs (שׁלח and קרא) that can take both a direct object and עַל (on; upon), which he compares to the German *besiegen* (victory) and *siege über* (victory over).[93] Thus Day argues, "The force of *ʾal* can be rendered in English by translating 'was victorious *over*.'"[94]

---

89. Driver, "Review of M. Dahood," 112.
90. Emerton, "Enclitic *mem*," 377.
91. Ibid.
92. Spronk, *Afterlife*, 214.
93. Day, *Yahweh*, 167.
94. Ibid.

In light of the arguments presented above, Day's proposal seems to be the most simple and consistent way to account for the difficulties presented by this challenging phrase.

13 Scholarship has recently suggested several various ways of rendering the phrase לְכוֹכְבֵי־אֵל (the stars of God). Some have argued that the Hebrew references to divine names can be taken as epithets with an intensifying or superlative force.[95] Hence אל should be taken as a superlative and this phrase should be translated as "the highest stars."[96] Others have insisted that אל is a reference to the proper name of the Canaanite god אל, thus rendering the phrase as "the stars of El."[97] Wildberger has objected to the rendering of this phrase as a reference to the Canaanite god אל, "Since the present context of the poem places this word within material that gives witness to faith in Yahweh, אל (El) is a reference to Yahweh."[98] Thus, he argues that this phrase should be translated as "the stars of God." Wildberger's argument seems off target. As our analysis will later show, this text has wide-ranging resonances with the broader ANE mythology. It is unnecessary that a foreign tyrant would be presented as thinking in Yahwistic terms. There is no reason why he should not be presented as operating within the worldview which has the Canaanite god אל as the head of the divine order. It is to El's throne of that he aspires to ascend. Hence, following Spronk and others we lean towards rendering this phrase as "the stars of El."

17a There is a tension in the MT text here between the feminine תֵּבֵל (world) and וְעָרָיו (and his cities). LXX's reading omits the suffix and translates it as καὶ τὰς πόλεις (and the cities). Early on Hitzig proposed for תֵּבֵל to be taken as masculine.[99] Wildberger seems to be undecided between amending the text to read וְעָרֶיהָ (and her cities) and following the LXX reading.[100] One possible solution would be to take the pronoun to refer to the tyrant. This would be consistent with the rest of the verse. He is destroying his own cities and refusing to let his prisoners (אֲסִירָיו) to go home.

17b The phrase אֲסִירָיו לֹא־פָתַח בָּיְתָה (would not let his prisoners go home) has puzzled interpreters. LXX has rendered it as τοὺς ἐν ἐπαγωγῇ οὐκ

---

95. Thomas, "Expressing the Superlative," 210.
96. Pope, *El in the Ugaritic Texts*, 13.
97. Cassuto, *The Goddess Anath*, 57; Spronk, *Afterlife*, 215.
98. Wildberger, *Isaiah*, 45.
99. Hitzig, *Der Prophet*, 170.
100. Wildberger, *Isaiah*, 46.

ἔλυσεν (he did not release those in captivity). Peshitta similarly leaves the word בית (house) out and focuses on the release of the prisoners. The Vulgate ("eius non aperuit carcerem") and Targum retain the word בית (house) and interpret it as a reference to the prison where the prisoners have been kept. While all of our target translations emphasize the release of the prisoners' aspect of the text, two, KJV and NAB, leave out a reference to the house.

Wildberger, among many others, has suggested an extensive emendation to verses 17 and 18.[101] His rationale for emendation is based on the broken meter and the ambiguous use of the word בית (house). Wildberger claims that בית (house) is never used as "homeland." Furthermore the directional ה when added to בית (house) never brings out the meaning of "towards home" but rather "in the house." Wildberger proceeds to borrow the word כל (all) from the opening of v. 18 and moves the rest of that line down. As a result the text reads לאסיריו לא פתח בית הכלא (for his prisoners, he did not open their house of imprisonment).[102]

While Wildberger's suggestion seems appealing, one wonders both about the cogency of his arguments and the necessity of this emendation. First, as we have pointed out above (see note on 5a) the arguments about the broken meter seem ambiguous as there are several places in this text where the meter is imbalanced. Second, the ambiguous use of the word בית (house) should be probed further. While it is true that this word is not used in the meaning of "homeland," it is frequently used in reference to one's "household" in the sense of a family, as most memorably in Joshua 24:25 where Joshua affirms, "As for me and my household, we will serve the LORD." While the Joshua context is very different, one can still arguably envision the released prisoners returning to their households. Furthermore, Wildberger's insistence that the directional ה when added to בית (house) never brings out the meaning of "towards home" but rather "in the house" seems to be too ambiguous itself. For example, according to Williams's *Hebrew Syntax*, the directional ה is "used as a suffix on a noun to indicate a direction towards the thing named by the noun, often in reference to motion that ceases upon arrival."[103] One of two examples used by Williams is Genesis 43:16, "הָבֵא אֶת־הָאֲנָשִׁים הַבָּיְתָה" (Bring the men into the house). The presence of the directional ה, according to Williams, signals the meaning of

---

101. One other emendation worth mentioning is that of Ginsberg. He writes, "For MT, which is substantively insipid and linguistically suspicious, I read אסרי לפתח ביתה." He goes on to translate the phrase as "who chained to his palace gate" The phrase then is completed at the start of the verse 18 "all the kings of nations?" See Ginsberg, "Reflexes of Sargon," 52.

102. Wildberger, *Isaiah*, 47.

103. Williams, *Hebrew Syntax*, §62, 25.

"the direction of the house."[104] In the end, Erlandsson is surely correct that the lack of support from either the early translations or 1QIsa[a] makes this emendation "hardly possible."[105]

While one must agree that this phrase has valid reasons for scholarly puzzlement, the repointing of the MT text signaled by the marginal note in BHS suggests replacing פָּתַח with פִּתַּח.[106] This repointing, supported by HALOT would imply a meaning of "loose" or "release" thus making sense of the NRSV translation at hand.

18 The word translated as "tomb" is בית. While the actual meaning of the Hebrew word is "house," the context here dictates for it to be taken as "tomb," especially when it seems to be parallel with קבר (grave) in verse 19a.[107] Most of our target translations have chosen to render this word as "tomb" with the exception of KJV (house) and NCV (grave).[108]

19a The phrase "away from your grave" (מִקִּבְרְךָ) has been a focus of interesting scholarly discussion. LXX renders מִקִּבְרְךָ as ἐν τοῖς ὄρεσιν (on the mountains). Cheyne, Duhm, and Gray are among influential interpreters who have followed this reading. According to Erlandsson, Ziegler has proposed the most plausible rationale for this translation, "[LXX] die Lesart des MT in ihrer Vorlage gehabt und sie in exegesierender Weise gedeutet: weg von deinem Grabe=ohne Grab= in den Bergen."[109] Erlandsson provides the following Old Testament texts that link the mountains with corpses (Isa 5:25; 34:3; Ezek 32:5).[110]

While few recent scholars have followed the LXX lead, Wildberger has made an interesting suggestion regarding a translation of the phrase "away from your grave" (מִקִּבְרְךָ).[111] According to him, the MT implies that the tyrant's body was thrown out of his grave. Wildberger argues that the narrative could hardly imply that the tyrant's body was cast away unburied. Thus, he claims that the reading should be emended to מְקֻבָּר (without having

---

104. Ibid.
105. Erlandsson, *Burden*, 36.
106. Similarly, early on Marti, *Jesaja*, 126.
107. Ginsberg, "Reflexes," 52.
108. Page suggests that "house" is a reference to temples. See Page Jr., *The Myth of Cosmic Rebellion*, 136.
109. Joseph Ziegler, *Untersuchungen zur Septuaginta des Buches Isaias*, 113.
110. Erlandsson, *Burden*, 37.
111. Wildberger, *Isaiah*, 46.

a grave) where the preposition מִן functions as privative.¹¹² Several other scholars have argued along the same lines.¹¹³ As suggestive as this proposal might be, verses 9–11 might suggest a different picture. The dead tyrant is pictured as arriving to Sheol. Furthermore he is envisioned as covered with maggots which presumably means the natural decomposition of his body that would be consistent with a body being buried. Olyan has argued that the king's punishment for his numerous atrocities was exhumation and subsequent exposure away from his grave.¹¹⁴ Our subsequent discussion will consider at a greater length this tension in the text between burial (vv. 9–11) and non-burial (vv. 19–20), but for now it is sufficient to state that the suggested textual emendation in verse 19 is probably unnecessary.

19b The MT here likens the tyrant's dead body to נצר (shoot/branch). This reading stands in contrast with some early translations including the LXX reading of ὡς νεκρὸς ἐβδελυγμένος (like a detestable corpse). This reading seems to be based on the alternative reading containing נפל (miscarriage) instead of נצר (shoot/branch). Other significant early sources that reflect this reading include Symmachus' reading of ἔκτρωμα and Targum's rendering of it as כיחט both meaning "miscarriage." These early emendations seem to driven by the by the modifier נתעב (loathsome). Would a mere branch elicit such strong negative description? At least three major modern translations (NRSV, NJPS, and NAB) seem to have felt the weight of that question and have chosen to emend נצר with נפל and translate it as "carrion." Wildberger has been the formidable contemporary voice in support of this emendation. He writes, "A miscarried birth is abhorrent because it is believed that some evil forces have been at work and may have caused such an event."¹¹⁵ Wildberger goes on to reject the Masoretic reading and translates it as "a stomach-turning 'miscarriage.'"¹¹⁶ He opts for this emendation as he finds no reasonable explanation as to why a branch however detestable should be buried.

Despite these weighty witnesses the majority of the modern translations have followed the Masoretic reading translating it as "branch" (ESV, NIV, NASB, KJV, CEB, NCV, NJB) or "shoot" (NET). The Masoretic reading has a strong support of early sources such as 1QIsa9, the Vulgate, and

---

112. On the privative מִן, see Waltke and O'Connor, *An Introduction to Biblical Hebrew Syntax*, 214 and Williams, *Hebrew Syntax*, §321, 122.

113. Brichto, "Kin, Cult, Land and Afterlife—A Biblical Complex," 25. Fohrer, *Das Buch Jesaja*, 173; Kilian, *Jesaja*, 105.

114. Olyan, "King," 423–26.

115. Wildberger, *Isaiah*, 46.

116. Ibid., 42.

Peshitta. The focus of this comparison is rejection. It is the rejection precipitated by YHWH rather than malevolent cosmic forces halting the natural birth process in the womb. The king who has aspirations for human greatness finds himself disposed as a rejected broken-off piece of wood.

19d The MT reads יוֹרְדֵי אֶל־אַבְנֵי־בוֹר (who go down to the stones of the pit). On the one hand, all of our target English translations as well as some key early translations (Peshitta, Aquila, and Theodotion) render the phrase אֶל־אַבְנֵי־בוֹר as "to the stones of the pit" or close to it—"the stony pit" (CEB), "the deep rock pit" (CEV), "a rocky pit" (NCV), "the rocks of the abyss" (NJB). On the other hand, Wildberger's lament that this text, as it stands, makes little sense without further explanation seems to express a shared scholarly puzzlement.[117] Some have understood אֶל־אַבְנֵי־בוֹר to be a reference to a grave. Duhm argues that this is a reference to an ignoble treatment of a slain body by an enemy, tossed into a common grave without any respect or proper care. He writes, "Der Dichter meint die schimpfliche Beseitigung der Leichen durch die Feinde, man schleppt sie in Gruben und wirst Steine daraus."[118] Somewhat different, but still referring to a grave is Gesenius' understanding, anticipated already by Calvin,[119] of it as a reference to the "costlier sepulchers hewn in the rock."[120] Finally, Hitzig claims that אַבְנֵי־בוֹר is a reference to "der Stein, welcher die Oeffnung der Gruft schliefst." Thus, as stones covering an entrance of the sepulcher, argues Hitzig, they function similarly to the great stone at the entrance of Jesus' rock-hewn tomb (Matt 27:60).[121] More recently, Erlandsson argued that it is a reference to a "stone-lined grave."[122]

This view has been sharply criticized by Wildberger, who has specifically singled out Duhm's reference as "fantasy-filled explanation."[123] He argues that this attribution of בוֹר to a grave, be it a costly rock-hewn sepulcher or a common war-time burial spot, ignores the fact that ירד בור is a "fixed formula, used to describe the descent into the underworld"[124] as seen in

---

117. Ibid., 71.

118. Duhm, *Das Buch*, 121. Similarly, but without the pejorative nuance of Duhm, was Orelli's thought that this is a reference to a war-time common grave, "Those slain on the battlefield must go down without further formality under the stones of the pit." See Orelli, *The Prophecies of Isaiah*, 95.

119. Calvin, *Isaiah*, 1:448.

120. GKC, 120.

121. Hitzig, *Der Prophet*, 171.

122. Erlandsson, *Burden*, 38.

123. Wildberger, *Isaiah*, 71.

124. Ibid.

Isaiah 38:18, Ezekiel 26:20; 31:14–16; 32:18 among others. This is also similar to the Ugaritic *yardm arṣ* (he goes down into the Pit). Thus, Wildberger argues this is simply a reference to the cistern-shaped Sheol.[125] The stones, Wildberger hypothesizes, are either a pavement of Sheol or resting pillows for the dead who reside there.[126]

Wildberger's position has a weighty support from LXX and earlier commentators. LXX translates יוֹרְדֵי אֶל־אַבְנֵי־בוֹר as καταβαινόντων εἰς ᾅδου (going down to Hades). Early on Gray, along with BHS and others,[127] suggested that אבני should be emended to אדני (cf. Job 38:6), thus supplying a reading of "the bases of the pit," which would be in line with both Symmachus (ἐπὶ θεμελίους λάκκου) and the Vulgate (*ad fundamenta laci*). Gray argues that this emendation would bring it in parallel with אֶל־יַרְכְּתֵי־בוֹר (to the depth of the Pit) in verse 15 where it clearly refers to Sheol.[128]

As suggestive as Gray's emendation is, one wonders if it is necessary. The conceptualization of Sheol as a cistern-shaped underworld might allow room for a more natural explanation of אַבְנֵי (stones) than has been envisioned. Keel's insightful research on the spheres of death has shed a significant light on the meaning of the word בור as "cistern." Cisterns were hollowed out spaces in the ground without any lateral access. Water and rain were supposed to enter in from the shaft-like opening at the top. Plastered walls were designed to keep the water from leaking out. Keel writes, "Because a great deal of dust and earth naturally enters the cistern along with the water, the cistern floor is generally covered with sediment. The depth of sediment depends on the length of time since the last cleaning."[129] Seen in this light אֶל־אַבְנֵי־בוֹר could be a reference to Sheol as the untended cistern-shaped space, full of rocky sedimentary muck.

20-21a The references to מְרֵעִים (evildoers) in verse 20 and אֲבוֹתָם (their fathers) in verse 21 are rendered as singulars in the LXX and Peshitta. Earlier commentators have tended to follow their lead.[130] Kaiser has insisted that the singulars were original and were later emended to plurals when verses 22 and following were interpolated into the original poem.[131]

---

125. Ibid., 68.
126. Ibid., 72.
127. Marti, *Jesaja*, 126.
128. Gray, *Isaiah I–XXVII*, 260.
129. Keel, *The Symbolism of the Biblical World*, 71.
130. Duhm, *Das Buch*, 122; Marti, *Jesaja*, 127.
131. Kaiser, *Isaiah 13–39*, 29.

NRSV's rendering of the MT plural of אֲבוֹתָם (their fathers) as a singular "their father" reflects the current diversity of scholarly opinion regarding this issue. It is well represented in our target English translations. Several translations have chosen to render both of these phrases as plurals: ESV ("evildoers" and "their fathers"), KJV ("evildoers" and "their fathers"), NASB ("evildoers" and "their fathers"), NET ("the wicked" and "their ancestors"), NIV ("the wicked" and "their ancestors"). Only one translation has rendered both of these phrases as singulars—CEB ("evil offspring" and "their father"). The rest of them have been split, translating one phrase as singular and the other one as plural: CEV ("you evil monster" and "their ancestors"), NJPS ("evildoers" and "their father"), NAB ("evil" and "their fathers"), NCV ("evil people" and "their father"), NJB ("the wicked" and "their father").

Marti has explained the plural זֶרַע מְרֵעִים (seed of evildoers) as reflective of Isaiah 1:4 where the same phrase appears. Commenting on the use of זרע (seed) in Isaiah 1:4, he writes, "זֶרַע bekommt erst durch den Zusammenhang die üble Nebenbedeutung *Brut* vgl. γέννημα ἐχιδνῶν Mt 3:7. Sie sind eben eine schöne Sippschaft—von Bösewichtern."[132] This parallel hinges on how זרע (seed) is to be taken. If it is taken as a construct form, then the phrase זֶרַע מְרֵעִים would be rendered as "seed of evildoers." But if is taken as an absolute, then זרע (seed) stands in opposition to מרעים (evildoers), thus the phrase should be translated as something like a "seed consisting of evildoers." This seems to be the way Marti has taken the phrase זֶרַע מְרֵעִים.[133] As suggestive as Marti's thought might be, it has failed to differentiate the way the phrase is used in Isaiah 1:4 and 14:20. The context of Isaiah 1:4 does point to the appositional form. The corrupt present generation is described as זרע (seed). They are the rebellious children who stand in opposition to YHWH (1:2). He lays at their feet his charge (1:4) which includes a reference to them as זֶרַע מְרֵעִים, which could be reasonably rendered as NRSV does as "offspring who do evil." Turning to Isaiah 14, we are faced with a different situation. There are no references to the children of the tyrant having acted wickedly. The word מרעים (evildoers) clearly refers to the sinfulness of the previous generation. The children of the tyrant are זרע (seed) which faces annihilation by the virtue not of their own wickedness but of family association. Here is a reference to ancient *realpolitik* rather than ethics. Hence Wildberger's translation of זֶרַע מְרֵעִים as "this wicked family line" seems to nicely capture the intended meaning of complete annihilation of the tyrant's family without undue emendation of the MT text.[134]

---

132. Marti, *Jesaja*, 5.
133. Interestingly, Shipp translates it as "the offspring who do evil." See *Dirges*, 133.
134. Wildberger, *Isaiah*, 42.

Regarding the phrase בַּעֲוֺן אֲבוֹתָם (because of the guilt of their fathers), Rinaldi and Wildberger have argued persuasively that it is an often repeated phrase in the prophetic corpus (Isa 65:7; Jer 11:10; 14:20; 32:18; Ezek 18:17), as well as other parts of the Old Testament (Exod 20:5; 34:7; Lev 26:39; 26:40; Num 14:18; Deut 5:9; Ps 109:14; Dan 9:16; Neh 9:2). It appears to be a formula that envisions the sons being recipients of retribution incurred by the guilt of the fathers. Hence, Wildberger is surely correct in his assessment that the emendation of the plural is unnecessary.[135]

21b *BDB* translates the *hapax legomenon* noun מַטְבֵּחַ (slaughter) as "slaughtering place."[136] It is reflected in Wildberger's translation of it as "the slaughtering bench."[137] Similarly two recent monographs have translated it as "slaughtering block"[138] and "slaughtering place."[139]

Hays has made an interesting observation regarding two roots, טבח and זבח. The root זבח is used predominantly in reference to sacrificial acts while טבח refers to the slaughtering of humans.[140] To this we must add that this figurative use of the root טבח is most prevalent in the poetic sections of the prophetic literature. Of these, Isaiah uses it most frequently (14:21; 34:2; 34:5; 53:7; 65:12). All five references to the root טבח in Isaiah are figurative of human slaughter.

In its discussion of the word מַטְבֵּחַ *HALOT* draws a parallel with the word מִזְבֵּחַ which is used 400 times which means "an altar" as a place of animal sacrifices.[141] It seems preferable then that מַטְבֵּחַ should be translated as "slaughtering place" where the tyrants' sons will face their dreadful end.

21c There seems to be an uncertainty regarding the reading of עָרִים (cities). Gray, following Duhm and Marti, has argued that both עָרִים (cities) and פְּנֵי (face of) might be a later addition to the text that had a parallelism of *earth* and *world* akin to what one finds in Isaiah 24:4 and 34:1.[142] LXX reads πολεμων (wars), BHK emends it to עִיִּים (ruins), while Targum and Gesenius render it as צָרִים (enemies). Considering the option of "enemies," Calvin writes memorably, "All wicked men are enemies of the human race,

---

135. Ibid., 47.
136. "מַטְבֵּחַ," n.p. *BDB* Electronic adaptation.
137. Wildberger, *Isaiah*, 42.
138. C. B. Hays, *Death*, 206.
139. Shipp, *Dirges*, 133.
140. C. B. Hays, *Death*, 206.
141. "מַטְבֵּחַ," n.p. *HALOT on CD-ROM*.
142. Gray, *Isaiah I–XXVII*, 261.

or rather of the whole earth; and, therefore, ... the Lord provides for the safety of all, when he takes them out of the midst; for the earth would otherwise be choked by them as by thorns and briers."[143] These alternative readings to the "cities" highlight the destructive impact of the tyrant's quest for greatness. In the end it populates the world with conflict and tends to divide humanity into polarized enemies. Despite the fact that these readings make good sense of the flow of the text, scholarly preference leans towards the MT reading that claims that the tyrant's intent is to cover the globe with cities.[144] Having considered other alternatives, Calvin opts for the translation of "cities." The rationale is found in the old proverb "a bad reed grows quickly" which is brought to imply that the wicked tend to have a "numerous progeny."[145] Thus Calvin writes, "The wicked men would fill the whole earth not only with men, but also with towns, if the Lord did not beforehand perceive and guard against this evil, and diminish their number."[146]

22-23 Tension exists between the NRSV rendering of these two verses as prose in contrast with the *BHS* editor's choice to lay out the MT text as poetry. While other issues surrounding these verses have attracted much scholarly discussion, many commentators have been virtually silent about this tension. On the one hand, Oswalt has rendered these verses as poetry in his translation.[147] On the other hand, Gray has taken the opposite view, "This is scarcely either poetry or the original continuation of vv. 4b-21."[148] The reasons for this silence could be due to the fact that as far as the content and interpretation is concerned not much hinges on the form of these verses. Hence a decision to read these verses as poetic must be tentative.

23 The word קפד (hedgehog) designates a wild animal of uncertain type. The LXX has translated this word as ἐχῖνος (hedgehog). Calvin similarly opts for the "hedgehog" translation while Lowth and Rosenmüller go with "porcupine."[149] *BDB* designates it as derivative of the verb קפד which in the piel has a meaning of "roll up" and appears only in Isaiah 38:12. Hence *BDB* gives it a meaning of "porcupine" as describing an animal which tends to roll

---

143. Calvin, *Isaiah,* 1:454.
144. NRSV, NIV, ESV, NASB, KJV, NCV, CEV, CEB, NJB, NAB translates it as "cities," while NJPS translates it as "towns."
145. Calvin, *Isaiah,* 1:454.
146. Ibid.
147. Oswalt, *Isaiah,* 325.
148. Gray, *Isaiah I-XXVII,* 262.
149. Calvin, *Isaiah,* 1:456.

itself together.¹⁵⁰ This would equally apply to a hedgehog. But Blenkinsopp has made an interesting observation, "Hedgehogs do not haunt watery wastelands if they can help it."¹⁵¹ Wastelands equally do not qualify as a natural habitat for porcupines who are mostly found in forests, rocky hillsides or deserts.¹⁵² In the absence of a consensus, modern translations have variously translated it as a hedgehog (ESV, NASB, NJB), a porcupine (RV), a bittern (KJV, NJPS), a heron (CEB), or an owl (NIV, NCV, NAB). Some modern translations (CEV, NET) have chosen to leave this issue unresolved and translate it as "wild animals."

150. "קפד," n.p. *BDB* Electronic adaptation.
151. Blenkinsopp, *Isaiah*, 285.
152. Deal, *Wildlife*, 173.

3

The Meaning of משל

IN THE PREVIOUS CHAPTER the enigmatic nature of the word משל which means a *proverb* or a *saying* was highlighted. It is worth noting that the conventional translation of משל as "parable" derives from the LXX which was first to render it as *parabole*.[1] As mentioned earlier, the conundrum surrounding the word משל revolves around its frequent rendering as a *taunt*, which was first suggested by Budde in 1882.[2] Budde's proposal was soon further elaborated by Lohman and Jahnow. Lohmann's research into our text's genre (Gattung) has posited a fusion of two genres, namely of *Spottlied* (taunt song) and *Leichenlied* (funeral song).[3] He writes, "Das prophetische Spottlied kleidet sich in das Gewand einer Totenklage, wie man sie sonst an der Totenbahre anzustimmen pflegte, um die Vorzüge und Heldentaten des Dahingeschiedenen zu besingen und seinen Verlust zu beklagen."[4] Not long after, Jahnow also suggested that the author of Isaiah 14 poem made a conscious transformation of the genre of funeral song.[5] The fact that this issue is far from being settled is clearly indicated by the fact that Shipp's dissertation on this text submitted to the faculty of Princeton Theological Seminary in 1997 spends over thirty pages wrestling with its literary genre citing the "difficulties and the lack of clarity" that surround it.[6]

---

1. Stern, *Parables*, 10.

2. Budde, "Klageleid," 1–52.

3. Lohmann, *Prophetien*, 21.

4. "The prophetic taunt dressed in the garb of lament to be sung at the bier, usually used to sing the merits and exploits of the deceased and to mourn his loss." In Lohmann, *Prophetien*, 21.

5. Jahnow, *Leichenlied*, 242.

6. Shipp, *Dirges*, 33. On pages 34–42 Shipp supplies a helpful summary of the recent discussion regarding משל. He brings this scholarly discussion into conversation with ancient Near Eastern texts such as the Bel-eṭir inscription which parodies the king of Egypt. While Shipp's discussion of משל is both instructive and controversial (see pages 214–15 of the review by D. M. Clemens in *JNES* 66.3 [2007], 213–16), it does not represent a major advancement in the conversation so it will not be treated at length here.

Before proceeding to offering a reading of Isaiah 14:3–23 it is significant to step back and reflect further on this longstanding issue of the use of the משל designation in the text at hand. What is at stake is the tone of the whole poem. Prior to exploring *what* the text means one must reasonably deduce *how* the text means.[7] According to Eco, "every act of reading is a difficult transaction between the competence of the reader (the reader's world knowledge) and the kind of competence that a given text postulates in order to be read in an economic way."[8] Hence this discussion invites us to become more nuanced and competent readers of Isaiah 14:3–23.

Discussion of the Literary Genre of משל.

While the issues raised by Budde, Lohmann, and Jahnow are still with us, there has been a marked shift in the conversation.[9] Characteristically, Curkpatrick would recently insist that the meaning of משל is "fluid, being contingent . . . on context."[10] This shift in the משל discussion is a part of the larger developments in the scholarly understanding of genre.

Determination of a text's genre has been a staple of form-critical scholarship. Collins has defined genre as "a group of written texts marked by distinctive recurring characteristics which constitute a recognizable and coherent type of writing."[11] In line with this definition, the majority of classic form-critical scholarly effort went into demarcating and cataloguing recurring features of texts for the sake of genre classification. Schipper sums up the traditional form-critical work well:

> According to this approach, a text or speech act belongs to a given genre when it exhibits some minimally required number of properties or features that make up that genre in its hypothetically pure or ideal form. The notion that genres have pure or ideal forms, which can become impure when altered, has been popular in Hebrew Bible form criticism since at least the time of Hermann Gunkel near the turn of the last century.[12]

---

7. Berlin, *Poetics*, 17.

8. Eco, "Between Author and Text," 68.

9. Schipper, *Parables*, 1–22. For other insightful reviews of scholarly discussion regarding משל, see Boadt, "Understanding the Mashal," 172–76; Gowler, *Parables*, 42–46; and Niditch, *Folklore and the Hebrew Bible*, 67–87.

10. Curkpatrick, "Between *Mashal* and Parable," 59.

11. Collins, "Introduction," 1.

12. Schipper, *Parables*, 7.

Yet Newsom has signaled a change, "Over the past quarter century . . . genre theorists have become increasingly dissatisfied with an approach that defines genres by means of lists of features."[13] She points to two major objections.

First, some have argued that such cataloguing approach does not represent well how genres actually function. As Fowler has insisted, "[Genre] is an instrument not of classification or prescription, but of meaning."[14] Genres are a part of human communication which makes them inherently dynamic, while form-critical classifications are by their very essence static. To use Fowler's memorable analogy, classic form-critical classifications approach genres as pigeonholes, while in reality they are more like pigeons.[15] Newsom writes, "'Mere' classification obscures the way in which every text—however it relates to similar texts—whether 'by conformity, variation, innovation, or antagonism' will change the nature of the genre and indeed give rise to new genres."[16]

Furthermore, the classic form-critical cataloguing approach to genres comes under attack from post-structuralists. Derrida dismisses the notion that texts can *belong* to a genre. Rather he prefers to speak of "a sort of participation without belonging—a taking part in without being part of, without having membership in a set."[17] Newsom represents well the current scholarly shift in understanding genre when she writes, "There is much to be said for following Derrida's lead and thinking of genre in relation to a text's rhetorical orientation so that rather than referring to texts as belonging to genres one might think of texts as participating in them, invoking them, gesturing to them, playing in and out of them, and in so doing, continually changing them."[18]

Schipper has argued that this larger shift of emphasis on genre as "providing a rhetorical orientation for the text or speech rather than as the categorization of a text or speech" has set the context of the scholarly rethinking of the משל designation in the Old Testament texts.[19] According to him, the משל conversation is no longer dominated by attempts to define a משל by its type or form, but rather by its content and function.[20]

---

13. Newsom, "Spying Out the Land," 20. Quoted in Schipper, *Parables*, 8.
14. Fowler, *Kinds of Literature*, 22.
15. Newsom, "Spying Out the Land," 21.
16. Ibid.
17. Derrida, "The Law of Genre," 230. Quoted in Ibid.
18. Ibid.
19. Schipper, *Parables*, 9.
20. Ibid., 2.

While the works of scholars such as McKane,[21] Landes,[22] and Suter[23] were instrumental in facilitating the scholarly recalibration of the משל designation we will focus on Polk's recent exploration of the "paradigmatic-parabolic" quality of משל as a prime example of the mature distillation of several decades of scholarly discussion.[24] Based on Wittgenstein's work, Polk highlights the noetic function of these speech-acts.[25] He argues that משל intends to go beyond merely imparting information to its hearers. Polk writes, "The *māšāl* seems always to have an affective component such that to understand it, we cannot merely say what it means (indeed, this may be impossible); we must *see* what it *does*."[26] He claims that this characteristic of משל that seeks to evoke a certain response makes it especially suitable for religious discourse, as for example in Ezekiel where it "involves its addressee, or target, in self-judgment."[27] Polk's observations on the enduring value of משל are very instructive:

> The comparisons are not there for their own sake, preserved out of some purely antiquarian interest. They must have been thought to model a reality always capable of impinging upon a particular readership. Hence, when the elements of the passage turned metaphorical, then the depiction of Israel's history as one of judgment and salvation became paradigmatic such that Israel's history becomes *trans*historical and the passage can say, "Here is Israel's death and life and destiny, and not just sixth-century Israel's." Now representative and paradigmatic, the passage can take on existential import.[28]

Seen in this light, משל is a powerful tool in the hands of the author who furnishes this larger-than-life paradigmatic comparison in order to shape his readers' response.

Having situated the משל discussion in the broader form-critical conversation regarding genre, we are now able to turn our attention to the exploration of the way the משל designation works in Isaiah 14.

---

21. McKane, *Proverbs*.
22. Landes, "Jonah," 137–46.
23. Suter, "*Māšāl*," 193–212.
24. Polk, "Paradigms," 564.
25. Ibid., 569.
26. Ibid., 567.
27. Ibid., 570.
28. Ibid., 582–83.

The Function of משל in Isaiah 14:3–23

Schipper has argued that the recent developments in the genre conversation are more reflective of a shift in emphasis rather than a totally new understanding. He cautions against pressing too far the differences between the old and recent modes of inquiry. He writes:

> Even though biblical scholars have traditionally emphasized a text's formal properties when studying genre throughout the last century, they have often tried to reconstruct how genres operated within a particular situation in life in the ancient Near East (setting-in-life or *Sitz im leben*). In this sense, such studies do not ignore the rhetorical functions of a genre even when trying to isolate its pure or ideal form.[29]

The wisdom of Schipper's caveat can be seen in the way Budde and his successors paid close attention to the rhetorical function of משל in Isaiah 14:3–23. A fine example of that would be one of the giants of the Old Testament scholarship, Otto Eissfeldt, whose research on use of משל in the Old Testament dates to the beginning of the twentieth century. Eissfeldt claimed that Isaiah 14:4–21 is "the most powerful prophetic dirge which we possess in the Old Testament."[30] He reflects on the widespread use of משל in ancient Israel. According to him the משל function was to express Israel's heartfelt commitment to its way of life and equally passionate rejection of its enemies and their *modi operandi*. He writes,

> Just as in the life of the individual, the mocking saying represented a weapon of great power, so the mocking song was a terrible political weapon, which provided protection and security for one's own people, but consigned the enemy to contempt and destruction. The mocking song was for the foreign policy of ancient Israel what today is represented by newspaper propaganda which, when it becomes really intense, goes back in words and pictures to the crudities of the ancient method. As far as Israel is concerned, the ancient mocking poetry appears to have been forced more and more into the background with the rise of prophecy, and to have been replaced by the prophetic threats against foreign nations.[31]

---

29. Schipper, *Parables*, 9.
30. Eissfeldt, *Introduction*, 93.
31. Ibid.

Eissfeldt demonstrates that משל achieves its intended purpose by painting in stark contrast the former glory and present dishonor. Reversal of fortunes imbedded in a משל juxtaposes the pride that preceded the downfall with the pathetic catastrophe that followed it. Commenting on Isaiah 33:2–16, he points out that there exists "the enormous contrast between former glory and present darkness, between former power and present insignificance, and to heighten the effect of contrast, there are borrowings from myth with its vividly glaring colours."[32]

A prominent recent example of someone combining the old form-critical instincts and recent modes of inquiry is Gail Yee. While the suggestion that a funeral dirge has been recast to function as a taunt in Isaiah 14 goes back to Budde and Eissfeldt, it was Gail Yee's insightful article that tipped the scale in producing a degree of scholarly consensus.[33] One can hear the echoes of the recent scholarly shift as she writes, "As with all parody, biblical parody has no anatomy of its own but assumes the shape of that which it impersonates."[34] Yet she does not eschew the classic form-critical inquiry. Her form-critical analysis compares Isaiah 14:4b–21 with David's dirge over the slain Saul and Jonathan in 2 Samuel 1:19–27. According to Yee, the funeral service was the most likely *Sitz im Leben* of the lament form. The hero's life would have been described in poignant and dramatic fashion, using the hyperbolic language to accentuate the person's worth and accomplishments. Based on 2 Samuel 1:19–27 Yee outlines six features common for the lament form:

> We see then that the dirge form, as it is represented by David's lament over Saul and Jonathan, is composed of six typical features: (A) a rhetorical introduction announcing the death; (B) the suppression of news of death from enemies; (C) a description of nature at the person's death; (D) a description of the person's life; (E) a call to mourners to weep; (F) an expression of the singer's personal grief.[35]

When she turns her attention to Isaiah 14:4b–21 Yee detects the author imitating the lament form but with a twist. Yee writes, "The Isaian poet, while adhering strictly to the conventions of the traditional lament, is able to manipulate them to create a marvelous parody ridiculing a nameless tyrant."[36] On the one hand, the poet crafts a dirge, but on the other hand, he

32. Eissfeldt, *Introduction*, 96–97.
33. Yee, "Anatomy," 565–86.
34. Ibid., 582.
35. Ibid., 573.
36. Ibid., 582.

is able to insert a completely foreign content or play on the elements in such a way as to bring a complete reversal of expectations. The poem does open (v. 4b) with a rhetorical introduction that announces the death by the use of typical features of the lament form, particle *'êk* and the *qînâ* meter.[37] Furthermore, verses 5–6 do give us a description of the dead person's life. The author plays on the customary use of the portrayal of the hero's weapons and describes his staff and scepter as symbolic of his abuse of power. Next, nature's reaction to the death is portrayed in verses 7–8. Classic lament envisions the hero's death, inviting nature to mourn. Here the whole earth is at rest. Trees rejoice. Creation is experiencing relief. From here things get even more grotesque. Instead of a call for mourners to weep, in verses 16–17 we witness a bloody corpse as the audience stares and raises mock lament. Finally, verses 18–21 reverse all expectations for the singer's personal grief over the dead person. The motif of a lack of a proper burial for a fallen military hero is a familiar one. Away from home, one might be left at the battle field without proper honor and dignified final rest. Yet here the author affirms such a gruesome finish as an appropriate end for the tyrant and expresses hope that a similar fate would be awarded to his offspring as well.

Yee's explanation of what happens in Isaiah 14 is instructive:

> The poet of Isa 14:4b–21 imitates a known literary form, viz., the dirge, but "with a difference." He imposes upon the form a completely alien content, a content which actually reverses the customary intent and purpose of laments. He manipulates the typical features and conventions of the dirge form in such a way as to achieve irony, humor, and satire. The target of attack is not the literary form itself, as is the case with some parodies, but rather the tyrant to whom the poem refers. The Isaian parody thus becomes a vehicle for social, rather than literary, criticism.[38]

The line going from Budde to Eissfeldt to Yee represents a major scholarly tradition regarding the function of משל in Isaiah 14:3–23.[39] The poem shaped as a funeral dirge that functions as a taunt sets up a definitive mood for reading. As Weisman aptly states, "From beginning to end this satire against the king of Babylon is an exemplar of the taunt elegy, whose connection with the model of the dirge is only formal, that is, in its structure

---

37. O'Connell, "Isaiah XIV 4B–23," 407; Sweeney, *Isaiah 1–39*, 517–19.

38. Yee, "Anatomy," 581.

39. Blenkinsopp, *Isaiah*, 286; Brueggemann, *Isaiah*, 125; Childs, *Isaiah*, 127; Clements, *Isaiah*, 139; Dempsey, *Isaiah*, 34; Goldingay, *Isaiah*, 102; Kaiser, *Isaiah*, 29; Oswalt, *Isaiah*, 316; Seitz, *Isaiah 1–39*, 134; Sweeney, *Isaiah*, 228–29; Tucker, *Isaiah*, 158; Tull, *Isaiah*, 277–78; Wildberger, *Isaiah*, 50; Watts, *Isaiah*, 207–8.

and form; it is unconnected with respect to mood and essence of the experience."[40] Positioning this משל to be read as a playful improvisation on the well-known genre of funeral dirge invites a sardonic mood akin to any first-rate political satire. When encountering this משל designation at the opening of our poem, the perceptive reader could be justified in asking, "Might one anticipate finding in this poem an ancient analog to Voltaire, Jonathan Swift or George Orwell?"

If the cogency of this interpretive trajectory that perceives the משל as a precursor of a political satire is granted, one must be allowed to raise a question of its intended *telos*. Or to put this question differently, "What does this משל intend to accomplish?" In order to address this question we must turn our attention to the nature of irony in the Old Testament and subsequently discuss the work of Robert Alter who insightfully builds on and in essential ways complements Yee's thoughts on this issue.

Good's classic work argues that irony is used frequently in the Old Testament as a tool to awaken the reader to "the grotesque and absurd" in what they have taken for granted.[41] Satire's vehicle for doing that is the ridicule.[42] As a form of sarcasm, Good argues, satirical texts, such as parody, elicit laughter, yet it is far from being lighthearted—it is "the laugh . . . tinged with bitterness."[43] Similarly, Weiseman insists that a satire carries the mood of animosity and insult.[44] The intention is to both expose and ridicule and thus in the process to declare a victory over one's enemy, if not on the battlefield, then at least in the hearts of those huddled around to hear the taunt. Yet is this merely a temporary release from otherwise problematic realities of life?

Booth has argued that the purpose of irony can be compared with "the notion of reconstructed buildings and relocated inhabitants."[45] He defines the reconstruction as "the tearing down of one habitation and the building of another one on a different spot."[46] Our grasp on reality is settled and firm, hence resembling a permanent place of habitation. The frontal attack on it might yield very little. Irony acts subversively from the inside. Spoken by the one who shares that place, it subtly and unobtrusively exposes that place as uninhabitable. Booth writes,

40. Weisman, *Satire*, 77.
41. Good, *Irony*, 26.
42. Ibid., 27.
43. Ibid., 28.
44. Weisman, *Satire*, 7.
45. Booth, *Rhetoric*, 33.
46. Ibid., 33.

> I do not convince you that our king is a menace by saying so . . .
> I must convince you that I know of qualities and actions of his
> that you will think *imply* a threat to your welfare or a violation of
> your values. If I cannot find some point of contact with your no-
> tions of what implies threat, some point on which we can stand
> in agreement as we explore our disagreements, I can never hope
> to change your mind.[47]

Thus, irony assumes a subtle posture that excludes any coercion. Its inviting mode beckons the reader to "a kind of morally active engagement."[48] It taps into the values and priorities of the reader and spurs him or her into action. The relocation into the new place of habitation then happens when, as a reader, "I make the new position mine with all the force that is conferred by my sense of having judged independently."[49]

Booth's notion of irony inviting a morally active engagement is very much compatible with Alter's discussion of the purpose of the משל designation in Isaiah 14. Even without much reference to the discussion above, it is clear that Alter stands on the mature continuum of the ongoing scholarly conversation both about genre in general and משל in particular. His interests clearly lie with the rigorous exploration of how poetic texts function in the context of the larger rubric of prophecy. He argues that the language of poetry in most biblical prophecy leans towards "aligning statements that are addressed to a concrete historical situation with an archetypal horizon."[50] Seen in this light, the book of Isaiah, while presenting a message as designed for the eighth-century audience, does not merely represent the "transcription of a historical document," but rather a body of work that "continues to speak age after age, inviting members of otherwise very different societies to read themselves into the text."[51] Thus, Alter insists that poetry in biblical prophecy is not just "a set of techniques for saying impressively what could be said otherwise." Rather, he claims, "it is a particular way of imagining the world."[52]

In this context Alter considers משל as an example of "vocative poetry" with "the archetypifying force."[53] The prime example of it is Isaiah 14:4–21, where Alter argues "the provoking pretensions of the satiric target invite a

---

47. Ibid., 34.
48. Ibid., 66.
49. Ibid., 41.
50. Alter, *Art*, 146.
51. Ibid., 146.
52. Ibid., 151.
53. Ibid., 146.

mythological scale of mimicry."[54] What interests Alter is not the origin of the word משל but its playful and evocative use by the prophetic text. Having briefly mentioned that משל is a "literary term of shifting meaning that in the Prophets usually refers to songs of mockery," Alter proceeds, "The poet . . . play[s] with the term by referring to the king metonymically as "the rod of rulers" (*moshlim*) and then later invoke still another sense of the root *m-sh-l* when the denizens of the underworld ask the king how he has "become just like" (*nimshalta*) them."[55]

Read in this light, the משל of Isaiah 14 renders irrelevant the historical identity of the king who it addresses. Alter insists that the language of evocative poetic משל makes him "the very archetype of self-deifying (and hence self-deluding) earthly power."[56] Alter's summary of how this משל functions is both profound and instructive,

> From the global perspective through which the poem views the tyrant, his career becomes an exemplary instance of how man overreaches himself in his unslaked thirst for power and by so doing turns civilization into desolation. As a powerful exemplum, the poem possesses a quality of timelessness: though particularly inspired, we may assume, by the historically specific barbarity of Assyrian imperialism in the eighth or early seventh century B.C.E., it gives body and weight to a grim image of political perversion that we have known all too well in the century of Hitler and Stalin.[57]

Conclusion

As Muecke has stressed, the irony sheds light on "something in order to have it rejected as false."[58] Reflecting on Yee and Alter, one comes away with a sense that the משל of Isaiah 14 is a raw and in places grotesque picture that exposes what is arguably one of the most grave and "perennially problematic dimensions within human response to God."[59] The danger is to allow human beings to persist in their blind unawareness of how uninhabitable is their old house of unrestrained self-seeking. Without a sophisticated mode of confrontation they might opt out to "dwell in happy ignorance in the

54. Ibid., 147.
55. Ibid. For similar observations see also Godbey, "The Hebrew Mashal," 99.
56. Alter, *Art*, 150.
57. Ibid.
58. Muecke, *Irony and the Ironic*, 56.
59. Moberly, *Theology*, 281.

shaky edifice, thus adding to its absurdity."⁶⁰ The scandalizing taunt might be the only hope for awakening the readers from slumber of self-exaltation and inviting them into creative and imaginative engagement in life before God.

One can hear the resonances of such prophetic impulses in one of the most intriguing twentieth-century novelists, Flannery O'Connor. Her trademark writing style could be summed up as violent plots filled with grotesque characters and laced with sarcasm. O'Connor's own rationale for producing such outlandishly smug characters as Ruby Turpin and depressing plots as "A Good Man is Hard to Find" is very instructive,

> The novelist with Christian concerns will find in modern life distortions which are repugnant to him, and his problem will be to make these appear as distortions to an audience which is used to seeing them as natural; and he may well be forced to take ever more violent means to get his vision across to this hostile audience. When you can assume that your audience holds the same beliefs you do, you can relax a little and use more normal ways of talking to it; when you have to assume that it does not, then you have to make your vision apparent by shock—to the hard of hearing you shout, and for the almost blind you draw large and startling figures.⁶¹

O'Connor's rationale is congruent with what seems to be going on in Isaiah 14. In the end, the משל of Isaiah 14 might not be a jejune cameo intended for mere jeering, but a thoughtful vehicle for change. To put it differently, the משל might not care if the tyrant hears the taunt or not, but it hopes against all odds to get a reflective and thoughtful response from those it seeks to transform. Towards that end it whimsically yet shamelessly draws very large and startling figures.

---

60. Booth, *Rhetoric*, 41.
61. O'Connor, *Prose*, 34.

4

Imaginative World of Isaiah 14:3–23

THE PREVIOUS CHAPTER SOUGHT to stress the significance of the fact that Isaiah 14:3–23 is a משל and as such it seeks an engaged reader who will be open to change upon encountering its imaginative portrayal of the world. Wilder, writing insightfully about the parables of Jesus, sheds light on what is at stake in taking texts with imaginative seriousness,

> [A] true metaphor or symbol is more than a sign, it is a bearer of the reality to which it refers. The hearer not only learns about that reality, he participates in it. He is invaded by it. Here lies the power and fatefulness of art. Jesus' speech had the character not of instruction and ideas but of compelling imagination, of spell, of mythical shock and transformation.[1]

Inherent in any attempt to paint a world is an assumption that there are other ways of doing the same thing. Telling a story is an exercise of entering into the realm of contested imaginations. Thus, with its large and graphic images, the משל of Isaiah 14:3–23 paints an evocative picture of reality and invites its reader to enter its world laced with mythic echoes and satirical twists. In what follows we enter the imaginative world of the משל of Isaiah 14:3–23. Our hope is to get a sense of a poem as a whole—to hear its unique voice that seeks to persuade readers that its construal of the world has more enduring value than any of the other alternatives.

A Reading of Isaiah 14:3–23

> **3** When the LORD has given you rest from your pain and turmoil and the hard service with which you were made to serve, **4a** you will take up this taunt against the king of Babylon. (Isa 14:3–4a)

---

1. Wilder, *Early Christian Rhetoric*, 84.

The מָשָׁל proper is introduced with a note in 14:3–4a, which sets up its context and serves to link it with the material in chapter 13 bringing together a collection of oracles under the rubric of מַשָּׂא בָּבֶל (oracle against Babylon). The downfall of Babylon described in Isaiah 13 is reiterated in Isaiah 14 as explicitly bound up with the deliverance of Israel from bondage.

The vision of the future is marked by the removal of pain, suffering, and enslaving labor. The language of rest (נוח) is often linked in the Old Testament with YHWH's presence. A noteworthy reference is found in Exodus 33:14. As Israel prepares to depart from Sinai, Moses pleads with YHWH to show his ways. YHWH replies, "My presence will go with you, and I will give you rest (נוח)." As then so now, YHWH will furnish rest for his people from the enslaving enemy.

> **4b** "How the oppressor has ceased!
>   How his insolence has ceased!
> **5** The LORD has broken the staff of the wicked,
>   the scepter of rulers,
> **6** that struck down the peoples in wrath
>   with unceasing blows,
> that ruled the nations in anger
>   with unrelenting persecution.
> **7** The whole earth is at rest and quiet;
>   they break forth into singing.
> **8** The cypresses[2] exult over you,
>   the cedars of Lebanon, saying,
> "Since you were laid low,
>   no one comes to cut us down." (Isa 14:4–8)

Isaiah 14:4b–8 envisions the enemy as the king of Babylon. Bolstered by YHWH, his people will burst into a song against their adversary. As sharp and evocative as these opening lines are in their own right, it may help to feel the force of this מָשָׁל if the reader initially stands back and reflects on some of the claims for greatness that were typically made by the Babylonians. Hearing the self-aggrandizing aspirations of ancient Babylon for the role of the cosmic epicenter sharpens the force of a reading of the downfall of the tyrant. While there is an abundance of primary sources and secondary

---

2. In my discussion in chapter 2 I have argued that a preferable translation would be "Phoenician junipers."

literature, a couple of targeted examples should suffice to create a flavor of Babylon's quest for greatness.³

The *Enuma Elish*, one of the oldest Mesopotamian creation myths dating from the second millennium BC, envisions the building of Babylon as the climactic point of the creation epic. The perplexed and frightened assembly of gods turns to Marduk in hopes of overcoming the threat posed by Tiamat. In exchange for averting the Tiamat threat Marduk is granted the supreme authority over the divine assembly.

> They erected him a princely throne.
> Facing his fathers, he sat down, presiding.
> "Thou art the most honored of the great gods,
> Thy decree is unrivaled, thy command is Anu.
> Thou, Marduk, art the most honored of the great gods,
> Thy decree is unrivaled, thy word is Anu.
> From this day unchangeable shall be thy pronouncement.
> To praise or bring low—these shall be (in) thy hand.
> Thy utterance shall be true, thy command shall be unimpeachable.
> No one among the gods shall transgress thy bounds!
> Adornment being wanted for the seats of the gods,
> Let the place of their shrines ever be in thy place.
> O Marduk, thou art indeed our avenger.
> We have granted thee kingship over the entire universe."⁴

The story culminates with the building of Babylon as Marduk's abode. Grateful gods inquire of Marduk,

> "Now, o lord, thou who has caused our deliverance,
> What shall be our homage to thee?"⁵

Brightly glowing Marduk replies,

> "Construct Babylon, whose building you have requested,
> Let its brickwork be fashioned. You shall name it 'The Sanctuary.'"⁶

---

3. For Babylon's role in antiquity see Arnold, *Who Were the Babylonians?*; Brinkman, *A Political History*; Roux, *Ancient Iraq*; Saggs, *The Greatness*. Especially helpful is the annotated bibliography in Arnold's volume (*Babylonians*, 107–12).

4. *ANET*, 66.

5. Ibid., 68

6. Ibid.

A marvelous feast at Marduk's temple celebrates the momentous occasion of Babylon's construction as other gods confer on him fifty names, asserting that this patron god of Babylon is the chief god of the pantheon. This account positions Babylon for its due prominence in the world.

In a similar vein, Nabopolassar's inscription dating from the seventh century BC, praises the walls of Babylon as marking off the favorite residence of the gods,

> The great fortification wall of Babylon, the original boundary-post which has been made manifest since olden days, the solid border as ancient as time immemorial, the lofty mountain peak which rivals heavens, the mighty shield which locks the entrance to the hostile lands, the wide enclosure of the Igigi, the spacious courtyard of the Anunnaki.[7]

The city's cosmic status was further affirmed by linking it with "the staircase to heaven, the ladder to the netherworld."[8] The architecture from times immemorial was a handmaid of propaganda. As an epitome of human accomplishment Babylon undoubtedly aimed to exalt the kings who stood behind such grand undertaking.

As stunning as Babylon and her kings could be to the ancient mind, the author of our text is not impressed. Different assumptions of human greatness seem to be operating here that refuse to join the ancient chorus of praise for the Babylonian royal rule. In a peculiar fashion the king of Babylon is not introduced in verse 4 by his name but rather with a pejorative designation of נגש (oppressor). While the significance of the text's refusal to name this king will be discussed at length later, the designation of him as נגש signals the text's own intentionality in highlighting the fact that this king exercises his reign in such a way that leads to destructive violence. Memorable use of the word נגש is in Exodus 3:7 where it refers to the Egyptian task-masters who exerted unbearable pressure on the Hebrew slaves till their groans and agonizing cries moved YHWH to summon Moses to lead them out of captivity. The reader is invited to imagine the groans of the oppressed across the earth as the tyrant, in his insolent fury,[9] goes on striking down the peoples with unceasing blows. His reign is tainted by the anger that poured out the cosmic portions of unrelenting persecution (14:6).

---

7. *COS* 2:307.

8. Ibid.

9. As pointed out in chapter 2 we follow the scholarly consensus in rendering the word מדהבה as "insolent fury" in verse 4. Modern scholarship has assumed the dalet-resh (ד-ר) confusion based on the evidence of the Qumran scroll 1QIsaᵃ and has emended מדהבה to מרהבה (marhevah, fury).

The staff and the scepter, ubiquitous symbols of royal authority in the ancient Near East, originated in a pastoralist context due to the association of the king with a shepherd of people.[10] Symbols of guidance and protection at the disposal of a wise shepherd, they become instruments of enslavement when placed in the wrong hands. The participle forms of both נכה (strike) and רדה (rule) suggest a repeated or ongoing nature of violence perpetrated by the tyrant's staff and scepter.

It is hard to disagree with Seitz that here we find "the epitome of unjust oppression, the culmination of all evil."[11] Rather than a cosmic display of human greatness, Babylon is envisioned here as one of the worst of human undertakings. Although the Babylonian power was not in fact universal, the poet imagines the tyrant's downfall as so massive that it is as though the whole earth is affected by it. Seitz writes, "This is no mere instance of earthly persecution, or even an outstanding example of absolute power corrupting absolutely: the whole earth was made to feel the oppressive weight of Babylon's rule."[12] Thus, reflecting back on the tyrant's life, the text feels the weight of the tyrant's oppression casting an ominous shadow across the globe. "It appeared as though no force on earth could contend with the might and terrifying force of Babylon the Great."[13] At this low point of global history, the text envisions YHWH's intervention. YHWH breaks (שׁבר) the symbols of the tyrant's oppression. This language of שׁבר is very characteristic of the divine punitive action in antiquity. The Code of Hammurabi contains stern warnings for a king who would deviate from the laws set out by this third millennium BC Babylonian king,

> In the days to come, for all time,
> let the king who appears in the land observe
> the words of justice which I wrote on my stela;
> let him not alter the law of the land which I enacted,
> the ordinances of the land which I prescribed;
> let him not rescind my statutes . . . .
> If that man did not heed my words which I wrote on my stela,
> and disregarded my curses,
> and did not fear the curses of the gods,
> but abolished the law which I enacted,
> has distorted my words,

10. Fischer, "Sticks and Staves," 7–8
11. Seitz, *Isaiah*, 134.
12. Ibid., 135.
13. Ibid.

has altered my statutes,
effaced my name inscribed (thereon)
and has written his own name . . .
may mighty Anum, the father of the gods, who proclaimed my reign,
deprive him of the glory of sovereignty,
may he break his scepter, may he curse his fate![14]

Similarly, in the Old Testament YHWH is frequently the subject of the verb שבר. The likes of the yoke of the king of Babylon (Jer 28:2), the Pharaoh's arm (Ezek 30:21), the gate bars of Damascus (Amos 1:5), Nebuchadnezzar's yoke (Jer 28:11), Elam's bow (Jer 49:35), and the Assyrians themselves (Isa 14:25) become the recipients of YHWH's symbolic disciplinary action of breaking. Thus, our text reinforces what the rest of the Old Testament affirms, namely that no matter how powerful one who wields his power in a way that oppresses is, he will eventually meet his match in YHWH. As Brueggemann says, "In a world governed by Yahweh, nobody is free to practice exploitative brutality, but the tyrant always learns that too late."[15]

The aftermath of YHWH's intervention is described in almost idyllic terms (vv. 7–8). First, the whole earth enjoys rest (נוח) and quiet (שקט). As was discussed earlier, the scope envisioned here undoubtedly goes beyond the boundaries of Israel and includes the entire world as known to the author of this משל, which most likely included the lands that felt the impact of the Babylon's power. Wildberger reminds us that Israel's idea of נוח was inextricably linked with the appropriation of the land YHWH had promised which was accompanied with the release from "the anxieties of a nomadic way of life in order to be settled permanently in one place." This rest ultimately anticipated a tranquil existence at peace from all the enemies (Deut 12:10; 25:19; Josh 23:1).[16] As we saw earlier, the framing of the משל in verse 3 envisions precisely this sort of a rest—one that sees the removal of pain, turmoil, and enslaving labor at the hands of the oppressor. Similarly, the idea of שקט is associated frequently in Joshua, Judges, and Chronicles with the tranquility and rest that follow the cessation of warfare.[17] For example, Joshua 11:23 records what follows the end of Joshua's military campaign, "Joshua took the whole land, according to all that the LORD had spoken to Moses; and Joshua gave it for an inheritance to Israel according

---

14. *ANET*, 178–79.
15. Brueggemann, *Isaiah*, 126.
16. Wildberger, *Isaiah*, 49–50.
17. See Brueggemann, *Isaiah*, 126 and Gray, *Isaiah I–XXVII*, 255.

to their tribal allotments. And the land had rest (שׁקט) from war." Also, Jehoshaphat's twenty-five-year reign is marked with tranquility, "So the realm of Jehoshaphat was quiet (שׁקט), for his God gave him rest (נוח) all around" (2 Chr 20:28). Finally, שׁקט in the book of Judges often characterizes the condition of the land after a judge, raised up by YHWH, delivers Israel from bondage. Judges 8:28 reports the result of Gideon's deliverance, "So Midian was subdued before the Israelites, and they lifted up their heads no more. So the land had rest (שׁקט) forty years in the days of Gideon."

Furthermore, YHWH's intervention prompts singing. Scholarship has frequently pointed out that singing in view of deliverance is a characteristic feature of the book of Isaiah. While it is more frequent in Second and Third Isaiah (35:10; 43:14; 44:23; 48:20; 49:13; 51:11; 54:1; 55:12), the idea of exuberant singing in response to deliverance does appear in First Isaiah beyond Isaiah 14 (24:14,16; 26:1,19). Peculiarly, the phrase פָּצְחוּ רִנָּה (break forth in singing) is uniquely Isaianic, only appearing here as well as 44:23, 49:13, 54:1 and 55:12.[18] The subject of this singing that breaks forth is not clear. Who are "they" who engaged in this exuberant singing? Presumably, it refers to those who inhabit the whole earth—peoples who are enjoying the rest and quiet brought about by YHWH's breaking of the oppressor's violence. Yet Tull has pointed out that this Isaianic phrase designates "the joy of inanimate objects in this poem and in Second Isaiah, where mountains and forests (44:23), mountains (49:13), the city itself (54:1), and mountains and hills (55:12) likewise 'burst into song.'"[19] While one is tempted to improve on Tull's somewhat awkward way of grouping these references as "the joy of inanimate objects," her point is none the less significant. Coupled with the reference to the whole earth, this picture of joyful singing seems to indicate that the exuberance at the downfall of the tyrant is both global and creation-wide, encompassing every aspect of the world.

This reference also prepares the reader for the next aspect of what follows YHWH's decisive intervention. Verse 8 pictures the junipers and the cedars of Lebanon joining the joyful celebration of the tyrant's demise. The reason for their celebration is that with the demise of the oppressor no one is coming up to cut them down. Cedars of Lebanon were the source of numerous ancient Near Eastern construction projects. Timber was a precious commodity in antiquity—a fact further reinforced by rapid deforestations

---

18. Oswalt, *Isaiah*, 317. Unfortunately, Oswalt erroneously leaves out its use in 54:1 and 55:12. See Gray, *Isaiah I–XXVII*, 253.

19. Tull, *Isaiah*, 278.

due to high demand for quality building materials.[20] The Assyrian king Esarhaddon reports,

> All these I sent out and made them transport under terrible difficulties, to Nineveh, the town (where I exercise) my rulership, as building materials for my palace: big logs, long beams (and) thin boards from cedar and pine trees, products of the Sirara and Lebanon (*Lab-na-na*) mountains, which had grown for a long time into tall and strong timber.[21]

Similarly, The Old Testament records several instances of the cedars of Lebanon being used for royal constructions projects.[22] The coveted building materials from the lush forests of Lebanon continued to be the objects of royal desire down through the centuries.[23] We have a record as late as 316 BC when Antigonus Monophthalmus had thousands of cedars of Lebanon cut down to build a fleet for his invasion of Egypt.[24]

Isaiah 14:4–8 bears a poignant witness to what appears to be true in every age, namely that human grasping for divine majesty indeed comes out as cruelty, abuse, and violence on the global scale. This text raises questions whether the peaceful denouement of human history could be a result of human goodwill. Rather, Isaiah insists that it comes on the heels of YHWH asserting his power in the affairs of humanity. His intervention brings about the stunning reversal of fortunes where the unmitigated quest for human greatness finds an unexpected end. Forceful abasement of the cosmic tyrant appears to be a prerequisite for universal peace.

Excursus: Some Hermeneutical Difficulties in Isaiah 14:8

A. *On Junipers and Cedars of Lebanon*

While a straightforward reading of Isaiah 14:8 could assume that the junipers and cedars of Lebanon represent nature joining the global chorus

---

20. Harrison, *Forests*, 17.

21. *ANET*, 291.

22. King David's house was made of cedar (2 Sam 7:2; 1 Chr 17:10). Solomon negotiated with king Hiram of Tyre to procure timber from Lebanon for his building projects (1 Kgs 5).

23. Other Mesopotamian sources include the accounts of Ashurnasirpal II (*ANET*, 175) and Nebuchadnezzar (*ANET*, 307). One should also mention several sources from other regions of ANE, namely accounts from Egypt (*ANET*, 27, 240, 243) and from Ugarit (*ANET*, 134).

24. Briant, *Persian Empire*, 421.

of praise of those released from the tyrant's exploitative reign, some scholars have suggested that there is more going on here than mere halting of timber-gathering expeditions. Nielsen has insisted that the reference to the trees in Isaiah 1–39 are metaphorical references to political realities that the text seeks to bring to the light.[25] For example, Isaiah 2:12–13 pronounces judgment on the cedars of Lebanon,

> **12** For the LORD of hosts has a day
> against all that is proud and lofty,
> against all that is lifted up and high;
> **13** against all the cedars of Lebanon,
> lofty and lifted up;
> and against all the oaks of Bashan

According to Nielsen this is not a reference to YHWH's anger against the tall trees of Lebabon, rather it is a metaphorical depiction of the arrogance of the rulers who are cast in the imagery of cedars of Lebanon, tall and imposing to anyone who sets their eyes on them.[26] When it comes to Isaiah 14, Nielsen, following early Christian commentators such as Eusebius,[27] insists that the clearly metaphorical reference to the trees rejoicing should be seen as representing vassals of the tyrant who now can breathe a sigh of relief at the downfall of the oppressor.[28]

Nielsen's idea is definitely suggestive as her observation that the language of trees functions metaphorically in First Isaiah is indeed on target. Yet Nielsen's own programatic statement insists that the metaphorical language in biblical texts is frequently reused in other contexts, which invites the possibility of reinterpretation. She writes,

> The metaphorical function of a word is not part of the meaning of the word itself. No words are born as metaphors, but a word can in a concrete context be used as a metaphor. We therefore have to know the context in order to determine whether a word

---

25. Hays has recently proposed a position similar to Nielsen. According to Hays, Nabonidus' inscription which refers to his mother's funeral reports the delegates from various regions of his empire being present. In a similar vein, Hays suggests that the cedars of Lebanon are a metaphorical reference for the representatives of this region being present at the tyrant's funeral. This, according to Hays creates a "carnival rendition of real mourning practices." See Hay, *Death*, 208–9.

26. Nielsen, *Tree*, 178.

27. Eusebius, *Isaiah*, 77.

28. Nielsen, *Tree*, 162–63.

must be taken literally or metaphorically. And a word in its context is a word in function.²⁹

In other words, Nielsen does not advocate an inflexible metaphor that functions in the same way in every text, but one that is rather moldable in use depending on the context. The trees of Lebanon do indeed function metaphorically in 14:8, yet the question is what they represent. In Isaiah 2:13–14 cedars of Lebanon stand for *human* pride and haughtiness, but that is clearly conditioned by the context of verses 11–12 and 17 that bracket it. The immediate context of Isaiah 14:8 is somewhat different. If we take seriously both the global context of the verse 7 and Tull's observations about the uniquely Isaianic phrase פָּצְחוּ רִנָּה (break forth in singing) as referring to "the joy of inanimate objects," then it seems that the language of junipers and cedars of Lebanon functions as a metaphor within a larger metaphor. The text's internal logic moves from peoples and nations in verse 6 to broader creation-wide impact of the tyrant's downfall in verse 7. The stock imagery of fertile Lebanon with its beautiful forests which has approximately seventy biblical references according to Nielsen, rounds out the sweeping picture of global celebration. Thus, the junipers and cedars of Lebanon are a reference to real forests of Lebanon that are painted into a metaphorical picture of the jubilant creation released from the oppressive bondage of the tyrant.

Unlike Nielsen's metaphorical approach, some have suggested that the reference to the trees of Lebanon stems from a mythological milieu. Stolz proposed that behind this text stands the concept of a garden of God located at the top of the Lebanon mountain range.³⁰ The evidence does point to the fact that the imposing luxuriant Lebanon was considered a prototype of "gardens of gods."³¹ For example, the seventh-century BC Assyrian text, *A Vision of the Nether World* describes the temple of Assur as "the Garden of Plenty, the image of Lebanon."³² The Old Testament echoes the similar sentiment when Ezekiel 31:8 refers to Lebanon as a "garden of God."

Stolz draws parallels between Ezekiel 31 and Isaiah 14 as a way of opening the door for grasping the mythological context of the verse 8,

> Der Vers lässt sich völlig «unmythologisch» verstehen. Man wird dann darauf hinweisen, dass die assyrischen und babylonischen Könige je und dann Holz für Bauten und Kriegsgeräte aus dem Libanon bezogen. Doch es ist zu fragen, ob nicht derselbe

---

29. Nielsen, "Metaphors," 129.

30. Stolz, "Die Baume der Gottesgartens," *ZAW* 84 (1972), 141–56. It was reprinted in Stolz, *Religion*, 139–53. Our citations are from this latter volume.

31. Keel, *The Song of Songs*, 170.

32. *ANET*, 110.

> Hintergrund anzunehmen ist, wie in Ez 31. Dann wären die Libanonzedern die Bäume des Gottesgartens; sie zu fällen, erschiene hier als überheblicher Frevel; und als Konsequenz wäre wieder das Motiv der Unterweltsfahrt zu beobachten, das hier freilich nicht fur umgehauenen Bäume gälte, sondern für den frevelnden Baumfaller.[33]

Stolz postulates that, seen in this mythological context, the tyrant is envisioned as someone who is assaulting the abode of God. Rather than merely attempting to procure timber for his building projects, he is seen as impiously pushing his way into the divine dwelling place,

> Was sich der König von Assur nach diesem Textzeugnis vornimmt, ist genau das, was der in Jes 14:8 verspottete, gestürzte Herrscher ausgefuhrt hat: Er will den Libanon-Waldgarten fällen und bis zuoberst vordringen; dort ist eine Behausung—nach dem ursprünglichsten Zusammenhang wohl die Behausung eines Gottes. Dieses Vorhaben wird hier als Frevel Jahwe gegenüber verstanden. Man kann aus dem Zusammenhang aller bisher besprochener Stellen demnach vermuten, dass in gewissen Kreisen Jahwe als Besitzer des Libanon-Gottesgartens galt; ein Anschlag darauf tastet Jahwes Herrschaft an.[34]

Thus the trees of Lebanon rejoicing are not merely representing the nature that has been spared of the tyrant's exploitation, but rather a relief of the part of the divine abode that has come under the assault from this tyrant of Babylon.

Wildberger has picked up Stolz' thesis and developed it in his commentary. He has provided the following reconstruction of the myth that could be standing in the background of Isaiah 14:8,

> a foolhardy rascal climbs up into the Lebanon, forces his way into the garden of God, and commits the sacrilege of touching the trees of El. . . . It is not the "tree," as in Ezekiel, but the intruder who is driven by hubris, who is to be handed over into the power of one who is stronger, one who would deal with him on the basis of his evil nature. . . . There is no question that, from the very first, the trees of the garden of God were symbolic of life and fruitfulness. . . . If the evildoer climbs up to them in order to fell them, he is trying to take hold of the elements that constitute life itself. It poses a deathly threat to the "whole earth" when this

---

33. Stolz, *Religion*, 141.
34. Ibid., 142.

impious one forced his way to the junipers and cedar trees in the garden of God.³⁵

The strength of the Stolz/Wildberger argument is supported by two pieces of evidence. First, Isaiah 37:22–29 envisions the downfall of the Assyrian king Sennacherib. Verse 24 describes the arrogance of Sennacherib in the language very much reminiscent of the משל of Isaiah 14:

> By your servants you have mocked the LORD,
>   and you have said, "With my many chariots
> I have gone up the heights of the mountains,
>   to the far recesses (ירכתים) of Lebanon;
> I felled (כרת) its tallest cedars,
>   its choicest cypresses;
> I came to its remotest height,
>   its densest forest."

Beyond an overlap in the words used, such as "far recesses" (ירכתים) echoing the "heights of Zaphon" in 14:14 and "felled" (כרת) resonating with "no one comes to cut us down" in 14:8, Sennacherib's arrogant attitude as he storms the far recesses of Lebanon has the thematic parallel with the tyrant's attempt to ascend to heaven to sit on the mount of assembly on the heights of Zaphon—both arrogantly aspire for the divine realm.

An impious tone that one would envision accompanying a brazen assault on the divine abode presumed in Wildberger's reconstruction of the myth could be detected in Sennacherib's traversing the terrain of Lebanon. There is no suggestion in this text that Sennacherib's intent is to plunder the timber of the forests of Lebanon. His expedition appears to be a mere display of his arrogant power even if presumably providing much coveted timber for royal construction projects—arrogance easily detected in the tyrant of Babylon in Isaiah 14 as well.

Furthermore, the idea of an adventurous king trespassing the dwelling place of gods figures prominently in the Sumerian epic "Gilgamesh and the Land of the Living"—a tale of the king Gilgamesh's first heroic venture beyond the walls of Uruk which takes him and his royal servant and friend Enkidu to the Cedar Mountain. The variant of this story is also found in the famous Akkadian account *The Epic of Gilgamesh*. Two aspects of this account are significant for our purposes.

---

35. Wildberger, *Isaiah*, 59.

First, *The Epic of Gilgamesh* gives us a clear picture of what this king has his sights set on. As Gilgamesh and Enkidu arrive to the border of the Cedar Mountain, this is the sight they encountered,

> They stood still and gazed at the forest,
> They looked at the height of the cedars,
> They looked at the entrance to the forest.
> Where Humbaba was wont to walk was a path,
> Straight were the tracks and good was the going.
> They beheld the cedar mountain, abode of gods,
> > Throne-seat of Irnini.
> From the face of the mountain
> > The cedars raise aloft their luxuriance.[36]

Guarded by the fear-inducing monster Humbaba, this Cedar Forest is both imposing and awe-inspiring. Gilgamesh and Enkidu are clearly aware of the danger they face as seen in Enkidu's fear and Gilgamesh's plea to Shamash for help.[37] Trespassing into the divine realm is clearly a perilous undertaking for any human being.

Second, the Sumerian version answers the obvious question that would be in the reader's mind, namely: why would Gilgamesh attempt such an undertaking? Trying to enlist god Utu's favor on his journey, Gilgamesh exclaims,

> "O Utu, I would enter the 'land,' be thou my ally,
> I would enter the land *of the cut-down* cedar, be thou my ally."
> Utu of heaven answers him:
> ". . . verily thou art, but what art thou to the 'land'?"
> "O Utu, a word I would speak to thee, to my word thy ear,
> *I would have it reach thee*, give ear to it.
> In my city man dies, oppressed is the heart,
> Man perishes, heavy is the heart,
> *I peered over* the wall,
> Saw the dead bodies . . . *floating on* the river;
> As for me, I too will be served thus; verily 'tis so.
> Man, the tallest, cannot stretch to heaven,
> Man, the widest, cannot cover the earth.

---

36. *ANET*, 82.
37. Ibid., 83.

> Not *(yet) have brick and stamp* brought forth
> > *the fated end,*
> I would enter the 'land,' I would set up my name,
> In its places where the names have been raised up, I would
> raise up my name
> In its places where the names have not been raised up, I would
> raise up the names of the gods."[38]

Gilgamesh peers over the walls of Uruk and encounters the bodies of the dead floating down the river. Whether some sort of ancient Sumerian funerary ritual[39] or an aftermath of catastrophe,[40] Gilgamesh encounters not just dead bodies, but rather his own mortality. Human being, however great, could neither reach the heights of heaven nor cover the breadth of the earth. Trapped in his humanity, Gilgamesh's assault on the Cedar Forest is an attempt to transcend the limitations of being a mere mortal.

While one must admit that there are certain overlapping thematic lines between Gilgamesh's assault on the divine forest and the tyrant's aspirations, this parallel is less than convincing. As Shipp has pointed out, the rationale for YHWH's anger against the tyrant is different from the divine wrath that Gilgamesh's effort precipitates. While one might envision a parallel between Gilgamesh's effort to force his way into the divine forest and the tyrant's longing for a seat in the divine assembly (14:12–15), our text insists that YHWH breaks the staff of the wicked because it "struck down the peoples in wrath with unceasing blows" and "ruled the nations in anger with unrelenting persecution" (14:6). Furthermore, in the Gilgamesh account it is Enkidu rather than Gilgamesh who receives the curse from Humbaba and is eventually slain by Ishtar.[41] Finally, the linking of the Cedar Forest in the Gilgamesh account with the lush forests of Lebanon has been contested. For example, Hansmann has argued that *erĕnu*-wood in the Sumerian version of the Gilgamesh account should be translated as "juniper" rather than "cedar" and the forest should be located in the ancient territory of Elam, east of Sumer, which would be to the south-west of Iran rather than to the north-west in Syria or Anatolia.[42]

---

38. Ibid., 48. *ANET*'s italics. "Italics within translations have been used for two purposes: first, to designate a doubtful translation of a known text; secondly, to indicate transliterations" (*ANET*, xxii)
39. Harrison, *Forests*, 16; Raine, *Guardianship*, 203.
40. Forsyth, *Enemy*, 25.
41. Shipp, *Dirges*, 11
42 Hansmann, "Gilgamesh," 23–35.

While one cannot completely dismiss the possibility of a myth standing behind the imagery of Isaiah 14:8, at the very least it is not as straightforward as Stolz and Wildberger might suggest. The well-attested fact of the forests of Lebanon being recipients of the excessive deforestation due to numerous royal projects seems to provide a plausible and sufficient explanation over against a tentative reconstruction of a myth we do not at the moment possess.

> **9** Sheol beneath is stirred up
> to meet you when you come;
> it rouses the shades to greet you,
> all who were leaders of the earth;
> it raises from their thrones
> all who were kings of the nations.
> **10** All of them will speak
> and say to you:
> "You too have become as weak as we!
> You have become like us!"
> **11** Your pomp is brought down to Sheol,
> and the sound of your harps;
> maggots are the bed beneath you,
> and worms are your covering. (Isa 14:9–11)

With verses 9–11, eerily resembling Dante's "All hope abandon, ye who enter in!," the scene shifts from the peaceful earth to the agitated Sheol. The tyrant is dead. Life on the earth could move on. But if the משל is to have its full impact, the poet deems it necessary to linger with the dead body. Hence the picture of divine abasement of human aspirations for ill-shaped greatness is further elaborated in the reception that awaits this tyrant upon his entrance into Sheol.

According to Yamauchi, "The issues of life, death, and afterlife were of vital concern to the ancient Near East."[43] Thus, the poet's shifting of the lens to Sheol in Isaiah 14:9–11 seems to be very much in line what one would anticipate in the ancient Near Eastern milieu to be a natural progression of the thought upon the news of the tyrant's death. Verse 9 portrays Sheol busily making arrangements to prepare for the tyrant's arrival

---

43. Yamauchi, "Life, Death, and the Afterlife," 21. Yamauchi's article presents a good starting point laying out the similarities and differences that exist in the way these issues were understood in Egypt, Mesopotamia, Ugarit, Persia, and Israel. See also Lewis, "Dead," *ABD* 2:101–5.

to her abode. This is a peculiar picture of Sheol when seen against the broader ancient Near Eastern context. Consistent with ANE cosmology, the Old Testament texts envision the three-tiered universe where YHWH dwells in the heavenly realm, humans inhabit the earth, and the dead occupy the depths of Sheol.[44] On the one hand, Sheol is a final destination for all who pass away (Job 3:13–19).[45] On the other hand, it is pictured as a devouring cavernous beast (Ps 141:7).

The peculiarity of the portrayal of Sheol here is that this abode of the dead is personified as the "mistress of the kingdom of the underworld."[46] The personification of Sheol stands in contrast with the ancient Near Eastern tendency to deify death—most famously, in the Ugaritic god Mot, the son of El who reigns over the subterranean world and is often portrayed battling Baal.[47] Tromp has argued that this tendency to personalize death is universal. He even goes as far as referring to it as "archetypal." Tromp has

---

44. Walton, *Ancient Near Eastern Thought*, 165–78; Wright, *History of Heaven*, 53–54.

45. The minority view is represented by Alexander Heidel who claims that Sheol "applies to the habitation of the souls of the wicked only." (Heidel, *The Gilgamesh Epic*, 184). See also Barth, *Die Errettung vom Tode*, 144–45; Bückers, *Die Unsterblichkeitslehre des Weisheitsbuches*, 74; and Rosenberg, "Biblical Sheol," 174–75.

Contra Heidel and others, Levenson refuses to smooth over the two conceptions of Sheol in the Hebrew Bible, "The inconsistency is best seen as a tension between two competing theologies. The one that sees Sheol as the universal destination comports well with ancient Mesopotamian and Canaanite notions of human destiny as finally one of pure gloom. This conception survives in the Hebrew Bible, especially Wisdom literature, the category to which most of these exceptional passages belong. But it is very much at odds with most of the relevant texts, which instead assume a destination between those who go to Sheol and those who die blessed, like Abraham, Moses, and Job." Thus Levenson claims that this is a tension between two theologies. The older theology affirmed that Sheol was a final destination of all humanity, while the younger theology affirmed YHWH's capacity to deliver some from that dreaded end. (Levenson, *Resurrection*, 75).

Somewhat similarly, Day approaches this topic from the diachronic perspective and argues that Israel's beliefs about afterlife underwent significant developments from the "gloomy underworld cavern" to a "more worthwhile afterlife" in the post-exilic times. (Day, "Life after Death," 231). Barr has also pointed out that a wide variety of beliefs about afterlife could be detected within the Old Testament and the denial of this would be tantamount to allowing one's ideology to trump the evidence at hand. (Barr, *The Garden of Eden*, 99). Finally, noteworthy is Bailey's cautious exhortation regarding differing biblical perspectives on death, "It is precarious to speak of the biblical response to death. Rather, there is a variety of responses, depending upon the time and circumstances." (Bailey, *Biblical Perspectives on Death*, 97).

46. Kissane, *Isaiah*, 172.

47. Healey, "Mot," 1122–32; Leick, *Dictionary*, 119.

questioned whether those who would dismiss texts like those describing Mot as merely poetic are really taking the phenomenon seriously. He writes,

> For Israel's neighbors Death was an extremely real and concrete reality, a monstrous personal power waylaying fertility and life. Of course in Israel itself the divine Mot was dethroned by Jahwism, but "zu den am längsten beiseite geschobenen und darum von Jahwäglauben lange nicht durch gestaltenen kanaanäischen Elementen gehören die Vorstellungen von Tod und postmortalem Dasein." Consequently the experience of death was not fundamentally changed in Israel and in the light of this fact the many occasions where Death is personified acquire a pregnant meaning.[48]

The truth of Tromp's observation is evident in the way personification in general works in the book of Isaiah as well is in the way it handles Sheol. Reading of the desert rejoicing (35:1), mountains breaking forth into singing (44:23), and the trees clapping their hands (55:12), the reader gets a sense that the personification appears to be one of the book's significant literary techniques. Scholarship has long acknowledged that the female personification (mother, daughter, bride, widow) of Zion/Jerusalem is an important aspect of Second Isaiah.[49] Similarly, of the nine references to Sheol in the book of Isaiah, five appear to be a personification. The most memorable ones besides the reference to Sheol stirring up the shades to properly prepare for the tyrant's arrival (14:9), are the references to Sheol having an enlarged appetite and opening its mouth wide to swallow her prey (5:14) and Sheol as a covenant partner shaking hands with the scoffers of Jerusalem (28:15).

While the Isaiah 14:9–11 account of Sheol as the abode of the dead lacks the deification elements of its ancient Near Eastern counterparts, it might be heuristically helpful to consider one memorable Akkadian myth as a way to better understand how this משל intends to use the personified Sheol for its rhetorical purposes. *Descent of Ishtar to the Nether World* recounts the journey of the goddess Ishtar through the seven gates of the underworld to find her beloved Tammuz.[50] She arrives at the gates of the Land of No Return, a realm which is described in gruesome colors,

---

48. Tromp, *Death and the Netherworld*, 100–101. Tromps' quote refers to Maag's article, "Tod und Jenseits," 17–37, esp. 17.

49. Darr, *Isaiah's Vision*, 165–204; O'Connor, "Second Isaiah's Use of Daughter Zion," 281–94; Dille, *God as Mother and Father*, 128–62.

50. This point is a subject of recent scholarly reconsideration. There is evidence from other texts that the goddess Ishtar herself sent her husband Tammuz to the underworld. See Smith, *Biblical Monotheism*, 11–14; Yamauchi, "Tammuz and the Bible,"

To the Land of no Return, the realm of [Ereshkigal],
Ishtar, the daughter of Sin, [set] her mind.
Yea, the daughter of Sin set [her] mind
To the dark house, the abode of Irkal[la],
To the house which none leave who have entered it,
To the road from which there is no way back,
To the house wherein the entrants are bereft of li[ght],
Where dust is their fare and clay their food,
(Where) they see no light, residing in darkness,
(Where) they are clothed like birds, with wings for garments
(And where) other door and bolt is spread dust.[51]

This dusty and lowly-lit realm of the underworld is ruled by Ishtar's sister, Ereshkigal, the goddess of death and sterility, who is threatened by her arrival. Presumably Ereshkigal's fear is that Ishtar has come to take over her reign. Hence Ishtar has to force her way into the underworld by threatening the guard at the entrance,

O gatekeeper, open thy gate,
Open thy gate that I may enter!
If thou openest not the gate so that I cannot enter,
I will smash the door, I will shatter the bolt,
I will smash the doorpost, I will move the doors,
I will raise up the dead, eating the living,
So that the dead will outnumber the living.[52]

Subsequently, Ishtar descends through seven gates, being progressively stripped of her clothes and jewelry, till finally naked, she faces Ereshkigal who orders her vizier Namtar to release sixty diseases against her. Only the intervention of the great gods, at the request of the vizier named Papsukkal revives and brings Ishtar back to the land of the living. The story seems to end with Ishtar's beloved Tammuz playing on a flute of lapis.

The picture of goddess Ereshkigal, personified death, who is alarmed by the perceived assault of her abode might help the reader navigate his or her way through the Sheol segment of Isaiah 14 with more imaginative precision. The trembling (רגז) that the earth has felt during the life-time of the tyrant (14:16), is now passed on to Sheol as she is stirred up (רגז) at the

---

283-90; Yamauchi, "Additional Notes on Tammuz," 10-15.

51. *ANET*, 107.

52. Ibid.

thought of his arrival (14:9). The primary meaning of רגז is "to tremble" or "be caught in restless motion."⁵³ The idea of shaking in anticipation is a common way of interpreting רגז in Isaiah 14:9. Yet shaking produced by fear is also attested in texts like Isaiah 32:10–11, Joel 2:1–2, and Micah 7:16–17. Two weighty examples worth mentioning here would be Exodus 15:14–16 and Deuteronomy 2:24–25. Exodus 15:14–16 reports the fear-filled response of trembling that the nations experience as YHWH's people pass by,

> 14 The peoples heard, they trembled (רגז);
> pangs seized the inhabitants of Philistia.
> 15 Then the chiefs of Edom were dismayed;
> trembling (רעד) seized the leaders of Moab;
> all the inhabitants of Canaan melted away.
> 16 Terror and dread fell upon them;
> by the might of your arm, they became still as a stone
> until your people, O LORD, passed by,
> until the people whom you acquired passed by.

Similarly, in Deuteronomy 2:24–26 YHWH's command for Israel to march on and cross Wadi Arnon is accompanied with YHWH's promise to cause the fear-filled trembling in all who hear about them,

> 24 Proceed on your journey and cross the Wadi Arnon. See, I have handed over to you King Sihon the Amorite of Heshbon, and his land. Begin to take possession by engaging him in battle. 25 This day I will begin to put the dread and fear of you upon the peoples everywhere under heaven; when they hear report of you, they will tremble (רגז) and be in anguish because of you.

Thus it is possible to envision that the dominant emotion that has gripped Sheol at the news of the tyrant's impeding arrival is not anticipation, but fear. This fear that was felt across the whole earth, now leads Sheol to rouse her inhabitants to face this ominous foe. Sheol appears not to be organizing a welcome party, but rather, in alarm, is mustering up a shadowy army to fend off the enemy. While the word קרא (to meet) in verse 9a is a by-form of קרה means to "meet or encounter someone,"⁵⁴ in the context envisioned here it appears to be used in a way analogous to its use in texts like Joshua 11:20 where the enemy with a hardened heart comes up (קרא) against Israel in battle.

---

53. "רגז" n.p. *HALOT on CD-ROM*.
54. "II קרא" n.p. *HALOT on CD-ROM*.

Kaiser's description of the anticipation of the רפאים is fittingly evocative and gruesome,

> In the darkness and half-light of the great cistern of the underworld, the shades of the kings, surrounded by their shadowy armies, sit motionless upon their thrones. Then the gate of the underworld opens. The underworld shakes and the shadows spring up from their thrones.[55]

The realm of Sheol has been readied to face the notorious enemy.

In verse 10 the רפאים begin to speak, yet it is not clear how much they really say. The quotation marks supplied by NRSV reflect a modern conventional way of demarcating the direct speech—a technique unknown to the MT. Thus, the extent of the speech of the רפאים needs to be addressed. According to NRSV, the mocking speech ends in verse 10. This judgment is supported by CEB, ESV, NIV, and NCV. A major alternative would be to extend the quotation to include verse 11, as done by CEV, NAB, NASB, and NJPS. Other options include NJB's decision to extend the quote to the end of verse 15. NET extends it even further to the end of verse 17. KJV does not use quotation marks which makes it hard to determine what the translators had in mind.[56] It is worth noting that NET's judgment has the weighty support from Sweeney's major commentary which argues that verses 9–17 represent Sheol's response to the downfall of the tyrant.[57]

Surely the decisive factor should be the literary shift in verse 12. The presence of the definitive feature of the funeral dirge, introductory אֵיךְ (how), in verse 12 seems to signal the start of a new segment—a dirge within the dirge. This would limit the scope of the speech of the רפאים to either verse 10 or 11. Of these two options either one seems equally defensible. So our choice of extending the quote to include verse 11 cannot be more than a plausible preference.

The רפאים have been duly awakened and readied by Sheol. They are prepared to face the arriving tyrant. Yet upon careful examination of the tyrant the shades breathe a sign of relief, "You too have become like us!" These former leaders, powerful in their own right, but by now weakened, express simultaneously unguarded astonishment and rancorous delight at the sight of this tyrant. Weakened just like them, the tyrant no longer

---

55. Kaiser, *Isaiah*, 37.

56. The lack of scholarly consensus can be seen also in the fact that two recent PhD dissertations, which handle this text at considerable depth, offer two differing interpretive decisions. Hays limits the speech of the רפאים to verse 10 (Hays, *Death*, 204), while Shipp extends it to verse 11 (Shipp, *Dirges*, 130).

57. Sweeney, *Isaiah 1–39*, 225.

presents a threat (14:10). Instead of trembling in fear, they can now mock him (14:11). While other kings rest on their thrones in their shadowy existence in Sheol, this tyrant finds his opulent lifestyle replaced with a bed of maggots and a blanket of worms (v.11). Brueggemann, moving quickly to the world in front of the text, writes memorably about the rhetorical impact this construal of the world seeks to have on its reader,

> Whereas the rhetorical dismantling in all its harshness may have been aimed at Babylon, in canonical form the onslaught means to school the imagination of the community of faith. It intends to provide a world in which abusive power is seen to be flimsy and precarious, and sure to pass.[58]

Excursus: Famous Underworld Journeys in Antiquity

The motif of underworld journey is recurrent across the ages and cultures.[59] Several great epics arising from the Western literary tradition have structured their narratives around a descent into the underworld. While the impact of Dante's *Inferno* and Milton's *Paradise Lost* on the Western mind are widely recognized, two memorable ancient accounts of the underworld journey are worth highlighting here.[60]

Homer's *Odyssey* recounts the wanderings of Odysseus following his victory in the Trojan War. At a certain point during his journey home, Odysseus barely survives a violent storm sent by Zeus and ends up with the Phaiakians. Beneficiary of their generous hospitality, Odysseus tells them the story of his adventures. It is here that we hear about Odysseus' descent to Hades. According to Odysseus, he was told by the goddess Kirkê that before his return home he must descend to Hades in order to consult the shade of the blind Theban prophet, Teiresias. The fear that Odysseus felt upon hearing that he must descend to "the cold home of Death" (10.624) reveals the Greek dread of death (10.551–57),

> At this I felt a weight like stone within me,
> and, moaning, pressed my length against the bed,
> with no desire to see the daylight more.

---

58. Brueggemann, *Isaiah*, 128.

59. Bauckham, *The Fate of the Dead*, 9–48.

60. Iannucci, *Dante, Cinema and Television*; Tillyard, *The Elizabethan World Picture*; Luke, *Journey and Transformation in Dante's Divine Comedy*; Lewis, *A Preface to Paradise Lost*; Markos, *Heaven*; Durham and Pruitt, *Reading Milton Deeply*.

> But when I had wept and tossed and had my fill
> of this despair, at last I answered her:
> "Kirkê, who pilots me upon this journey?
> No man has ever sailed to the land of Death."[61]

Journey to the underworld implies for Odysseus facing both his own mortality and the fate of the soul after death—the task he is willing to undertake despite his tears. According to Markos, Odysseus must descend to Hades because "he, like all the great heroes of Greek mythology (Orpheus, Hercules, and Theseus) must brave the fearsome pit. What better way to test one's mettle, one's courage, one's capacity for despair than to descend bodily into the underworld, to come face-to-face with death itself?"[62] The willingness to face this daunting task rewards Odysseus with a glimpse into his future. Teiresias tells Odysseus that he will return home and die a peaceful death surrounded by his family and his people (11.148-51),

> ... Then a seaborne death
> soft as this hand of mist will come upon you
> when you are wearied out with rich old age,
> your country folk in blessed peace around you.[63]

His journey to Hades comes to an abrupt end as Odysseus gets swarmed by "shades, rustling in a pandemonium of whispers, blown together" (11.751). The sight of thousands of dead spirits pressing in on him induces panic in Odysseus. As the story ends, forsaking any further fraternizing with the dead heroes, he makes a swift run back to his ship (11.755-59),

> I whirled then, made for the ship, shouted to crewmen
> to get aboard and cast off the stern hawsers,
> an order soon obeyed. They took their thwarts,
> and the ship went leaping toward the stream of Ocean
> first under oars, then with a following wind.[64]

Virgil's *Aeneid* describes Aeneas descending to the underworld with Deiphobe, the Sibyl of Cumae. The purpose of his journey, different from Odysseus, is to see his father, Anchises. At the climactic point of the reunion Aeneas tries, three times, to embrace his father, but only grabs air—a painful

---

61. Homer, *The Odyssey*, 180.
62. Markos, *Heaven*, 16.
63. Homer, *Odyssey*, 189.
64. Ibid., 206.

moment that highlights both the bond and the tragedy of separation. The only comfort is that Anchises reveals the great future that is in store for Aeneas and his descendants, which will lead to Romulus and eventually to Caesar Augustus, Rome's first Emperor and, incidentally, Virgil's own benefactor (VI. 1048–50),

> Now turn your two eyes here, to look upon
> your Romans, your own people. Here is Caesar
> and all the line of Iülus that will come
> beneath the mighty curve of heaven. This,
> this is the man you heard so often promised-
> Augustus Caesar, son of god, who will
> renew a golden age in Latium.[65]

Reading these memorable accounts, one possibly earlier and the other certainly later than Isaiah 14, one can hear interesting resonances with the משל of Isaiah 14. First, the inhabitants of the underworld retain a degree of continuity with their former existence. In Isaiah 14, they are still recognizable as they were on earth, but they are now are either referred to as shades (14:9) or as those who have been weakened (14:10). Both Odysseus and Aeneas try to embrace their dead parents, but both fail. While Anchises remains silent about the reasons for this phenomenon, Antikleia tells her son Odysseus (11.248–52),

> All mortals meet this judgment when they die.
> No flesh and bone are here, none bound by sinew,
> since the bright-hearted pyre consumed them down—
> the white bones long examinate—to ash;
> dreamlike the soul flies, insubstantial.[66]

Furthermore, the realm of the underworld is eerily dark and lifeless—not a place any human being would want to inhabit willingly. Isaiah 14:11 envisions the tyrant's descent into Sheol as the cessation of enjoyable and lavish earthly existence.[67] Odysseus weeps at the thought of the descent into Hades. While having a conversation with Achilles, Odysseus expresses his envy, "We ranked you with immortals in your lifetime ... and here your

---

65. Virgil, *Aeneid*, 164.
66. Homer, *Odyssey*, 192
67. For an insightful summary of the ancient, particularly Mesopotamian, view of the gloominess of the underworld see Cooper, "Death and Afterlife in Ancient Mesopotamia," 19–33, esp. 27.

power is royal among the dead men's shades."[68] Achilles' response is both shocking and instructive (11.576–81),

> He answered swiftly: Let me hear no smooth talk
> of death from you, Odysseus, light of councils.
> Better, I say, to break sod as a farm hand
> for some poor country man, on iron rations,
> than lord it over all the exhausted dead.[69]

Finally, whether the reason for the descent is an oracular consultation, testing the hero's courage, or death on the battlefield—one gets a sense that the journey to the underworld is a sophisticated literary tool in the hands of a skillful poet. While the reader is guided through the twists and turns of poetry to the depths of the underworld, the journey turns out to be an imaginative way to reflect on life here. For Virgil it is the affirmation of the Roman way of life. For Homer it is the concern for the heroic endurance in facing human fears.[70] For Isaiah 14 it is a thoughtful reflection on the transient nature of human power. In each case the account of the underworld journey is a means of rendering the world in accordance to the imaginative construal of the poet who stands behind it.

> **12** How you are fallen from heaven,
> O Day Star, son of Dawn!
> How you are cut down to the ground,
> you who laid the nations low!
> **13** You said in your heart,
> 'I will ascend to heaven;
> I will raise my throne
> above the stars of God;
> I will sit on the mount of assembly
> on the heights of Zaphon;
> **14** I will ascend to the tops of the clouds,
> I will make myself like the Most High.'
> **15** But you are brought down to Sheol,
> to the depths of the Pit. (Isa 14:12–15)

---

68. Homer, *Odyssey*, 201.
69. Ibid.
70. According to Markos, "after the *Odyssey*, no hero can truly qualify as an *epic* hero without enduring the awe and terror of the land of the dead." (Markos, *Heaven*, 17.)

With verses 12–15 we come to the rhetorical center of the poem. According to Erlandsson, Isaiah 14:12–15 "constitutes the core of the song."[71] Its weighty significance is apparent both in the way it functions in the משל and by its voluminous reception history. Appropriately these verses anticipate much lengthier discussion in the next chapter. Here the discourse will be limited to several ground-clearing observations and preliminary comments that will set up the trajectory for fuller engagement to follow.

The arrival of the tyrant to the underworld allows the poet to take a step back and ponder the magnitude of the event that had just unfolded before the reader. The poet creatively reflects on the transient nature of the abusive power by highlighting the unexpected reversal of fortunes. In essence, verses 12–15 paint a picture of the ultimate contrast precipitated by the tyrant's global reach. His arrogant quest for power is juxtaposed with his colossal downfall.

This astonishing reversal of fortunes is cast in memorable imagery. The tyrant is portrayed as הֵילֵל בֶּן-שָׁחַר (the Day Star, Son of Dawn), presumably luminous and distinct (14:12). A peculiar handling of the identity of the tyrant is significant to the way this section and the entire משל is read. As mentioned above, at the opening of the משל, verse 4 leaves the king of Babylon unnamed. Rather, he is introduced as נגש (oppressor). Now verse 12 casts him as the figure of הֵילֵל בֶּן-שָׁחַר. This ambiguous *hapax legomenon* phrase has generated an extensive scholarly discussion which attempts to understand both its origin and meaning. At this juncture it is important to note that whether הֵילֵל בֶּן-שָׁחַר is Mesopotamian, Canaanite, or Greek in its origins, this image seems to be at home within the mythological milieu of the ancient Near East. Hence, the lack of the reference to the identity of the king and the thoroughgoing shared ancient Near Eastern mythopoetic presuppositions have to be taken with imaginative seriousness in order to grasp the narrative world that the poet paints here—all of which will be more fully addressed in the following chapter. While enigmatic in its origin this image seeks to highlight a simple fact. The tyrant's reign is both luminous and short-lived. He rises to the heights of power but soon finds his destructive reign brought to abrupt end.

The text envisions the tyrant's ambition in categories that are not distinctly Israelite but rather those that could be used by a non-Yahwistic Babylonian king. Five statements in verses 13–14 each of which are rendered in NRSV as starting with "I will" phrase exploit such staple ancient Near Eastern mythological imagery as the human ascent to heaven, the mount of assembly (הַר-מוֹעֵד), heights of Zaphon (בְּיַרְכְּתֵי צָפוֹן), and the divine name

---

71. Erlandsson, *Burden*, 123.

עֶלְיוֹן. In vivid colors, the poet displays the tyrant's intent to scale the heights of heaven in order to set up his throne above the stars of God (14:13). The tyrant has picked out the assembly of the gods on mount Zaphon as a suitable place for himself (14:13). The ultimate goal of his ambition was to make himself equal to the Most High (14:14). Yet the attempted encroachment on the divine power ends in the lamentable fall into the far recesses of the underworld (14:15). Yee sums up succinctly the main thrust of these verses,

> By embedding this dirge in the center of the overall lament, the poet assimilates the tyrant to this primordial figure, identifying the tyrant's rise and fall with that of Hêlēl, the Bright One. Thus, for the poet, the tyrant's transgression, his harsh oppression of the people, is ultimately traceable to his consummate arrogance in desiring to be like God. As Hêlēl climbed higher and higher only to fall deeper and deeper, so too the tyrant's fate.[72]

The tyrant's attempts at self-exaltation are bracketed by forceful pictures of abasement. The enduring image of the Day Star falling from heaven is reinforced with two images of גדע (cut down) in verse 12 and ירד (bring down) in verse 15. Here the peculiarity of Hebrew grammar is put to the service of the poet's imaginative construal of the world. The word גדע (cut down) in verse 12 is passive (nifal). The word ירד (bring down) appears in verses 11 and 15. These are the only two occurrences of the verb ירד in passive form. In both cases it appears in hofal. The passive forms of these two verbs on the surface of things mask the agent of action. Yet one can reasonably argue that we are faced here with a divine passive. According to Hurtado the biblical texts where "actions are described in passive verb forms with no subject explicitly mentioned but where God is to be understood as the subject of the verbs"[73] represent examples of the divine passive. Similarly, Macholz has referred to this phenomenon in the Old Testament as "passivum regium."[74] The use of the divine passive that signals YHWH's decisive abasement of the evil tyrant brackets his relentless pursuit of self-exaltation that would put him on par with God. It is envisioned as a fitting divine response to the human attempt to craft one's self in the likeness of God.

Most evocatively our text's use of the imagery of divine abasement is connected with a word-play on יְרֵכָה (extremity) that reinforces the dynamic of exaltation and abasement. The tyrant's desire to reach the heights of Zaphon (יַרְכְּתֵי צָפוֹן) in verse 13 is matched with his relegation to the depths of the Pit (יַרְכְּתֵי-בוֹר) in verse 15. This is a movement from one extreme to

---

72. Yee, "Anatomy," 577–78.
73. Hurtado, "GOD," 271.
74. Macholz, "Das 'Passivum Divinum,'" 247–53, esp. 248.

another. Human self-exaltation that craves the divine abode at the heights of Zaphon is crushed by the weight of divine abasement as it finds itself relegated to the extremity of Sheol. As Eichrodt would put it, "In dem gewaltigen Gegensatz von Himmel und Totenwelt, der die Strophe beherrscht, ist alle menschliche Vergeltungs—sucht verschwunden und Gott allein die Ehre gegeben."[75]

> 16 Those who see you will stare (שׁגח) at you,
>   and ponder (בין) over you:
> "Is this the man who made the earth tremble,
>   who shook kingdoms,
> 17 who made the world like a desert
>   and overthrew its cities,
>   who would not let his prisoners go home?" (Isa 14:16–17)

In verses 16–17 the focus of the imaginative world of the text shifts back to earth where people gather to look at the corpse of the tyrant. The crowd of onlookers stares (שׁגח) and ponders (בין) the unexpected outcome the tyrant's reign. Those gathered examine the fallen tyrant and wonder, "Is this the man who made the earth tremble, who shook kingdoms, who made the world like a desert and overthrew its cities, who would not let his prisoners go home?" (14:16). Or to paraphrase as Kilpatrick has done, "Is this he who strode the world like a Colossus, and looked pitilessly on the lands he ruined and the hearts he broke?"[76]

Does the onlookers' question imply gloating? While the downfall of the widely despised oppressor could be easily perceived eliciting a sense of triumphant gloating, the text seems to suggest something different. The question of "Is this the man who made the earth tremble, who shook kingdoms, who made the world like a desert and overthrew its cities, who would not let his prisoners go home?" is placed on the lips of people who are both staring (שׁגח) and pondering (בין) the corpse. This tandem of words creates a distinctive picture.

The Hebrew word שׁגח means to "gaze." The precise meaning of this rare word is "to look at closely and to examine critically."[77] This is not simply a disdainful staring but rather an intense observation. It signals the crowd's true astonishment as this is the most unlikely place and state for such a powerful individual.

---

75. Eichrodt, *Jesaja 13–23 und 28–39*, 25.
76. Kilpatrick, "Exposition of Chapters 1–39," 5:262.
77. "שׁגח" n.p. *HALOT on CD-ROM.*

Furthermore, the Hebrew word בין means to "understand" or "know." When in hitpolel as here (יִתְבּוֹנָנוּ), it acquires a nuance of close examination with the apparent implication of getting a better understanding and more accurate perception of reality as in 1 Kings 3:21 where the distraught nursing mother is envisioned examining closely the dead infant to discover to her relief that this was not the child she had borne.[78] As the crowd encounters the corpse, they stand in disbelief. This could not possibly be the king of Babylon. So they look and examine carefully. To their astonishment their initial guess turns out to be true. The most unthinkable scenario seems to reflect reality. The man who terrorized the earth is laying dead in front of them.

The apparent disbelief implied in the onlookers' wonderment is precipitated by the type of far-reaching power this ruler possessed. Brueggemann, in his characteristically memorable way states, "Here is the quintessential evil one, the cosmic brutalizer of the innocent who wants to usurp the throne room of the good."[79] The tyrant is an epitome of someone who has so absolutely wielded power that apparently there is no force in the universe that can contend with him. The whole earth trembles, the kingdoms shake, and the world turns into a desert as this ruler administers his reign (14:17). The British historian Edward Gibbon famously called history "little more than the register of the crimes, follies, and misfortunes of mankind."[80] Faced with the depiction of the tyrant's impact in Isaiah 14:17, one can see some resemblance this statement.

An obvious question facing the reader of these verses is the identity of the onlookers. Whom does the text envision being gathered around the dead tyrant? One possible option is that these are the shades who were marshaled by Sheol to face the arriving tyrant back in verses 9–11.[81] In this scenario verses 16–17 do not represent a return of the narrative focus back to earth but rather stand in parallel with verses 9–11 in their depiction of the tyrant's reception in Sheol.

While this is a possible scenario perhaps a better option is reading these verse in conjunction with the material in verses 18–21, which depict the tyrant's corpse as lacking a proper burial. In this case the crowd of staring and pondering onlookers is situated on the earth. Such an earth-bound audience could be made up more generally of anyone who saw the tyrant's

---

78. "בין" n.p. *HALOT on CD-ROM*.

79. Brueggemann, *Isaiah*, 129.

80. Gibbon, *Fall of the Roman Empire*, 1:46.

81. Among others see Brueggemann, *Isaiah*, 130; Clements, *Isaiah*, 143; O'Connell, "Isaiah XIV 4B–23," 407–8; Sweeney, *Isaiah 1–39*, 225; Tucker, *Isaiah*, 159.

former glory[82] or more specifically of those who pick up the משל of Isaiah 14:3–23. Interestingly, if one envisions the likely scenario of the tyrant's death on the battlefield then the crowd could represent those who presumably witnessed the death of the tyrant during a battle. According to Tull, these are soldiers, possibly his own, who have survived in the battle and are now standing near the corpse and reflecting on the tyrant's life.[83] Alternatively, Wildberger suggests that these could be people charged with the responsibility of identifying the fallen soldiers in the aftermath of the battle and thus coming across the dead tyrant as they go through the battlefield.[84] Finally, this crowd could be made up of those who gather around the corpse at some later point in time after the body has been exhumed and thrown out of the grave. This alternative is closely linked with how one reads verses 18–19 so will be given further attention below.

With the crowd of onlookers standing around the corpse, the poet moves to the dramatic portrayal of the humiliating ending to the tyrant's spectacular political and military career. Smith has described the aftermath of the tyrant's death with these unforgettable words:

> Do we wish to know the actual punishment of his pride and cruelty? It is visible above ground; not with his spirit, but with his corpse; not with himself, but with his wretched family. His corpse is unburied, his family exterminated; his name disappears from the earth.[85]

Isaiah 14:18–23 matches the imagery of the paradigmatic fall from heaven and unmistakable divine cutting down of the brutal tyrant in previous verses with three vivid images of terrifying reality that follow his death. First, the tyrant's corpse lacks the proper burial (14:18–20a). Furthermore, the tyrant's family is slated to be exterminated (14:20b–21). Finally, YHWH himself pronounces the end of all that the tyrant stands for (14:22–23). We will consider each of these images here in order.

> **18** All the kings of the nations lie in glory,
>   each in his own tomb;
> **19** but you are cast out, away from your grave,
>   like loathsome carrion,
> clothed with the dead, those pierced by the sword,

---

82. Kissane, *Isaiah*, 173.
83. Tull, *Isaiah*, 281.
84. Wildberger, *Isaiah*, 69.
85. G. A. Smith, *Isaiah*, 431–32.

> who go down to the stones of the Pit,
> like a corpse trampled underfoot.
> **20** You will not be joined with them in burial,
> because you have destroyed your land,
> you have killed your people.

Verses 18–20a envision the tyrant's exposed corpse. While other earthly kings receive a dignified end of their life, he is cast away from his grave like a rejected carrion (14:18–19). The textual difficulty regarding the MT reading of נצר (shoot/branch) and proposed emending it to נפל (miscarriage) reflected here in NRSV's translation "carrion" has been discussed at length above. Whether an image of "a stomach-turning 'miscarriage'"[86] or more likely image of a useless twig thrown away without much further thought, the poet seems to point to one gruesome reality—the tyrant is denied the basic human right, namely a decent human burial. Rather than being given a proper honorable burial the tyrant is covered with dead bodies pierced by the sword. His body is trampled underfoot like an ordinary casualty of a military campaign (14:19).

This ignoble end is linked with the tyrant's handling of his domestic affairs, namely his people and his land. Thus, verse 20a offers a particular moral reason for the king's fate. While verse 6 envisioned the creation-wide jubilation at the downfall this tyrant due to his mistreatment of them, here we see the particularization of that response. According to verse 20a, his lack of burial is associated with his abuse of his own land and his own people. It shows that even among his own people the tyrant will not be given any honor because of the way he had dealt with them.

A close reading of these verses reveals a peculiar tension. Verse 19 which envisions an exposed corpse laying on the battlefield appear to stand in contrast with verses 9–11, which seemingly imply the burial of the tyrant. In other words, a careful reader is faced with a question of whether the reference to the tyrant's dead body being cast out, away from his grave in verse 19 implies non-burial, exhumation, or something else. Before considering these options it might be helpful to step back and provisionally reflect on the implications of the lack of a proper burial in antiquity as a way of grasping the poignancy of the imagery put by the poet before the reading or listening audience.

---

86. Wildberger, *Isaiah*, 42.

Excursus: Significance of Proper Burial in Antiquity

It is a well-attested fact that in the ancient Near East an honorable burial was a prerequisite for one's entrance to the underworld.[87] The elaborate mourning rituals and burial rites were designed to facilitate a person's separation from his community and transition to the postmortem existence.[88] The grave site was the link between the land of the living and the underworld.[89] Marking the burial site well was paramount, as the evidence from Mesopotamia indicates the urgency of proper entombment of the remains so that the loved ones could bring an offering.[90]

While the prevalence of the cult of the dead in pre-exilic Israel is still a debatable issue,[91] the explicit opposition of key biblical texts such as Leviticus 19:18 and Deuteronomy 18:10–11 seems to indicate that this was an ongoing struggle for those who sought to be faithful to YHWH.[92] Hence the awareness of and interest in the postmortem existence was as alive in Israel as in the cultures that surrounded her, which does not seem surprising as the care for the well-being of one's loved ones is a universal human experience

---

87. Abusch, "Ghost and God," 327–78.

88. Cohen, *Death*, 15–26; Scurlock, "Death and the Afterlife," 1883–93.

89. Harris' analysis of all sixty-five occurrences of the word Sheol in the Old Testament have led him to the following conclusion, "It is used almost exclusively in poetic passages. . . . Many times Sheol clearly means just 'grave.' Its parallels are 'death,' 'pit' (which predominantly means a hole in the earth), or 'sepulcher.' Its accompaniments are worms, dust, armor, etc. Its characteristics are darkness, being forgotten . . . , lack of wisdom, lack of work, and absence of praise. The only passages that speak of activity in Sheol are those in Isaiah 14 and Ezekiel 31 and 32 which are pretty clearly the 'grave' with some figurative treatment. The New Testament usage of Psalm 16:10 and Hosea 13:14 depends on Sheol being interpreted as 'the grave.' Sheol is not a cavern way below the earth's crust; it is a grave dug into the ground. All go to Sheol without moral distinction because the grave is our common end. There is no clear case for punishment in Sheol because the grave is not applicable to the grave." (Harris, "The Meaning of the Word Sheol," 135). This view has not gained much support as many scholars have voiced significant reservations about it. See Johnston, *Shades*, 73–75; Knibb, "Life and Death in the Old Testament," 403; Yamauchi, "Life, Death, and the Afterlife," 43.

90. Bottéro, "La mythologie de la mort en Mésopotamie ancienne," 37–38.

91. The most complete account arguing for the existence of a vibrant cult of the dead in Israel is found in Bloch-Smith's volume (Bloch-Smith, *Judahite Burial Practices*). Her examination of the archeological data from the burial sites in Judah ranging from eleventh to ninth century BC, leads her to postulate a thesis that the ancestral veneration was very much a part of the early Israelite experience, which was later suppressed and marginalized by the editors of the Bible following the reforms of Hezekiah and Josiah. On page 126 she points to Deuteronomy 26:14 as an example of a biblical text that is making room for the offering of food to the dead. See also Hallote, *Death, Burial, and Afterlife*, 54–68.

92. Xella, "Death and the Afterlife," 2067.

which does not stop with the termination of their earthly existence. The same could probably be said about the opposite human emotion. Human capacity to hate one's enemy beyond their death also seems to be universal.

Hence, while the concepts of death and afterlife varied significantly throughout the ancient world, there seems to be a consensus that "for human beings in ancient times it was a great comfort to count on having an appropriate and fitting burial."[93] For example, the third-millennium-BC Egyptian account of the campaigns of Pepi-nakht from his tomb at Qubbet el Hawa records the attempt to recover, at the command of Pharaoh Pepi II, the body of Enenkhet, the naval commander, who was murdered while overseeing the construction of a boat for an expedition to Nubia,

> Now the majesty of my lord sent me to the country of the Asiatics . . . to bring for him the sole companion, [commander] of the sailors, the caravan conductor, Enenkhet . . . , who was building a ship there for Punt, when the Asiatics belonging to the Sanddwellers . . . slew him, together with a troop of the army which was with him.[94]

Reflecting on the challenges accompanying ancient military campaigns, Hamblin writes,

> Dying in a foreign land, and thereby missing a proper burial in Egypt was a serious eternal concern to ancient Egyptians. Without a proper burial, ritual, and grave goods, the soul of the departed would suffer in eternity. This would have been of great concern to soldiers and officers going on foreign military expeditions. To die and have one's corpse left rotting in a foreign battlefield was tantamount to a condemnation to hell, probably creating a type of "leave no man behind" mentality among Egyptian soldiers.[95]

Thus, Hamblin argues, Pepi-nakht's expedition was not just a punitive action, but was also designed to boost the morale of the Egyptian army by demonstrating that their dead would not be left behind in the battle, but rather every effort would be made to provide for the Egyptian warriors a proper burial in their homeland.[96]

According to the Mesopotamian records, the burial constituted a rite of passage. It was a way of integrating the dead into the cosmic order. Proper

---

93. Wildberger, *Isaiah*, 70.
94. Breasted, *Ancient Records of Egypt*, 194.
95. Hamblin, *Warfare in the ancient Near East*, 350.
96. Ibid.

burial was a conduit to establishing a link between the living and the dead. According to Abush,

> The body must be buried; otherwise, the ghost will have no rest and will not find its place in the community of the dead, usually associated with the netherworld. In addition, burial is crucial for future care, for the dead are to be the recipients of ongoing mortuary rites, which include invocations of the name of the deceased, presentation of food, and libation of water. In this way, the dead are cared for and kept (alive) in memory.[97]

Lindenlauf argues that the ignoble disposal of the dead human body constituted a major insult in ancient Greece. The social memory of convicted criminals such as traitors and temple robbers was erased by disposing their dead bodies outside the communal boundary, submerging them into the sea, or offering them to animals for consumption. Especially insightful are Lindenlauf's observations on the symbolic significance of the dead body's mistreatment,

> The exhumation of burials, resulting in the careless deposition of their contents, was necessarily a symbolic statement of disgrace. In cases where people were executed and punished "in the same way as," for example, a traitor, the disposal method was used as a powerful means to express the esteem in which the individual was held either by individuals or by social and political group in power.[98]

Johnston has argued persuasively for the importance of burial in Israel. He points out that accounts of death of the many major figures in the Old Testament are accompanied with references to their burial. Furthermore, various Old Testament texts speak of significance of a burial in the family tomb. Johnston turns to texts like 2 Samuel 19:37 where the aging Barzillai refuses David's hospitality in order to return home, "so that I may die in my own town, near the grave of my father and mother." Finally, the Old Testament reflects the belief that everyone deserves burial. Deuteronomy 21:23 states that even the executed criminal's corpse must not remain all night upon the tree. It must be buried that same day.[99]

Johnston goes on to consider an alternative of *non-burial*. He writes, "Burial should be universal and immediate, and non-burial was a sign of

---

97. Abusch, "Ghost and God," 373.
98. Lindenlauf, "Disposal of the Dead in Ancient Greece," 86–99, esp. 96.
99. Johnston, *Shades*, 51.

particular opprobrium, in Israel as throughout the ancient world."[100] After the conquest of Ai at Joshua's command the body of the executed king was taken down from the tree at the sunset and thrown at the entrance of the gate of the city and stones were piled over it. (Josh 8:29). Jeremiah warns that the people of Judah have defiled YHWH's house. Their building of the high place of Topheth with accompanied human sacrifices is about to bring an outpouring of his wrath. The valley of the son of Hinnom will be renamed into the valley of Slaughter. The gruesome picture of YHWH's judgment is accentuated with a reference to non-burial, "The corpses of this people will be food for the birds of the air, and for the animals of the earth; and no one will frighten them away" (Jer 7:33). Thus, whether as a sign of divine judgment or a terrible fate of a defeated king on the battlefield, *non-burial* was understood as a ghastly aberration of the widely held norm.

Having explored the significance of the proper burial in antiquity we are ready to return to the scene of onlookers being gathered around the corpse of the tyrant in verse 19. Given the fact that the tyrant's body ends up in such dishonored state, the curious question to consider is whether the text envisions the body not buried or temporarily buried only to be exhumed at a later point to underscore the judgment that this tyrant evoked from those around him.

The majority of scholarship reckons that the tyrant was never buried.[101] The Hebrew phrase ואתה השלכת מקברך (but you are cast out, away from your grave) at the opening of verse 19 has evoked two major interpretive options among those who argue for the lack of burial. First, some have argued that this is a case of a corpse being left far away from a place of proper burial. Keil and Delitzsch suggested, "The Chaldean lay far away from the sepulcher that was apparently intended for him."[102] While every other king receives his proper burial within his own house, i.e. the premises of his palace, this tyrant is denied that rite.[103] Second, some have argued that everything hinges on the way a preposition מִן is used here. Wildberger, among others, has insisted that the text could hardly mean the corpse being thrown out

---

100. Johnston, *Shades*, 55.

101. The classic formulation of the non burial goes back to Duhm who writes, "Aber es ist unwahrscheinlich, dass der König erst in Frieden stirbt und begraben und darauf aus dem Grabe gerissen wird, denn die Schwertdurchbohrten sind doch gewiss Babylonier, mit denen der König fallt, auch v.20 scheint dazu nicht zu passen, und ganze Gedicht setzt voraus, dass der Tod des Königs und der Fall der babylonischen Herrschaft zu gleicher Zeit erfolgen." (Duhm, *Das Buch*, 121).

102. Keil and Delitzsch, *Isaiah*, 314.

103. Recently Shipp (See *Dirges*) argued similarly for the tyrant's abandonment away from his tomb (157). But his position stands at odds with his actual translation of this phrase as "you are cast out from your grave" (132).

of the grave. Rather he suggests that מִ is privative, thus the word, slightly emended, should read מִקֶּבֶר (without grave).[104] According to Wildberger, the corpse being left without a proper burial fits more naturally in situations where a corpse that is "cast forth" describes someone who dies on the battle field and either no one is available or willing to bury them (1 Kgs 13:24–25; Isa 34:3).[105] Several other scholars have argued along the same lines.[106]

Early on Kissane suggested another way of envisioning this picture of the dead corpse being exposed to be seen by onlookers. According to him, מקברך seems to imply that the tyrant was buried and at a later point cast out of his grave. Hence, he insists that the most natural way of reading this verse is to envision interment followed by exhumation at a later point.[107] This minority view has been advanced also by Olyan,[108] who argues that the idiom שלך in passive (Hophal) with מן occurs throughout the Old Testament with the unambiguous meaning of "to cast /be cast from locus A (to locus B)."[109] Some of the examples he provides include Psalm 51:13, Judges 15:17, and Nehemiah 13:8. Olyan goes on to point out, "Exhuming and scattering or transporting buried human remains are frequently understood as acts of hostility to the dead, and are mentioned or alluded to in a number of West Asian texts, including the Hebrew Bible."[110] He points to texts such as Jeremiah 8:1–2 which announces the exhumation of the remains of the kings of Judah,

> **1** At that time, declares the LORD, the bones of the kings of Judah, the bones of its officials, the bones of the priests, the bones of the prophets, and the bones of the inhabitants of Jerusalem shall be brought out of their tombs. **2** And they shall be spread before the sun and the moon and all the host of heaven, which they have loved and served, which they have gone after, and which they have sought and worshiped. And they shall not be

---

104. Wildberger, *Isaiah*, 46. Clements similarly suggest that here is a case of *min privativum* and should read "without a proper burial chamber." (Clements, *Isaiah*, 144). See also Oswalt, *Isaiah*, 324.

105. Wildberger, *Isaiah*, 70.

106. Brichto, "Kin," 25; Fohrer, *Jesaja*, 173; Gray, *Isaiah I–XXVII*, 259; Kilian, *Jesaja*, 105; Oswalt, *Isaiah*, 324.

107. Kissane, *Isaiah*, 173.

108. Olyan, "King," 423–26. Others who have also embraced this view include de Jong, Isaiah, 142–43; Holladay, "Text," 633–45, and Schöpflin, "Ein Blick in die Unterwelt," 299–314.

109. Olyan, "King," 425.

110. Ibid.

gathered or buried. They shall be as dung on the surface of the ground.

Furthermore, Olyan examines Ashurbanipal, Eshmunazor and Si'gabbar inscriptions. Ashurbanipal's inscriptions report his desecration the graves of the kings of Elam and the subsequent transportation of their remains to Assyria as a way of denying them proper rest in afterlife. Both the Eshmunazor and Si'gabbar inscriptions reflect a fear that the tomb may be vandalized and that the remains of the dead may be removed.[111] In light of the evidence at hand, Olyan insists that Isaiah 14:19 should be understood in the similar fashion, "The king will be punished through exhumation and exposure on account of his depredations during life."[112]

In the end, whether the tyrant was temporarily buried or not, the poet invites the reader to reflect on the evocative impact of this scene of onlookers observing the corpse of a man who exerted enormous power during his reign. Here we might heuristically consider resonances with Jeremiah 22 which record the words of prophet Jeremiah directed against Jehoiakim, the king of Judah. Jeremiah 22 portrays Jehoiakim in ways analogous to the king of Babylon in Isaiah 14. His reign is characterized by similar violent and oppressive tendencies,

> 17 But you have eyes and heart
>   only for your dishonest gain,
> for shedding innocent blood,
>   and for practicing oppression and violence.

Similar to the king of Babylon, Jehoiakim's oppression will be met with divine retribution,

> 18 Therefore thus says the LORD concerning Jehoiakim the son of Josiah, king of Judah:
> "They shall not lament for him, saying,
>   'Ah, my brother!' or 'Ah, sister!'
> They shall not lament for him, saying,

---

111. Ibid.

112. Ibid. De Jong has suggested that the onlookers observing the tyrant's dead body are the kings in Sheol. Hence he envisions a peculiar scenario, "The kings of the nations cast the tyrant from Sheol. He is not allowed to stay in their company for he has destroyed his land and killed his people (14:20)." (de Jong, *Isaiah*, 140.) Here he follows the earlier lead of Holladay who links the exhumation of the tyrant's corpse with the rejection of him from Sheol. (See Holladay, "Text," 642–43.) De Jong writes, "The phrase 'you are cast out from your grave' (14:19) on one level refers to the disinterment of the tyrant's corpse, but on a deeper level to the tyrant's ejection from Sheol."

'Ah, lord!' or 'Ah, his majesty!'
19 With the burial of a donkey he shall be buried,
  dragged and dumped beyond the gates of Jerusalem."

Moberly has summed up well the thrust of this passage,

> The result . . . will be that when Jehoiakim dies people will not lament him with the usual expressions of grief heard at funerals; rather his end will be that of an animal, unlamented, unceremonious, and uninterred. . . . One might perhaps paraphrase the sense of the passage by saying that because Jehoiakim has denied the humanity of others, treating people as mere objects for oppression and exploitation, so at his dying his humanity too will be denied, and he will be treated as a mere object of heedless neglect.[113]

It seems that the poet of Isaiah 14 embodies a similar moral vision. Whether never interred or exhumed at a later point in time, the exposed corpse of the dead tyrant signals the denial of humanity to the one who denied others their humanity during his oppressive reign.

20b May the descendants of evildoers
  nevermore be named!
21 Prepare slaughter[114] for his sons
  because of the guilt of their father.
Let them never rise to possess the earth
  or cover the face of the world with cities.

The second image of the aftermath of the tyrant's death is given in verses 20b-21 where the tyrant's family is poised to be exterminated. The command is issued to prepare a place for his sons' slaughter. In the ominous move the tyrant's progeny will be held responsible for his brutality. The intention is to wipe them all out so that his offspring will never be even named.

The aftermath of warfare in the ancient Near East was marked with unmistakable violence towards those who experienced defeat. Especially noteworthy was the Assyrian propensity towards brutality in relation to those they conquered. The captives' noses, ears, and limbs are reported to have been routinely cut off. Both male and female prisoners were burnt. Many were impaled or blinded. Ninth-century-BC Assyrian king

---

113. Moberly, *Prophecy and Discernment*, 69-70.

114. In my discussion in chapter 2, I have argued that a preferable translation would be "place of slaughter."

Ashurnasirpal II boastfully referred to himself as the "trampler of all enemies ... who defeated all his enemies (and) hung the corpses of his enemies on posts."[115] Ashurnasirpal's words describing a typical account of sacking a city are unsettling,

> In strife and conflict I besieged (and) conquered the city. I felled 3,000 of their fighting men with the sword.... I captured many troops alive: I cut off some their arms (and) hands; I cut off of others their noses, ears, (and) extremities. I gouged out the eyes of many troops. I made one pile of the living (and) one of heads. I hung their heads on trees around the city; I burnt their adolescent boys and girls. I razed, destroyed, burnt, and consumed the city.[116]

Sennacherib's eighth-century-BC account is equally disturbing,

> I cut their throats like lambs. I cut off their precious lives (as one cuts) a string. Like the many waters of a storm, I made (the contents of) their gullets and entrails run down upon the wide earth. My prancing steeds harnessed for my riding, plunged into the streams of their blood as (into) a river. The wheels of my war chariot, which brings low the wicked and the evil, were bespattered with blood and filth. With the bodies of their warriors I filled the plain, like grass. (Their) testicles I cut off, and tore out their privates like the seed of cucumbers.[117]

The fate of the royal household was especially liable to violent treatment. Tiglath-pileser III reports his violent treatment of a royal household of Nabû-ushabshi,

> Nabû-ushabshi, their king, I hung up in front of the gate of his city on a stake. His land, his wife, his sons, his daughters, the treasure of his palace, I carried off. Bit-Amukâni I trampled down like a threshing (sledge). All of its people, (and) its goods, I took to Assyria.[118]

Concerted efforts were made to ensure that the entire royal household, including the dead, received a humiliating treatment. The seventh-century-BC Babylonian king Ashurbanipal's abuse of the royal dead of Elam is typical,

---

115. Grayson, *Inscriptions*, 120.
116. Ibid., 126.
117. *ARAB*, vol. 2, secs. 254.
118. *ARAB*, vol. 1, secs. 584–85.

> The sepulchers of their earlier and later kings, who did not fear Assur and Ishtar, my lords, had plagued the kings, my fathers, I destroyed, I devastated, I exposed to the sun. Their bones I carried off to Assyria. I laid restlessness upon their shades. I deprived them of food-offerings and libations of water.[119]
>
> The bones of Nabu-shum-eresh, which they had brought from Gambulu to Assyria, these bones I had his sons crush in front of the gate inside Nineveh.[120]

Wildberger explains of rationale for such violent mistreatment of the defeated royal household,

> Whenever a ruler was overthrown in the ancient Near East, there was a concerted effort to exterminate his family as well, so that no family member could come back and claim to have a legitimate right to regain power.[121]

Old Testament resonances are noteworthy. Baasha conspires against Jeroboam's dynasty and kills Nadab, thus capturing the throne in Israel. 1 Kings 15:29 tells us, "As soon as he was king, he killed all the house of Jeroboam; he left to the house of Jeroboam not one that breathed, until he had destroyed it." Fast forward a quarter of a century and the same pattern repeats itself. Elah, the son of Baasha begins his reign over Israel in Tizrah. Two years into his reign, Zimri, one of the commanders of the king's chariots conspires against him. Following a drunken feast in Tirzah, Zimri slaughters the king and takes the reins of Israel. 1 Kings 16:11–12 tells us, "When he began to reign, as soon as he had seated himself on his throne, he killed all the house of Baasha; he did not leave him a single male of his kindred or his friends. Thus Zimri destroyed all the house of Baasha."

Isaiah 14:21 is clear as to what is the reason for this cruel treatment of the despot's family, "Let them never rise to possess the earth or cover the face of the world with cities." The uncertainty regarding the reading ערם (cities) has been discussed at length above. While LXX (πολεμων, wars) and Targum (צרם, enemies) renderings appear to be imaginatively suggestive, the current scholarly consensus, reflected in virtually unanimous rendering in modern English translations, is to follow the MT and read the tyrant's intent as to cover the globe with cities.

Wildberger claims that in the ancient world the establishment of cities was a most effective means of maintaining absolute control over a land

---

119. *ARAB*, vol. 2, sec. 810.
120. *ARAB*, vol. 2, sec. 866.
121. Wildberger, *Isaiah*, 72.

that been conquered.[122] The control of multi-ethnic empires was indeed a struggle in antiquity. Establishment of colonies, loyal to the center and reflective of the imperial culture was crucial for a creation of trans-ethnic identity. For example, Eusebius mentions Nebuchadnezzar's establishment of the Babylonian colony at the mouth of the Euphrates, "He also walled off the inundation of the Red Sea and built the city of Teredon against the incursions of the Arabs."[123] While new colonies were at times created from scratch, this was usually accomplished through forced population movement and repopulation, which essentially amounted to the creation of new cities—the reality reflected in such biblical texts as 2 Kings 17:23-24 which address the exile and repopulation of the Northern Kingdom.

Parpola argues that population movement was a crucial strategy for the Assyrian assimilation and integration.[124] Mass deportations were first introduced by Ashurnasirpal II and reached their height during the reigns of Shalmaneser III and Tiglath-pileser III. Parpola estimates that between 830 and 640 BC 4.5 million people were dislocated from their homes and resettled in other areas of Assyria, mostly in large urban centers. Parpola's summary of the process of colonization and its far-reaching impact is worth quoting at length,

> The massive deportations of foreign people into Assyria, and the concomitant reorganization of the conquered areas as Assyrian provinces, subjected huge numbers of new people to a direct and ever-increasing Assyrian cultural influence. This included, among other things, the imposition of taxation and military service, a uniform calendar, judiciary, and conscription system, as well as imperial weights, measures, and other standards. In addition, Assyrian royal ideology, religious ideas and mythology were incessantly propagated to all segments of the population through imperial art, emperor cult, religious festivals, and the cults of Aššur, Ištar, Nabû, Sîn and other Assyrian gods. The peoples of the newly established provinces routinely became Assyrian citizens. While the process of Assyrianization thus put under way undoubtedly worked fastest in the big cities of central Assyria, it must have proceeded rapidly in the new provinces as well, as they were no longer the countries they used to be.

---

122. Wildberger, *Isaiah*, 73.

123. Eusebius, *Preparation for the Gospel*, 485. Though the presence of this town is well attested by the time of Alexander the Great, Retso has recently raised the possibility of Nebuchadnezzar's involvement with the Arabs being apocryphal. See Retso, *The Arabs in Antiquity*, 181.

124. Parpola, "Identity," 5-22.

> Their intelligentsia had been deported to Assyria and replaced with Assyrian administrators, their capitals had been razed and rebuilt in Assyrian fashion, and their populations now included, in addition to deportees from other parts of the Empire, also considerable numbers of Assyrian immigrants and colonists.[125]

Parpola's account of the process of Assyrianization has instructive resonances with Isaiah 14:21. While the poet might not be aware of the intricacies of the Assyrian colonization strategies, this ancient example allows the reader to imaginatively envision the kind of reality that would stand behind the threat of the sons of the tyrant rising to possess the earth (יקמו וירשו ארץ) as they cover the face of the world with cities. Parpola's account helps the reader construct the type of impact a city-building could have in the ancient world and why the divine halting of these architectural projects by the tyrant's sons could be envisioned as welcome news. Once this despot controlled the known world via loyal cities. The wiping out of his entire family assures the world that it will never again be subjected to his terrorizing rule.

> **22** I will rise up against them, says the LORD of hosts, and will cut off from Babylon name and remnant, offspring and posterity, says the LORD. **23** And I will make it a possession of the hedgehog, and pools of water, and I will sweep it with the broom of destruction, says the LORD of hosts.

As the final image of the aftermath of the tyrant's death, verses 22–23 envision a complete annihilation of everything this tyrant represents—Babylon itself. The poet's lens shifts once again away from the scene of onlookers being gathered around the dead tyrant and zooms out in the attempt to reflect on the significance of all that has been seen so far.

Scholarship for a long time has understood these verses being a result of editorial activity that sought to reaffirm the identity of the king as a Babylonian ruler (14:4a) and to link his death with the downfall of Babylon's global rule (13:19–22). Within the imaginative world of the משל of Isaiah 14:3–23, these verses—while, as discussed earlier, possibly different in style (prose rather than poetry) from verses 4b–21 which precede them—round out where the משל has been going all along. Marked with the weighty prophetic formula נאם־יהוה (declares the LORD), verses 22–23 make it clear that Babylon will no longer terrorize the earth in general and Israel in particular. Clements is surely correct that these verses were "designed to

---

125. Parpola, "Identity," 10.

affirm the finality of the fate that has overtaken Babylon."[126] Going beyond that affirmation, these verses seek to underscore that behind that fate stands none other than YHWH. By utilizing the first person speech, YHWH is positioned as the speaking voice of these verses.[127] YHWH himself puts the weight of his authority as the assurance of the finality of the imagined downfall of the tyrant.

In some ways the reader gets an impression that verses 22–23 do not add much more content to the imaginative world of the משל of Isaiah 14:3–23. When this thought is coupled with the possibility that these verses are a prose addition to the otherwise poetic texts of the משל proper, it is easy to see how these verses could be easily overlooked when envisioning the imaginative world of the משל. Yet, as discussed earlier, the disagreement between the NRSV rendering of these verses as prose and the *BHS* rendering it as poetry highlights the complexity of the issue of editorial activity. To that we might add the ambiguity of the fruitfulness of attempting to reconstruct that process for the purposes of grasping the imaginative world of Isaiah 14. Hence, without unduly historicizing the issue, it is worth withholding the judgment and asking whether verses 22–23 merely repeat the material in the preceding verses or seek in their own nuanced way to underscore the finality of YHWH's judgment of the tyrant's reign.

The climactically positioned voice of YHWH begins its utterance at the start of verse 22. With the downfall of the tyrant vividly portrayed in previous verses one would anticipate YHWH speaking directly into that situation by possibly addressing the humiliated ruler as other speaking voices have done so far—the cypresses and cedars of Lebanon (14:8), the shades (14:10–11), and the narrator (14:8, 12–21). Yet instead, YHWH turns his attention to a different target. He says, "I will rise up against them." Whom might the puzzling phrase עֲלֵיהֶם (against them) be envisioning? While critical scholarship, well represented in Wildberger, might be correct that form-historically speaking "we are in a completely different setting,"[128] in the imaginative world of the משל this phrase comes right on the heels of the command to prepare the sons of the tyrant for slaughter (14:21). YHWH's focus in rising up against the sons of the tyrant is to cut off from Babylon name and remnant, descendants and posterity. Keil and Delitzsch, among others, suggest that the combination of these phrases "name and remnant" (שֵׁם וּשְׁאָר) and "offspring and posterity" (נִין וָנֶכֶד) in verse 22 stands

---

126. Clements, *Isaiah*, 145.

127. Meier speaks of "intense concentration" of the phrase (צבאות) נאם יהוה which is used here three times in the span of two verses. See Meier, *Speaking*, 245.

128. Wildberger, *Isaiah*, 73.

as "two pairs of alliterative proverbial words"¹²⁹ which are used to signify "the whole, without exception."¹³⁰ The termination of the name, remnant, offspring and posterity point to one overarching reality—the memory of the tyrant disappears from the earth. This is YHWH's ultimate goal. Rather than a vindictive retributive action against the despised despot, the voice of YHWH addressing the tyrant's descendants reflects his commitment to ensure that when this king falls everything he represents goes down with him.

Those steeped in the Old Testament world quickly pick up on the ominous outlook on the despot's future when the poet announces that YHWH will cut off the name and remnant, offspring and posterity from Babylon. Grassi points out that in the Old Testament immortality was linked to living on through children who carried on the name of their parents.[131] In Genesis 48 we find elderly Jacob with Ephraim and Manasseh on his knees pronouncing his blessing on them. He prays, "In them let my name be perpetuated, and the name of my ancestors Abraham and Isaac; and let them grow into a multitude on the earth" (Gen 48:16). For the tyrant in Isaiah 14 this prayer is not an existential possibility.

Being forgotten by posterity seems to have been considered one of the major tragedies in life in the ancient world. The Akkadian *Myth of Etana* tells the story of king Etana, the ruler of Kish, "a shepherd, the one who to heaven ascended."[132] Upon his ascent to the divine abode Etana is entrusted by gods to bring humanity the security and blessing of kingship. The *Myth of Etana* reflects this sentiment of one's memory being perpetuated in one's progeny when it reports the king pleading with the god Shamash to give him an heir, "Remove my burden and produce for me a name!"[133]

Schmidt summarizes well what appears to be a widely shared attitude in antiquity towards post-mortem memory,

> While it may be difficult, if impossible to imagine, for us as moderns to imagine, let alone embrace, a world where physical continuity persists beyond the grave merely as a shadow of our existence, the inhabitants of ancient Israel, Ugarit, and Ebla could not only conceive of, but openly embrace, the belief in such a physical existence. A shadowy, feeble, physical existence

---

129. Keil and Delitzsch, *Isaiah*, 316.

130. Ibid. Similar thought is suggested by Gray who furnishes the texts where these alliterative phrases are used. For נִין וָנֶכֶד see (Gen 21:23; Job 18:19; Sir 41:5 and 47:22). For a language similar to שֵׁם וּשְׁאָר see 1 Sam 24:1 and 2 Sam 14:7. (Gray, *Isaiah I–XXVII*, 262).

131. Grassi, "CHILD, CHILDREN" *ABD* 1:904.

132. Jacobsen, *The Sumerian King List*, 81.

133. *ANET*, 117.

in the netherworld was a given. It was acceptable because it did not constitute the central focus of their efforts in constructing a worthwhile life beyond death. The energy and resources of the living, in anticipation of death, were concentrated instead on establishing, even institutionalizing, one's immortality by the preservation of one's deeds, position, or personhood in the mind of those one left behind long after one's departure from this world. This form of immortality—supported by institutional infrastructures—political, legal, and religious—served to counter the dreaded "death after death" in ancient Mediterranean West Asian societies.[134]

According to Keel, this sentiment was acutely felt in Egypt. He writes, "From the most ancient times in Egypt, stelae erected beside the graves further assisted the recollection of the dead."[135] It can also be seen in the fact that the ancient funerary text the *Book of Dead* dedicates two chapters (25 and 90) under the title "Of restoring the memory of the deceased by magical means." Here is a snapshot of the ancient wish,

> May the memory of my name always remain with me
> when I dwell there in the light,
> walled in by the fiery walls of the underworld.[136]

Similar ways of thinking are evident in ancient Mesopotamia. Bottéro writes,

> One kept the memory of the deceased alive, but ordinarily without going back further than three generations: those that came before, with the exception of the most illustrious, were henceforth only the objects of a collective and vague memory. In their gloomy, sleepy existence they had been absorbed by the great universal forgetting—the true death of a person.[137]

YHWH threatens to do to this tyrant what his own Mesopotamian culture considers a final blow. In the absence of descendants and posterity this tyrant is indeed facing the true death of being forgotten. John Oswalt insists that here the taunt eulogy reaches its climax,

> Instead of wishing that the deceased's name will endure after him and that his children will bring honor to that name through

---

134. Schmidt, "Memory as Immortality," 100.
135. Keel, *Symbolism*, 69.
136. Ibid.
137. Bottéro, *Religion in Ancient Mesopotamia*, 110.

their own long and productive lives, the singer wishes the opposite:may the earth quickly be delivered from even having to remember that this man was.[138]

The picture of complete destruction is further elaborated as the poet envisions Babylon's fate being reversed in verse 23. Babylon will go from the known and revered center to a muddy swampland inhabited by hedgehogs. Wildberger offers an interesting insight in the way he handles the presence of hedgehogs in the midst of swamps which is not their natural habitat. He writes that whether קִפֹּד is indeed a hedgehog or some other type of animal this rare word seems to be stock imagery portraying a complete destruction of a well-populated area (Isa 34:11 and Zeph 2:14)[139]—one of the sort of stock images of the devastated fortified city that are prevalent in the Old Testament (Isa 25:2; 27:10–11; Ezek 16:35–41; Mic 3:12).[140]

Resonances with Sennacherib's account of his devastation of Babylon in 689 BC are striking,

> The city (its) houses, and walls, I destroyed, I devastated, I burned with fire. The wall and outer wall, temples and gods, temple-tower of brick and earth, as many as there were, I razed and dumped them into the Araḫtu-canal. Through the midst of that city I dug canals, I flooded its site with water, and the very foundations thereof I destroyed. I made its destruction more complete than that by a flood. That in days to come the site of that city, and (its) temples and gods, might not be remembered, I completely blotted it out with (floods) of water and made it like a meadow.[141]

Hence Babylon, this awe-inspiring human undertaking, comes to despicable end. The one whose name was on the trembling lips of the terrorized world will be eventually swept away by YHWH's broom of destruction along with whatever remains of Babylon without leaving a trace.

Smith's evocative words are hard to improve upon and thus form a fitting finale for this chapter,

> Man's arrogance and cruelty are attempts upon His [God's] majesty. He inevitably overwhelms them. Death is their penalty:

---

138. Oswalt, *Isaiah*, 325.

139. Wildberger, *Isaiah*, 74.

140. For an insightful analysis of the imagery of the destroyed city encapsulated in the metaphor of a violated woman see Kelle, "Wartime Rhetoric," 95–112.

141. *ARAB*, vol. 2, secs. 341.

blood and squalor on earth, the concourse of shuddering ghosts below.

> *The kings of the earth set themselves,*
> *And the rulers take counsel together,*
> *Against Yahweh and against His Anointed.*
> *He that sitteth in the heavens shall laugh;*
> *The Lord shall have them in derision.*

He who has heard that laughter sees no comedy in aught else. This is the one unfailing subject of Hebrew satire, and it forms the irony and the rigor of the . . . ode.[142]

---

142. G. A. Smith, *Isaiah*, 432–33. Smith's italicized quote is Psalm 2:2, 4. This quote is from the revised edition of Smith's commentary. It refers to "Yahweh" while the original edition has "the Lord." Also, the original edition has this material on page 412.

5

Myth and History in Isaiah 14:3–23

Isaiah 14:3–23 is a משל that paints a memorable picture of an unnamed tyrant of Babylon who is cast in the language of ancient mythology. It would be easy to envision a timeless moralizing reading that smooths over any historical contingencies or controversies. Yet we would be wise to heed the words of Childs,

> The witnesses of the Bible bear all the marks of their historical conditioning. To be correctly understood they must be heard in their particular period of history, through the culture-formed vehicles of language and thought patterns, and mediated through the individual and corporate personalities of authors and redactors. This characteristic of Biblical revelation offers a warrant for the historicocritical study of the Bible. There is the full necessity for taking seriously the original context of every Biblical passage.[1]

While he is often accused of flattening the historical realties that undergird the biblical text in favor of canonical reading, Childs highlights the indispensable role of historical-critical inquiry for the reading of biblical texts,

> In my judgment, the genuine contribution of this history of scholarship has been to point out a variety of difficult problems which, when once seen, prevent all efforts at glossing over homiletically.[2]

Hence, in this chapter we seek to highlight three significant issues surrounding Isaiah 14:3–23. First, we will give special attention to the mythological background and function of הֵילֵל בֶּן-שָׁחַר image in Isaiah 14:12–15. Second, the historical referent of the king of Babylon will be discussed in light of the fact that the משל leaves him unnamed. Third, we will map historical-critical approaches to the formation of the Oracles Against the Nations in Isaiah 13–23, which is the canonical home of Isaiah 14:3–23.

1. Childs, *Biblical Theology*, 112.
2. Childs, *Introduction*, 450.

The Mythological Background and Function of הֵילֵל בֶּן-שָׁחַר Image in Isaiah 14:12–15

In the previous chapter we proposed that Isaiah 14:12–15 represented the rhetorical center of the poem. The enduring value of these verses has been well-captured by Margulis who referred to them as "a mythological allegory unequalled in all of biblical literature."[3] Laced with the imagery reflective of substantial continuity and shared mythopoetic presuppositions that governed the way people thought about their world in antiquity, Isaiah 14:12–15 affirms the validity of Cross' insistence on "a perennial and unrelaxed tension between the mythic and the historical" in Israelite religion.[4]

> 12 How you are fallen from heaven,
>   O Day Star, son of Dawn!
> How you are cut down to the ground,
>   you who laid the nations low!
> 13 You said in your heart,
>   "I will ascend to heaven;
> I will raise my throne
>   above the stars of God;
> I will sit on the mount of assembly
>   on the heights of Zaphon;
> 14 I will ascend to the tops of the clouds,
>   I will make myself like the Most High."
> 15 But you are brought down to Sheol,
>   to the depths of the Pit.

The downfall of the king of Babylon is envisioned here as the falling from heaven of an enigmatic figure of הֵילֵל בֶּן-שָׁחַר (the Day Star, Son of Dawn). The rationale for this rejection from the heavenly abode is his mistreatment of those around him. As a retributive action, his laying low of the nations is matched with his own cutting down to the ground. The ambiguous *hapax legomenon* image of הֵילֵל בֶּן-שָׁחַר has generated a voluminous array of scholarly proposals regarding its mythological background. So we turn our attention to the range of options considered by modern scholarship.

---

3. Margulis, "Weltbaum and Weltberg in Ugaritic Literature," 15.
4. Cross, *Canaanite Myth*, viii.

Search for Mesopotamian Cognates of the Mythological Background of Isaiah 14:12–15

Prior to the discovery of the Ras Shamra texts it was a commonly held hypothesis that this mythological imagery came from some unknown Mesopotamian original.[5] Gallagher has recently attempted to revive the Mesopotamian hypothesis. He posits that הֵילֵל is a West Semitic equivalent of the Mesopotamian Enlil/Illil.[6] He writes, "One could reasonably expect *hll* to be the West Semitic form of *illil*. As the Ebla tablets suggest, *Illil* came into West Semitic directly from Sumerian."[7] Gallagher draws parallels between Isaiah's description of this figure and what is known of Enlil. According to Isaiah 14, הֵילֵל laid the nations low (v. 12), aspired to set up his throne above the stars of El (v. 13) and craved the seat among the mount assembly at the heights of Zaphon (v. 13). Similarly, Enlil is portrayed as a devastator. Among Enlil's noteworthy epithets are "lord of weapons" and "the bull which makes the heavens and the earth quake."[8] He has a prominent place among the divine assembly, occupying the highest place in the Mesopotamian mythology until the close of the second millennium. Even the downfall of these two figures could be compatible. הֵילֵל falls into the depths of the pit (14:15). According to Mesopotamian mythology, Marduk eventually defeats older deities including Enlil and Anu. As a result, Enlil is cast into the abyss and consigned to the underworld of gods. For Gallagher this association of the king of Babylon with הֵילֵל in Isaiah 14:12 is not accidental. He argues for Sargon's close linkage with the Mesopotamian god Ellil. Here he points to Sargon's own designation of himself as *šaknu/šakin ellil*, i.e., appointee of Ellil.[9] This was the prominent epithet in Sargon's inscriptions between 722 and 710 BC. Furthermore, Gallagher postulates that the reference to הֵילֵל climbing the heights of Zaphon is probably an allusion to the place of Sargon's death, as he was most likely killed in Tabal, not far from Zaphon.[10] Gallagher concludes, "Sargon's religious orientation and propaganda gave Ellil a special distinction unmatched by any Neo-Assyrian or Neo-Babylonian king."[11]

---

5. Gray, *Isaiah I–XXVII*, 255–56; Smith, *Isaiah*, 430; Skinner, *Isaiah I–XXXIX*, 122.
6. Gallagher, "Identity," 131–46.
7. Ibid., 131.
8. Ibid., 140.
9. Gallagher, *Campaign*, 88.
10. Ibid.
11. Ibid., 89.

As interesting as Gallagher's suggestion might be, there are several lines of criticism against his position. First, Day has dismissed this view based on the fact that *Enlil* was already the supreme god and hence did not need to strive to ascend the heights as הֵילֵל does in Isaiah 14:12–15.[12] Furthermore, Shipp has cast doubt on this alternative due to Gallagher's failure to adequately explain how *Illil* could function as the "son of Dawn."[13]

Another Mesopotamian option worth mentioning is Robert O'Connell's suggestion that Isaiah 14 intentionally evokes the familiar storyline of the Epic of Gilgamesh.[14] He writes,

> Thematic correspondence between this Mesopotamian classic and Isa. xiv strongly suggest that the author of Isaiah was deliberately using the device of allusive cueing to evoke the themes of this familiar Mesopotamian story so as to invert its storyline as a parody of the fall of this legendary (and thus archetypical) king of Babylon.[15]

Among the parallels brought together by O'Connell, several are worth noting here. The broad similarity of the reversal of fortunes can be seen in the shocked reaction of the dead kings as they encounter the king of Babylon entering the realm of Sheol. O'Connell points to the similar reaction of Gilgamesh, the Mesopotamian king himself, when he encounters the final state of Utnapishtim, the only mortal who has achieved the immortality Gilgamesh so desires.[16] The thematic parallel highlights a human being who craves to transcend his human limitations and in this transgression infringe on the divine realm. Furthermore, O'Connell highlights some Isaianic paraphrases of key points in the Mesopotamian myth: "you have become weak like us" (Gilg. XI.3–4 and Isa 14:10), "you lie indolent on your back" (Gilg. XI.6 and Isa 14:10), and "staring in startled amazement" (Gilg. XI.2–4 and Isa 14:16).[17] Thus, according to O'Connell, the author of Isaiah purposefully inverts the theme of power and weakness by the allusion to the well-known story in order to complement what he has sought to do via a concentric structure of the poem. He concludes, "Isa. xiv 4b–21 is thus a subtle reversal of royal-mythic themes well-rehearsed in Mesopotamian culture. It is de-

---

12. Day, *Yahweh*, 168.
13. Shipp, *Dirges*, 131.
14. O'Connell, "Isaiah XIV 4B–23," 407–18. We must note that O'Connell relies heavily on and develops the arguments of Van Leeuwen. See Van Leeuwen, "Isa 14:12," 173–84.
15. O'Connell, "Isaiah XIV 4B–23," 413–14.
16. Ibid., 415.
17. Ibid.

signed to evoke recognition that it is YHWH who vanquishes the pride of the Mesopotamian king(s)."[18]

O'Connell's theory might contain interesting parallels, but as Hays pointed out it hardly explains the mythic background of הֵילֵל.[19] Furthermore, there are limits to parallels with this story. As Shipp has insisted, Gilgamesh does not ascend to heaven in the Neo-Assyrian version of the story. It is true that in later texts he is identified as a major deity, but these texts are clearly late, dating to the first millennium BC.[20] While Shipp's argument does stand against O'Connell's use of a Neo-Assyrian version, it must be admitted that depending on one's dating of Isaiah the later divine attribution to Gilgamesh could make it contemporary with Isaiah 14 material.

Search for Greek Cognates of the Mythological Background of Isaiah 14:12–15

Some scholars have suggested an alternative Greek mythological background for Isaiah 14:12–15.[21] While a number of them have mentioned the myth of the Titans, it is the myth of Phaeton that has occupied much of the scholarly attention in considering a possible Greek mythological

---

18. Ibid., 414.

19. Hays, *Death*, 214. The same criticism has been raised against Langdon's proposal of the possible parallels with the Babylonian myth of the underworld deity Negral-Irra (Langdon, "Star," 172–74). He quotes the following threat from Irra, "The brilliance of the god Shulpae will I cause to fall, and the stars will I cause to be suppressed." The name Shulpae is a well known title of Marduk. The planet Jupiter is regularly linked with him during the Babylonian period. Langdon writes, "The passage in the Irra myth, where it occurs in prophecy against Babylon, undoubtedly refers to Jupiter the planet of Marduk-Bel, the god of Babylon" (173). Langdon argues that הֵילֵל is really a Babylonian loan-word for Jupiter or Marduk. According to Langdon, the title *ilu ellu*, "the bright god," is often used in reference to Marduk. He writes, "The principal Sumerian name of Marduk, Asarludug, is explained by the Babylonians of the late period as *ilu ellu mullil alakti-ni*, 'Bright god who brightens our way'" (173). Hence, Langdon claims, the author of Isaiah 14:12–15 must have borrowed *ellu* in the construct form êlil which would be transcribed as Hêlêl. (For further critique of Langdon's proposal see Day, *Yahweh*, 168).

20. Shipp, *Dirges*, 95–96.

21. Among the notable early commentators to suggest this option were Delitzsch, *Prophecies of Isaiah*, 311; Duhm, *Das Buch*, 92; and Gunkel, *Creation*, 90. Wildberger also mentions the work of Gruppe dating back to 1883 (Wildberger, *Isaiah*, 64).

forerunner.²² Grelot²³ and McKay ²⁴ have been the leading proponents of the myth of Phaethon.²⁵ Phaethon, whose name means "shining one," is a somewhat enigmatic figure. According to Hesiod, he was a son of the goddess Eos and her lover, Cephalus.²⁶ Ovid insists that he is the son of Helios and the Oceanid Clymene.²⁷ Helios was a personification of the Sun, a handsome god who drove his chariot drawn by solar steeds across the sky every day. Phaethon, wounded by the doubts of Epaphus, son of Zeus, that he was indeed of the divine stock, confronts his mother. She assures him that he is indeed Helios' son, but encourages him to inquire of Helios himself. Helios reassures Phaethon that he is his son. Having secured his father's oath to do anything for him, Phaethon demands to be allowed to drive Helios' chariot. Helios tries to dissuade his son, but fails. The fiery steeds recognize the inexperienced driver and take their chance to rush across the sky with furious speed and get off-course. As a result they come too close to the earth, drying up rivers and setting the ground on fire. Zeus, facing this tragic turn of events, strikes Phaethon with a lightning bolt. Phaethon is thrown from the sky. His corpse falls into the River Po.

If one allows the transfer of the story from Phaethon the son of Helios (Sun) to Phaethon, the son of Eos (Venus), the parallels between this myth

22. The myth of the Titans might deserve a more careful consideration, as relatively few scholars have mentioned it at all. Bamberger, *Fallen Angels*, 10; Cheyne, *Isaiah*, 89; Forsyth, *The Satanic Epic*, 201; Gowan, *Man*, 61–62; Louden, *The Iliad: Structure, Myth, and Meaning*, 212; Morgenstern, "Psalm 82," 29–126; Pope, *El*, 97, 103; Reade, *Sacred Poems*, 69; Shipp, *Dirges*, 13; Soggin, *Introduction to the Old Testament*, 52; Wildberger, *Isaiah*, 67–68. It is peculiar that the recently published volume of papers presented at the symposium entitled "Der Fall der Engel—The Fall of the Angels'" held in 2001 by the University of Groningen and the Eberhard-Karls University of Tübingen (*The Fall of the Angels*) contain both a paper that deals with Isaiah 14:12–15 and one dealing with the myth of the Titans, but neither mentions each other's topic. See Bremmer, "Remember the Titans!" 35–61, and Albani, "The Downfall of Helel, the Son of Dawn: Aspects of Royal Ideology in Isa 14:12–13," 62–86.

23. Grelot, "Isaïe," 18–48.

24. While Grelot's article preceded McKay by fourteen years, we will mainly focus on the later as he summarizes and then expands on Grelot's arguments. See McKay, "Helel," 451–64.

25. See also Baumgartner, *Zum Alten Testament und seiner Umwelt*, 157–58; Koenig, "Lucifer," 479; Schmidt, "Lucifer als gefallene Engelmacht," 167; Stolz, *Strukturen und Figuren*, 211.

26. Hesiod, *Theogony*, 2–86.

27. James Diggle provides a helpful overview of the traces of the Phaethon myth in Greek and Latin Literature. While our summary here follows the version presented in Ovid's *Metamorphoses* I.803–II.400, according to Diggle there are references to this myth in Euripides, Aeschylus, Plato, Diodorus Siculus, Strabo, Longinus, Plutarch, Seneca, Cicero, and Lucretius. See Diggle, *Euripides*, 4–9.

and Isaiah 14:12–15 become apparent. Both of the myths seem to utilize the astral phenomenon to amplify the theme of ascending and descending the divine realm. One question that comes up is, "how could this Greek myth make its way into Isaiah 14?" Here McKay provides a suggestive hypothesis, "When the Greek myth entered Canaan it underwent change and modification in such a way that it became, to all intents and purposes, a wholly Canaanite tale and, although the *dramatis personae* remained unchanged, their roles became modified in the light of the more familiar Canaanite mythology."[28] He argues that by the time this myth was introduced in Syria-Palestine, the myth of Athtar, son of Athirat, who failed to occupy the throne of Baal was already in circulation. McKay argues that the similarities between Athirat and Eos as well as between Phaethon and Athtar led to the confusion of these two myths. Phaethon's ascent to the heights was recalibrated as a desire to occupy the throne of the most high god. Rather than modifying the names Phaethon and Eos they were simply translated. This, according to McKay, is due to the fact that "they corresponded well with the astral phenomenon of Venus as the dawn star which never reaches the summit of heaven but is always compelled to return to earth as a 'weakling above the nations', eventually descending below the horizon into Sheol."[29] Finally, McKay argues that שחר appears without the definite article in a number of the MT texts, which indicates that it was perceived as a female deity, a Dawn-goddess, who makes it possible to establish a correspondence with Eos, the Greek goddess who according to Hesiod's version of the myth was the mother of Phaethon.[30]

Despite these valiant efforts, the Greek alternative has not gained much traction among the scholarly community. While Day's argument that the reason for Phaethon's ascent is incongruent with that of the king of Babylon in Isaiah 14 needs to be sharpened through direct engagement with McKay's hypothesis of the way this myth entered into the Semitic realm, his insistence that there is no known myth in Greek mythology that refers to

---

28. McKay, "Helel," 463.

29. Ibid., 464.

30. John C. Poirier offers an interesting alternative. Building on W. S. Prinsloo's insight that Isaiah 14:12–15 contains "an intermingling of divergent mythologies," he postulates the presence of two different myths, one in verse 12 and a different one in verses 13–15. They are not linked in a narrative fashion but rather sit side-by-side aiming at one goal, the elucidation of the king's hubris. Verses 13–15 are a "free rendering of a nondescript coup-of-heaven" while verse 12 is a myth of Phaethon. Here Poirier seeks to strengthen the argument in favor of the myth of Phaethon by exploring the third-century Alexandrian inscription of the poet Callimachus who tells his readers of the fallen Hesperus in *Epigram* 56. See Poirier, "Parallel," 371–89 . For Prinsloo's insights see Prinsloo, "Humiliation," 432–38.

Phaethon son of Eos (Venus), but only one who is the son of Helios (Sun) is noteworthy.[31] Furthermore, Hays is surely correct when he points out that "the story of a hot-headed boy borrowing power from his father and accidentally inflicting harm does not seem a natural wellspring for an allusion about a vicious tyrant."[32]

Search for Ugaritic Cognates of the Mythological Background of Isaiah 14:12–15

Having looked at the Mesopotamian and Greek alternatives, we are now ready to turn our attention to the Ugaritic realm.[33] Childs succinctly sums up the current scholarly interest, "With the discovery of the Ugaritic texts, the evidence mounted for seeing a far closer parallel with Canaanite mythology."[34]

While considering the Ugaritic mythology some scholars have argued, based on the lexical affinity, for the identification of הֵילֵל with the Hilâlu, the god of the crescent moon.[35] Others have noticed some degree of affinity with the Ugaritic ritual narrative about the birth of gods Shahar and Shalim, the morning and the evening stars.[36] According to the *Poem of the Birth of the Gracious Gods*, El encounters two goddesses pouring water. They are both brought to his house and seduced. Each goddess gives birth to a son. The names of these two deities born on the same day are Shachar (Dawn) and Shalim (Dusk).[37] Wildberger writes, "One of the Ugaritic texts (SS) portrays the procreation of Shachar by El and his birth from one of El's consorts, at which point comparisons have been made with Shalim, the god

31. Day, *Yahweh*, 174–75.

32. Hays, *Death*, 212.

33. Albright, *Archeology*, 84; Albright, *Yahweh and the Gods of Canaan*, 201–2; Childs, *Isaiah*, 126; Clements, *Isaiah*, 142; Coogan and Smith, *Stories from Ancient Canaan*, 14; Fohrer, *Jesaja*, 179–80; Gray, *The Legacy of Canaan*, 209; Kaiser, *Isaiah*, 39; Motyer, *The Prophecy of Isaiah*, 144; M. S. Smith, "Athtar," 627–40; Quell, "Jesaja 14:1-23," 156–57; Watson, "Helel," 746–50; Wildberger, *Isaiah*, 63.

34. *Isaiah*, 126.

35. For the association with Hilâlu see *Wörterbuch der Mythologie*, 447; Korpel, *A Rift in the Clouds*, 575–76; Spronk, *Afterlife*, 224. Spronk later changed his position and linked Helel with the Sun. See Spronk, "Mythological Background of Isa. 14:12," 717–26. It is noteworthy that *HALOT* makes this lexical association of Helel with Hilâlu. See "הלל," n.p. *HALOT on CD-ROM*.

36. See Huffmon, "Shalim," in *DDD*, 755–57; Kaiser, *Isaiah*, 39; Parker, "Shahar," 754–55; Wyatt, "Theogeny Motif," 395–419.

37. *KTU* 1.23. For the English translation see Gibson, *Canaanite Myths and Legends*, 123–27.

of the evening dusk. The way Shachar is used in personal names in Ugarit provides further evidence that it was considered a deity."[38]

The myth of Athtar (Ashtar) has also been a focal point of discussion. According to this myth, the slaying of Baal by Mot precipitated a need for a suitable replacement. Athtar ascends to the throne of Baal on mount Zaphon being appointed by El following the mediation of Anath and Asherah. Yet Athtar soon discovers that he is not physically large enough to occupy Baal's place, as his feet do not reach down to the footstool, nor his head reaches up to the top of the throne. So Athtar descends from the throne to rule the earth.[39]

One of the cogent proponents of this Ugaritic antecedent to Isaiah 14:12–15 has been Craigie. He has pointed out that the meaning of the name Helel, "shining," which comes from the Akkadian *ellu* corresponds well with Athtar's epithet, "Athtar the Luminous." Furthermore, Craigie highlights Athtar's character as a warrior. According to Craigie, in the Babylonian cuneiform text listing members of the Ugaritic pantheon (RS 20.24), the god Aštabi, which is the Hurrian equivalent to Ugaritic Athtar, is linked with certain Babylonian warrior gods. Thus he insists, "Athtar is the "shining one," the warrior, but essentially he is inadequate and falls; he forms a close parallel to the aspiring Babylonian warrior king, whose act of hubris would lead to his downfall."[40] Craigie rejected the Greek antecedent, such as the myth of Phaethon because the evidence seems to point in the direction of Near Eastern influence on Greek literature rather than vice versa. In the end, he argues that "the differences between the account of Helel and its Ugaritic counterpart are to be explained by poet's license in adaptation, rather than in seeking a closer, though very dubious, parallel in Greek mythology."[41]

Oldenburg has added interesting elements to this conversation.[42] He has argued that the origins of this myth are to be found in the Ancient South Arabian religion, where Athtar played a much more prominent role than El.[43] It was Athtar, not El who was the supreme god whom all of South Arabian nations venerated under the same name. Oldenburg furnishes evidence that seems to point to the fact that Athtar was identified with the

---

38. Wildberger, *Isaiah*, 63.
39. *ANET*, 139–40.
40. Craigie, "Helel," 223–24.
41. Ibid., 225.
42. Oldenburg, "El in Ancient South Arabic Religion," 187–208.
43. For Athtar in the South Arabian Religion see Ryckmans, "South Arabia," 171–76.

planet Venus and postulates that at some point the cult of El was displaced by the cult of Athtar.[44]

Page has brought a helpful corrective to the scholarly understanding of the Athtar figure in the Ugaritic texts. He argues against the view suggested by Gaster back in 1950 that Athtar is "a god of inferior status who aspires to domination over both the earth and the water but who is regarded in each case as not fully qualified to wield it."[45] Gaster's view has been widely accepted, as evidenced by the works of Oldenburg, Gibson, de Moor and Smith.[46] Page's comprehensive analysis of the Ugaritic texts paints a quite contrary picture. Athtar is a son of El and Asherah, who always serve as his political benefactors. He is a king, who is said to be "terror inspiring." While it is true that he is painted as physically weaker than Baal and "minute in strength," it is noteworthy that there is no criticism of his stature by El when he descends from Baal's throne. So this might be a comparative weakness as Baal is the king of gods and the major actor in the myth. Commenting on Athtar's profile, Page writes, "While it is different from that of Baal it in no way suggests that he is pathetic or impotent. The most that can be said is that he is *enigmatic*."[47] While Baal tends to seek El's opinion, Athtar acts independently. Without any advice from his benefactors he steps down from the throne of Baal and makes himself the king of the underworld. Page writes, "Athtar is a mysterious (no home, very little personal property, refuses to retain power given to him by his political patrons) yet active and intelligent comic force with power over the underworld."[48]

Heiser has been a significant recent voice in this discussion.[49] He leans on the findings of Page, but is dissatisfied with his conclusions. First, he argues that Page's discussion of the figure of Athtar does not merit his conclusion that Athtar became construed as a rebellious deity—a construal that is not inherent in the Athtar myth itself.[50] Heiser argues that Athtar is indeed a rebellious god. Prior to being offered Baal's throne, Athtar complains about not having his own house. After giving the throne of Baal a try he has the audacity to despise the position given to him by El. This, argues Heiser, is consistent with the pattern of Athtar's challenging of El's decrees as seen

---

44. Ibid., 23–4.

45. Page, *Myth*, 63. This quote come from Gaster, *Ritual, Myth and Drama in the ancient Near East*, 126.

46. Gibson, *Canaanite Myths and Legends*, 19; de Moor, *Religious Texts*, 415; Oldenburg, *El and Ba'al in Canaanite Religion*, 42; Smith, "Athtar," 627–40, esp. 640.

47. Page, *Myth*, 78.

48. Ibid., 67.

49. Heiser, "Mythological Provenance," 354–69.

50. Ibid., 361.

in *KTU* 1.2.III.15–24.[51] Second, while Page is convinced that some aspects of Isaiah 14:12–15 are Canaanite in origin, he is hesitant in applying his findings to the question of the mythological provenance of this text—the hesitation that Heiser finds unwarranted. He tackles this issue head on by posing a question, "Why would the author of Isa. xiv 12–15 use a myth that itself is not about the usurpation of a throne to recount a tale whose main character clearly intends to unseat his superior?"[52] Heiser argues that the point of Isaiah 14 is not the take over of the throne but arrogance. It is here that the reconstruction of Athtar as an arrogant rebellious deity becomes crucial. Heiser writes, "I believe the Baʻal-ʻAthtar tale fits this perfectly, for it describes a striking act of insolence ... Hēlēl ben-Šaḥar (and so ʻAthtar) wanted to be like the Most High *not* in terms of usurping a position, *but in his desire for decretive control*."[53]

As suggestive as the Athtar option might be, Gowan's critique of Oldenburg is worth noting, "Oldenburg ... has added more information about Athtar in South Arabia but must still admit there is no trace of the myth presumed to lie behind Isa. 14."[54] A similar voice of caution was issued by Watson, "No mythological episode in Ugaritic connects either *hll* or *šḥr* with the presumption of rising to heaven and instead being thrust into the underworld."[55] Some have argued the realm of *arṣ* over which Athtar rules after descent from Baal's throne is the Underworld. Heiser, who otherwise supports the Athtar proposal, rejects it, "Baal and Mot were 'co-regents' of the *arṣ*, but ... the *arṣ* over which the co-regency is held is not the Underworld. Hence one cannot argue that when Athtar briefly became king over the *arṣ* before Baal's resurrection, that realm was the Underworld ... It makes more sense to see the realm Athtar took for himself after his defiant rejection of Baal's position over other gods as the earth."[56] Heiser goes on to argue that this incongruence lies with the author of Isaiah 14:12–15, "The theology of the author of Isa. xiv 12–15 mandated a disastrous end for the rebel: an abrupt and permanent expulsion to the realm of the dead."[57] This appeal to the theological grid of the author of Isaiah 14:12–15 is an interesting proposal but lacks hard historical evidence.

---

51. Ibid., 365.
52. Ibid., 365
53. Ibid., 365.
54. Gowan, *Man*, 163 n.16.
55. Watson, "Helel," 393.
56. Heiser, "The Mythological Provenance of Isa. XIV 12–15," 367.
57. Ibid., 368.

Search for Canaanite Cognates of the Mythological Background of Isaiah 14:12–15

A noteworthy alternative suggested by Day that has not yet generated much scholarly discussion deals with a Canaanite cognate. He postulates that a Jebusite myth was appropriated by the author of Isaiah 14:12–15.[58] Day marshals several intriguing arguments to support his hypothesis. First, the Isaiah 14:14 reference to Elyon is significant because it is the distinctive name of the Jebusite deity of Jerusalem in Genesis 14:19 and 22. Furthermore, Psalm 110 has a reference to the Davidic king having a role of priest in the order of Melchizedek. Day points out that in Genesis 14 Melchizedek is the Jebusite priest of El-Elyon, so it must be that "the royal priesthood after the order of Melchizedek reflects a fusion of the Israelite and Jebusite royal ideologies effected soon after the conquest of the city."[59] Finally, the origin of the name of Jerusalem is "the foundation of the god Shalem." Shalem is argued to be the god of dusk. As we have seen above, in Ugaritic mythology Shahar [dawn] and Shalem [dusk] were twin brothers whose father was El. So Day postulates, "if the god Shalem ('dusk') was prominent in Jebusite Jerusalem mythology, it is only natural that his brother Shahar, 'dawn', would appear there too."[60] As suggestive as Day's proposal might be, at this point we do not have any extra-biblical evidence for the Jebusite god named Elyon or any reference to Shahar.

The Fruitfulness of the Search for the Ancient Cognates of הֵילֵל בֶּן-שָׁחַר Image for the Reading of a Paradigmatic מָשָׁל of Isaiah 14:3–23

Having laid out all of the proposed options for the mythological background of Isaiah 14:12–15, we are faced with an almost overwhelming array of options to consider. In reading a paradigmatic מָשָׁל found in Isaiah 14 one may come to ask about the fruitfulness of this attempt to pin down the enigmatic myth.

Scholarship has been careful to acknowledge the limitations of this search for the mythic background for Isaiah 14:12–15.[61] It is worth mentioning that serious doubts regarding the mythological background have

---

58. Day, *Yahweh*, 179–80.
59. Ibid., 180.
60. Ibid.
61. Sweeney, *Isaiah 13–39*, 237–38.

been raised based on historical-critical grounds. Following Spronk's earlier lead, Albani has argued, "Isa. 14:12ff. does not reflect any myth about a deity named *Helel* son of *Shahar,* but rather it alludes by way of criticism to the royal notion of the postmortal apotheosis of the king."[62] Furthermore, Kaiser's cautionary caveat issued on the heels of discoveries of the Ugaritic texts in Northern Syria still stands. While they have been extremely helpful in illuminating some of the individual features, "they have not so far provided any direct parallel to the present passage."[63]

If one is serious about the shared mythopoetic presuppositions that were in operation in antiquity, then room must be made for the weaving together of different motifs in the Isaiah text at hand. Hays' recent comment seems to bear the validity of that observation. He writes, "It is important to recognize that Isa. 14 is best deemed a particularly Israelite employment of a widespread mythic tradition."[64] Search for *the* myth that stands behind this text might be a valid activity in its own right but in the end seems to fail to take this substantial continuity of ancient worldview seriously. The poet who pens these verses brings to the table the widely held grid and puts it to use in painting the imaginative world of the משל of Isaiah 14:3–23.

The Historical Referent of the King of Babylon

Isaiah 14:3–4a informs us that this is a משל about the king of Babylon. A small cottage industry has been created by the simple fact that this king is not named. Much scholarly ink has been spilled in search of the historical referent of the king to whom this song refers.

Before attempting to handle this conundrum, we need to take a step back and situate this issue in its broader literary and historical-critical contexts. The Assyrian Empire and the surrounding *Realpolitik* issues of the eighth century BC are dominant in Isaiah 1–12. When the Oracles Against the Nations open in Isaiah 13, the reader encounters a collection of material dealing with Babylon. This peculiar shift from Assyria to Babylon in Isaiah 13–14 has been a topic of spirited scholarly discussion in its own right. Early on, Calvin attempted to solve the puzzle by suggesting that Babylon was a figure for Assyria.[65] As Seitz has pointed out, "Assyria and Babylon

---

62. Albani, "Downfall," 62–86. For Spronk's thought see "Down," 717–26.

63. Kaiser, *Isaiah,* 38–39.

64. Hays, *Death,* 214.

65. See Seitz' insightful comments on Calvin's interchangeable use of Babylon and Assyria in his commentaries (Seitz, "History," 1–6).

are for Calvin figures of the selfsame divine purpose, whatever one might understand by their discrete locations in historical time."⁶⁶ Although Calvin does not discuss the typology in his comments on the משל we can see that it comes up in the material immediately following it in Isaiah 14:24–27. He reads these verses figuratively, albeit the other way around, "Isaiah, though he is speaking of *Babylon*, describes the whole of its force under the name of *Assyria*."⁶⁷ Since the time of Duhm, critical scholarship has assumed that the context of these oracles against Babylon in Isaiah 13–14 was the Neo-Babylonian Empire of the sixth century BC, which was eventually devastated by the Medes and Persians led by the king Cyrus in 539 BC.⁶⁸ This shift precipitated by Duhm's proposal of multiple authorship of Isaiah has led the majority of scholarship to consider Isaiah 13–14 as a work of an exilic or post exilic redactor. Despite Erlandsson's weighty argument for the eighth century BC Babylonian context of the kingdom ruled by Merodach-baladan and its final destruction by Sennacherib in 689 BC, the majority of recent scholarship has treated Isaiah 13–14 as post-Isaianic, thus underscoring the complex nature of the book as it stands and its composition history.⁶⁹

Literary and historical-critical issues as just outlined have shaped the way this issue of the historical referent of the king of Babylon has been handled in modern critical scholarship. The peculiar relationship between the Assyria and Babylon materials placed side-by-side in the canonical setting of Isaiah and the ambiguity of the historical setting for these oracles against Babylon have framed the modern scholarly exploration of the historical referent of the unnamed Babylonian tyrant via proposals of various individual kings.⁷⁰ Much hinges on how one reads the introductory verses of Isaiah 14:3–4a, which frame the poem:

66. Seitz, "History," 1.

67. Calvin, *Isaiah*, 1:458.

68. For a succinct discussion of history of dating Isaiah 13–14 see Gray, *Isaiah I–XXVII*, 235–36.

69. Erlandsson, *Burden*, 86–92. For a fair summary and judicious critique of Erlandsson see Childs, *Isaiah*, 115.

70. It is worth noting that many early commentators allowed for the view that the individual king was a representative figure. Eissfeldt writes, "It is clear that it is directed at one of these two world powers (Assyrian or Babylon), represented by the person of their king, under which Israel had so terribly suffered, and it is from this that we may explain the magnificent pathos of passionate and triumphant satisfaction with which the fall of the king, presented as if it has already taken place, is derisively lamented." (Eissfeldt, *Introduction*, 97.) Similarly Dillmann sees the king as "Zusammenfassung des Volks und der Macht der Babylonier." (Dillmann, *Der Prophet*, 134.) Yet this representative role was still tied with an actual historical referent and thus was a far cry from a king as a paradigmatic figure which would emerge in later research.

> 3 When the LORD has given you rest from your pain and turmoil and the hard service with which you were made to serve, 4 you will take up this taunt against the king of Babylon.

Some scholars argue that all of the מָשָׁל of Isaiah 14:3–23 was composed as a reference to an eighth-century-BC Babylonian king. Others tend to see the introduction of Isaiah 14:3–4a as a later framing device that allows the poet to recycle a poem, which was originally penned with the eighth-century-BC Assyrian king in mind to now apply to a sixth-century-BC Babylonian king. Still others posit an even later Greek referent based on the larger paradigmatic role assigned to Babylon in late antiquity.

Search for an Eighth-Century-BC Babylonian Referent for the King of Babylon

A. *Tiglath-pileser III (745–727 BC)*

It might seem odd to start our survey of options for a Babylonian referent with a discussion of a prominent Assyrian king, but this reflects both Babylon's exalted status in antiquity and the peculiar relationship of some of the Assyrian rulers in regards to this venerated political and religious center.

Erlandsson, the main proponent of this eighth-century-BC referent, has pointed out that for centuries Babylon was the place of worship as well as of commerce. He claims that Babylon in antiquity played a role analogous for Rome in the Middle Ages. The great Assyrian cities of Nineveh and Kalaḫ paled in comparison.[71]

Tiglath-pileser affirmed Babylon's dominant political position in Mesopotamia when he assumed the title of *šàr Bābili* (king of Babylon) in 727 BC. At least two other prominent Assyrian monarchs, Sargon and Sennacherib, would follow his example. Additionally, in the act of humble submission, Tiglath-pileser reassured the prominence of the Marduk priesthood by presenting himself on the New Years Day and performing the ceremony of grasping the hand of Marduk in 728 BC.[72] Thus, Erlandsson argues, "the ideology which Babylon represented . . . became the official religion in the Assyrian empire, and to a great extent the gods of Babylon superseded the Assyrian gods."[73] In this linking of the Assyrian royal power with the prominence of Babylon, Erlandsson sees it very fitting that the Oracle Against Babylon would be addressing this prominent Assyrian king. "That same

---

71. Erlandsson, *Burden*, 88.
72. Ibid.
73. Ibid., 163.

pride which the city of Babylon represents, is in the ode personified by the Assyrian tyrant."[74]

We will see Tiglath-pileser's name come up again, as the scholarship has attempted to reconfigure this Assyrian referent in a different way. While lengthier evaluative note will come at that point, it is worth mentioning here that the details of his death do not line up well with the way Isaiah 14 envisions the tyrant's death.

B. *Marodach-baladan (722–710 BC)*

Smith has been an another notable proponent of the eighth century reference to a Babylonian king. He claims that the introduction of Isaiah 14:3–4a and the whole of the poem were composed with the Babylonian king Marodach-baladan in mind.[75] Smith assumes the Isaianic authorship of the book and argues for the eighth century composition of this text. He sees the historical realities outlined in Isaiah 39:1–9 forming the narrative background for this poem. Hezekiah's attempt to form a political alliance with Merodach-baladan against Assyria was a risky gambit. It gave a temporary infusion of hope, but with Sennacherib's devastating blow to Babylon in 689 BC came the crashing of Judah's dreams. Smith considers the death of Merodach-baladan as a terrible news for Judah. He writes,

> The death of this pivotal Babylonian ally would be a terrible blow to Judah, and many in Judah naturally lament his passing. His death would undermine their coordinated plan to rebel against Assyria and dash their hopes of maintaining their freedom from Assyrian domination. . . . Thus it is not so much a taunt of the king but a sober lament. Many will weep, for God is going to end the life of the Babylonian king that Judah was trusting.[76]

Smith's hypothesis hinges on a radically different reading of the entire משל. It is hard to see how one would embrace this option without making a prior move of reading this poem not as paradigmatic taunt shaped as a lament song, but rather as a real lament about the downfall of the trusted political ally.

---

74. Erlandsson, *Burden*, 163–64.
75. Smith, *Isaiah 1–39*, 310–11. See also Watts, *Isaiah*, 188.
76. G. A. Smith, *Isaiah*, 310.

Search for an Eighth-Century-BC Assyrian Referent for the King of Babylon

Some scholars have suggested that the משל of Isaiah 14:3–23 was originally composed with one of the Assyrian tyrants in mind. Peter Machinist's superb analysis of the portrayal of Assyria in First Isaiah gives a rationale for this line of thinking. His survey of the relevant texts in Isaiah shows that Assyria was perceived as

> an overwhelming military machine, destroying all resistance in its path, devastating the lands of its enemies, hauling away huge numbers of spoils and captives to its capital or elsewhere in its realm, and rearranging by this devastation and deportation the political physiognomy of the entire region.[77]

This perception was very much in line with how the Assyrian imperial propaganda set out to portray itself in various Neo-Assyrian royal inscriptions.[78] For example, Sargon II, who was a contemporary of Isaiah claims,

> The immense armies of Aššur I mustered, (and) went out to conquer those [citie]s. With powerful battering-rams I [smashed] their fortified walls and reduced them [to] the ground. [The people] together with their possessions I took as booty. T[hos]e [cities] ... [I devastated, I destroyed, I burned w]ith fire. ... Because of the sin which they committed I tore them away from their homes and settled them i[n the land of] Ḫatti [of Amurru].[79]

If in Isaiah's mind the Assyrian Empire was a quintessential military machine, then its downfall could be naturally envisioned as a theological counterpoint to its global uprise. So Machinist tentatively suggests that when it comes to Isaiah 14, words that were initially applied to the death of Sargon II were later reinterpreted against the background of the Neo-Babylonian Empire. He claims that some of the old Assyrian images were reused but other Mesopotamian motifs, coming now from the Babylonian milieu, were also added.[80]

---

77. Machinist, "Assyria," 722.
78. Ibid., 723–28.
79. Lie, *Inscriptions*, 9. Quoted in Machinist, "Assyria," 723.
80. Machinist, "Assyria," 736–37.

Our analysis will focus on three main Assyrian referents that have dominated the modern scholarly discussion. We will consider in chronological order Tiglath-pileser II, Sargon II, and Sennacherib.[81]

A. *Tiglath-pileser III (745-727 BC)*

A traditional view, represented by Hayes and Irvine, identifies the king with the Assyrian ruler, Tiglath-pileser III, who assumed the Babylonian throne after its conquest in 729 BC. Hayes and Irvine have argued vigorously for the essential Isaianic authorship of the material found in Isaiah 1-39. Towards that end they attempt to read the material in sequential order. Thus, contextually, they place Isaiah 14:1-27 between 731-729 BC and 727 BC. Their rationale is that Isaiah 13 reflects the historical realities recorded in an Assyrian eponym list that shows that an Assyrian king fought a battle in Babylon in 731 BC, remained at home in 730 BC, and eventually claimed the Babylonian throne in 729 BC.[82] On the other end, the material in Isaiah 14:28-32 deals with the time of Ahaz's death which took place in 727 BC. This leads Hayes and Irvine to argue that Isaiah 14:1-27 has to be interpreted against the backdrop of the international political realities in the years 729 BC and 727 BC, which revolve around Tiglath-pileser.[83] According to them the text's description of the king of Babylon fits well with Tiglath-pileser's own "royal braggadocio"[84] as one of the Assyrian inscriptions reads,

> Palace of Tiglath-pileser, the great king, the mighty king, king of the universe, king of Assyria, king of Babylon, king of Sumer and Akkad, king of the four regions of the world; the brave hero, who, with the help of Assur, his lord, smashed all who did not obey him, like pots, and laid them low, like a hurricane, scattering them to the winds; the king, who, advancing in the name of Assur, Shamash and Marduk, the great gods, brought under his sway the lands from the Bitter Sea of Bit-Iakin to Mount Bikni, of the rising sun, and to the sea of the setting sun, as far as Egypt—from the horizon to the zenith, and exercised kingship over them.[85]

---

81. The last two Assyrian kings, Sin-Shar-ishkun (627-612) and Ashur-uballit II (612-607) do fit the context of Isaiah 14:19 that describes the slaughter of the king of Babylon. (See Gallagher, *Campaign*, 87-8).
82. Hayes and Irvine, *Isaiah*, 227.
83. Ibid.
84. Hayes and Irvine, *Isaiah*, 231.
85. *ARAB* I § 787. Quoted in Ibid.

Hays' otherwise favorable summary of this option presented by Hayes and Irvine raises two significant reservations. First, while Hayes and Irvine speculate that Tiglath-pileser died during the campaign against Damascus in 727 BC, there no evidence of that in the Assyrian accounts. Neither is there any evidence that he did not receive a proper burial. At best, what Hayes and Irvine suggest regarding this king's death is an argument from silence. Second, while Tiglath-pileser would have been known in Israel and Judah, an awareness of the Assyrian would have heightened after the destruction of Samaria in 722 BC. Based on that hypothesis Hays claims that Sargon would fit the profile better than Tiglath-pileser.[86]

B. Sargon II (722–705 BC)

One of the most widely considered options for an Assyrian referent has been Sargon II.[87] Ginsberg has argued that this poem is an ode on the death of Sargon that reflects a "spontaneous reaction" to the news of his downfall.[88] Exilic and post-exilic redactors have added verses 3–4a as well as verses 22–23 updating it to reflect their current realities. Ginsberg points to Sargon's "notorious Babylonism."[89] By this he implies Sargon's three year-long residence in this ancient city, acquisition of Babylonian titles and lavish endowments to the inhabitants and temples. He also points back to arguments brought up by Orr and Winckler that the description of the fate of the king of Babylon in Isaiah 14:18–19 fits well with what is known about Sargon's fate. He appears to have been killed and abandoned at the battlefield as reflected in the cuneiform text K 4730 which states, "Sargon ... was not buried in his house."[90] According to this document Sargon's gruesome end has prompted his son and successor Sennacherib to initiate an investigation by inquiring of his soothsayers as to what sort of sin could have caused such severe punishment.[91]

Sweeney comes to similar conclusions regarding a possible Sargon reference in this text. He points out that Sargon was responsible for the devastation of Samaria and deportation of the population of the northern

---

86. Hays, *Death*, 217.

87. Barth, *Die Jesaja-Worte in der Josiazeit*, 135–36; Bonkamp, *Die Bibel im Lichte der Keilschriftforschung*, 426–27; Childs, *Isaiah*, 127; Gottwald, *All the Kingdoms of the Earth*, 176; Shipp, *Dirges*, 158–62; Sweeney, *Isaiah 1–39*, 232–33; Tull, *Isaiah*, 284; Wilke, *Jesaja und Assur*, 84; Winckler, *Keilinschriften*, 74–75; Younger, "Sargon II" 288–329.

88. Ginsberg, "Reflexes," 49.

89. Ibid.

90. Ibid., 50.

91. Ibid.

kingdom of Israel in 721 BC. He also made threats towards Jerusalem during his campaign in 720 BC. All this, most likely, amounted to the perception of Sargon as a terrifying threat. Hence, Sweeney wonders if this song was composed by Isaiah in response to the news of Sargon's death reaching Jerusalem around 705 BC. It constitutes Isaiah's public utterance regarding Sargon whom he denounced in Isaiah 10:5–34 for his arrogant boasting.[92]

While the parallels with Sargon are indeed impressive, it is not clear what Isaiah would gain by referring to Sargon, the king of Assyria, as the king of Babylon while Assyria was the dominant political superpower of that day. Furthermore, despite Sargon's clear identification with Babylon he never identified himself as the "king of Babylon" in his titles. His choice epithet was "governor of Babylon" (šakkanak Bābili).[93] Finally, while the astute modern student of the history of the ancient Near East has access to the details of Sargon's "notorious Babylonism," would Isaiah's audience in Israel and Judah be familiar with them?

c. Sennacherib (705–681 BC)

Less frequently mentioned among the options for an Assyrian king is Sennacherib.[94] One of the first scholars to suggest this option was Hugo Winckler.[95] In his brief note written in 1894, he was arguing for the Isaianic authorship of Isaiah 14:4–21. According to Winckler the violent death of the king of Babylon described here must be referring to the slaughter of Sennacherib in 682 shortly after his withdrawal from Palestine.[96] He points to the poem's close affinity with 2 Kings 19:21–28 which records Isaiah's prophecy of Sennacherib's downfall.[97] Winckler seems to be convinced that the affinity is due to the fact that one poem anticipates Sennacherib's overthrow and the other one describes its aftermath.[98]

Another proponent of the Sennacherib option was Cobb. His approach to identifying the historical referent has focused on the four characteristics

---

92. Sweeney, *Isaiah 1–39*, 233.
93. Gallagher, *Campaign*, 90.
94. See also Staerk, *Weltreich*, 144–47.
95. Winckler, *Forschungen*, 193–94.
96. Winckler writes, "Da offenbar auf einen gewaltsamen tod angespielt wird, so ist kaum ein zweifel, das die ermordnung Sanheribs im jahre 682 gemeint ist, welche stattfand, nachdem dieser aus Palästina hatte abziehen müssen.» in *Forschungen*, 193–94.
97. Winckler, *Forschungen*, 194.
98. Winckler later would change his mind in light of new evidence emerging that Sargon "was not buried in his house." See Winckler, *Keilinschriften*, 74–75.

that the poem ascribes to the king of Babylon.[99] First, he was an oppressive tyrant. He is marked by arrogance (14:4), lays low the nations (14:12) and destroys his own land and his people (14:20). Second, he was a world-ruler. This tyrant smote the peoples of the world in anger (14:6). Upon his downfall the whole earth is finally at rest (14:7). He made the whole earth tremble (14:16) and turned the world into wilderness (14:17). Third, he was famous for pomp and pride. His pomp is brought down to Sheol (14:11). The tyrant desired to ascend the divine abode (14:13–14). Fourth, he was brought to an inglorious end. The tyrant is brought down to the ground (14:4). He ends up in the uttermost parts of the abyss in Sheol (14:15). His corpse is cast away from his grave in dishonor (14:19–20). Cobb's analysis of the historical referents leads him to conclude, "All four points in the historical situation described meet in Sennacherib; to the best of my knowledge and belief, they *all* meet in no one else."[100]

Some of the questions raised about Sargon II equally apply to Sennacherib. Especially, in light of the notoriety that this Assyrian king received due to his bloody but failed campaign to capture Jerusalem in 701 BC, one wonders about the plausibility or reasoning for referring to him as the king of Babylon.

Search for a Sixth-Century-BC Babylonian Referent for the King of Babylon

Childs is one of many who have suggested that the משל of Isaiah 14:3–23 was originally composed with the eighth-century Assyrian ruler in mind and was later recycled to apply to a sixth-century Neo-Babylonian monarch by adding the framing reference to the king of Babylon in Isaiah 14:3–4a.[101] The most plausible of Neo-Babylonian candidates whom this recalibrated poem envisioned addressing seem to be Nebuchadnezzar (605–562 BC) and Nabonidus (556–539 BC).[102]

---

99. Cobb, "Ode," 25–26.
100. Ibid., 28. Italics are Cobb's.
101. Childs, *Isaiah*, 127.

102. Another lesser explored Babylonian ruler option which has not gained much traction is Belshazzar. Sawyer points to the Daniel 5 text. This "quite unhistorical legend," as Sawyer puts it, reports a story of Belshazzar's feast using the utensils brought from the temple in Jerusalem. This monstrosity of using sacred utensils during a drunken royal orgy prompts YHWH's swift response. Daniel 5:30 reports that king Belshazzar dies that very night. In this Sawyer sees "the most illuminating parallel in terms of dramatic force and prophetic significance." See Sawyer, *Isaiah*, 143.

A. Nebuchadnezzar (605–562 BC)

Blenkinsopp claims that Nebuchadnezzar and Nabonidus are "the only Neo-Babylonian dynasts of sufficient distinction to be considered."[103] In favor of Nebuchadnezzar Blenkinsopp mentions his arrogant claim to have torn down cedars of Lebanon with his bare hands as a reference to Isaiah 14:8. Yet for Nabonidus he points to the fact he was not a popular ruler and might have even been at war with his own people in connection with his abdicating the throne for a retirement at the Tema oasis.[104]

John Day has also argued in favor of Nebuchadnezzar. Unlike Nabonidus, Nebuchadnezzar was indeed a great conqueror. Day points to the discovery of the Chaldean Chronicle that reveals that Nebuchadnezzar's actions were very much parallel to those taken by the Assyrian kings, namely annual military campaigns, impositions of heavy tribute, and harsh punishment of those defeated. In light of that he concludes, "It seems unnecessary to suppose that Isaiah 14:4b–21 originally referred to an Assyrian king, and there is every reason to believe that the king in view here is Nebuchadrezzar."[105]

Wildberger has suggested that there might be a wordplay on Nebuchadnezzar's name in the word נצר (carrion) in verse 19, though admitting the uncertainty of this suggestion.[106] Furthermore, he claims that due to Nebuchadnezzar's harsh dealings with Israel, he of all options fits best the "typological profile" of a brutal tyrant portrayed in Isaiah 14.[107]

Sweeney has summed up well the doubts surrounding the Nebuchadnezzar option. He argues that of all Babylonian kings Nebuchadnezzar indeed alone had amassed the power and greatness that could reflect the self-aggrandizing boasting reflected in Isaiah 14:13–14. Yet Sweeney rejects this option due to the fact that this king was succeeded by his son Amel-Merodach rather than suffering the cut off of his dynasty that Isaiah 14:21 envisions. Besides, there is no evidence that he was left without a burial or that his corpse was desecrated the way Isaiah 14:18–19 suggest about the tyrant.[108]

---

103. Blenkinsopp, *Isaiah*, 287.
104. Ibid.
105. Day, *Yahweh*, 182–83.
106. Wildberger, *Isaiah*, 53.
107. Ibid., 55.
108. Sweeney, *Isaiah 1–39*, 232.

b. Nabonidus (556–539 BC)

While mainly favored by earlier commentators,[109] the Nabonidus option has found fresh attention in Clements' commentary. Clements considers Nebuchadnezzar as a very viable option among the Babylonian kings. He argues this on the basis of the fact that Nebuchadnezzar's conquests had the most devastating effect on Judah. Yet, according to Clements the imagery of the tyrant of Babylon in Isaiah 14 does not simply refer to a single ruler's reign but rather to someone who encapsulates the tyrannical dynasty and its final ending.[110] It is this aspect of the dynastic finality that leads him to eventually settle on Nabonidus, the last of the Babylonian rulers whose reign culminated in the destruction of Babylon in 538 BC, as the most fitting option.[111]

The Nabonidus proposal does not cohere well with the outcome of tyrant's life envisioned in Isaiah 14 as was acknowledged early on by Duhm.[112] The third-century-BC Babylonian writer Berossus reports Cyrus' magnanimous treatment of the deposed Nabonidus. Josephus[113] and Eusebius[114] refer to Berossus and while diverging on details agree that after removing him from the Babylonian throne Cyrus made Nabonidus a governor the province of Carmania in eastern Persia.[115]

Search for a Late Non-Babylonian Referent for the King of Babylon

So far we have seen that the tension of Assyrian and Babylonian material placed side by side in the early chapters of Isaiah and the editorial framing of Isaiah 14:3–4a linking the poem with the downfall of the Babylonian tyrant has been understood by many as the reworking of the earlier Assyrian material and reapplying it to Babylon. Goldingay argues that this reapplication "reflects how the Old Testament can see the succession of superpowers (Assyrian, Babylon, Persia, Greece) as the embodiment of one phenomenon."[116]

---

109. Driver, *Literature of the Old Testament*, 212; Jahnow, *Leichenlied*, 242; Marti, *Jesaja*, 128.

110. Clements, *Isaiah*, 141.

111. Ibid., 140.

112. Duhm, *Das Buch*, 90.

113. Josephus, *Against Apion*, 20–1.

114. Eusebius, *Preparation*, IX, 41.

115. The cogency of this evidence has been questioned. See the pertinent discussions in Dandamaev, *Political History*, 49–50; Glassner, *Mesopotamian Chronicles*, 81; Nissen and Heine, *Mesopotamia*, 105.

116. Goldingay, *Theology*, 41.

The cogency of Goldingay's observation can be seen in the way Ezra 6:22 refers to the king of Babylon as the king of Assyria.

Speaking specifically about the way the references to Babylon might be functioning in the Old Testament, Goldingay points out that at the heart of the collection of the Oracles Against the Nations in Isaiah 13–23 sits Isaiah 17:12–14 which reads,

> **12** Ah, the thunder of many peoples,
>   they thunder like the thundering of the sea!
> Ah, the roar of nations,
>   they roar like the roaring of mighty waters!
> **13** The nations roar like the roaring of many waters,
>   but he will rebuke them, and they will flee far away,
> chased like chaff on the mountains before the wind
>   and whirling dust before the storm.
> **14** At evening time, lo, terror!
> Before morning, they are no more.
> This is the fate of those who despoil us,
>   and the lot of those who plunder us.

This oracle reassures YHWH's people that every superpower that arises raging and roaring across the world will eventually fall. Any terror and plunder is temporary. YHWH will ultimately rebuke the oppressors and chase them away as a mere chaff.

Goldingay observes that Hebrew has no terms that would designate "the superpower" or "the empire." The language here is merely that of "the nations" and "the peoples" who are set over against Judah. Goldingay insists that this reality gives rise to the use of Babylon as the language for the archetypal superpower. He writes, "Babylon become(s) *the* symbol of a nation set over against God, as it is in the revelation to John. The collage's arrangement[117] may imply it is already becoming such a symbol. The Babylon whose fall is described is then not merely the historical Babylon, Israel's conqueror, but also the symbolic Babylon. Its fall signifies the dethroning of every power opposed to God."[118]

This movement towards perceiving Babylon as the paradigmatic figure, lies at the heart of the search for a late non-Babylonian referent of the king of Babylon in Isaiah 14:3–4a. So we turn to the final alternative to consider

---

117. Goldingay considers the book of Isaiah a collection of five collages. The collage he refers to here is Isaiah 13–27. See Goldingay, *Theology*, 12–13.

118. Ibid., 41.

for an individual king—Alexander the Great. Charles Torrey argues that the book of Isaiah came into its final shape during the Greek period.[119] He writes, "Redactional operations in variety, occasionally of considerable extent, sometimes only verbal additions, can be shown with greater or less distinctness to have been made after the conquests of Alexander."[120] Torrey insists that the scope of Assyrian or Babylonian domination is minuscule in comparison to that of Alexander. He truly was the world-wide ruler whose conquest "shook the earth." Torrey's comment, indicative of the intuitive reading strategy in antiquity, is instructive,

> Readers of Is 14 in the third century B.C., men whose fathers had seen the onrush of the Greek armies, and who knew how western Asia had been thrilled by the news of the great Macedonian's death, could hardly fail to find this the true historical background, in spite of the Babylonian label.[121]

One piece of textual evidence pointing in this direction is the possible linking of Alexander with Isaiah 14:21–23, which calls for the slaughter of the king's sons lest they fill the world with cities. According to Torrey, this reference to the cities is "senseless if the poem referred to a king of Babylonia or Assyria" but becomes potent when one considers the dread of the multiplying Greek cities that threatened to turn the Semitic western Asia into a Greek province.[122]

As suggestive as Torrey's thoughts might be, the details of Alexander the Great's death and subsequent treatment of his body do not concur with the fate of the tyrant of Babylon in Isaiah 14. First, Alexander the Great died in Babylon in 323 BC of disputed causes—malaria, typhoid, or poisoning have been suggested, but the death on the battlefield can be ruled out.[123] Second, despite his dying wish to have his body thrown into the river as a way of perpetuating the myth of his immortality, he was buried in honorable fashion in a tomb in Memphis, Egypt. At a later time Alexander's body was transferred from Memphis to Alexandria and laid to rest there.[124] Third, rather than being despised by posterity, his subjects wept at the news of his death and some shaved their heads as a sign of mourning.[125]

119. Torrey, "Operations," 109–39.
120. Ibid., 110.
121. Ibid., 117.
122. Ibid.
123. For a succinct and engaging discussion of the possible causes of Alexander's death see Phillips, *Alexander the Great*.
124. Bunson, *Encyclopedia of Ancient Egypt*, 21.
125. Freeman, *Alexander the Great*, 320–21.

The Fruitfulness of the Search for a Historical Referent of the King of Babylon

How does one properly assess this dizzying variety of options for the historical individual that stands behind this text? As we have seen above, none of the possible referents fit the details of the Isaiah 14 description of the tyrant exactly in the light of our limited knowledge. Commenting on this reality, Kaiser made a passing comment that could prove to be very significant for our evaluation, "A detail which contradicts our historical knowledge might present no objection to the identification of the ruler, because we cannot necessarily assume that the poet possessed the knowledge which we have from our study of sources."[126] In other words, the search for a historical correspondence should not inadvertently presuppose some kind of omniscience on the part of the poet. One must in principle allow for the poet's limited or even erroneous grasp on the details of this tyrant's life. If that is the case, then the whole enterprise of constructing the identity of the tyrant is analogous to building a jigsaw puzzle with a possibility that the box contains pieces from different sets—a task of insurmountable complexity, a source of continual frustration, and a goal most likely out of reach.[127]

Early on Kissane anticipated the modern debate about the identity of the king of Babylon. He argues that the vagueness of the description of the king of Babylon is due to the fact that the historical realities fade into the background as the author "merely applies the current teaching on the justice of God to the case of the empire which is oppressing Israel."[128] According to Kissane, the poem's description of the downfall of the tyrant as a past event could be explained by the use of the prophetic perfect which he finds to be analogous to Isaiah 9:1–6. He writes, "It is a past event only in the mind of the prophet."[129] Kissane argues that when compared with texts like Job 15:20–35, 18:5–21, 20:6–29, as well as Psalm 27, it is evident that the poem represents the conventional description of the fate of the wicked rather than a reporting of the downfall of a specific tyrant. Among the typical stock-pictures of the sacking of the wicked Kissane points to abrupt turn of fortunes, wiping out of their wealth and power, depriving of proper burial, and lack of posterity.

---

126. Kaiser, *Isaiah*, 31.

127. Vermeylen's survey of viable options ends in memorable conclusion that we are faced with "autant d'hypothèses invérifiables." (Vermeylen, *Du Prophète Isaïe à l'Apocalyptique*, 1:293–94).

128. Kissane, *Isaiah*, 167.

129. Ibid.

Wildberger has been the most formidable modern voice of dissatisfaction with the attempts to pinpoint the historical context for identify of the king,

> In the final analysis, the wide variety of suggestions simply points out that a question has been confronted that can produce little more than idle speculations. The anonymity of the evildoer and the absence of tangible historical links must be respected; these realities have made it easier to reactualize the details of this song, over and over again, within the context of new historical circumstances.[130]

Several things must be mentioned about Wildberger's position. First, Wildberger's position is not driven by concerns about a single eighth-century authorship. He is convinced that Isaiah 14:3–23 could not have been authored by Isaiah.[131] During Isaiah's time, Babylonian kings did not wield the sort of power that Isaiah 14 ascribes to this Babylonian ruler. So it would have seemed grotesque to picture the sort of world-wide jubilation over his downfall. Also, the fall of a Babylonian king would imply further consolidation of the Assyrian grip, which anyone in Israel would be hard pressed to consider salutary.

Furthermore, Wildberger thinks that it is reasonable to suggest that this text was originally addressed to a non-Babylonian ruler but was later redacted to fit a different context. If pressed hard, he would admit that Nebuchadnezzar most accurately fits the bill, but he is careful to point out other historical figures that have been considered by various scholars—Sargon, Sennacherib, Ashur-uballit, Nabonidus, and Alexander the Great.[132]

Finally, while making room for extended and extensive history of editing and reapplication of this text, Wildberger's ultimate aim is to understand the actual text at hand. His commitment to respect the text's anonymity about the identity of this king leads Wildberger to suggest that the final editor uses "Babylon" as a code word for any world authority. In the end, the original person to whom this text was addressed fades away. In Wildberger's mind, what bears weight is the type of person, not the actual historical individual.[133] His summary is worth quoting here,

> The name "Babylon" must function as a symbolic name used to identify the "world power" for this redactor, who initially had

---

130. Wildberger, *Isaiah*, 55.
131. Ibid., 53–54.
132. Ibid., *Isaiah*, 54–55.
133. Ibid., 54.

the Persian Empire in mind. There is apparently not a single threat against this empire in the entire OT. . . . This cannot be explained simply by presuming that Israel had accepted the Persian rule, at least after the time of Haggai/Zechariah. This odd state of affairs can be explained by the fact that pseudonyms are used when referring to this kingdom. This technique might have come into vogue after human beings who spent time studying the rise and fall of a number of world powers learned that, in addition to whatever was unique about a particular world empire that happened to be in control at the moment, with its own plans and important figures, in the final analysis one could also identify general characteristics that would apply to each and every "world power."[134]

Wildberger's dissatisfaction with various historicizing moves has found increasing resonance. One of the most recent is Vanderhooft's analysis of Babylon in the latter prophets. He finds a significant distinction in the way Babylon is treated in the First Isaiah and Second Isaiah material. Vanderhooft argues that in Second Isaiah, written he assumes by a prophet who spent part of his career in Babylon, there is ample reference to the Mesopotamian milieu. He highlights the satirical descriptions of the Babylonian construction and worship of divine images as found in Isaiah 40:18-20, 46:1-2, 42:8, 47 and many other texts. These are suggestive of an eyewitness who is keenly aware of their details and effects on the Judean community in exile. Vanderhooft writes, "The prophet's diatribes against the idols of the Babylonians and the vaunted expertise of Babylonian religious experts provide the most sustained effort to challenge the imperial worldview."[135] Vanderhooft argues that references to Babylon in the First Isaiah material lack this kind of specificity as they do not refer either to Babylonian imperial ideas nor to its practices. Instead, Babylon is cast in the mold of an archetypical wicked city akin to Sodom and Gomorrah. This leads him to tentatively propose that when it comes to the First Isaiah material, "perhaps this shows that the responsible writers viewed Babylon in strict typological terms."[136]

If Wildberger's notion of symbolic use "Babylon" for "world power" is on target then the search of the historical setting that gave rise to Isaiah 14:3-23 would miss the point of its canonical setting in the midst of an archetypal oracle. What are the options for paradigmatic readings that have been suggested by a few scholars?

134. Ibid., 49.
135. Vanderhooft, *Empire*, 208.
136. Ibid., 134.

In addition to Wildberger's reading, Oswalt comments, "The attempt to identify a precise historical figure is probably futile. Isaiah is using a concrete representation to discuss the nature and end of human pride."[137] He argues that the king of Babylon represents Babylon as a whole standing in opposition to God and thus displaying the essence of human pride.[138]

Kaiser argues that in the figure of the king of Babylon we meet a typical or idealized figure which symbolizes the power hostile to God. He writes,

> The possibility always remains that the first news, or some unknown occasion, of the death of an emperor stimulated the imagination of the poet. But this interpretation borders on another, which has largely been preferred to it, that in his song the poet is expressing the certain hope of the end of a hated ruler. In this case it is impossible to decide whether the emperor intended is an Assyrian, Babylonian or Persian king, or even Alexander the Great, since there are no criteria to be found within the poem for its dating. For basically there are no limits to the poetic imagination. And a detail which contradicts our historical knowledge might present no objection to the identification of the ruler, because we cannot necessarily assume that the poet possessed the knowledge which we have from our study of the sources.[139]

According to Kaiser, brilliant poetic imagination invites the people of God to reflect on the downfalls of Assyrian and Babylonian kings as a means of realizing "the transitoriness of every world power and every tyrant, to the last of whom the true Lord of the world would deliver the final blow."[140]

---

137. Oswalt, *Isaiah*, 314.
138. Ibid., 325.
139. Kaiser, *Isaiah*, 30–31.
140. Ibid., 31.

Oracles Against the Nations in Isaiah 13–23[141]

Historical-critical approaches to the study of the Oracles Against the Nations go back to the eighteenth century.[142] For the last two hundred years the issues of authentic/inauthentic oracles, process of corpus formation, and dating of the oracles have dominated the field. Since Isaiah 14:3–23 is a part of this larger collection of oracles, this section will provide a broad overview of scholarly conversation. The aim is to ultimately ask whether the dominant emphases of that larger conversation have much bearing on helping one read the paradigmatic משל of Isaiah 14:3–23 with more precision.

Scholarship generally agrees that the מַשָּׂא superscriptions are crucial for this material.[143] This introductory formula is used in Isaiah 13–23 nine times (13:1; 15:1; 17:1; 19:1; 21:1; 21:11; 21:13; 22:1; 23:1) and only one other time (30:6) in the whole book of Isaiah. Wildberger writes, "This use of the same designation to introduce each of the individual sections in chaps. 13–23 binds them all together and shows that this was formed into a single, large unit, constructed intentionally by a redactor."[144] Williamson agrees with this assessment.[145] According to him, "The disagreements among scholars are . . . concerned not so much with general principle as with the detail of which passage or section is to be ascribed to which stage of composition or redaction."[146]

---

141. It is worth noting that recent scholarly trends argue that Isaiah 13–27 is a single literary unit. For example, Blenkinsopp argues that "the Isaian Apocalypse" of Isaiah 24–27 lacks any sort of introductory formula or structural markers that would demarcate it from what precedes it. Furthermore, Blenkinsopp goes on to argue that much of the material in these chapters containing the psalm (25:1–5), the prayer (26:7–19), and the song (27:2–5) could hardly classify as apocalyptic. He proposes that scholarship ought to explore the relation between Isaiah 13–23 and Isaiah 24–27 further (Blenkinsopp, *Isaiah*, 272). While the evaluation and detailed engagement with this proposal lies outside the scope of our discussion, it is worth noting that Isaiah 13–23 seems to retain a degree of intentionality forming a context for the material of Isaiah 24–27. Thus, even if one grants the validity of these recent observations, it seems that Isaiah 13–23 could still be taken as a subunit within the larger literary unit of Isaiah 13–27.

142. See Sweeney's survey of critical scholarship that anticipated the arrival of Duhm's monumental commentary on the book of Isaiah (Sweeney, "Duhm," 243–63). Sweeney's broad discussion helps map out the trajectory of the scholarly conversation surrounding the Oracles Against the Nations in Isaiah. Especially pertinent are his discussions of Eichorn, Gesenius and Ewald.

143. Liebreich, "The Compilation of the Book of Isaiah," 46:259–77; 47:114–38; Sweeney, *Isaiah 1–39*, 212–17 and Weis, "Maśśa."

144. Wildberger, *Isaiah*, 1.

145. Williamson, *Book Called Isaiah*, 156–83.

146. Ibid., 156.

The editorial activity involving the מַשָּׂא superscriptions has sparked one of the significant but inconclusive debates regarding Isaiah 13–23. This debate dealing with the process of formation of the corpus of Isaiah 13–23 has been summed up well by Cook.[147] On the one hand, some scholars have argued that the collection of מַשָּׂא oracles was added to preexisting material. Marti was a significant voice representing the scholarly tendency early on to focus on the distinction between מַשָּׂא and non-מַשָּׂא texts in the process of the corpus formation.[148] Cook writes, "According to Marti, the earliest group of oracles consisted of a small amount of Isaianic material, primarily within what is now Isa 17; 18; 20; 22. Perhaps during the third or second century B.C.E. a complete collection of מַשָּׂא oracles was broken up and distributed among these early texts, along with the addition of Isa 24–27."[149] Cook raised three substantial questions regarding the view that perceives the מַשָּׂא oracles were added to earlier texts.[150] First, the underlying assumption that there was such a collection of oracles lacks any empirical support and needs further evidence. Second, the dating of such a collection is very challenging and is often done on the basis of only some of the oracles, thus overlooking the fact that there are מַשָּׂא oracles (14:28–32) in Isaiah 13–23 that could be easily dated back to the eighth century BC. Third, this approach assumes the existence of a coherent non-מַשָּׂא collection—the assumption that Cook challenges by pointing out the non-uniformity of these texts.

On the other hand, a few scholars have insisted on the primacy of the מַשָּׂא oracles. The early proponent of this view was Cheyne, who claimed that the initial מַשָּׂא collections were supplemented with non-מַשָּׂא material original to Isaiah (14:24–27; 17:12–14; 18:1–7; 20:1–6) for the purposes of giving the sense of authenticity to the entire collection.[151] A similar view could be more recently attributed to Kaiser.[152] He argues for the late dating of the whole corpus. Since the oracles regarding Babylon could not have been earlier than the exilic period he claims that the מַשָּׂא oracles as a collection came into existence at that time. At an even later period the non-מַשָּׂא material was added. These proponents of the primacy of the מַשָּׂא collection of oracles receive an equally perceptive set of probing questions from Cook. Contra Cheyne, Cook points out that the argument that the later non-מַשָּׂא

---

147. Cook, *Redactional Formation of Isaiah 18–20*, 1–25. The evaluation of Cook's own proposal that seeks to move beyond the time honored ways of understanding the process of formation of Isaiah 13–23 is beyond the scope of this discussion.

148. Marti, *Jesaja*, xvi–xix.

149. Cook, *Sign*, 3.

150. Ibid., 8–9.

151. Cheyne, *Introduction to the Book of Isaiah*, xxiv–xxv.

152. Kaiser, *Isaiah*, 1–5.

material was added to bring authenticity to the entire corpus does not stand. While Cheyne claims that the non-מַשָּׂא material that was added comprises of 14:24–27, 17:12–14, 18:1–7, and 20:1–6, only Isaiah 20:1–6 explicitly refers to Isaiah, so it is not clear how this added material could bring the weight of authenticity to the whole collection.[153] Kaiser's suggestion evokes the same set of questions that Cook has raised regarding those who claimed the primacy of the non-מַשָּׂא oracles—namely that the underlying assumption of existence of a block of מַשָּׂא oracles has yet to be proven.

Though inconclusive, the debate about the process of formation of the collection of the Oracles Against the Nations has highlighted several aspects of scholarly agreement. First, this collection brings together very diverse material. Some of it dates back to the eighth-century prophet Isaiah and some of it arguably belongs to the exilic period or later. Furthermore, while not all of the material is marked with it, the presence of the מַשָּׂא superscriptions reflects what Williamson calls a "degree of conscious compilation at some stage in the formation of these chapters."[154] Finally, there is a substantial agreement that this corpus reaches its final form in the late exilic or post-exilic period.

One crucial factor in determining the date of the final editing of the collection of the Oracles Against the Nations has been the way scholarship has understood the oracle against Babylon found in Isaiah 13:1—14:23. Several things are peculiar about this oracle. First, though not chronologically prior, this oracle opens the collection of Oracles Against the Nations. Furthermore, while the superscription of Isaiah 13:1 introduces it as מַשָּׂא בָּבֶל, there is another oracle against Babylon in this collection (Isaiah 21). Finally, it is much lengthier that any other oracle in this corpus.

For the solution to these puzzling aspects of the oracle against Babylon in Isaiah 13:1—14:23 we turn to Williamson, who has argued that the author of Deutero-Isaiah was responsible for bringing this oracle together during the time of the Babylonian exile.[155] According to Williamson, this

---

153. Cook, *Sign*, 10.

154. Williamson, *Book Called Isaiah*, 156.

155. While the majority of critical scholarship has accepted an exilic dating of this oracle, Gosse has argued on linguistic as well as historical grounds for the post-exilic date of Isaiah 13–14. (Gosse, *Isaïe 13,1—14,23*). Williamson's superb analysis of Gosse's work concludes with a fair evaluative summary, "Gosse's work has succeeded in showing that, taken in isolation, many elements in Isaiah 13–14 could as well have been penned in the post-exilic as in the exilic period, but not that they must have been" (Williamson, *Book Called Isaiah*, 175). Also worth noting is Begg's observation that all of the references to Babylon in Isaiah occur between chapters 13 and 48 (Begg, "Babylon," 121–25). This would presumably limit the scope of dating to the exilic period. Finally, particularly challenging for Gosse's position is the reference to the Medes in

unknown exilic redactor combines together two lengthy poems, 13:2–22 and 14:4b–21, via the editorial material of 14:1–4a and 14:22–23.[156]

Isaiah 14:1–4a accomplishes two things. First, it links the downfall of Babylon with the reversal of fortunes for Israel. In other words it contextualizes the news of the demolishing of the Babylonian empire as YHWH's good news for his people. Furthermore, it sets up a context for the משל of Isaiah 14:4b–21. Williamson claims that the style of this editorial comment "differs sharply from the surrounding material."[157] This difference, according to Williamson, is due to the fact that the vocabulary in Isaiah 14:1–4a is distinctively Deutero-Isaianic.[158]

The other editorial material, Isaiah 14:22–23, serves the purpose of linking the משל of Isaiah 14:4b–21 with Babylon. The goal according to Williamson is to "move beyond the death of a single king to the fall of the city as a whole."[159] In so doing, the material regarding the fate of the king of Babylon in chapter 14 is linked with the material regarding the fate of Babylon as a nation in chapter 13, thus providing a fitting finale to the whole of מַשָּׂא בָּבֶל in Isaiah 13:1—14:23.

The oracle against Babylon in Isaiah 13:1—14:23, specially edited and prominently placed at the beginning of the collection of the Oracles Against the Nations, is designed to function paradigmatically portraying the fate of any human superpower that arises against YHWH and oppresses his people. Even if one is successful at determining whether Isaiah 13 was penned with Assyria or Babylon in mind, the thrust of the oracle against Babylon takes up its historical referent and utilizes it for its own purpose. Childs is surely correct when he argues that here we find an announcement of a sweeping apocalyptic consummation of human history. The focus, Childs argues, is on the capacity of YHWH to bring the old age to an end. According to him, this text

> envisions the eschatological end of world history coinciding with the fall of Babylon, the archenemy. The "day of the LORD," in which finally the wrath of God is unleashed against all human arrogance, is identified with God's historical intervention

---

13:17, which indicates a date prior to Cyrus takeover of Media around 550 BC. In the end, Sweeney's conclusion represents the current scholarly grasp on the Oracle against Babylon. Sweeney argues that Isaiah 13:1—14:23 was "edited into their present form in the mid- to late-6th century, in that they anticipate the fall of Babylon to the Medes and the end of the Babylonian ruling house" (Sweeney, *Isaiah 1–39*, 234).

156. Williamson, *Book Called Isaiah*, 158.
157. Ibid.
158. Ibid., 165–67.
159. Ibid., 158.

against Babylon. It is a final consummation of a quality of judgment only foreshadowed in the overthrow of Sodom and Gomorrah (13:9).[160]

The editorial decision to place the Oracle Against Babylon at the head of the collection signaled its paradigmatic function, shaping how this entire corpus is to be read. Our interaction with issues about the Oracles Against the Nations in Isaiah 13–23 can sharpen our appreciation of the rhetoric of the paradigmatic משל of Isaiah 14:3–23.

---

160. Childs, *Isaiah*, 179.

6

Isaiah 14:12–15 in Reception History

> At Lucifer, though he an angel were
> And nat a man, at hym wol I bigynne.
> For though Fortune may noon angel dere,
> From heigh degree yet del he for his synne
> Doun into helle wheren he yet is inne.
> O Lucifer, brightest of angels alle,
> Now artow Sathanas, that mayst nat twynne
> Out of miserie, in which that thou art falle.[1]

THESE WORDS DRAWN FROM the "Monk's Tale" by Chaucer highlight two aspects of the fascinating history of reception of the משל of Isaiah 14:3–23. First, in the history of reception the focus narrows, as four verses, namely Isaiah 14:12–15, rather than the poem as a whole have a lasting impact. Second, the reason for the interest in these four verses is that early on in Christian interpretation they came to be seen as describing the downfall of Satan.

In this chapter we will provide a close reading of two biblical interpreters who have played a significant role in how Isaiah 14:12–15 has been read throughout the ages. Origen (182–254 AD) appears to have been one of the first to apply these verses to Satan's downfall in the third century AD. Over the course of the centuries his reading became dominant in the church as the likes of Jerome (347–420 AD),[2] Augustine (354–430 AD),[3] and Gregory

---

1. Allen and Fisher, *Poetry and Prose of Geoffrey Chaucer*, 286.

2. Jerome, "Against Jovinianus," 2.4 in *NPNF2* 6:391; "Dialogue against Pelagians," 3.14 in *NPNF2* 6:480; *Commentariorum in Isaiam Prophetam* 5.14:12–14 and 6.14:12 in *CCSL* 73:168–169; "Letter XXII:To Eustochium" XXII.4 in *NPNF2* 6:23; Letter CXXXIII:To Ctesiphon" CXXXIII.1, in *NPNF2* 6:272.

3. Augustine, *City*, 11:15, p. 469; *The Confessions of Saint Augustine*, 10.36.58, p. 267; "Exposition on the Psalms" 36.15; 48.3; 89.12 in *NPNF1* 8:90, 165, 433; "Homilies on the Gospel of St. John: Tractate III on Chapter 1:15–18" III.17 and "Homilies on the Gospel of St. John: Tractate XVII on Chapter 5.1–18" XVII.16 in *NPNF1* 7:21, p. 116.

the Great (540–604 AD)[4] embraced it. This long-standing interpretation was dismissed by the Reformers in the sixteenth century AD, most notably by Calvin (1509–64 AD). This was indeed a tectonic shift, as by the twentieth century AD most major commentaries do not even mention Origen's interpretation, while at least one premier evangelical interpreter argues strongly against it.[5] Yet matters are not as simple as they might seem. While biblical scholarship has long been suspicious of Origen's reading of Isaiah 14:12–15, traces of it are still found in the writings of contemporary systematic theologians as well as in wider Western culture. Hence, we will attempt to trace this reception history in more detail and reflect on possible ways of fruitful engagement with contemporary theology.

Origen's Reading of Isaiah 14:12–15

Origen has long been considered as one of the most notable representatives of the so-called Alexandrian school. While posthumously denounced by the church for some of his more daring theological speculations, Origen has recently received fresh academic interest.[6] The earlier theories of gnostic influences on his interpretive approach have been questioned as evidence has emerged that points to the impact of Jewish exegesis on the Alexandrian tradition.[7] It is fair to say that not everyone has been notably sympathetic,

---

4. Gregory the Great, "The Book of Pastoral Rule and Selected Epistles," II.6 in *NPNF2* 12:14; "Epistle XVIII: To John, Bishop" in *NPNF2* 12:166; "Epistle XXI: To Constantina Augusta" in *NPNF2* 12:172 and *Homiliae in Hiezechihelem*, in *CCSL* 142:326–27.

5. Oswalt, *Isaiah*, 320.

6. Among many see Daniélou, *Origen*; Hanson, *Allegory*; Heine, *Origen*; Louth, *Discerning the Mystery*; De Lubac, *History*; Martens, *Origen and Scripture*; Torjesen, *Procedure*; Trigg, *Origen*.

7. Childs, *The Struggle to Read Isaiah as Christian Scripture*, 63. Greer early on suggested that the source of Christian allegory found in the Alexandrian school lies with Jewish Alexandrian allegorical method most notably represented by Philo (Greer, *Theodore of Mopsuestia*.). Greer writes, "In Alexandria a quite different method of exegesis had grown up, a method undoubtedly influenced by Hellenistic allegory. Philo is the best representative of this allegorical school. He attempted to see in the Hebrew scriptures the Platonic philosophy he held on other grounds" (89). See also Niehoff, *Jewish Exegesis*. Niehoff argues for a close connection between Jewish biblical exegesis and Homeric scholarship in Alexandria thus demonstrating a complex relationship between Judaism, Hellenism, and Rome. Niehoff acknowledges the recent emphasis on Philo as the representative of the Hellenistic Judaism who paved the way for Clement and Origen, but seeks to broaden the question of influence beyond allegory. Niehoff writes, "Thus far, the connections between Christian and Jewish exegesis have been investigated with a view to allegory, remaining regrettably isolated from studies of the relationship between Christian exegesis and Greek scholarship. It is now time to

as is evident in Hanson's consistently scathing comments such as his reference to Origen's use of allegory as "largely a façade or a rationalization whereby he was able to read into the Bible what he wanted to find there."[8] Yet one bears in mind the words of Didymus the Blind, the head of the Catechetical School of Alexandria in the fourth century AD, who described Origen as "the greatest teacher in the Church after the Apostles."[9] Daniélou is surely correct in asserting that alongside of Augustine, Origen is indeed one of the "greatest geniuses of the Early Church."[10] It is no wonder that von Balthasar pays high complement to Origen, "His work is aglow with the fire of a Christian creativity that in the greatest of his successors burned merely with a borrowed flame."[11]

Context of Origen's Reading of Isaiah 14:12–15

Origen encounters Isaiah 14 in the midst of his battle with gnostic views of creation with their parallel thoughts of original darkness and matter as evil.[12] According to Martens, "the triumvirate of Valentinus, Basilides, and Marcion proved to be one of the decisive forces that shaped Origen's ecclesiastical career."[13] Engaging in disputes with these gnostic figures, Origen saw himself as the church's ambassador—the one who carried out these debates in the arena of biblical scholarship.[14] In *Contra Celsum* (IV.65) we can see what interests Origen when he comes to read Isaiah 14,

> No one will be able to know the origin of evils who has not grasped the truth about the so-called devil and his angels, and who he was before he became a devil, and how he became a devil, and what caused his so-called angels to rebel with him. Anyone who intends to know this must possess an accurate understanding of daemons, and be aware that they are not God's creation in so far as they are daemons, but only in so far as they are rational beings of some sort. And he must understand how

---

integrate these different elements and examine scholarly as well as allegorical aspects of Christian exegesis in light of Greek and Jewish hermeneutics" (15–16).

8. Hanson, *Allegory*, 258.
9. Quoted in Prestige, *Fathers and Heretics*, 52.
10. Daniélou, *Origen*, vii.
11. Balthasar, "Preface," xi.
12. Although the term "Gnostisim" has been challenged is some recent scholarship, I retain it here for convenience, as nothing of significance hinges on the term.
13. Martens, *Scripture*, 111.
14. Ibid., 112.

they came to be such that their mind put them in the position of daemon. Accordingly if there is any subject among those that need study among men which is baffling to our comprehension, the origin of evil may be reckoned as such.[15]

Origen's agenda is to repaint the picture of existential reality as created good but fallen as a result of the free will. In his monumental work on the origins and development of the Satan figure in antiquity, Forsyth writes,

> For Origen, all rational creatures, heavenly powers and men alike, fall not by their nature but by their will. The cause of this prehistoric disturbance is thus, by implication, a rebel; he is not created such. He is evil not in essence but by accident, so to speak.[16]

An important view in the early church, based on the Ethiopic Book of Enoch, was that evil was caused by the Watchers, the lustful angels assigned to guard the earth. While the Enoch material lacks coherence and reflects several stages of editing, Forsyth is able to give the general contours of the story which represented a commonly held view of the origin of evil,

> A group of angels join their leader in a plot to violate their assigned role; they descend to the earth and have sexual intercourse with the daughters of men; as a result, the earth is corrupted and eventually cries out in its agony to heaven; God intervenes and sends down good angels, among them Michael, to put a stop to the goings-on and imprison the rebels; at the same time, God foretells the ultimate end of all this—after seventy generations in prison, the rebels will be permanently locked away in torment, while all wrong is destroyed from the earth and a new world is born in righteousness and peace.[17]

By the dawn of the third century AD, the lustful Watchers theory was losing its original appeal as it became clear it was based on the obscure passages from the book of Enoch that was not widely accepted as scripture among the churches. If the lustful Watchers theory is deemed suspect, what might be an alternative explanation for the origin of evil? Writing roughly during the same time as Origen, Tertullian in *Against Marcion* (II.10) turned to Ezekiel 28 which portrays a downfall of the king of Tyre as describing the downfall of Satan. Tertullian considers that evil was present in the world prior to the sin of Adam and Eve. If the devil is the instigator of human sin,

15. Origen, *Contra Celsum*, 236–37.
16. Forsyth, *Enemy*, 370.
17. Ibid., 163.

then he wonders where devil's wickedness came from. It is that question that sets up Tertullian's reflection on Ezekiel 28,

> Now, whence originated this malice of lying and deceit towards man, and slandering of God? Most certainly not from God, who made the angel good after the fashion of His good works. Indeed, before he became the devil, he stands forth the wisest of creatures; and wisdom is no evil. If you turn to the prophecy of Ezekiel, you will at once perceive that this angel was both by creation good and by choice corrupt. For in the person of the prince of Tyre it is said in reference to the devil: "Moreover, the word of the Lord came unto me, saying, Son of man, take up a lamentation upon the king of Tyrus, and say unto him, Thus saith the Lord God; Thou sealest up the sum, full of wisdom, perfect in beauty" (this belongs to him as the highest of the angels, the archangel, the wisest of all); "amidst the delights of the paradise of thy God wast thou born" (for it was there, where God had made the angels in a shape which resembled the figure of animals). "Every precious stone was your covering, the sardius, the topaz, and the diamond, the beryl, the onyx, and the jasper, the sapphire, the emerald, and the carbuncle; and with gold have thou filled thy barns and thy treasuries. From the day when though were created, when I set thee, a cherub, upon the holy mountain of God, thou wast in the midst of stones of fire, thou wast irreproachable in thy days, from the day of thy creation, until thine iniquities were discovered. By the abundance of thy merchandise thou hast filled thy storehouses, and thou hast sinned," etc.[18]

It is interesting to note how Tertullian links the king of Tyre with Satan. While a modern reader, shaped by contemporary literary conventions would tend to read the Ezekiel 28 passage as a metaphorical depiction of the opulent reign of the king of Tyre, Tertullian makes a radically different interpretive move. He considers the king of Tyre himself as a metaphor for Satan,

> This description, it is manifest, properly belongs to the transgression of the angel, and not to the prince's: for none among human beings was either born in the paradise of God, not even Adam himself, who was rather translated there; nor placed with a cherub upon God's holy mountain, that is to say, in the heights of heaven, from which the Lord testifies that Satan fell; nor

---

18. *ANF*, 3:305–6.

detained among the stones of fire, and the flashing rays of burning constellations, whence Satan was cast down like lightning.[19]

Hence, in the imagery of the king of Tyre Tertullian finds an alternative explanation for the origin of evil,

> It is none else than the very author of sin who was denoted in the person of a sinful man: he was once irreproachable, at the time of his creation, formed for good by God, as by the good Creator of irreproachable creatures, and adorned with every angelic glory, and associated with God, good with the Good; but afterwards of his own accord removed to evil.[20]

Tertullian's move is analogous to the way Origen will read the reference to the king of Babylon in Isaiah 14. Origen rejects interpretations that read the king of Babylon as referring to Nebuchadnezzar. He does so by questioning whether any human being has "fallen from heaven" or has been known as "Lucifer," the bearer of light (IV.3.9),

> And as for the numerous statements made about Nebuchadnezzar, especially in Isaiah, how it is possible to interpret them of that particular man? For the man Nebuchadnezzar neither "fell from heaven," nor was he the "morning star," nor did he "rise in the morning" over the earth.[21]

In a move akin to Tertullian, Origen's argument comes to the issue from the opposite end of what might be expected by the modern reader. Rather than seeing the reference to "falling from heaven" or bearing light as an metaphorical way of describing the earthly reality, he sees it as a very concrete reality—as concrete and historically grounded as any Babylonian king.

Both Tertullian and Origen come to their reading of Ezekiel 28 and Isaiah 14 respectively looking for trans-human origins of evil. The hermeneutical moves they make are influenced by their search. Thus, in their readings, the appeal to allegory allows for the figures of kings of Tyre and Babylon to function metaphorically describing much larger existential realities of evil and its genesis.

It is interesting to note that in his discussion of the origin of evil in *Against Marcion* (II. 10), Tertullian does not turn to Isaiah 14. This is peculiar, as in two other places in this volume he does refer to it as describing Satan. First, contra Marcion, Tertullian claims that the reference to the "god

---

19. *ANF*, 3:306.
20. Ibid.
21. Origen, *On First Principles*, 302.

of this world" in 2 Corinthians 4:4 is not a reference to a different God, but rather to Satan (V.11). Tertullian claims that while Marcion's arguments could be easily dismissed on grammatical grounds, he is able to offer a much simple explanation,

> A simpler answer I shall find ready to hand in interpreting "the god of this world" of the devil, who once said, as the prophet describes him: "I will be like the Most High; I will exalt my throne in the clouds." The whole superstition, indeed, of this world has got into his hands, so that he blinds effectually the hearts of unbelievers, and of none more than the apostate Marcion's.[22]

Furthermore, Tertullian turns to Isaiah 14 when refuting Marcion's interpretation of Ephesians 2:1–2. Marcion seems to read the phrase "they had walked according to the course of this world, according to the prince of the power of the air, who worketh in the children of disobedience" in reference to God. Yet Tertullian claims that Marcion has no grounds for interpreting the "world" as "the God of the world." Also, he argues that the descriptions of the prince of the power of the air or the instigator of unbelief do not suit God. Rather than a reference to God, this is a description of Satan,

> There is another being to whom they are more applicable—and the apostle knew very well who that was. Who then is he? Undoubtedly he who has raised up "children of disobedience" against the Creator Himself ever since he took possession of that "*air*" of His; even as the prophet makes him say:"I will set my throne *above the stars*; . . . *I will go up* above the clouds; I will be like Most High." This must mean the devil, whom in another passage (since such will they have apostle's meaning to be) we shall recognize in the appellation *the god of this world*. For he has filled the whole world with the lying pretense of his own divinity. To be sure, if *he* had not existed, we might then possibly have applied these descriptions to the Creator.[23]

It is obvious from these references that Tertullian is clearly aware of Isaiah 14 as a suitable candidate for an extended discussion on the origin of evil, yet to the best of our knowledge he never links it with Ezekiel 28, an impulse apparent already in Hippolytus (170–236 AD) who appeals to these two texts as predicting the downfall of the Antichrist.[24] Nevertheless, in Tertullian's reading the interpretive ground was readied for Origen's

---

22. *ANF*, 3:454.
23. *ANF*, 3:466. Italics are original to the translated text used.
24. Hippolytus, "Treatise on Christ and Antichrist," in *ANF* 5:215.

sustained argument that introduced Isaiah 14 text as an explanation for the origin of evil.

Origen first turns to Isaiah 14 in his *Contra Celsum* as he is rethinking the lustful Watchers theory of the origin of evil, precipitated by Celsus' attack on Christianity. Celsus raises questions regarding the basis of Christian faith and its supposed angelic origin. He appears to be making a reference to the theory of Lustful Watchers in his appeal. Origen quotes him at length to provide a context for his own response (V.52),

> We leave on one side the many arguments which refute what they say about their teacher; and let us assume that he really was some angel. Was he the first and only one to have come? Or were there also others before him? If they were to say that he is the only one, they would be convicted of telling lies and contradicting themselves. For they say that others also have often come, and, in fact, sixty or seventy at once, who became evil and were punished by being cast under the earth in chains. And they say that their tears are the cause of hot springs.[25]

Furthermore, Celsus is dismissive of the Christian notion of Satan (VI. 42),

> That they make some quite blasphemous errors is also shown by this example of their utter ignorance, which has similarly led them to depart from the true meaning of the divine enigmas, when they make a being opposed to God; devil, and in the Hebrew tongue, Satanas are the names which they give to this same being.[26]

Celsus considers it ridiculous that there would be such a being, created by God, who would have power to oppose God, especially when he wants to confer some benefit on mankind. Celsus appeals to ancient Greek myths in the writings of Heraclitus, Pherecydes and Homer that hint at a sort of divine war. He concludes that the most scandalizing aspect of the Christian portrayal of the devil is his relationship with Jesus (VI.42),

> The punishment of the Son of God by the devil is to teach us that when we are punished by the same being we should endure it patiently. All this also is ludicrous. In my opinion he ought to have punished the devil; certainly not to have pronounced threats against the men who had been attacked by him.[27]

---

25. Origen, *Contra*, 305.
26. Ibid., 357.
27. Ibid., 359.

Origen's reply is to go back to the Old Testament and show that texts, which are older than these Greek authors Celsus mentions, teach the existence of the wicked power that fell from heaven. Origen first turns to references to the devil he finds in the passages that he attributes to Moses, such as the serpent of Genesis 3, the destroyer of Exodus 12:3 and Azazel of Leviticus 16:8, 10. The clearest support for his argument is found in Job's portrayal of the devil as standing in the presence of God and asking for his permission afflict Job. This text (Job 1), according to Origen was even older than Moses. Having considered these scriptural passages for the existence of the wicked power that fell from heaven which predate the Greek texts referred to by Celsus, Origen bolsters his argument with an appeal to Ezekiel 28 and Isaiah 14 (IV. 43),

> I have not yet mentioned also the examples from Ezekiel where he speaks, as it were, of Pharaoh, or of Nebuchadnezzar, or of the prince of Tyre, or the passage from Isaiah where the dirge is sung for the king of Babylon. From these scriptures one would learn not a little about evil, of the character of its origin and beginning, and how that evil came to exist because of some who lost their wings and followed the example of the first being who lost his wings.[28]

This reference to Isaiah 14 is not long, but none-the-less we can see here the germinating of the thought that will come to fruition in his book *On First Principles* and will be discussed at length below. Here it is worth stating that Forsyth is surely correct in crediting Origen's use of Isaiah 14 with the ultimate displacement of the Watchers myth with a "rebel angel myth" as the cause of evil.[29] Origen's reading would dominate the church's reading of Isaiah 14 till the time of Reformation.

Origen's Hermeneutical Approach

Origen is arguably one of the intellectual giants of his time, writing in a frame of reference that is far removed and at times very foreign for contemporary readers. Furthermore, as Heine has argued persuasively, there is decisive shift in the middle of Origen's life.[30] The move from Alexandria to Caesarea forces Origen to revise his earlier formulations and at times reformulate his positions, which makes it difficult to present a simplified

---

28. Ibid., 360.
29. Forsyth, *Enemy*, 372.
30. Heine, *Origen*, vii–viii.

summary of Origen and his theological stance. Hence ours will only be a selective introduction that will not touch on many of the topics in Origen's writings, but rather will note aspects of his approach to reading scripture.

Torjesen's recent work has provided a succinct summary of Origen's interpretive presuppositions,

> Origen's doctrine of Scripture would read as follows: Scripture is nothing other than the teachings of Christ; the divinity of Scripture is nothing other than the divine power and effectiveness of these teachings. The inspiration of Scripture is nothing other than the divine origin of these teachings.[31]

She goes on to argue, "The essential task of exegesis in Origen had been decisively organized around the figure of the hearer/reader."[32] In striking resemblance to Paul Ricoeur, Origen sees the transformation of a reader as the main purpose of reading.[33] Torjesen insists that for Origen the scriptures are the ground for twofold pedagogy of the Logos, "Origen's exegesis moves from the saving doctrines of Christ once taught to the saints (the historical pedagogy of the Logos) to the same saving doctrines which transform his hearers today (the contemporary pedagogy)."[34] The historical pedagogy deals with the literal, grammatical sense of the text. The contemporary pedagogy takes the spiritual sense of the text and applies to new audiences. While different in form, these two approaches refer to the same spiritual reality that undergirds them. As Childs points out, "the move from the literal to the spiritual is not an alien transference to bridge a double meaning, but rather a generalization to a universal scope of the historical particularity, because the literal sense has already opened up the spiritual reality."[35]

De Lubac has been a powerful recent voice in helping us understand ancient and medieval exegetical practices in general and Origen in particular. One cannot understand Origen apart from the inherent hermeneutical stance towards scripture that ancient and medieval exegetes assumed. De Lubac writes,

> Scripture is like the world: "undecipherable in its fullness and in the multiplicity of its meanings." A deep forest, with innumerable branches, "an infinite forest of meanings": the more one gets in it, the more one discovers that it is impossible to explore

31. Torjesen, "Origen's Theory of Exegesis," 288.
32. Torjesen, *Procedure*, 12.
33. Potworowski, "Hermeneutics," 161–66.
34. Torjesen, *Procedure*, 13.
35. Childs, *Struggle*, 69.

> it right to the end. It is a table arranged by Wisdom, laden with food, where the unfathomable divinity of the Savior is itself offered as nourishment to all. Treasure of the Holy Spirit, whose riches are as infinite as himself. True labyrinth. Deep heavens, unfathomable abyss. Vast sea, where there is endless voyaging, "with all sails set." Ocean of mystery.[36]

One could argue that this sense of scripture as the unfathomable abyss is precisely what accounts for Origen's overall hermeneutical approach and even his excesses. De Lubac is aware of typical reservations about Origen and is willing to admit, "A certain fervor of soul joined to an impetuous spirit launch him at times onto reckless paths."[37] Yet de Lubac's key point is that these excesses cannot dismiss Origen's overall reading of scripture. He argues that despite the caricatures, Origen's reading was not arbitrary or cavalier. De Lubac insists that Origen's allegorical reading is inseparable from Origen's understanding of the Bible as the church's book. He writes, "Concern for orthodoxy and attachment to the faith of the church, love for the 'dogmas of the truth', are one of the reasons of Origen's allegorism."[38]

According to Origen, "just as man . . . is said to consist of body, soul and spirit, so also does the holy scripture, which has been bestowed by the divine bounty for man's salvation" (IV.2.4).[39] The scripture is given by God to guide its hearers to spiritual perfection, preparing them for eternal union with God. The goal of all three senses of scripture, Origen argues, is the edification and nourishment of God's people. Thus, in *Genesis Homily XIII* he explains his own role as an exegete, "Each of us who serves the word of God digs wells and seeks 'living water', from which he may renew his hearers."[40] Hence, in Origen's mind, "the purpose of seeking the 'spiritual meaning' of Scripture is to nourish oneself from it, it is to treat it as Catholic, *verbum Dei catholice tractari* (to handle the Word of God in the Catholic way)."[41] De Lubac captures well what is at stake for Origen in his reading of scripture,

> It (the spiritual meaning) is to receive it (the Word of God) from the hands of Jesus and to have it read by him. It is to act as "a son of the Church." If there is a fundamental obligation for the Christian, it is that of being "attached to the rule of the heavenly Church of Jesus Christ, according to the succession of the

---

36. De Lubac, *Medieval Exegesis*, 75.
37. De Lubac, *History*, 380.
38. Ibid., 72.
39. Origen, *First*, 276.
40. Origen, *Homilies*, 189.
41. De Lubac, *History*, 73.

apostles"; now, concretely, what is this rule? Saint Irenaeus had already said it: it is the spiritual interpretation of Scripture.[42]

In the end, Torjesen is surely correct in insisting that it is the theological structure of Origen's exegesis which is crucial for understating Origen. She writes,

> Once we have understood the theological structure of Origen's exegesis and its roots in his doctrine of Scripture and theology of exegesis, we can see why Origen's exegesis is fundamentally oriented around the three-way relationship of text, interpretation, and hearer. Exegesis is the mediation of Christ's redemptive teaching activity to the hearer.[43]

Origen's Reading of Isaiah 14

Having outlined some basic issues surrounding Origen's exegetical practice we turn our attention to Origen's reading of Isaiah 14 in his *On First Principles*. According to Heine, "The *On First Principles* is Origen's effort to pull together his understanding of the major doctrines of the Christian faith."[44] As it would turn out, this was the last book he would write in Alexandria due to the controversy that it stirred. Heine reflects on the sad irony inherent in the mixed reception of this volume in Alexandria,

> If my suggestion above is correct, that the *On First Principles* was written out of Origen's desire to clarify and unify the Christian understanding of the teachings of the apostles and to defend these apostolic doctrines against those who were eroding their authority, it is ironic that the publication of this document was the final blow that broke his relationship with the hierarchy of the Alexandrian Church and made him a borderline heretic for centuries.[45]

One of the topics that Origen gives his sustained attention to in this book is what Heine calls the apostolic doctrine of creation.[46] It is under this rubric of the doctrine of creation that Origen discusses the creation and function of rational natures or minds.

42. Ibid.
43. Torjesen, *Procedure*, 13-4.
44. Heine, *Origen*, 130.
45. Ibid., 143-44.
46. Ibid., 142.

Heine argues that the fact that Origen addresses the doctrine of natures several times in this volume as well as in his commentary on the Gospel of John shows that at least some in the Christian circles in Alexandria still accepted it.[47] Most likely this was precipitated by an exposure to Valentinian determinism which, according to Heine, "claimed that humanity is made up of three predetermined natures: a material one that is doomed to perish, a spiritual one associated with spiritual powers, and animate or psychic one that is intermediate between the other two and with the help of the spiritual can be saved."[48] Another noteworthy influence would have been Heracleon, especially his view that the devil was wicked because God made him of that particular essence. Similarly Heracleon claimed that some people are unable to hear the gospel because they are of the essence of the devil.[49] It is against this backdrop of the battle against problematic teaching that Origen writes (I.5.2),

> Every being which is endowed with reason and yet fails to adhere to the ends and ordinances laid out by reason, is undoubtedly involved in sin by this departure from what is just and right. Every rational creature is therefore susceptible of praise and of blame; of praise, if in accordance with the reason which he has in him he advances to better things; of blame, if he departs from the rule and course of what is right, in which case he is also rightly subject to pains and penalties.[50]

For Origen, this rational capacity is an attribute of created beings, which includes the devil himself and his angelic cohort. Origen rejects the notion that either wickedness or goodness are a part of one's essence. Rather, he insists (II.9.2), "whatever may have been the goodness that existed in their being, it existed in them not by nature but as a result of their Creator's beneficence."[51] The decisive thing for Origen is his understanding that God endows his creatures with free will. By the exercise of this free will the creatures can make this gift of goodness their own or by rejecting it descend into wickedness (II.9.2),

> The Creator granted to the minds created by him the power of free will and voluntary movement, in order that the good that was in them might become their own, since it was preserved by

47. Ibid., 128.
48. Ibid., 127.
49. Ibid., 128.
50. Origen, *First*, 44.
51. Ibid., 130.

their own free will; but sloth and weariness of taking trouble to preserve the good, coupled disregard and neglect of better things, began the process of withdrawal from the good. Now to withdraw from the good is nothing else than to be immersed in evil; for it is certain that to be evil means to be lacking in good. Hence it is that in whatever degree one declines from the good, one descends into an equal degree of wickedness.[52]

Thus, regarding the devil and his angels, he concludes (I.5.4), "these opposing and wicked powers were not so formed and created by nature but came from better conditions and changed for the worse."[53] Isaiah 14 is the text that he turns to for the explanation of this process of going from better to worse.

To explain the downfall of the devil Origen quotes at length from Isaiah 14:12-22 (I.5.5),

> How has Lucifer, who arose in the morning, fallen from heaven. He who assailed all the nations is broken and dashed to the earth. Thou saidst indeed in thy heart, I will ascend into heaven; above the stars of heaven I will place my throne; I will sit upon a lofty mountain above the lofty mountains which are towards the north; I will as send above the clouds; I will be like the Most High. But now shalt thou be cast down to the lower world, and to the foundations of the earth. All who see thee shall be amazed over thee and say: This is the man that afflicted the whole earth, that moved kings, that made the whole round world a desert, that destroyed cities and did not loose those who were in chains. All the kings of the nations sleep in honor, each one in his own house; but thou shalt be cast forth upon the mountains, as an accursed dead man, with the many dead that have been pierced through with swords and have descended to the lower world. As a garment clotted and stained with blood will not be clean, so too shalt thou not be clean, because thou hast ruined my land and killed my people. Thou shalt not abide henceforth for ever, thou most wicked seed. Make ready thy sons for slaughter for the sins of their father, that they rise not up and possess the earth by inheritance and fill it with wars. And I will rise up against them, saith the Lord of Sabaoth, and I will cause their name to perish and their remnant and their seed.[54]

52. Ibid.
53. Ibid., 47.
54. Ibid., 49-50.

Origen utilizes the LXX text which is evident in the reference to the dead body of the Babylonian king being "cast forth upon the mountains" (14:19) and in the comparison "as a garment clotted and stained with blood will not be clean, so too shalt thou not be cleaned, because thou hast ruined my land and my people" (14:20), which are absent from the Hebrew text. He succinctly sums up the whole passage this way (I.5.5),

> It is most clearly proved by these words that he who formerly was Lucifer and who "arose in the morning" has fallen from heaven. For if, as some suppose, he was a being of darkness, why is he said to have formerly been Lucifer or light-bearer?[55]

Three things are worth highlighting in Origen's reading of Isaiah 14. First, he connects his reading of this text with the words of Jesus, "The Savior teaches us about the devil as follows: 'Lo, I see Satan fallen as lightning from heaven.' So he was light once."[56] Origen's move is not surprising when seen in the light of the use of the Old Testament in the early church. Childs' words are instructive here:

> Christians understood that the biblical text pointed beyond itself and was not to be a "dead letter" (*gramma*). The controversy which shortly arose between Christians and Jews turned on the different understandings of the reality to which scripture pointed. For Christians the Old Testament was not a flat, self-contained text which could be bent at will, but a witness to God's purpose revealed in the history of Israel, which Christians saw as continuing in the life, death, and resurrection of Christ.[57]

In quoting Luke 10:18 Origen bolsters his appeal to Isaiah 14 by linking it with the authority of Jesus' own teaching.

Furthermore, in his reflection on the nature of Satan's downfall Origen utilizes an intertextual reading of scripture. Young speaks of "the profound importance of intertextuality and cross-reference in early Christian exegesis."[58] She defines intertextuality as "the principle of looking for the reference and exploiting cross-reference in order to substantiate proposed exegesis in a rational way."[59] Young argues that this exegetical strategy is absolutely crucial in understanding the way the early church was reading the scriptures. Young's thorough analysis demonstrates the significance of

---

55. Ibid., 50.
56. Ibid.
57. Childs, *Theological Reflection*, 226.
58. F. M. Young, *Exegesis*, 133.
59. Ibid., 137.

intertextuality for Origen. This strategy which was so pervasive in ancient literature "became more sophisticated in the hands of such as Origen and Eusebius."[60] This is very evident in the way Origen employs intertextuality as he reflects by the way of contrast on the light that Satan was and the world as the place of his exile upon his rejection from heaven.

The reference to the Lucifer who "rose in the morning" in Isaiah 14 leads Origen to intertextual reading of the *light* that Satan once was. Origen writes,

> Our Lord, who is the truth, compared even the power of his own glorious advent to lightning, in the words: "For as the lightning shineth from one end of heaven to the other, so shall also the coming of the Son of Man be" (Matthew 24:27). Yet he also compares Satan to lightning, and says that he fell from heaven, in order to show thereby that he was in heaven once, and had a place among the holy ones, and a share in that light in which all the holy ones share, in virtue of which the angels become "angels of light" (2 Corinthians 11:14) and the apostles are called "the light of the world" (Matthew 5:14) by the Lord.[61]

It is Origen's thesis that "among all rational creatures there is none which is not capable of both good and evil" (I.8.3).[62] This is inherently the work of the Triune God. The Father bestows on his creatures the gift of existence (I.1).[63] The Son, by the virtue of him being the Word of God, endows them with the rational capacity (I.2).[64] The Spirit enables those beings who are not holy in essence to be made holy (I.3.8).[65] The work of the Triune God is precisely a gradual formation of beings who can behold the holy and blessed life. Origen evocatively outlines this formation (I.3.8), "The more we partake of its blessedness, the more may the loving desire for it deepen and increase within us, as ever our hearts grow in fervor and eagerness to receive and hold fast the Father, the Son and the Holy Spirit."[66] The tragedy of Satan is that he once shared the light with the holy ones and had access to virtue, hence he could have embarked on this journey towards blessed life.

---

60. Ibid.
61. Origen, *First,* 50. Scripture references are not in the original text.
62. Ibid., 69.
63. Ibid., 7–14.
64. Ibid., 15–28.
65. Ibid., 29–39, esp. 38.
66. Ibid., 39.

But the fact that he was capable of good, does not, argues Origen, imply that he either desired it or made any effort to accrue virtue (I.8.3).[67]

For Origen, falling away is analogous to a man skilled in geometry or medicine gradually losing his knowledge. At first "he loses interest in these exercises and neglects to work" (I.4.1).[68] Then, tragically, "through this negligence his knowledge is gradually lost, a few details at first, then more, and so on until after a long time the whole vanishes into oblivion and is utterly erased from his memory" (I.4.1).[69] This is a tragic path, open to all rational creatures endowed with the free will. The path was first taken by Satan, but is equally open for all.

In order to highlight the magnitude of the reversal of fortunes brought about by Satan's refusal to seek virtue, Origen reflects intertextually on the *world* as the place where Satan fell to,

> In this way, then, even Satan was once light, before he went astray and fell to this place, when "his glory was turned into dust." So he is called the "prince of this world" (John 12:31; 16:11), for he exercises his princely power over those who are obedient to his wickedness, since "this whole world" (and here I take "world" to mean this earthly place) "lieth in the evil one" (1 John 5:19) that is, in this apostate. That he is an apostate, or fugitive, the Lord also says in Job, in the following words, "Thou wilt take with a hook the apostate dragon" (Job 40:20 LXX), that is, the fugitive dragon. And it is certain that the dragon means the devil himself.[70]

This turning of glory into dust as Satan is ejected from heaven is consistent with the foundational thought for Origen that God "dispenses all his gifts in proportion to the merits and progress of each recipient" (I.8.4).[71] Every angelic office, according to Origen, is a "reward of merit." This is equally true of holy and wicked angels. He writes (I.8.4),

> We must think of the opposing powers in precisely the same way. These have become attached to their particular place or office, so as to be "principalities," or "powers," or "rulers of the darkness of the world," or "spiritual hosts of wickedness," or "malignant spirits," or "impure daemons," not because they hold it essentially not because they were so crated; on the contrary,

67. Ibid., 70.
68. Ibid., 40.
69. Ibid.
70. Ibid., 50.
71. Ibid., 71.

these ranks in wickedness have been assigned to them in proportion to their bad conduct and the progress they have made in wrong-doing.[72]

As a tragic denouement of persisting in wickedness (I.8.4),

There exists that other order of rational creatures, who have so utterly abandoned themselves to wickedness that they lack the desire, rather than the power, to return, so long as the frenzy of their evil deeds is a passion and a delight.[73]

Finally, having reflected on Origen's linking of Isaiah 14 with the words of Jesus and his use of intertextuality, we turn our attention to the goal of Origen's exegesis. In *Homily XXVII on Numbers* Origen has stated plainly the value of scriptures in human life, "Every rational nature needs to be nourished by foods of its own and suitable for it. Now the true food of a rational nature is the Word of God."[74] In light of Origen's understanding of the role of scripture to nourish the people of God, some scholars recently have insisted that for Origen "the task of the exegete was to enable scripture to function pedagogically for the hearer, assisting the journey of the soul."[75] This is very evident in the direction Origen's exegesis of Isaiah 14 takes him.

Having demonstrated that the origin of evil lies with corruption of the devil and his cohort of angels, he moves on to reflect on the nature of holiness. According to Origen, holiness has an "accidental quality," i.e. rather than belonging to a category of essence it is something determined by one's actions. "What is accidental may also be lost."[76] It is this accidental quality that stands behind the origin of evil. "These opposing powers . . . were once stainless and dwelt among those that have continued stainless until now."[77] From this foundation Origen is able to broaden his pedagogical appeal to his readers,

All this shows that no one is stainless by essence or by nature, nor is any one polluted essentially. Consequently it lies with us and with our own actions whether we are to be blessed and holy, or whether through sloth and negligence we are to turn away from blessedness into wickedness and loss; the final result of which is, that when too much progress, if I may use the word,

72. Ibid.
73. Ibid., 71–2.
74. Origen, *Works*, 245.
75. Young, *Exegesis*, 242.
76. Origen, *First*, 50.
77. Ibid.

has been made in wickedness, a man may descend to such state (if any shall come to so great a pitch of negligence) as to be changed into what is called an opposing power.[78]

Origen and the Western Church

One final issue to address in our discussion of Origen's reading of Isaiah 14:12–15 is related to the widespread acceptance of his reading in the Western church. What makes this issue peculiar is the fact that Origen carried out his writing and teaching career in Alexandria and later in Caesarea. He was posthumously condemned as a heretic by the Fifth Ecumenical Council in Constantinople in 553 AD.[79] How did the reading of the condemned heretic from Alexandria become widely accepted in the church in the West?

Heidl's recent monograph on Origen's influence on young Augustine helps shed the light. He writes,

> Origen and Augustine are two giants—some would say *the* two giants—of the early Christian theological world. Each of them pondered fundamental questions of belief in a world marked by suffering and imperfection. For each the interplay of Divine justice, Providence, grace, human freedom and the love of the Creator for creatures was a problem that demand a cosmic solution. Both addressed this problem with one eye on the Bible, the other on contemporaneous philosophical discussion. Addressing the most sophisticated critiques of Christianity, each contested the claim that later Platonism was most appropriately melded with traditional Greco-Roman religion rather than with Christianity. Each argued strenuously in intra-ecclesial disputes over correct doctrine—and thus contributed to the determination that certain views fell short and were therefore to be considered heretical. Both were "men of the church" who in the course of their lives dedicated ever-increasing proportions of their prodigious literary output to the explication of the Bible, often in the form of sermons preached to the faithful.[80]

Heidl's analysis seeks to demonstrate that these similarities are not coincidental, but rather are a result of Augustine's exposure to Origen's writings early on in his life. Heidl argues that it is reading Origen, albeit in translation,

---

78. Origen, *First*, 50–51.

79. Trigg, *Origen*, 62–66. The Council's stated rationale for Origen's condemnation could be found in "The Anathemas against Origen," in *NPNF2*, 14:318.

80. Heidl, *Influence*, v.

that Augustine is prompted to return to the church and plunge into debates with the Manichaeans. In support of his hypothesis that Augustine had the first-hand knowledge of Origen, Hedl demonstrates a close linguistic affinity between Augustine's first exegetical work, *De genesi contra manichaeos* and Origen's writings. Augustine's allegorical interpretation of Genesis, Heidl claims, was influenced by Origen's homilies and commentary on Genesis, an exposure to which, Heidl conjectures, came from Simplicianus.[81] While Heidl's proposal is fresh and in some ways speculative, anticipating further work and broader discussion, his work is suggestive in tracing the possible path for wider acceptance of Origen's reading of Isaiah 14 via one of the most influential figures in the Western church. Hence we turn to Augustine's reading of Isaiah 14 as a way of exploring a close affinity with Origen.

Augustine turns to Isaiah 14 during his struggle with Manichaean cosmological dualism according to which the universe was composed of two fundamentally opposed natures—good and evil. According to Mann, Manichaeism "offered a straightforward solution for the problem of evil: God is doing the best he can against evil, but finds himself facing an independent opponent as formidable as he."[82] Writing in his *On the Morals of the Manichaeans* (I.1), Augustine argues that the Manichaean dualism is clearly wrong,

> The chief good is that which is properly described as having supreme and original existence. For that exists in the highest sense of the word which continues always the same, which is throughout like itself, which cannot in any part be corrupted or changed, which is not subject to time, which admits of no variation in its present as compared with its former condition. This is existence in its true sense. For in this signification of the word existence there is implied a nature which is self-contained, and which continues immutably. Such things can be said only of God, to whom there is nothing contrary in the strict sense of the word. For the contrary of existence is non-existence. There is therefore no nature contrary to God.[83]

From here Augustine goes on to affirm that God is the author of all natures and substances. If this is so, then does it follow that God is the author of evil? Augustine's answer is "No." This answer stems from Augustine's definition of evil (*On the Morals of the Manichaeans* I.5),

---

81. Heidl, *Influence*, 35.
82. Mann, "Augustine on Evil and Original Sin," 40.
83. *NPNF* IV:69.

> What is evil? Perhaps you will reply, Corruption. Undeniably this is a general definition of evil; for corruption implies opposition to nature, and also hurt. But corruption exists not by itself, but in some substance which it corrupts; for corruption itself is not a substance. So the thing which it corrupts is not corruption, is not evil; for what is corrupted suffers the loss of integrity and purity. So that which has no purity to lose cannot be corrupted; and what has, is necessarily good by the participation of purity. Again, what is corrupted is perverted; and what is perverted suffers the loss of order, and order is good. To be corrupted, then, does not imply the absence of good; for in corruption it can be deprived of good, which could not be if there was the absence of good. Therefore that race of darkness, if it was destitute of all good, as you say it was, could not be corrupted, for it had nothing which corruption could take from it; and if corruption takes nothing away, it does not corrupt. Say now, if you dare, that God and the kingdom of God can be corrupted, when you cannot show how the kingdom of the devil, such as you make it, can be corrupted.[84]

Thus, Augustine denies that evil is a nature of any sorts. It is, rather, a corruption of the good nature created by God.

In formulating the notion of evil as the corruption of the good nature, Augustine has to deal with the possible New Testament rebuttal from the Manichaeans. 1 John 3:8 states that the devil sinned from the beginning. For the Manichaeans this verse amounted to the proof that "the devil is sinful by nature."[85] Augustine insists that they misinterpret this text. If the devil was created to be evil by nature then how might one understand texts such as Isaiah 14 and Ezekiel 28,

> For Isaiah representing the devil under the figure of the prince of Babylon, says: "How art thou fallen, O Lucifer, son of the morning!" Also, Ezekiel says: "Thou hast been in Eden, the garden of God; every precious stone was thy covering"; and by this we are to understand that the devil was for some time without sin. For, a little later, it is more expressly said: "Thou was perfect in thy ways." And if no other more fitting interpretation of these verses can be found, then we must also understand this one, "He abode not in the truth," to mean that the devil was once in the truth, but did not remain in it.[86]

---

84. *NPNF* IV:71.
85. Augustine, *City*, 11:15, p. 469.
86. Ibid.

Augustine argues that 1 John 3:8 reference does not mean that the devil was sinful from the beginning of his existence, rather "from the beginning of his sin, because it was by his pride that sin first came to be."[87] Rather than the devil being created evil,

> His beginning ... is the Lord's handiwork. For there is no nature, even the least and lowest of the beats, which was not wrought by him from Whom comes all the measure, all the form and all the order without which nothing can be found or conceived to exist. How much more, then, is the angelic creation, which surpasses in dignity all apse that He has made, the handiwork of God![88]

Reading Augustine's defense of classic Christian formulations of cosmology, nature and origin of evil it is clear that he stands in substantial continuity with Origen. As Origen, he comes to this text searching for the origin of evil. His battles with the Manichaeans were very similar with those Origen engaged against the gnostic writers of his time. In search for support he too turns to Isaiah 14 where he finds a textual answer to the question of the origin of evil that plagues him. Augustine's turn to Isaiah 14 in such weighty work as *The City of God* as well as allusions to it in *The Confessions*[89] and homilies[90] paved the way for the widespread acceptance of this text referring to the downfall of Satan in the Western church. Thus, the man whose influence on the Western church was simply staggering becomes the impetus for preserving Origen's reading of Isaiah 14 even when Origen's own writings were rejected as heretical.

Summary

Our reading has sought to briefly enter into Origen's conceptual world and analyze his exegetical approach in order to make sense of his reading of Isaiah 14. Origen's reading of Isaiah 14 is far from being a haphazard collection of exegetical moves congenial to him. As a true "son of the church" he comes to this text interested in understanding broader issues of the origins of evil and its intersection with the free will—issues that are dominating the thinking of the broader church community at that time. His allegorical

87. Ibid.
88. Ibid., 11:15, p. 469–70.
89. Augustine, *Confessions*, 10.36.58, p. 267.
90. Augustine, "Exposition on the Psalms" 36:15; 48:3; 89:12 in *NPNF1* 8:90, 165, 433; "Homilies on the Gospel of St. John: Tractate III on Chapter 1:15–18" III.17 and "Homilies on the Gospel of St. John: Tractate XVII on Chapter 5.1–18" XVII.16 in *NPNF1* 7:21, 116.

reading of the downfall of the king of Babylon as descriptive of the downfall of Satan is very much consistent with an ancient approach to reading the Bible as sacred scripture. Origen does not come to Isaiah 14 expecting to merely receive an understanding of the past, rather he comes to it in search of meaning that bears weight on how one lives faithfully before God. Origen, it seems, would very much agree with one of his leading contemporary interpreters that scripture

> is not a document handed over to the historian or the thinker, even to the believing historian or thinker. It is a word, which is to say, the start of a dialogue. It is addressed to someone from whom it awaits a response. More precisely, it is God who offers himself through it, and he awaits more than a response: a return movement.[91]

Calvin's Reading of Isaiah 14:12–15

John Calvin (1509–64) was a principal figure of the sixteenth-century Protestant Reformation. His impact on the Western world has been aptly summed up by McGrath,

> Calvin's theological heritage has proved fertile perhaps to a greater extent than any other Protestant writer. Richard Baxter, Jonathan Edwards and Karl Barth, in their very different ways, bear witness to the pivotal role that Calvin's ideas have played in shaping Protestant self-perception down the centuries. While the scholarly debate over the nature and extent of Calvin's influence over the development of modern capitalism, the emergence of the natural sciences and the shaping of modern views of human rights will continue, there is no doubting Calvin's role in contributing to the shaping of modern Protestant attitudes in these areas. It is impossible to understand modern Protestantism without coming to terms with Calvin's legacy to the movement which he did so much to nourish and sustain.[92]

In considering the cultural impact of Calvin it is crucial to keep in mind the influence of Renaissance Humanism on Calvin's thought. Bouwsma writes, "All of his life Calvin inhabited the Erasmian world of thought and breathed its spiritual atmosphere; he remained in major ways always a

---

91. De Lubac, *History*, 346–47.
92. McGrath, "Protestantism," 64.

humanist of the late Renaissance."[93] Bouwsma is careful to document how the writings of Calvin reveal someone profoundly shaped by this massive intellectual and cultural movement:

> His writing is filled with powerful imagery, unexpected imaginative insights, psychological aperçus, rhetorical elaborations, digressions, and repetitions that were intended to serve a polemical, instructional, or other purpose. Calvin expressed himself in the style of Renaissance humanism.[94]

Renaissance Humanism was not merely interested in discovering timeless truths. On the contrary, its primary focus was on the transformation of the contemporary world. Words of Bouwsma are instructive,

> Humanism, as a movement, had always displayed a remarkable sensitivity to the concrete historical circumstances in which it had unfolded. It was, broadly speaking, a self conscious reform movement, concerned to reform not all times but *its own time*, sometimes in narrower, sometimes in broader ways. It did so with a sense of urgency that was a major element in its rejection of speculative system-building, which seemed a kind of luxury that the times could ill afford. The times called for action![95]

The resurgence of learning based on classical sources, which was a characteristic of Renaissance Humanism, made a profound mark on Calvin. As the humanists turned to the ancient texts in search for wisdom to transform the society around them, Calvin brought his vast humanist learning to the service of the church. He entered the scene as the second generation of the Reformers who sought to correct the practices of the church in the sixteenth century. George sums up well this basic reality of Calvin's circumstances,

> Calvin brought to the Reformation the militancy of a convert of the second generation. When he was born in northern France in 1509, Luther was already giving lectures at the university of Erfurt and Zwingli was hurrying about his pastoral duties in rural Switzerland. . . . When Calvin became a Protestant in the early 1530s, he inherited a tradition and a theology already well defined by nearly two decades of controversy.[96]

---

93. Bouwsma, *Portrait*, 13.
94. Bouwsma, "Artifact," 35.
95. Ibid.
96. George, "Introduction," 16.

What contribution was Calvin's humanist education to offer to the efforts of the Reformers? Muller, who provides a scathing rebuttal of what he perceives to be an overly psychological portrait of Calvin presented by Bouwsma's account of the Reformer's life, still cautions against attempts to understand Calvin's contribution in contemporary dogmatic categories. As he embarks on his examination of Calvin's *Institutes* as the "body of Christian teaching," Muller is careful to point out,

> Such an examination, while maintaining the *Institutes*' identity as a sixteenth-century form of theological system, must point away from modern dogmatics and towards Calvin's exegetical task as the proper context for understanding the document. Calvin, after all, did not think of himself as a dogmatician in the modern sense of the term: rather, like most of the other theologians of his time, he understood himself as a preacher and exegete, and he understood the primary work of his life as the exposition of Scripture.[97]

Calvin's focus as the biblical exegete who puts his humanist learning to the service of the church could be summed up succinctly in Calvin's own words from his commentary on Matthew 3:7, "It would be really a frigid way of teaching if the teacher did not determine carefully the needs of the times and what suits the people concerned, for in this regard nothing is more unbalanced than absolute balance."[98] Calvin's immersion in Renaissance Humanism shaped him into a brilliant teacher of the Bible who saw his calling as one who would become a careful and attentive shepherd nurturing the faith of his flock in Geneva.

Our consideration of Calvin is due to the fact that his reading of Isaiah 14:12–15 overturned the centuries-old reading of the this text as a reference to the origin of evil. While not the first one to reject the reading of Isaiah 14:12–15 as depicting the downfall of Satan, Calvin was undoubtedly one of the most influential.

Calvin's Hermeneutical Approach

Before exploring Calvin's reading of Isaiah 14:12–15 we need to turn our attention to his hermeneutical approach. How Calvin understands his own undertaking is crucial in us grasping the interpretive moves he makes when he reads this passage.

---

97. Muller, *The Unaccommodated Calvin*, 5.
98. Quoted in Bouwsma, "Artifact," 38.

The difficulty of outlining Calvin's hermeneutical approach has been captured well by Leith, "Calvin, to my knowledge, never formally summarized his hermeneutical principles beyond his various statements on the need for brevity and clarity, on the importance of the natural sense of scripture."[99] The reason for that is broader than just Calvin's neglect to provide such summary. According to Leith, "For the Reformers, generally, method grew out of the reality of what they were doing."[100] Nevertheless, we will turn to Childs' insightful account of Calvin's actual exegetical strategies.

Childs highlights five main issues at stake in understanding the Reformer's hermeneutical approach.[101] First, Childs underscores the complexity of the plain sense of the biblical text in Calvin's writings. One gets the most forceful statement of Calvin's emphasis on the plain sense of the text in one of his commentaries, "Let us know, then, that the true meaning of Scripture is the natural and simple one (*verum sensum scripturae, qui germanus est et simplex*), and let us embrace and hold it resolutely."[102] Yet we are wise to head the caution of Steinmetz, "For Calvin as for Origen the meaning of the Bible could not be collapsed into a bare historical account of the activities of ancient Semites. Calvin did not have a modern, that is, historical-critical, understanding of letter and the literal sense."[103] In other words, Calvin's "natural sense" is not equivalent to a modern "historical sense." On the one hand, Calvin's commentaries on the Bible reflect the humanist attention to the authorial intent, grammatical details, geography, philology, style, and literary context of a text he engages with.[104] Yet, on the other hand, Childs is careful to note,

> This is only part of the task; the relation between the human and divine nature of scripture requires a much more subtle approach. It would be a mistake, however, to suppose that Calvin simply joins the humanist study of the literal sense of a biblical text with an additional theological step. Rather, it is crucial to understand that what Calvin means by a text's literal sense is not simply identified with its verbal or historically reconstructed meaning.[105]

---

99. Leith, "Calvin's Doctrine," 214.

100. Ibid.

101. Childs, *Struggle*, 210-17.

102. Calvin, *Galatians, Ephesians, Philippians and Colossians*, 84.

103. Steinmetz, "Calvin and the Irrepressible Spirit," 103.

104. See two excellent summaries of Calvin's exegetical practices: Kraus, "Calvin's Exegetical Principles," 8-18 and Zachman, "Gathering Meaning," 1-26.

105. Childs, *Struggle*, 211.

Childs takes seriously Greene-McCreight's argument that for Calvin the plain sense of scripture in inseparable from a ruled reading. According to Greene-McCreight, a plain sense of the text "involves negotiating between the constraints of verbal sense and Ruled reading . . . respecting the verbal and textual data of the text as well as privileging the claims about God and Jesus Christ which cohere with the Rule of faith."[106] The Rule of Faith (*regula fidei*) encompasses the overarching theological framework based on the history of the divine redemption in Jesus Christ. The biblical narrative that stretches from the creation account in the opening chapters of the book of Genesis to the eschatological consummation of history in the kingdom of God envisioned by the book of Revelation provides the context for Calvin's plain sense of the text. Childs insists that for Calvin this literary framework stretching from creation to consummation serves as a necessary and sufficient theological restraint rendering irrelevant any recourse to a different textual level in search of a spiritual meaning. Childs argues that for Calvin, "The literal sense is the true and genuine meaning of scripture."[107]

Second, Childs reflects on the intersection of human and divine intentionality in Calvin's reading of biblical texts. On the one hand, Calvin sees biblical texts as products of human authors (*mens authoris*). In his his preface to the commentary on Romans Calvin writes, "Since it is almost [the interpreter's] only task to unfold the mind of the writer whom he has undertaken to expound, he misses his mark, or at least strays outside his limits, by the extent to which he leads his readers away from the meaning of his author."[108] Yet, on the other hand, Calvin is careful to point out in his *Institutes* that the Bible reflects God's intentionality (*Dei consilium*) as he insists, "The Scripture exhibits clear evidence of its being spoken by God."[109] Furthermore, Calvin affirms that the illuminating work of the Holy Sprit sears into human hearts this conviction about the divine authorship of scripture,

> Enlightened by [the Holy Spirit], we no longer believe, either on our own judgment or that of others, that the Scriptures are from God; but, in a way superior to human judgment, feel perfectly assured—as much so as if we beheld the divine image visibly impressed on it—that it came to us, by the instrumentality of men, from the very mouth of God.[110]

---

106. Greene-McCreight, *Ad Litteram*, ix.
107. Childs, *Struggle*, 212.
108. Calvin, *Romans and Thessalonians*, 1.
109. Calvin, Institutes I.7.4, 71.
110. Ibid., I.7.5, 72.

Childs refers approvingly to Puckett's analysis of the interrelationship between human and divine intentionality in Calvin's reading of biblical texts.[111] He agrees with Puckett when he states, "Calvin is unwilling to divorce the intention of the human writer from the meaning of the Holy Spirit."[112] He is ready to concede the general conclusion drawn from Puckett's analysis that there is really no easy way to distinguish between these aspects of Calvin's reading. Childs claims that while this is indeed true for Calvin, "there is also within the ruled reading a strong force exerted to extend the meaning by adapting the biblical text to the present usage of the church."[113] An *anagoge* (literary analogy) is the form of figuration, that, according to Childs, is Calvin's means of extending the text's meaning—the extension which "derives from the overarching purpose of God with Israel and the world into which the message of human writers are observed."[114]

Third, Childs elaborates on Calvin's understanding of history. According to Childs, "Calvin's understanding of Old Testament history is shaped completely by his theological stance that it is the divine will that gives meaning and direction to all earthly events."[115] Here Childs leans heavily on Parker's analysis of Calvin's thought. Parker insists that for Calvin the Old Testament is "the book that recounts and describes the childhood and growing up of the Church."[116] Or to be much more precise, "since this was no sailing a calm sea in halcyon days, it recounts and describes the way in which God preserved his Church in the midst of disasters and persecutions."[117] Parker stresses the idea that for Calvin the Old Testament recounts the growth of the church from its infancy (*pueritia*) till it reaches the full adulthood (*virilis aetas*) at the dawn of Incarnation. In his commentary on Isaiah 54:2 Calvin insists that this chapter has the kingdom of Christ in mind and that the promises contained here were fulfilled when the gospel began to be preached. He writes,

> This prophecy began to be fulfilled under Cyrus, who gave the people liberty to return, and afterwards extended to Christ, in whom it has its full accomplishment. The Church therefore conceived, when the people returned to their native country; for the body of the people was gathered together from which Christ

---

111. Puckett, *Exegesis*.
112. Childs, *Struggle*, 212–13.
113. Ibid., 213.
114. Ibid.
115. Ibid.
116. Parker, *Calvin's Old Testament Commentaries*, 83.
117. Ibid.

should proceed, in order that the pure worship of God and true religion might again be revived. Hitherto, indeed, this fertility was not visible; for the conception was concealed, as it were, in the mother's womb, and no outward appearance of it could be seen; but afterwards the people were increased, and after the birth the Church grew from infancy to manhood, till the Gospel was preached. This was the actual youth of the Church; and next follows the age of manhood, down to Christ's last coming, when all things shall be fully accomplished.[118]

Childs argues that this type of historical understanding in Calvin is sustained by two sophisticated hermeneutical moves, namely accommodation and typology. According to Childs, accommodation implies that "God condescends in his dealings with fallible human beings by accommodating his teaching to mankind's limited capacity."[119] Closely related to accommodation is the idea of typology. Childs comments, "Because history is the unified expression of the will of God for his creation, Calvin envisions a meaningful pattern of events within God's unfolding purpose."[120]

What Childs refers to as sophisticated hermeneutics to some seems like Calvin's acknowledgment, however subtle, that Origen was not totally off-base regarding his allegorical reading after all. Steinmetz writes, "Calvin ridiculed Origen and set out to extirpate allegorical interpretations of the Bible. He discovered that the nature of the book he sought to interpret did not allow the abolition of allegory but only the pruning of its excesses."[121] Thus Steinmetz insists that both allegory and typology were a part of Calvin's exegetical repertoire alongside of his literal-historical tools. His comments on Calvin's understanding of history are worth quoting at length,

> The word "anagogy" made a brief appearance in Calvin's exegesis, though it is not altogether clear whether by its use Calvin meant anagogy in the strict sense or merely analogy. At any event, the literal-prophetic sense as Calvin used it embraced a good deal of what earlier interpreters had meant by anagogy. The line which Calvin drew from the kingdom of Israel to the messianic kingdom is both literal-prophetic and anagogical. When Calvin moved from a discussion of the kingdom of Israel to the church and from the church to the messianic kingdom

---

118. Calvin, *Isaiah*, 4:135–36.
119. Childs, *Struggle*, 214.
120. Ibid.
121. Steinmetz, "Spirit," 105.

of God, he was, from our point of view if not always from his, teaching the spiritual sense of Scripture.¹²²

All this seems to amount to quiet readmittance of Origen through the back door. Hence Steinmetz concludes,

> Calvin can be admired as a biblical theologian, not because he returned to the literal sense of scripture (which, after all, had never been lost), but because he recognized that the literal sense of scripture was, as the Church had known for more than a millennium, never enough. Calvin used allegory, typology, and tropology because the nature of scripture required it. If I listen carefully, I can hear the faint laughter of Origen.¹²³

Fourth, Childs' critical eye turns to Calvin's understanding of the relationship between the testaments. On the one hand, Childs is very approving of Calvin's approach, "Calvin is fully right in formulating a biblical theology of both testaments in which there is an overarching unity between the two."¹²⁴ The differences between testaments are not those of substance, but of the administration of God's unified will. Childs writes,

> The Old Testament promises are couched as earthly blessings in contrast to the heavenly blessings of the New Testament. The old covenant is one of shadow and is temporal; the new covenant is clear and eternal. The old covenant is of the letter rather than the spirit. Finally, whereas the old covenant is made with only one nation, in the new covenant the distinction between Jew and gentile has been removed.¹²⁵

According to Childs, Calvin's Old Testament exegesis is fundamentally shaped by this continuity of substance between the testaments.

Yet while appreciative of Calvin's emphasis on the overarching unity of the two testaments, Childs is critical of some of the moves that Calvin makes here. He finds Calvin's use of the New Testament citations of Old Testament at times a forceful attempting to harmonize or twist texts to achieve a coherent reading. Similarly, he finds unpersuasive Calvin's attribution to the people living under the old covenant a sort of Christian motivation, as he does when he claims that David knew he was only a type of the promised messiah. Commenting on Psalm 2:1 Calvin writes,

---

122. Ibid.
123. Ibid.
124. Childs, *Struggle*, 217.
125. Ibid., 215.

> But it is now high time to come to the substance of the type. That David prophesied concerning Christ, is clearly manifest from this, that he knew his own kingdom to be merely a shadow. And in order to learn to apply to Christ whatever David, in times past, sang concerning himself, we must hold this principle, which we meet with everywhere in all the prophets, that he, with his posterity, was made king, not so much for his own sake as to be a type of the Redeemer. We shall often have occasion to return to this afterwards, but at present I would briefly inform my readers that as David's temporal kingdom was a kind of earnest to God's ancient people of the eternal kingdom, which at length was truly established in the person of Christ, those things which David declares concerning himself are not violently, or even allegorically, applied to Christ, but were truly predicted concerning him.[126]

Childs finds this kind of an interpretive move dissatisfying,

> Calvin's approach runs the danger of projecting backward into the biblical narrative a meaning that is not derived from the Old Testament. The effect is that he christianizes the Old Testament by a form of psychologizing the unexamined motivation of its characters.[127]

Fifth, Childs reflects briefly on Calvin's homiletical use of the Old Testament. Childs insists that one of the post impressive elements of Calvin's exegesis is "his consistent attempt at adapting its message to his own time and to his Christian audience."[128]

Calvin's pastoral context in Geneva made him especially sensitive and adapt in relating the text to the needs of his flock. He was sensitive to the homiletical responsibility as a pastor,

> If I should enter the pulpit without deigning to glance at a book, and should frivolously think to myself, "Oh, well, when I preach, God will give me enough to say," and come here without troubling to read or thinking what I ought to declare, and do not carefully consider how I must apply Holy Scripture to the edification of the people, then I should be an arrogant upstart.[129]

---

126. Calvin, *Commentary on the Book of Psalms*, 1:11.
127. Childs, *Struggle*, 217.
128. Ibid.
129. *OC* 26, 473–74; Quoted in T. H. L. Parker, *John Calvin: A Biography*, 119.

Furthermore, Calvin was determined that the final goal of his exegesis was the edification and nourishment of his flock in the process of homiletical use of scripture (Sermon IV on 2 Timothy 2:16–18),

> When we come together in the name of God, it is not to hear merry songs, and to be fed with wind; that is, with a vain and unprofitable curiosity; but to receive spiritual nourishment. For God will have nothing preached in his name, but that which will profit and edify the hearer; nothing that which containeth good matter. But it is true, our nature is such, that we take great pleasure in novelty, and in speculations which seem to be subtle. Therefore, let us beware, and think as we ought; that we may not profane God's holy word. Let us seek that which edifieth, and not abuse ourselves by receiving that which hath no substance in it.[130]

Without a doubt Calvin was a remarkable student and teacher of scripture. His capacity to handle scripture was held in high esteem by supporters and bitter enemies alike. It is fitting to conclude this section with the words of someone who knew Calvin and his theology well and who was often perplexed by his hermeneutical moves. In a letter dated on May 3, 1607, not quite two years before his death, Jacobus Arminius would write,

> After the holy Scriptures (the perusal of which I earnestly inculcate more than any other person, as the whole university as well as the consciences of my colleagues will testify), I exhort [students] to read the Commentaries of Calvin. . . . For I tell them that he is incomparable in the interpretation of Scripture; and that his Commentaries ought to be held in greater estimation than all that is delivered to us in the writings of the Ancient Christian Fathers: So that, in a certain eminent Spirit of Prophecy, I give the preeminence to him beyond most others, indeed beyond them all. I add, that, with regard to what belongs to Common Places, his *Institutes* must be read after the Catechism, as more ample interpretation.[131]

---

130. Bentley, *Selection of Most Celebrated Sermons of M. Luther and J. Calvin*, 61.
131. Nichols, *The Works of James Arminius*, 1:295–96.

Calvin's Framing Comments Regarding the Burden of Babylon in Isaiah 13–14

Our discussion of Calvin's reading of Isaiah 14:12–15 necessarily begins with few observations about Calvin's framing comments regarding the Burden of Babylon in Isaiah 13–14 as close reading of Calvin's opening discussion on these chapters reveals what interests him as he comes to this section of Isaiah.

First, Calvin is aware of the fact that with the opening of the chapter 13, there is a shift in focus. He is not interested in the abrupt change of emphasis from Assyria in chapters 1–12 to Babylon in chapters 13–14. Rather, he emphasizes that "from this chapter down to the twenty-fourth, the Prophet foretells what dreadful and shocking calamities awaited the Gentiles and those countries which were best known to the Jews."[132] Calvin argues that when such calamities happen in the world around us, the tendency is to see them as random, or as he would put it, "directed by the blind violence of fortune."[133] Calvin decries the difficulty of convincing people that God is actually at work in their midst, "There is nothing of which it is more difficult to convince men than that the providence of God governs this world."[134] Even for believers this presents a serious challenge, "Many indeed acknowledge it in words, but very few have it actually engraved on their hearts."[135] Hence, according to Calvin, it seems that precisely this need to engrave God's sovereign activity in the world in the souls of believers stimulates Isaiah to pen these memorable words. To put it another way, Isaiah is driven by the need that "all might understand that those calamities did not take place but by the secret and wonderful purpose of God."[136]

One can hear the echoes of Calvin's words in his *Institutes* where he similarly points to the human propensity to downplay God's activity in the world,

> By an erroneous opinion prevailing in all ages, an opinion almost universally prevailing in our own day—viz. that all things happen fortuitously, the true doctrine of Providence has not only been obscured, but almost buried. If one falls among robbers, or ravenous beasts; if a sudden gust of wind at sea causes shipwreck; if one is struck down by the fall of a house or a tree;

---

132. Calvin, *Isaiah*, 1:406.
133. Ibid., 1:458.
134. Ibid., 1:406–407.
135. Ibid., 1:407.
136. Ibid.

if another, when wandering through desert paths, meets with deliverance; or, after being tossed by the waves, arrives in port, and makes some wondrous hair-breadth escape from death—all these occurrences, prosperous as well as adverse, carnal sense will attribute to fortune.[137]

Yet those who are immersed in scriptures, Calvin argues, can shun this erroneous opinion, "The Providence of God, as taught in Scripture, is opposed to fortune and fortuitous causes."[138] Thus, Calvin suggests that scripturally informed interpretation of realities of life would reflect openness to seeing God at work in the midst of them,

> Whoso has learned from the mouth of Christ that all the hairs of his head are numbered (Mt. x.30), will look farther for the cause, and hold that all events whatsoever are governed by the secret counsel of God.[139]

Furthermore, Calvin insists that Isaiah did not pen the burden against Babylon for the advantage of Babylon as these words probably never reached that nation. Rather the intent was to encourage the Jews who experienced oppression at the hands of the Babylonians. Calvin argues that the unchallenged power of Babylon's oppressive rule could shake the faith of YHWH's people,

> If the monarchy of Babylon had remained unshaken, the Jews would not only have thought that it was in vain for them to worship God, and that his covenant which he had made with Abraham had not been fulfilled, since it fared better with strangers and wicked men than with the elect people but a worse suspicion might have crept into their minds, that God showed favor to accursed robbers, who gave themselves up to deeds of dishonesty and violence, and despised all law both human and divine. Indeed, they might soon have come to think that God did not care for his people, or could not assist them, or that everything was directed by the blind violence of fortune.[140]

Hence, Isaiah's words were intended both to alleviate their grief over the pain experienced at the hands of the oppressors and to avert the despair when the realities of life clouded one's view of God. Calvin writes, "That they might not faint or be thrown into despair, the Prophet meets them with

---

137. Calvin, *Institutes* I.16.2, 173.
138. Ibid., I.16.2, 172–73.
139. Ibid., I.16.2, 173.
140. Calvin, *Isaiah*, 1:407–8.

the consoling influence of this prediction, showing that the Babylonians also will be punished."[141]

Once again, we hear the echoes of Calvin's discussion on the use to be made of the doctrine of Divine Providence in his *Institutes*. Calvin, whose life was lived out during the turbulent decades of the sixteenth-century Europe, is very honest about the dangers inherent in human life,

> Innumerable are the ills which beset human life, and present death in as many different forms. Not to go beyond ourselves, since the body is a receptacle, nay the nurse, of a thousand diseases, a man cannot move without carrying along with him many forms of destruction. His life is in a manner interwoven with death.[142]

Calvin's point is that if one jettison's the idea of God being at work in one's world then all one is left with is "the misery which man should feel, were he placed under the dominion of chance."[143] Even if we ourselves are not afflicted, watching others, "it is impossible not to fear and dread as if they were to befall us."[144] Hence Calvin exclaims, "What can you imagine more grievous than such trepidation?"[145] Calvin's answer is to find comfort in the Divine Providence (I.17.11),

> Once the light of Divine Providence has illumined the believer's soul, he is relieved and set free, not only from the extreme fear and anxiety which formerly oppressed him, but from all care. For as he justly shudders at the idea of chance, so he can confidently commit himself to God. This, I say, is his comfort, that his heavenly Father so embraces all things under his power—so governs them at will by his nod—so regulates them by his wisdom, that nothing takes place save according to his appointment; that received into his favour, and entrusted to the care of his angels neither fire, nor water, nor sword, can do him harm, except in so far as God their master is pleased to permit.[146]

Calvin also claims that the main reason behind Isaiah's Burden against Babylon is "to point out to the Jews how dear and valuable their salvation was in the sight of God, when they saw that he undertook their cause and

---

141. Ibid., 1:408.
142. Calvin, *Institutes*, I.17.10, 192.
143. Ibid., I.17.10, 193.
144. Ibid.
145. Ibid.
146. Ibid., I.17.11, 193.

revenged the injuries which had been done to them."[147] Calvin's main argument here is that "God takes a peculiar care of his own people, and gives his chief attention to them."[148] It is because of his providential care that he would stop at nothing, including first the chastisement of his own people, in order to bring about their deliverance. The goal of God's people has always been and continues to be a careful mindfulness of his salvific work,

> Whenever therefore we read these predictions, let us learn to apply them to our use. The Lord does not indeed, at the present day, foretell the precise nature of those events which shall befall kingdoms and nations; but yet the government of the world, which he undertook, is not abandoned by him. Whenever therefore we behold the destruction of cities, the calamities of nations, and the overturning of kingdoms, let us call those predictions to remembrance, that we may be humbled under God's chastisements, may learn to gather wisdom from the affliction of others, and may pray for an alleviation of our own grief.[149]

Yet one more time the echoes of Calvin's *Institutes* are heard. Calvin writes regarding the Christian attitude towards life in the light of this understanding of divine providence (I.17.6):

> The Christian, then, being most fully persuaded, that all things come to pass by the dispensation of God, and that nothing happens fortuitously, will always direct his eye to him as the principal cause of events, at the same time paying due regard to inferior causes in their own place.[150]

This proper attitude of confidence shatters any doubts that one's life is ever outside God's sovereign and protective care:

> He will have no doubt that a special providence is awake for his preservation, and will not suffer anything to happen that will not turn to his good and safety. But as its business is first with men and then with the other creatures, he will feel assured that the providence of God reigns over both. In regard to men, good as well as bad, he will acknowledge that their counsels, wishes, aims and faculties are so under his hand, that he has full power to turn them in whatever direction, and constrain them as often as he pleases. The fact that a special providence watches

---

147. Calvin, *Isaiah*, 1:408.
148. Ibid.
149. Ibid.
150. Calvin, *Institutes*, I.17.6, 188–89.

over the safety of believers, is attested by a vast number of the clearest promises.[151]

Ultimately the knowledge of divine providence guides God's people to sincere gratitude, knowing how deeply they are cared for by him:

> For the good and safety of his people, he overrules all the creatures, even the devil himself who, we see, durst not attempt any thing against Job without his permission and command. This knowledge is necessarily followed by gratitude in prosperity, patience in adversity, and incredible security for the time to come. Every thing, therefore, which turns out prosperous and according to his wish, the Christian will ascribe entirely to God, whether he has experienced his beneficence through the instrumentality of men, or been aided by inanimate creatures. For he will thus consider with himself: Certainly it was the Lord that disposed the minds of these people in my favour, attaching them to me so as to make them the instruments of his kindness. In an abundant harvest he will think that it is the Lord who listens to the heaven, that the heaven may listen to the earth, and the earth herself to her own offspring; in other cases, he will have no doubt that he owes all his prosperity to the divine blessing, and, admonished by so many circumstances, will feel it impossible to be ungrateful.[152]

As seen above, Calvin comes to Isaiah 14 with very different presuppositions and questions in mind than what we saw in Origen. As someone whose writer's desk is firmly planted in the local parish during the turbulent decades of sixteenth-century Reformation, Calvin is wrestling with theological and existential issues that are quite distinct. While as Origen, he too could claim the title of the "son of the Church," Calvin is interested in the questions of divine providence and God's protective and enduring care for his people. Hence, the questions that are in the forefront of his mind shape the focus of his exegesis of the of the משל of Isaiah 14 in general and verses 12–15 in particular.

---

151. Ibid., I.17.11, 189.
152. Ibid., I.17.7, 190.

Calvin's Paradigmatic Approach to the מָשָׁל of Isaiah 14

The following discussion focuses on Calvin's reading of the מָשָׁל of Isaiah 14. Understanding his paradigmatic approach to this text is vital for grasping the hermeneutical moves he makes when he comes to verses 12–15.

In the discussion of the opening verses of chapter 14 Calvin makes comments that give a distinct flavor of his reading of the text,

> Here, therefore, as in a picture, Babylon is contrasted with the Church of God; Babylon, I say, elevated to the highest power, which had plunged the Church into such a miserable and afflicted condition, that it was not probable that she could ever be raised up again.
>
> But the Lord casts down Babylon from her lofty situation, and thus testifies that he cares for his people, however mean and despicable they may be. It yields very great consolation to us to learn that the whole world is governed by God for our salvation. All things are directed to this object, that those whom he has elected may be saved, and may not be overwhelmed by any changes, however numerous, that shall befall them.[153]

Read in larger theological categories, this text is about the grand reversal of fortunes within divine providence. Babylon, who has made the life of God's people miserable, will be abased. The church of God despite her pitiful shape will be raised up again. That will be the Lord's doing on behalf of his people. This is a message of consolation. God's people are to learn that their God governs the whole world. He will bring salvation, so they are encouraged to not be overwhelmed by present turbulence, whatever it might be. All this clearly resonates with what we have seen emphasized both in Calvin's framing remarks regarding the Burden of Babylon in Isaiah 13–14 and in relevant passages from his *Institutes*.

Calvin's reflection on the meaning of the word מָשָׁל reveals further the kind of reading he is undertaking. Though without recourse to the lament form, he acknowledges the fact that its meaning goes beyond the literal sense of "witty saying" or "parable." Read in broader theological context, the מָשָׁל shows that "the ruin of Babylon will be so great that it will even become a *proverb*, which usually happens in great and astonishing events."[154] Hence, Calvin could be rightly seen a forerunner of modern paradigmatic readings of this text.

153. Calvin, *Isaiah*, 1:433–34.
154. Ibid., 1:437.

Reading the text theologically and paradigmatically does not mean Calvin reads it naively or uncritically. The larger philological issues that still dominate the modern commentaries on Isaiah are discussed here. For example, based on the related to the Aramaic דהב (gold) the *hapax legomenon* word מדהבה in verse 4, Calvin argues, "denotes covetousness and insatiable greediness for gold, to which the Babylonians were subject."[155] While the majority of modern scholarship has doubted this association, at least one modern scholar has still insisted that מדהבה could be a word for the heavy tribute that was imposed by the conqueror. Hence, Erlandsson has proposed the meaning of "golden tribute."[156]

Consistent with the paradigmatic reading of this text as the *proverb*, Calvin interprets verses 5–8 as a display of God's sovereign work in punishing evil. The much-hated tyrant is dead. The entire creation responds with joyful singing. Even the fir-trees and cedars join in the chorus of praise. The stunning reversal has taken place, "as tyranny overturns everything, so when tyranny is done away, everything appears to be restored to its original condition."[157] Calvin insists that these verses are driving home a theological point, "This reminds us that at length God will not spare tyrants, though he may wink at them for a time."[158] He argues that when the brutal tyrants fall, this does not happen "at random or through the blind violence of fortune" but rather as a result of the providence of God at work.[159] God is the one who breaks the staff of the wicked and the scepter of the rulers. In the way, Calvin provides his readers with a simple guide to reading their times,

> Now, the ungodly are amazed at such works, and remain bewildered, because they do not see the reason; but the godly know that this ought to be ascribed to God. Let us therefore learn to admire the works of God, and while we are amazed at them, let us acknowledge him to be the Author; and let us think that any of them ought to be lightly passed over, especially when he displays his power for redeeming his Church, when by his wonderful power he delivers each of us from the bondage of the devil, from the tyranny of Antichrist, from eternal death.[160]

As the scene shifts to Sheol in verses 9–11, Calvin insists that the Sheol imagery here ought be read in a way analogous to the reference of

---

155. Calvin, *Isaiah*, 1:438.
156. Erlandsson, *Burden*, 30–31.
157. Calvin, *Isaiah*, 1:439.
158. Ibid.
159. Calvin, *Isaiah*, 1:438.
160. Ibid., 1:439.

the fir-trees and the cedars rejoicing over the downfall of the tyrant in verse 8, "As he had formerly attributed gladness to the trees, so now, by a similar figure, he attributes speech to *the dead*."[161] In other words, while there is a change in textual scenery, the paradigmatic painting continues. What is interesting is that the language that Calvin uses to describe this imagery gives the reader an impression that he wants to go out of his way to underscore the fact that this is literary imagery. In Calvin's description, "Isaiah pretends" that the dead are astonished.[162] On another occasion, Calvin refers to this as "fictitious representation."[163] While it is true that the Sheol imagery in verses 9–11 is a powerful and evocative literary construal of the poet, this does not preclude the fact that behind this imagery stands the widely shared ANE conception of the afterlife. This view stands at odds with Calvin's own configuration of the afterlife as he tends to insist in his *Institutes* that it is the resurrection of the body that matters, not the disembodied bliss:

> Since Scripture uniformly enjoins us to look with expectation to the advent of Christ, and delays the crown of glory till that period, let us be contented with the limits divinely prescribed to us—viz. that the souls of the righteous, after their warfare is ended, obtain blessed rest where in joy they wait for the fruition of promised glory, and that thus the final result is suspended till Christ the Redeemer appear. There can be no doubt that the reprobate have the same doom as that which Jude assigns to the devils, they are "reserved in everlasting chains under darkness, unto the judgment of the great day" (Jude, ver. 6).[164]

Hence, we wonder if it is this juxtaposition of perspectives which leads to such heightened need to underscore the literary nature of the image.

Calvin does not want to be distracted from what is the main point behind this imagery of Sheol, "This doctrine ought to be carefully pondered; for though men be well aware of their condition, and have death before their eyes, yet overrun by ambition, and soothed by pleasures, and even fascinated by empty show, they forget themselves."[165] In the end, Calvin argues that in verses 9–11 "there is . . . exhibited to us a lively painting of the foolish confidence of men, who, intoxicated with their present enjoyment

---

161. Ibid., 1:440. Italics in the text.
162. Ibid.
163. Ibid.
164. Calvin, *Institutes*, III.25.6, 267.
165. Calvin, *Isaiah*, 1:441–42.

and prosperity, flatter themselves."¹⁶⁶ This foolishness awaits verses 12–15 to be unpacked fully.

The depiction of the internal world of the tyrant in verses 12–15 reveals "the pride of the Babylonian monarch, who, relying on his greatness, ventured to promise to himself uninterrupted success, as if he had the power of determining the events of his life."¹⁶⁷ In his campaign to ascend to heaven he brutalizes others along the way. In an interesting move, which will be discussed at length later, Calvin reads these verses not just with the church in mind but as a reference to the church under the assault of the tyrant. While referring to the tyrant's oppressive reign, Calvin states, "The tyrant, by assailing the church, which was God's holy heritage, might be said intentionally to attack God."¹⁶⁸ Thus, rather than describing a downfall of Satan as envisioned by Origen, Calvin argues for verses 12–15 being a paradigmatic picture of the fate that awaits any tyrant who assails the church. The references to the church of God here are not anachronistic. Rather they are consistent with Calvin's view that the Old Testament paints a picture of the church in its infancy. As Parker insists, for Calvin "the Old Testament is the book that recounts and describes the childhood and growing up of the Church."¹⁶⁹ Parker argues that for Calvin the link between Israel and the church comes via YHWH's covenant with Abraham, which Calvin envisions being a the movement when God calls his church into existence.¹⁷⁰ Thus Calvin reads the משל of Isaiah 14 as referring to the struggle of Israel as God's people who find themselves in bondage to Babylon. Having established that, with this theological truth of God's covenant undergirding his reading, Calvin moves seamlessly to the contemporary "us" as the church.

Reading verses 16–23, Calvin further reflects on the aftermath of the tyrant's death. On the one hand, Calvin stresses the fact that the tyrant of Babylon had turned the world into a wilderness, overthrowing the cities and refusing to release the prisoners, is very characteristic of the way tyrants operate, "They think that the only way to reign is to strike terror into all by inexorable cruelty."¹⁷¹ On the other hand, Calvin, again, underscores the fact that evil will not prevail. Isaiah imagines a crowd of onlookers, whether dead or living, gathering to see the tyrant's corpse. In Calvin's mind, in the astonishing downfall of the tyrant of Babylon, Isaiah seeks to show that "this

---

166. Ibid., 1:441.
167. Ibid., 1:442–43.
168. Ibid., 1:445.
169. Parker, *Commentaries*, 83.
170. Ibid., 84.
171. Calvin, *Isaiah*, 1:447.

change proceeds from the hand of God, who, by the slightest expression of his will, can overturn the whole world."[172] While at times God could use tyrants as his instrument of chastising his people for their sins, he does not let them go unpunished. For Calvin, "tyrants, with all their cruelty, are like clouds, which pour down a sudden shower of rain or hail, as if they would destroy everything, but are scattered in a moment."[173] In God's decisive intervention, the reign of terror always vanishes completely. The tyrants receive their just recompense,

> This happens to all tyrants, that though, while they live, they are universally applauded and flattered, yet after they are dead, they and their posterity are universally abhorred. It is therefore evident that they re detested by God, by angels, and by men.[174]

Calvin's Reading of Isaiah 14:12–15

Having given a sense of Calvin's overall reading of the משל of Isaiah 14 we are ready to focus on verses 12–15. As we mentioned above, Calvin reads these verses as a reference to the church of God under the attack from the enemies of God. In this section we will analyze Calvin's reading of these verses more closely as a way to highlight several key hermeneutical moves Calvin makes that show both how and why he arrives to such reading.

Calvin opens his discussion by referring back to the imagery of Sheol in verses 9–11: "Isaiah proceeds with the discourse which he had formerly begun as personating the dead."[175] Isaiah's discourse that began as "personating the dead" leads to the conclusion here that the tyrant is no different from others, though he sought "to lead men to believe that he was some god."[176] In other words, Calvin sees verses 12–15 as a continuation of the imaginative construal of Babylon's oppressive reign. In describing this tyrant with god-like pretensions, Isaiah "employs an elegant metaphor, by comparing him to *Lucifer*, and calls him the *Son of the Dawn*; and that on account of his splendor and brightness with which he shone above others."[177] In one brief statement Calvin overturns Origen's venerated reading of Isaiah 14:12–15 as a reference to the origin of evil:

172. Ibid.
173. Ibid.
174. Calvin, *Isaiah*, 1:451.
175. Ibid., 1:442.
176. Ibid.
177. Ibid.

> The exposition of this passage, which some have given, as if it referred to Satan, has arisen from ignorance; for the context plainly shows that these statements must be understood in reference to the king of the Babylonians. But when passages of Scripture are taken up at random, and no attention is paid to the context, we need not wonder that mistakes of this kind frequently arise. Yet it was an instance of very gross ignorance, to imagine that *Lucifer* was the king of devils, and that the Prophet gave him this name. But as these inventions have no probability whatever, let us pass by them as useless fables.[178]

It is notable that in his dismissal of this view Calvin does not take an opportunity to attack Origen or anyone else who might be representing this view. This could be due to the lack of awareness on Calvin's part as to where this view had originated or it could be that it had become so widely accepted and common place that ascribing it to just Origen would have been excessive.

Rather than a reference to transhistorical rationale for the origin of evil, Calvin insists on Isaiah 14:12-15 being a metaphorical description of aberrant human realities. The internal speech of the tyrant in verses 13-14 is, according to Calvin, Isaiah's way of displaying the king's folly in relying on his own greatness in quest for "uninterrupted success."[179] While seeing this being a reference to Nebuchadnezzar, Calvin is clear that Nebuchadnezzar stands for a bigger paradigmatic realities of human evil,

> In him there is exhibited to us a mirror of the madness of pride with which ungodly men are swelled, and which sometimes they even vomit out. Nor ought we only to behold here the person of a single tyrant, but the blasphemous rage of all the ungodly, who form their resolutions as if they could dispose of everything according to their pleasure; as their plans are also beautifully described by James, "We shall go into that city, we shall transact business, we shall make gain, though at the same time they know not what tomorrow shall bring" (James iv.13) They do not consider that they are in the hands of God, but believe that they will do everything by their own ability.[180]

Filling out the picture of the "madness of pride" that has swelled up this tyrant, Calvin discusses his desire to ascend into heaven (14:13). According to Calvin, "In these words, and those that immediately follow, the boasting is so absurd that it is impossible to believe that they proceed from the lips

---

178. Ibid., 1:442-43.
179. Ibid.
180. Ibid., 1:443.

of a mortal man."[181] Calvin's comment is peculiar in light of his dismissal of the readings of the early church fathers such as Origen and Tertullian. It is precisely such language that seems to describe transhistorical realities that led them to conclude that this was a reference to the downfall of Satan.

Calvin resolves this issue by describing this statement as absurd. Isaiah did not intend to give his readers the actual words of Nebuchadnezzar. He merely placed this outrageous claim on the lips of this paradigmatically construed ruler in order to display how preposterous this self-aggrandizing pride could be. Yet despite such madness of pride, Calvin, asserts, those who claim for themselves more than human nature, will meet their due punishment because "every one who goes beyond the limits of his calling provokes the wrath of God against himself by his rashness."[182] This leads Calvin to admonish his readers to accept the limits that God sets,

> Let every one therefore be satisfied with his lot, and learn not to aim at anything higher, but, on the contrary, to remain in his own rank in which God has placed him. If God stretch out his hand, and lift us up higher, we ought to go forward; but no one ought to take it on himself, or to strive for it from his own choice.[183]

A further sign of the tyrant's foolishness is his intent to "sit on the mountain of the testimony, on the sides of the north" in verse 13. According to Calvin this statement amounts to an absurd attempt to make oneself equal to God. He does not envision the tyrant thinking in terms of ancient Near Eastern mythopoetic categories. He understands this mountain as "the mountain of testimony," thus envisioning the king setting his heart on scaling Mount Zion. In order to arrive at this reading Calvin needs to make two interpretive moves, namely providing a warrant for Zion being the mountain on the sides of the north and supplying linguistic grounds for rendering the word מועד in the phrase הר־מועד as having a meaning of covenant. Both of these moves will be discussed at length below. What is important for Calvin is that Zion is the place of God's dwelling among his people. By attacking Zion, the tyrant attacks God himself,

> Though he reasoned, after the manner of men, that he could obtain a victory over the Jews, yet, reckoning as nothing the assistance of God, by whom he had often heard that they were

181. Ibid.
182. Ibid.
183. Ibid.

protected, it was as if he had endeavored to destroy the very heavens.[184]

Closely related to the tyrant's attempt to assault Zion is his desire to ascend above the heights of the clouds in verse 14. Calvin's paradigmatic reading of this phrase sees this, once again, as a hardly believable ambition on the part of a daring human being who wishes to make himself equal with God. Calvin is amazed, "This thought could scarcely enter into the mind of a man without making him absolutely shudder."[185] What makes this statement so preposterous, Calvin argues, is that

> [t]here is a seed of religion implanted in us by nature, so we are constrained, even against our will, to entertain the belief of some superior being who excels all things; and no man is so mad as to wish to cast down God from his throne; for we are instructed by nature that we ought to worship and adore God.[186]

At this point Calvin shows his awareness that thinking in these categories could be problematic in reference to the Babylonian king. Because the gentiles are ignorant of God, "it may be thought improbable that the king of Babylon wished to drive out God, and to reign in heaven."[187] What is interesting is that while we might see this as Calvin's reading of the text in Yahwistic categories, he see it as Isaiah thinking of the king of Babylon in theological and closely related ethical categories. Thus, Calvin handles this possible objection in the theological framework:

> The Prophet does not accuse him falsely. Though the ungodly do not believe that they ought to reign instead of God, yet, when they exalt themselves more than is proper, they take away a portion of what belongs to him, and claim it for themselves, which is the same as if they wished to pull him down from his throne. And what did Satan say when he deceived our first parent? *Ye shall be as gods.* (Genesis iii.5.) Consequently, all who dare to ascribe more to themselves than God allows are chargeable with exalting themselves against God, as if they declared war against him; for where pride is, contempt of God must be there.[188]

The absurdity of the tyrant's desire to assault Mount Zion and take the place of God fully comes to fore in Calvin's concluding comments regarding

184. Ibid., 1:444.
185. Ibid.
186. Ibid., 1:445.
187. Ibid.
188. Ibid.

verses 13 and 14. To grasp Calvin's thoughts it is important to remember that in Calvin's writings there exists a close nexus of Zion/Jerusalem and the church. While this linkage will be further analyzed below, it is worth noting that in light of this nexus of Zion/Jerusalem and the church, it is understandable that Calvin would read Isaiah 14:12–15 in reference to the assault against the church. The tyrant's desire to scale Zion and take the place of God, for Calvin, are to be read in the context of threats against the church of God, "[The tyrant] is not accused of exalting himself above angels, but of endeavouring to crush the Church of God."[189] Calvin argues that the church is God's "holy heritage," hence anyone attempting to attack her "might be said intentionally to attack God."[190] Since the worship of God is not now confined to Zion alone, but rather is spreading across the world, these words now equally apply to any tyrant in any place who will try to oppress the godly. Any tyrant who attacks the church must understand that "he attacks not men, but God himself, who at length will not endure to be insulted."[191] On the basis of these observations Calvin is able to issue the memorable words of pastoral consolation for the church,

> Let us therefore know that we are under the protection of God in such a manner, that any one who gives us trouble will also have God for his enemy. *He that hurteth you, says he, hurteth the apple of mine eye.* (Zech. ii.8.) He likewise testifies that he *dwells in the midst of the Church*, (Ps. xlvi.5,) so that no one can attack the Church without receiving the first strokes; and therefore he will avenge the injuries which the Church endures, though he may permit her to be afflicted for a time.[192]

Before shifting the lens again in verse 16, Calvin pauses to reflect on the tragic downfall of the king expressed in the phrase "but thou shalt be brought down to the grave." Calvin highlights the reversal inherent in the play on the word "sides,"

> He had formerly said that the king of Babylon wished to be carried up *to Mount Zion, to the sides of the north*, because that was a very lofty situation, and widely seen. He now uses the word *sides* in an opposite sense, as if he had said that he would have an abode in the most contemptible part of a sepulcher, as when one is thrust into a mean and despicable corner. In a wide and large sepulcher they place the dead bodies of honorable men in

189. Ibid.
190. Ibid.
191. Ibid.
192. Ibid., 1:445–46.

the middle; but the Prophet means that he will be thrown into a corner, or into the outer edges.[193]

Such is the end of any tyrant who will rise up to oppress the church of God. The power of God is both swift and decisive in bringing complete end of any threat against his holy treasure.

Calvin's Key Hermeneutical Moves in Reading Isaiah 14:12–15

In our discussion of Calvin's reading of Isaiah 14:12–15 we briefly pointed out few places where he makes definitive hermeneutical moves that give shape to his reading. In this section we will highlight these three key hermeneutical moves in Calvin's reading of Isaiah 14:12–15 as a reference to the church of God under the attack by the enemies of God.

First, what is envisaged here by Isaiah, according to Calvin, is not a reference to a transhistorical rationale for the origin of evil, but an archetypal depiction of human hubris. Crucial for Calvin is his understanding of the identity of the tyrant and the way this figure functions in Isaiah's depiction of the paradigmatic picture of the evil threatening God's people. While identifying the tyrant of Babylon as Nebuchadnezzar, Calvin is aware of the fact that some of the details of the משל do not correspond to what actually happen to this ruler at his death. While reflecting on the difference between the honor that dead kings typically receive and the debasement of the tyrant's corpse in verse 18, Calvin writes, "This passage is the reason why I do not venture to limit, what Isaiah here foretells about the king of Babylon, to the person of Nebuchadnezzar alone; because it does not appear from history that he was denied burial."[194]

It is possible that this uncertainty led Calvin to change his mind regarding the identity of this tyrant several years later. Calvin's commentary on Isaiah was first published in 1551. His commentary on Acts which followed a year later still sees this as a reference to Nebuchadnezzar in his notes on Acts 12:23. Reflecting on Herod Agrippa's death, Calvin comments that he died because he failed to give glory to God. This failure, in Calvin's mind, is analogous to the fate of Nebuchadnezzar in Isaiah 14,

> We do not read that the king of Babylon was thus extolled; and yet the prophet upbraideth to him that he went about to make himself equal with God, (Isaiah xiv.13, 14.) Therefore this

---

193. Ibid., 1:446.
194. Ibid., 1:447–48.

sacrilege is a common fault in all proud men, because, by taking to themselves more than they ought, they darken the glory of God; and so, like giants, so much as ever they are able, they endeavor to pluck God out of his seat. Howsoever, they do not usurp the title of God, neither openly boast with their mouth that they are gods; yet because they take to themselves that which is proper to God, they desire to be, and to be accounted gods, having brought him under, furthermore, the prophet pointeth out the beginning of this evil in one word, when he bringeth in Nebuchadnezzar speaking on this wise, "I will go up," (Isaiah xiv. 13.)[195]

By 1557 there appears a change in perspective. In his comments on Psalm 48:2, while discussing Zion being on the side of the north, Calvin notes,

> We find the prophet Isaiah, with the view also of touching upon the excellence of this mountain, applying to it the very expression which is here employed. In the 14th chapter of his Prophecies, at the 13th verse, he represents Sennacherib as speaking thus:"I will ascend into heaven, I will exalt my throne above the stars of God: I will sit also upon the mount of the congregation, in the sides of the north."[196]

In the interesting turn of events, Calvin edited his Isaiah commentary and republished it in 1559. That edition, which has serves as a basis of English translations of Calvin's commentary, still attributes this text to Nebuchadnezzar. In the introduction dedicating the new addition to Queen Elizabeth I, Calvin claims that he has "bestowed so much care and industry" to producing it that "it ought justly to be reckoned a new work."[197] In light of Calvin's comments, it is possible to think that he once again changed his mind going back to his original thought of Isaiah 14 having Nebuchadnezzar as its historical referent. Yet a simpler explanation could also be possible. Steinmetz expresses the majority opinion that Calvin overstated the case of thorough revision. According to Stenmetz, the changes in 1559 edition of Calvin's commentary on Isaiah were most likely far less sweeping and were "more matters of style than of substance."[198] Hence, it is probable that the reference to Nebuchadnezzar in the 1559 edition is merely a result of cursory editing rather than an indication of changed perspective.

195. Calvin, *Acts of the Apostles*, 1:494.
196. Calvin, *Psalms*, 2:219.
197. Calvin, *Isaiah*, 1:xv.
198. Steinmetz, "John Calvin on Isaiah 6," 160.

What is interesting to note is that Calvin handles the fact of incongruence of textual details with Nebuchadnezzar's actual life by taking Isaiah's references to Nebuchadnezzar paradigmatically. For example, at one point he explains these discrepancies due to the fact that Isaiah "describes, not a single man, but a whole dynasty."[199] More broadly, Calvin seems to extend that picture even wider and go beyond the dynastic description to see in this tyrant of Babylon a "mirror of the madness of pride."[200] In other words, according to Calvin, Isaiah invites us to see not just one tyrant at one point of history, but rather a posture characteristic of all of throughout history who have chosen a path of self-sufficiency. It is a archetypal picture of "the blasphemous rage of all the ungodly."[201] While Origen would turn to this text with thoughts of where the creaturely exercise of the free will tragically leads, Calvin sees here the folly of human rejecting of God's sovereign rule and insisting on constructing the world according to "their own ability."[202] Yet this does not appear to be an existential possibility, as according to Calvin, whether they like it or not, "they are in the hands of God."[203]

It is also interesting to note that Calvin sees here a paradigmatic reference to Nebuchadnezzar, the sixth-century-BC Babylonian ruler, made by the prophet Isaiah who lived in the eighth century BC. While contemporary biblical scholarship has been uneasy about associating a long range prophecy with the Old Testament prophets, Calvin has no problems with attributing to Isaiah a predictive prophecy that foresees someone c. 150 years down the road of history.

Second, the sweeping aggrandizing language on the lips of the tyrant is not a reference to a primordial angelic aspirations to usurp the throne of God, but rather an evocative picture of the swelling human pride. The tyrant's desire to ascend into heavens in verse 13 invites these comments of Calvin, "In these words, and those that immediately follow, the boasting is so absurd that it is impossible to believe that they proceed from the lips of a mortal man."[204] Furthermore, the tyrant's desire to ascend above the heights of the clouds in verse 14 evokes a similar comment, "It might certainly be thought strange that the Prophet thus access the Babylonian monarch, as if he wished to make himself equal to God, since, as we have said, this thought could scarcely enter into the mind of a man without making him absolutely

---

199. Calvin, *Isaiah*, 1:448.
200. Ibid., 1:443.
201. Ibid.
202. Ibid.
203. Ibid.
204. Ibid.

shudder."²⁰⁵ As we pointed out, it is here that Origen and Calvin part ways. They both see these words as problematic when spoken by human beings, but, guided by their particular set of presuppositions and questions, they come to different interpretive solutions. For Origen this is a sign of transhistorical realities of the origin of evil, while for Calvin this is a picture of the gravity of human pride.

Third, the madness of human pride does not strive to ascend some mythical location but rather Mount Zion. As noted above, in order to arrive at this reading Calvin needs to make two interpretive moves. As his first move, Calvin faces a challenge of explaining how a mountain which is "on the sides of the north" could refer to Zion which geographically was located on the south side of Jerusalem. He turns to Psalm 48:2 for support of his argument, "For Mount Zion he uses the expression the sides of the north, according to the description, Mount Zion, on the sides of the north, the city of the great King (Ps. xlviii 2)."²⁰⁶ Interestingly, this move appears to be the opposite of what commentators do today. Most scholars today would take ירכתי צפון to be a reference to one of the great mountains in the north such as Zaphon or Olympus, which had significant mythological associations of being the abode of gods. Hence they would move from the mythopoetic language of Isaiah 14:13 describing the tyrant's ascent to the mythical mountain to Psalm 48:2 as a metaphorical rendering of Zion, rather than Zaphon or Olympus being on the sides of the north as highlighting the mountain's theological significance. Calvin goes the other way around. He turns to Psalm 48 and having found there a reference to Zion being on the sides of the north, he assumes that Isaiah 14 must be referring to it as well.

Furthermore, Calvin knows that linguistically the word מועד in the phrase הר־מועד signifies both an "assembly" and an "appointed day." But he chooses to refer to it as a "covenant." His rationale is as follows, "Here I prefer to view it as a *Covenant*; for the Lord, speaking by Moses, calls the tabernacle מועד, (*mōgnēd,*) [sic] and says, *I will meet with you there.* (Exodus 25:21, 22, 29:42.)."²⁰⁷ What is crucial for Calvin is that the place that the tyrant is after is the place of God's dwelling, "Let us not think, therefore, that it means an assembly of men, as when irreligious persons assemble to their fairs or festivals, but that the Lord intended to give a token of his presence, and there to ratify his covenant."²⁰⁸

205. Ibid., 1:444.
206. Ibid.
207. Ibid.
208. Ibid.

The significance of reading here a reference to Zion is further amplified by Calvin's close nexus of Zion/Jerusalem and the church. For example, while commenting on Psalm 87, Calvin identifies the words of the psalmist in verse 5, "And it shall be said of Zion, Man and man is born in her" as a promise that "new citizens shall be gathered into the Church of God from different parts of the world."[209] Furthermore, when the psalmist writes in verse 6, "The Lord will recount, when he written the peoples" Calvin sees this as an "effectual calling of God" which counts his people as "the citizens of Zion."[210]

The great Zion song, Psalm 48, which according to Calvin, "celebrate[s] some notable deliverance of the city of Jerusalem at a time when many kings had conspired to destroy it" is a prime example of this close linking of Zion and the church.[211] Opening three verses clearly speak of Zion, "the mountain of [God's] holiness." Jerusalem is YHWH's city built on Zion. Thus, Zion is seen as "the city of the great King." The psalmist describes it as "beautiful for situation" and "the joy of the whole earth."

Verses 4–7, which are our primary focus here, describe the assembling of the kings who gather together to assault and destroy Jerusalem. Calvin is uncertain of which historical occasion this threat refers to. Whether a reference to Sennacherib's attack (2 Kgs 19:35; Isa 37:36) or to the king of Ethiopia (2 Chr 14:9), Calvin insists that the psalmist here seeks to inform the reader that, "The Jews found from manifest experience that God was the guardian and protector of the holy city, when he opposed himself to the invincible power of their enemies."[212] That which is a clear reference of the foreign powers assault on Jerusalem, Calvin sees as talking about the church, "By these words [Isaiah] intimates that they had confederated and conspired together to destroy the Church."[213] Hence the lesson that the readers of this Psalm are to draw is very resonant with the words of Calvin's admonition to the readers of the משל of Isaiah 14,

> If in our day the Church is assailed by powerful adversaries, and has to sustain dreadful assaults; for it has been God's usual way from the beginning thus to humble his own people, in order to give more irrefragable and striking proofs of his wonderful power. At the same time, let us remember that a nod alone on the part of God is sufficient to deliver us; and that, although

209. Calvin, *Psalms*, 3:140.
210. Ibid.
211. Ibid., 2:216.
212. Ibid., 222.
213. Ibid.

our enemies may be ready to fall upon us on every side to overwhelm us, it is in his power, whenever he pleases, to strike them with amazement of spirit, and thus to make their hearts fail in a moment in the very midst of their efforts against us. Let this reflection serve as a bridle to keep our minds from being drawn away, to look in all directions for human aid.[214]

Summary

By the way of summary we can let Calvin himself speak one more time,

> For as the aged, or those whose sight is defective, when any book, however fair, is set before them, though they perceive that there is something written, are scarcely able to make out two consecutive words, but, when aided by glasses, begin to read distinctly, so Scripture, gathering together the impressions of Deity, which, till then, lay confused in our minds, dissipates the darkness, and shows us the true God clearly. God therefore bestows a gift of singular value, when, for the instruction of the Church, he employs not dumb teachers merely, but opens his own sacred mouth; when he not only proclaims that some God must be worshipped, but at the same time declares that He is the God to whom worship is due; when he not only teaches his elect to have respect to God, but manifests himself as the God to whom this respect should be paid.[215]

This evocative imagery of scriptures as glasses sums up what is at stake in Calvin's approach to the Bible. His pastoral aim was to sharpen the believers' view of God so that the church could accurately ascribe God his due worship. When he comes to Isaiah 14:12-15 Calvin is driven to overturn the centuries-old traditional reading of the downfall of Satan not as a hermeneutical maverick in search of novel things to say, but as a faithful interpreter of the text. His aim is to bring the theological affirmation of the Providence of God to bear on the maddeningly unpredictable realities of human life. The tyrants rise up to the stunning heights on the piles of groaning victims of their atrocities. Yet evil does not have the final say, God does. As God's "holy treasure" the church could remain confident that any threat directed at her will ultimately fail. In the blink of an eye, God will bring about a stunning reversal of fortunes, toppling the tyrants down to the far recesses of the

---

214. Ibid., 223.
215. Calvin, *Institutes*, I.6.1, 64-65.

grave. It is this theological truth of God's providential care that stands at the heart of Isaiah 14:12–15 which Calvin seeks to drive home.

Origen and Calvin: A Comparison

Comparing Origen and Calvin presents an interesting challenge, as Origen was labeled by the Reformers as a prime example of the sorts of hermeneutical excesses that they labored hard to correct. Allegorical readings, which Origen was well-known for, were held suspect as aiding in discovery of hidden meanings that had no connection to the plain sense of the text. As Luther would comment in his lectures on Genesis, "Ever since I began to adhere to the historical meaning, I myself have always had a strong dislike for allegories and did not make use of them unless the text itself indicated them or the interpretation could be drawn from the New Testament."[216] Origen became a prime target of what Luther abhorred in allegorical reading with the readings he strongly disapproved being labeled as "senseless allegories after the manner of Origen."[217]

The continuity of Calvin with the earlier Reformers' suspicion of Origen's interpretive moves is most notably evident in his commentary on Galatians. In his discussion of Galatians 4 dealing with Paul's treatment of the Old Testament passage regarding Hagar and Sarah, we encounter Calvin's bitter disagreement with Origen. Commenting on verse 22, Calvin writes,

> Origen, and many others along with him, have seized this occasion of twisting Scripture this way and that, away from the genuine sense *(a genuino sensu)*. For they inferred that the literal sense is too meagre and poor and that beneath the bark of the letter there lie deeper mysteries which cannot be extracted but by hammering out allegories. And this they did without difficulty, for the world always has and always will prefer speculations which seem ingenious, to solid doctrine. With such approbation the license increased more and more, so that he who played this game of allegorizing Scripture not only was suffered to pass unpunished but even obtained the highest applause. For many centuries no man was thought clever who lacked the cunning and daring to transfigure with subtlety the sacred Word of God. This was undoubtedly a trick of Satan to impair the authority

---

216. Luther, *Luther's Works*, 1:232–33.
217. Ibid., 1:122.

of Scripture and remove any true advantage out of the reading of it. God avenged this profanation with a just judgment when He suffered the pure meaning to be buried under false glosses.[218]

His primary critique of Origen is related to his perceived insistence that scripture has multiple meanings. Calvin is ready to embrace the complexity of scripture: "I acknowledge that Scripture is the most rich and inexhaustible fount of all wisdom."[219] Yet he is unwilling to follow what he deems to be the excess of allegorists: "I deny that its fertility consists in the various meanings which anyone may fasten to it at his pleasure."[220] Hence, it would appear that these two interpreters are miles apart not just chronologically but also hermeneutically. Yet a closer look might reveal that they have more in common than it would seem at the first sight.

Before we venture into making comments about the hermeneutical moves made by Origen and Calvin, it is worth noting the similarity of contexts in which they both write in. By his own admission, Origen sought to stand in the center of the church's life and have the church define his identity and theological thought (*Homily on Luke* 16: Luke 2:33–34),

> As for myself, my wish is to be truly a man of the Church, to be called by the name of Christ and not that of any heresiarch, to have this name which is blessed all over the earth; I desire to be, and to be called, a Christian, in my works as in my thoughts.[221]

Similar words could be true of Calvin as well. In his *Institutes* Calvin insists that "to those to whom [God] is a Father, the Church must also be a mother."[222] Thus, Calvin envisions the church as the tender mother "into whose bosom God is pleased to collect his children, not only that by her aid and ministry they may be nourished so long as they are babes and children, but may also be guided by her maternal care until they grow up to manhood, and, finally, attain to the perfection of faith."[223] The degree to which Calvin was nurtured by the church could be seen in his return to this imagery of the church as the loving Mother (IV.1.4),

> Let us learn, from her single title of Mother, how useful, nay, how necessary the knowledge of her is, since there is no other means of entering into life unless she conceive us in the womb

218. Calvin, *Galatians*, 84.
219. Ibid.
220. Ibid.
221. Origen, *Homilies on Luke:*, 66.
222. Calvin, *Institutes*, IV.1.1, 281.
223. Ibid.

and give us birth, unless she nourish us at her breasts, and, in short, keep us under her charge and government, until, divested of mortal flesh, we become like the angels (Matth. xxii.30). For our weakness does not permit us to leave the school until we have spent our whole lives as scholars. Moreover, beyond the pale of the Church no forgiveness of sins, no salvation, can be hoped for, as Isaiah and Joel testify (Isa. xxxvii.32; Joel ii.32).[224]

If our discourse above is correct, then both Origen and Calvin should be perceived as two faithful sons of the church albeit separated by the gap of time. What then makes their readings of Isaiah 14 so different from one another?

Neither Origen nor Calvin come to Isaiah 14 as disinterested exegetes. They both have a particular interest that leads them to this text. In other words, while being faithful sons of the church, they come to Isaiah 14 shaped by the different questions that are on the forefront of the church's mind. Origen's is a period of the struggle against the gnostic influences in the church which raise questions of the origin of evil. On the heels of Tertullian's discussion of Ezekiel 28, Origen comes to Isaiah 14 and in light of the ambiguity of larger-than-human language of self-aggrandizement on the lips of the tyrant of Babylon in verses 13-14 he sees a picture of the downfall of Satan.

Calvin, on the other hand, comes to this text during the age of anxiety that characterizes sixteenth-century Europe. According to Bouwsma, Calvin was very sensitive to the anxiety that was characteristic of his time, thus in his work both as a pastor in Geneva and as a theologian of the church he sought "to soothe a peculiarly anxious generation."[225] Calvin's remedy for the human anxiety was God's providential care for the church. Hence, when he comes to read Isaiah 14, his focus is radically different from that of Origen. He is not looking for an explanation of the origin of evil, he is interested in elevating the impact of the human evil intentionality that marks human existence in general and plagues his anxious generation in particular. In the swift and decisive termination of the tyrant's far-reaching oppressive reign, Calvin finds comfort for the church. This tragic reversal of fortunes that moves the tyrant of Babylon from the extremes of lofty heights to the despicable depth is an opportunity for Calvin to reaffirm his larger theological formulations with undoubtedly pastoral intent:

> The Lord from on high laughs at the pride of the ungodly, so that, when they shall have swallowed up everything by their

---

224. Ibid., IV.1.4, 284.
225. Bouwsma, *Portrait*, 32.

covetousness, and shall have burst through the clouds and heaven itself by their effrontery, he will at length expose them to the mockery of all, after having, in the twinkling of an eye, overturned their schemes.[226]

Hence, we would venture to suggest that the difference in Origen's and Calvin's readings of Isaiah 14 stems not primarily from their hermeneutics but their *theological presuppositions*. Our analysis above sought to demonstrate how significant was the emphasis on creaturely free will for Origen. He envisioned all creatures as endowed with free will. Holiness was not an essential quality but rather a derivative one—a result of one's choices and decisions. Matter was not created evil contrary to some gnostic teachings. He explicitly denies any link between matter and evil (*Contra Celsum* iv. 66-67), "But in our view it is not true that *the matter which dwells among mortals* is responsible for evils. Each person's mind is responsible for the evil which exists in him, and this is what evil is. Evils are the actions which result from it."[227] Evil was not caused by God, it's origin was a result of a prehistorical accident, to borrow Forsythe's phrase. In a fitting description Crouzel has memorably referred to Origen as "theologian *par excellence* of free will."[228]

Calvin's theological presuppositions are radically different as could be seen in his argument against the Stoics about the necessity of perpetual chain of causes contained in nature,

> We hold that God is the disposer and ruler of all things—that from the remotest eternity, according to his own wisdom, he decreed what he was to do, and now by his power executes what he decreed. Hence we maintain, that by his providence, not heaven and earth and inanimate creatures only, but also the counsels and wills of men are so governed as to move exactly in the course which he has destined.[229]

While Origen's mind dwelled on the fact that God endowed creatures with a capacity to choose, Calvin sees the world differently. In his mind, "men do nothing save at the secret instigation of God, and do not discuss and deliberate on any thing but what he has previously decreed with himself and brings to pass by his secret direction."[230] Hence Calvin insists that, "for

---

226. Calvin, *Isaiah*, 446.
227. Origen, *Contra*, 237.
228. Crouzel, *Origen*, 195.
229. Calvin, *Institutes*, I.16.8, 179.
230. Ibid., I.18.1, 199.

the man who honestly and soberly reflects on these things, there can be no doubt that the will of God is the chief and principal cause of all thing."[231]

Summary

It is apparent that Calvin, in line with other Reformers, was harsh towards Origen. The Reformers' dislike of allegorical reading has led to Origen becoming a proverbial easy target representing those who "without any restraint played all sorts of games with the sacred Word of God, as if they were tossing a ball to and fro."[232] Yet our analysis suggests that in Origen Calvin could in certain ways find a kindred spirit. They shared their firm commitment to the church as the fitting context for their work and thought. Rather than a haphazard mangling of the Word of God, Origen's exegesis was primarily driven by the desire to nourish the church, the desire very much resonant with Calvin's pastoral heart. When Origen and Calvin read Isaiah 14:12–15 they do come to different conclusions, but the variance, we would argue, is not in the vastly different set of hermeneutical tools or degree of proficiency in using them, but rather is a result of diverse set of theological presuppositions that guide their varying theological and existential interests.

---

231. Calvin, *Eternal Predestination*, 177.
232. Calvin, *2 Corinthians and Timothy, Titus & Philemon*, 43.

Reading Isaiah 14:3–23 as Christian Scripture Today

HAVING LOOKED AT TWO classical theological interpreters in the previous chapter, we are now going to begin our discussion of reading Isaiah 14:3–24 as Christian scripture today with a focus on two prolific contemporary Old Testament scholars who have written voluminously on the book of Isaiah, namely Walter Brueggemann and Christopher Seitz. It is our hope that in our dialogue with them we could make some modest proposals for reading the משל of Isaiah 14 as Christian scripture today.

Two Memorable Contemporary Readings of Isaiah 14:3–23 as Christian Scripture

Walter Brueggemann and Christopher Seitz represent some of the finest in the Old Testament scholarship, whose work is firmly situated in the context of the twenty-first-century church and whose writings have had a significant impact on the way the Bible has been read in that context as Christian scripture. The choice of these two interpreters is not arbitrary. While there are a number of fine commentaries written on Isaiah from confessedly Christian position, in our estimation, Brueggemann and Seitz represent a new wave of possibly fruitful approaches in the midst of the paradigmatic change highlighted by Rendtorff two decades ago. Even though Isaiah 14 does not figure prominently in their larger body of work on Isaiah, Brueggemann and Seitz have written commentaries on this book; hence their handling of this text could be both scholarly interesting and theologically engaging for those who seek to read Isaiah as Christian scripture.

Some might consider our choice of Seitz as less straightforward than Brueggemann. It is a well known fact that Seitz's work carries forward the canonical approach of Brevard Childs. While the choice of Childs alongside of Brueggemann would have been a more natural alternative, Childs' analysis of Isaiah 14 in his commentary of the book of Isaiah is rather concise.

Two pages devoted to Isaiah 14:4b–23 display a brilliant mind that has a thorough grasp on pertinent literature and is able to sum it all up in succinct and readable fashion. His brief but pointed comments on this passage focus on the *exegetical significance* of Isaiah 14:4–23 as preparing the reader for two oracles that follow, namely 14:24–27 and 14:28–31, that address Assyria and the Philistines and the *theological significance* of this text as pointing to "the selfsame reality of arrogance, which God's kingship is in the process of destroying and will in the end fully succeed as victorious."[1] This brevity, which is partly due to the limitations of a one-volume commentary, results in the unfortunate lack of detailed analysis that would display the force of Childs' canonical approach to reading this text as Christian scripture.[2] Yet, despite the brevity of Childs' own engagement with Isaiah 14, his approach overall has much to offer and Seitz is one of the most rigorous practitioners of Childs' canonical programme.

Walter Brueggemann

O'Brien has given one of the most generous endorsements of Brueggemann's work,

> A prolific writer and speaker, Walter Brueggemann perhaps comes the closest to anyone that Christian Old Testament scholarship might call a "celebrity." No other contemporary Old Testament scholar has written and worked more directly for the sake of the church or influenced more strongly the way that academics, pastors, and church leaders think about the Old Testament.[3]

Besides the lighthearted affirmation of Brueggemann's celebrity status, O'Brien has rightly emphasized the context of his writings as standing

---

1. Childs, *Isaiah*, 127.

2. This type of criticism is not new. R. W. L. Moberly, while building on and sharpening Childs' approach, has raised similar concerns, "In his recent works Childs has so concentrated on analyzing and engaging with the scholarly debates that he has failed to produce convincing and memorable exegesis and interpretation of the biblical text." See Moberly, "Theology of the Old Testament," 469. Similarly, Williamson decries that in reading Childs' commentary, "what we are left with is an extended example of the kind of material that normally features in the introductory paragraphs to each section of a standard commentary, a program for a commentary in which even the section headed "exposition" is more introductory than fully exegetical or expository." (Williamson, "Review of *Isaiah: A Commentary*," 121–24). For another balanced review of Childs' commentary on Isaiah see also Reimer, "Overwhelmed by Theology?" 51–54.

3. O'Brien, *Challenging Prophetic Metaphor*, 22.

on the border of the academic and ecclesial worlds, consciously seeking to calibrate his writings for the benefit of the church at large and with the person in the pew in mind. Thus, in this section we will provide an overview of Brueggemann's scholarly self-understanding and hermeneutical approach—an approach that could be characterized as reading the Jewish scripture as a Christian interpreter.

A. *Context of Brueggemann's Work*

Brueggemann's recent volumes have been self-revealing in regards to the formative influences on his life and scholarship. By his own admission, as a son of a Lutheran pastor, Brueggemann grew up in "an all-containing church culture of the old Evangelical and Reformed Church."[4] Several aspects of this peculiar context are worth highlighting. First, Brueggemann's was a church open to historical-critical study. He writes, "For the most part there were no battles in my church about historical criticism and literalism, and no theological 'tests' were imposed or contested."[5] Furthermore, the openness to the findings of historical-critical study was combined with the passion for social justice. Brueggemann talks with admiration about his father's commitment to "neighborly questions of justice."[6] Finally, Brueggemann claims that his childhood church was deeply shaped by the pietism that eschewed both the orthodox dogmatism of Missouri Synod Lutheranism and the rationalism of certain circles of German Lutheranism. He describes the Evangelical and Reformed church of his upbringing in almost idyllic terms, "That church, for which Frederick Schleiermacher was the formative theologian, was grounded in pietism that committed to an innocent, simple trust in Jesus of the Gospels without needing to settle all the theological issues implied in the affirmation of Jesus."[7]

As Brueggemann reflects on his life-long career as a biblical scholar he consciously identifies himself as a "church scholar."[8] While Brueggemann's work is carried out in the academic setting, he is very careful to point out that his reading of biblical texts is necessarily resonant with reading it in the setting of the church. This is evident in his emphasis on his reading to be spirit-led.[9] Brueggemann defines the spirit as "God's forceful, generative

---

4. Brueggemann, *Pathway*, xii.
5. Ibid.
6. Ibid., xiii.
7. Ibid.
8. Brueggemann and Sharp, *Countertestimony*, 72.
9. The use of the lower case "spirit" is puzzling. It is a clear choice of wording on

presence that repeatedly blows settled reality beyond itself, including the settled reality of the text."[10] Crucial for Brueggemann's understanding of the spirit-led reading is the notion that the text is spirit-inhabited. This idea is found in many places in his writings, most notably in his *Introduction to the Old Testament*,

> [I]n the text of Scripture we have something more and something other than the outcome of human imagination and human fidelity, which we signal by the term inspiration that is, the church takes Scripture as a gift of God and God's self-disclosure, even if humanly mediated.[11]

The spirit-led reading is informed by the insights of historical criticism and confessional dimensions, but ultimately the spirit-led reading takes place when "interpreter gives herself over to the text."[12] What does Brueggemann have in mind? In his *Testimony to Otherwise*, Brueggemann defines the spirit-led reading as a daring act of imaginative construal.[13] He is careful to point out that in his use of the language of imagination he does not imply a subjective and arbitrary use of an individual's imaginative capacities. Rather, it means "to let the Bible, its words and its claims, make contact with the life-and-death issues of our own time and place, contact not originally intended in the text, and contact that is not obvious or visible except by daring act of reconstrual."[14]

There appears to be real resonance between Brueggemann's approach and premodern approaches, as represented, for example, by Steinmetz' analysis of Luther's hermeneutic. According to Steinmetz, Luther understood the interpretation of scripture to be a God-dependent activity,

> Scripture is a gift of God to the Church, a gift which never resides simply in the Church's power. The prophets never stand at our beck and call and are not obliged to render up their secrets to the first doctor of divinity who schedules a series of university lectures on them. Luther has no intention of denigrating the role of theological learning, but learning has its limits. Scripture

---

Brueggemann's part—a choice that, to my knowledge, is not explained here or anywhere else in the text.

10. Brueggemann, *Pathway*, 26.
11. Brueggemann, *Introduction to the Old Testament*, 397.
12. Brueggemann, *Pathway*, 27.
13. Brueggemann, *Testimony*, 42.
14. Ibid.

imposes its own meaning. It is the Bible and not our learned exegesis which binds the soul to God.[15]

If God is the driving force of scripture interpretation, then it calls for a certain posture from the interpreter. While Brueggemann refers to that as the interpreter giving herself over to the text, Luther speaks of humility. Steinmetz sums up Luther's thought memorably,

> Exegesis is not merely an intellectual activity at which innate cleverness gives one an advantage over the slower-witted (though it is that, too). To interpret the Bible and interpret it correctly one must meet certain conditions which the text imposes on its interpreters. These preconditions are moral and spiritual as well as intellectual. What Luther has particularly in mind is humility. Humility opens the mind to God just as pride dulls the sharpest intellect and keeps it from the truth.[16]

One can detect a significant continuity with traditional approaches in Brueggemann's notion of spirit-led reading, even if nuanced and recast into a slightly different vocabulary.

In the end, it is interesting to note how this context shapes the way Brueggemann understands and evaluates his own scholarship,

> I don't think I want to take back anything about the main trajectory of my work, but I could have thought more or listened to more people or other people, or given better nuance to a lot of things. I suspect I am so much a child of the Church that I didn't push beyond that. I do think that the people who are extraordinarily skeptical and angry with the tradition are also children of the Church. They're just wounded children of the Church and I have not been wounded much by the Church. So I understand myself fairly well in context, and that's how it comes out.[17]

Moving beyond the ecclesial context of Brueggemann's work, we must also mention two formative academic influences dating back to the 1970s, namely the Critical Theory of the Frankfurt School and the writings of Paul Ricoeur.

At the core of the Critical Theory lies a critique of ideology. Marxist thought insists that a society is prone to developing a system of ideas and beliefs that masks the real workings of societal transactions which are always tilted to benefit those in control of political and economic power.

---

15. Steinmetz, *Luther and Staupitz*, 51.
16. Ibid.
17. Brueggemann and Sharp, *Countertestimony*, 96–97.

According to Geuss, the Critical Theory of the Frankfurt school "aim[s] at emancipation and enlightenment, at making agents aware of hidden coercion, thereby freeing them from that coercion and putting them in a position to determine where their true interest[s] lie."[18] Exposure to the Critical Theory convinced Brueggemann of "the capacity of theological interpretation to raise questions about social reality that were characteristically muted in conventional historical criticism."[19] This conviction would later be further reinforced by Brueggemann's interaction with Gottwald's volume, *The Tribes of Yahweh*, which highlighted "the sociological intentionality of the early traditions of Israel with reference to its ideological angle."[20]

Roughly at the same time Brueggemann encountered Ricoeur's *Freud and Philosophy*. The initial draw of Ricoeur for Brueggemann was in Ricoeur's identification of a "hermeneutic of suspicion" and a "hermeneutic of retrieval."[21] Here Brueggemann refers to two hermeneutical moves found in Ricoeur. Ricoeur's own summary is instructive,

> Hermeneutics seems to me to be animated by this double motivation: willingness to suspect, willingness to listen; vow of rigor, vow of obedience. In our time we have not finished doing away with idols and we have barely begun to listen to symbols.[22]

One can hear resonances of Ricoeur's thought on a hermeneutic of suspicion with the Critical Theory,

> [Hermeneutic of Suspicion] begins by doubting whether there is an object and whether this object could be the place of transformation of intentionality into kerygma, manifestation, proclamation. This hermeneutics is not an explication of the object, but a tearing off of masks, an interpretation that reduces disguises.[23]

Yet, for Ricoeur the hermeneutic of suspicion is not the final word. This is where he goes further with the hermeneutic of retrieval or recollection,

> The contrary of suspicion, I will say bluntly, is faith. What faith? No longer, to be sure, the first faith of the simple soul, but rather the second faith of one who has engaged in hermeneutics, faith that has undergone criticism, post critical faith.... It is a

---

18. Geuss, *Critical Theory*, 55.
19. Brueggemann, *Pathway*, xx.
20. Ibid., xxi.
21. Ibid., xx.
22. Ricoeur, *Freud*, 27.
23. Ibid., 30.

rational faith, for it interprets; but it is faith because it seeks, through interpretation of a second naïveté.²⁴

Thiselton has insightfully elaborated on what is at stake in each of these two moves of Ricoeur's hermeneutical theory,

> The first addresses the task of "doing away with idols," namely, becoming critically aware of when we project our own wishes and constructs into texts, so that they no longer address us from beyond ourselves as "other." The second concerns the need to listen in openness to symbol and to narrative and thereby to allow creative events to occur "in front of" the text, and to have their effect on us.²⁵

The magnitude of Ricoeur's influence on Brueggemann becomes clear when he writes,

> Eventually it became clear to me that Ricoeur's "second naïveté" is exactly the point of the work that I am able to do. By that phrase Ricoeur refers to readiness to take the Bible seriously as Scripture—as authoritative revelation—after one has abandoned a first simplistic naiveté and after one has seriously engaged criticism and pushed it as far as one can go. "Second naiveté" comes along with a full awareness of the epistemological crisis caused for faith by Enlightenment rationality. It does not invite a refusal to think critically, nor does it offer an option of being dishonest about the facts on the ground. It recognizes that in the midst of such rationality, there is nonetheless a "surplus" that cannot be vetoed by critical thought, but that continues to be generative when the text is heard in a kind of truthful innocence.²⁶

It is interesting to note the way Brueggemann was able to incorporate these formative influences of Critical Theory and Ricoeur's writings into his context as a church scholar. He writes, "It has slowly dawned on me that biblical exposition cannot be, in the context of the church, a scientific enterprise designed to recover the past as historical criticism has attempted; it is an artistic preoccupation that is designed to generate alternative futures."²⁷

The awareness of Ricoeur's hermeneutic of suspicion and Critical Theory's emphasis on "hidden coercion" leads to Brueggemann's formulating

---

24. Ibid., 28.
25. Thiselton, *New Horizons in Hermeneutics*, 26.
26. Brueggemann, *Pathway*, xx.
27. Ibid.

the notion of texts as means of "intentional advocacy."[28] Both in ancient times and today, the world is perceived through generated plausibility structures that interpret reality in specific ways. Brueggemann argues that whether it was the hub of royal imperial power or tribal oligarchy, the dominant life-world was always managed by those in control of social power via construction of narrative memory. Great temple liturgies were summoned to endorse this symbolic world and allowed people to place themselves in this carefully constructed script of reality.[29]

According to Brueggemann, when seen in this socially crafted matrix, texts are not innocent. Reading texts is an exercise in immersion into a certain type of reality that each given text advocates. Brueggemann insists that the dominant narrative engineered by socioeconomic, political, and military elites presses on and cajoles its hearers into submission by propagating deeply rooted and vividly enacted myths. Thus, Brueggemann sees texts as susceptible to becoming a vehicle by which those at the center are able to legitimize and maintain control over social power.

Here lies one of the controversial aspects of Brueggemann's program as his use of the hermeneutic of suspicion seems to fail to acknowledge how various types of texts fit into this sweeping paradigm, namely texts from the margins of society or poetic and lyrical texts. Moberly has also noted the indiscriminate appeal to a hermeneutic of suspicion in Brueggemann's writings, "It is vital that an appropriately (self-)critical hermeneutic of suspicion should not become indiscriminating and facilely brand all concern for structural, and sometimes hierarchical, order as intrinsically oppressive of the poor and marginalized. The biblical and historical Christian construal of institutional order as mandated by God, with power as a means of *service*, needs to be kept in view."[30] While acknowledging that Brueggemann could be correct in identifying the ways reading biblical texts has masked coercive use of power in certain contexts of the contemporary church, Moberly nonetheless insists that "it remains a gross travesty to tar all classic and ecclesial Christian theology with the brush of its abuse. One must always insist that abuse does not remove right use, and that the answer to poor use of Christian theology must be good use, not its caricature and abandonment."[31] In other words, a more cautious and nuanced application of a hermeneutic of suspicion is perhaps called for if Brueggemann's appropriation of Ricoeur's

---

28. Ibid., 2–3.
29. Ibid., 2.
30. Moberly, "Theology," 474.
31. Ibid., 476.

hermeneutic of suspicion in his notion of texts as means of intentional advocacy is to have a lasting impact.

While Ricoeur's hermeneutic of suspicion leads Brueggemann to formulate the notion of texts' intentional advocacy, Ricoeur's concept of hermeneutic of retrieval finds itself recalibrated as the task of redescribing the world. Brueggemann writes, "I propose that what we are doing in Scripture study, reading, and hearing is that we are *redescribing the world*, that is, constructing it alternatively."[32] At the core of Brueggemann's proposal is an assumption that the world is not what we are told it is. This is an invitation to see the world in a different light, to read the data at hand according to a different scale, to connect the dots of life against a different contextual map. Brueggemann writes,

> Every time the church takes up Scripture, it undertakes a serious challenge to dominant characterizations of our social world. It dares to propose an alternative reading of the world, an alternative version that is in fact a sub-version that rests beneath the dominant version in a less aggressive mode. That alternative reading of reality—alternative version, "sub" version—by its very nature, intends to subvert dominant readings of reality.[33]

This redescription, according to Brueggemann, entails three aspects. First, "Scripture intends to call things by their right names."[34] In other words, the Bible invites honest and passionate truth-telling about the world we inhabit. Second, "Scripture sees worldly data within a very different frame of reference; as a result the data is interpreted differently."[35] The reading of scripture invites us to connect the dots of reality in accordance to a different matrix than the paradigms of profit margins, military threat, or stock market volatility. Third, "the Bible redescribes the world by reference to YHWH, the key character in the history of the world and the creator of heaven and earth to whom all creatures owe glad, doxological obedience."[36]

It is perhaps peculiar that coming to read the Old Testament as a Christian interpreter, Brueggemann insists on the Jewishness of God. While we will return to this issue again when considering Brueggemann's reading of Isaiah 14, it is worth noting here the criticisms of Barr and Kaminsky. Barr's discussion of Brueggemann' *Old Testament Theology* raises questions about his "anxiously apologetic" tone when it comes to the Christian reading of

32. Brueggemann, *Pathway*, 4.
33. Ibid.
34. Ibid.
35. Ibid., 5.
36. Ibid.

the Jewish texts of the Old Testament.[37] Barr notes Brueggemann's desire to distance himself from "Christian supersessionism." He finds Brueggemann's use of this phrase confusing and ill-defined. It raises many questions, "What really can Christians claim? What exactly have they to stop thinking? If Christians abandon 'supersessionism', what view of their relation to the Hebrew Bible are they to adopt?"[38] If one follows Brueggemann's prescription of avoiding crowding the Old Testament into a confessional corner, "what *can* a Christian reading achieve?"[39] The answer, in Barr's view, is not very clear. Furthermore, Brueggemann's attempts to distance himself from Christian supersessionism leads him to affirm that Jews and Christians are co-believers. Barr is not convinced that is a feasible option, "This may be a good idea for Christians; but I am not sure that Jews *want* to be 'co-believers' with Christians."[40] One example of this could be the Jewish reticence about Brueggemann's handling of the biblical notion of justice. Kaminsky addresses this in his review of Brueggemann's *Old Testament Theology*,

> The proclivity to miss the particularistic bent of Israel's understanding of justice permits Brueggemann too quickly to universalize Israel's theological ideas and the historical experiences in which they are grounded. Thus Brueggemann's extrapolation of God's concern with the downtrodden leads him to assert that the biblical God "is a God who characteristically enacts exoduses, and who does so in many places, perhaps everywhere" (p. 178). His major evidence for a theological shift from reading God as initiator of Israel's exodus to God as "a restless agent of social newness" (p. 179) flows from his reading of a single verse, Amos 9:7. He claims that this verse shows that "the Exodus memory is left intact for Israel's affirmation, but the exclusiveness between Israel as an Exodus people and YHWH as an Exodus God is broken" (p. 178). Aside from placing an immense theological weight upon one verse, Brueggemann's reading doesn't acknowledge texts like Genesis 16 in which God commands Hagar to return to her abusive situation or Psalm 2 that speaks of the Davidic monarch ruling over all the nations of the world.[41]

It is interesting to hear Kaminsky's caution as well,

---

37. Barr, *Concept*, 549.
38. Ibid.
39. Ibid. Italics original to Barr.
40. Ibid., 550. Italics original to Barr.
41. Kaminsky, "Theology of the Old Testament," 3.

Although one is thankful that Christian scholars are finally taking account of Jewish interpretive techniques, it is important not to oversimplify Jewish biblical interpretation, nor to idealize Judaism and the Jewish people. Although being idealized is preferable to being demonized, it is better to be understood and respected.[42]

Hence, Brueggemann's insistence on the Jewishness of God as a Christian interpreter appears to be in need of further calibration.

One final note regarding the context of Brueggeman's work is his characteristic instance on a post-foundational reading of biblical texts. While not fully committed to the term *postmodern*, Brueggemann feels most at home in a post-liberal context. He is honest about the fact that he is a product of his times. Though precipitated by Karl Barth's work in the early twentieth century, it was in the 1970s that biblical scholarship saw the corrosion of the old liberal consensus in biblical studies, a corrosion that challenged scholarly confidence in their ability to reconstruct the past. The crisis of historical-critical certainty in biblical studies in the 1970s was closely linked with shifts in Western culture away from dominant categories of the objective and universal. Brueggemann credits this turn of affairs to events like the Vietnam War, Watergate, assassinations of Kennedy and Martin Luther King Jr, and student protest demonstrations in Paris in 1968. He writes, "The new skepticism about old consensus assumptions within the field of Old Testament studies, coupled with the new subversion that occurred externally and broadly in culture, combined to create a readiness for new ventures in interpretation."[43] The time was ripe for the post-liberal shift. Shaped by these larger realities Brueggemann is drawn to the adjective *post-foundational* when describing an interpretation of biblical texts. Post-foundational interpretation "recognizes that there is no governing certitude in interpretation, no ultimate 'final solution' to the text, because it is a living text that testifies to the living God."[44] In this context, faithfulness in interpretation entails being open-ended, refusing closure, and being ready to be "surprised by familiar texts."[45]

Levenson has wondered whether despite of all his rhetoric Brueggemann is truly a postmodern pluralist.[46] Brueggemann has insisted that "the

---

42. Brueggemann, "Theology," 5.
43. Brueggemann, "The Re-emergence of Scripture," 157–58.
44. Ibid.
45. Brueggemann, *Pathway*, 26.
46. Levenson, "Pluralist?" 265–94.

church has no interpretive monopoly on the Old Testament."[47] Hence, he has been a stout voice urging the church that "it must recognize the legitimacy of other interpretive communities, of whom the primary and principal one is the Jewish community."[48] While this appears to be a welcome move, Levenson is unsure what grounds Brueggemann has to make the following emphatic statement, "What Jews and Christians share is much more extensive, much more important, much more definitional than what divides us."[49] According to Levenson, this appears to be an odd attempt where "the differences between the two must be minimized in the pursuit of the common denominator."[50] As far as Levenson is concerned, Brueggemann has found "the Olympian perch from which both traditions are surveyed"[51]—the position hard to reconcile with truly postmodern pluralism. It is worth noting that Levenson does not deny the validity of Jewish-Christian dialogue and learning from one another. He writes, "Whatever the validity of Jewish, Christian, and historical-critical models of reading, and whatever the degree and the value of the overlap among them, at their deepest levels they are irreducibly different."[52] To Levenson, a true pluralist accepts and attends to these differences and "does not seek to minimize or dissipate diversity by appeal to commonalities, real or imagined."[53] There are thus perhaps open questions about the nature of Brueggemann's post-liberalism.

In summary, Brueggemann comes to read Isaiah 14 as a consciously self-aware Christian interpreter, one who has been nurtured in the ecclesial setting his entire life. Yet he also encounters this biblical text having been sharpened by two formative influences of the Critical Theory of the Frankfurt School and the writings of Paul Ricoeur which have nuanced and calibrated his critical awareness in such a way as to make him reticent of any possible dogmatic or coercive moves in interpretation especially when carried out in the post-foundational context. Yet as salutary as these influences might be, questions still linger regarding his use of a hermeneutic of suspicion as well as his insistence on the Jewishness of God.

47. Brueggemann, *Testimony, Dispute, Advocacy*, 733.
48. Ibid.
49. Ibid., 108.
50. Levenson, "Pluralist?" 271.
51. Ibid.
52. Ibid., 294.
53. Ibid.

B. Brueggemann's Approach to Reading the Book of Isaiah

"The book of Isaiah is like a mighty oratorio whereby Israel sings its story of faith."[54] With this opening statement Brueggemann frames his approach to reading the book of Isaiah. He insists that just like any other oratorio, the book of Isaiah "conveys its primary themes with great authority, so that they persist through the vagaries of many imaginative interpretations."[55] According to Brueggemann, the primary theme of this book is "the predominant and constant character of YHWH, who looms over the telling in holy sovereignty and in the faithful gentleness of a comforting nursemaid."[56] He is the "inscrutable Character"[57] whose story is told in the pages of the book of Isaiah.

According to Brueggemann, what we find in the book of Isaiah is not a product of the journalistic reportage that documents an unbiased account of events in history, rather it is a product of the intersection of history and theology. Brueggemann names that place of intersection *prophecy* which he defines as a *"redescription* of the public process of history through which the purposes of Yahweh are given in human utterance."[58]

As a Christian interpreter Brueggemann is careful not to ignore the "concrete particularity of the text."[59] The focal point of this book's account is the fate of Jerusalem. Brueggemann insists that the Isaianic oratorio is about the suffering and destiny of Jerusalem.[60] Having established that fact, he points out that we as Western Christian readers are not situated in Jerusalem, thus "we read only at a distance."[61] For Brueggemann, this is a distance that results in a respect of Jewish readings and a curbing of some hermeneutical habits that permit Christians to hijack this text. He writes, "It is legitimate to see how the book of Isaiah fed, nurtured, and evoked Christian imagination with reference to Jesus. But that is very different from any claim that the book of Isaiah predicts or specifically anticipates Jesus."[62]

On the other hand, we are not staring at some sort of a neo-Lessingian ugly broad ditch (*der garstige breite Graben*)[63] of history. We can and should

54. Brueggemann, *Isaiah*, 1.
55. Ibid.
56. Ibid.
57. Ibid.
58. Ibid., 2.
59. Ibid., 7.
60. Ibid., 2.
61. Ibid.
62. Ibid., 6.
63. Lessing, "Über den Beweis des Geistes und der Kraft," 140.

read *through* the concrete historical particularity. Brueggemann asserts, "Believing people (Jews and Christians) . . . dare to imagine that the same Holy One who acted in that time and place in disruptive and embracing ways still continues to disrupt and embrace even now."[64] The text remains relevant because our time and place are as much of an arena of YHWH's action as that time and place. Brueggemann claims that what gives this book its evocative power today is its theological frame that offers a "large rereading of historical reality that is strikingly pertinent to the current condition of Western culture."[65]

c. A Brief Survey of Brueggemann's Treatments of Isaiah 14:3–23

Brueggemann writes voluminously and in varieties of contexts. His treatments of the biblical texts range from scholarly monographs to sermon collections. Reading through Brueggemann's corpus, one gets a sense that certain theological themes and social concerns are significant for him, both as a scholar and as a Christian. A similar thing could be said of certain biblical texts that Brueggemann turns to in his writings. While the book of Isaiah as a whole features prominently in his writings, Isaiah 14:3–23 gets only limited attention.[66] It is worth noting that the Oracle against Assyria which follows this text in Isaiah 14:24–27 is referred to relatively often in Brueggemann's work.[67] To the best of my knowledge, Brueggemann's commentary is the only place that contains a sustained analysis of Isaiah 14:3–23, so we will focus our discussion there, while bringing in some of his summary thoughts from other places where appropriate.

---

64. Brueggemann, *Isaiah*, 7.

65. Ibid., 6.

66. Brueggemann, *Introduction*, 196; Brueggemann, *Isaiah 1–39*, 125–33; Brueggemann, *Out of Babylon*, 88; Brueggemann, *Testimony, Dispute, Advocacy*, 511, 519.

67. Brueggemann, *Interpretation and Obedience*, 89, 319; Brueggemann, *Isaiah 1–39*, 133–35; Brueggemann, *Old Testament Theology: An Introduction*, 251; Brueggemann, *Old Testament Theology: Essays on Structure, Theme, and Text*, 257; Brueggemann, *Out of Babylon*, 78; Brueggemann, *Peace*, 116; Brueggemann, *Theology of the Old Testament*, 355–56; Brueggemann, *The Creative Word: Canon as a Model for Biblical Education*, 61;

D. *Brueggemann's Framing Comments Regarding the Oracle against Babylon in Isaiah 13–14*

Brueggemann titles the section dealing with Oracles Against Nations in Isaiah 13–23 as "Yahweh's Rule in World Perspective."[68] He argues that while Isaiah 1–12 had the destiny of Judah and Jerusalem as its focus, the recurring emphasis on Assyria had signaled that "the larger horizon of this prophetic tradition is international in scope."[69] In other words, the destiny of Judah and Jerusalem could not be understood in a vacuum but as closely linked with ever-present geopolitical realities. Hence, the main thrust of Isaiah 13–23 is succinctly summed up by Brueggemann, "The primary theme of these chapters is the nonnegotiable, demanding, insistent rule of Yahweh before which every power must submit."[70] According to Brueggemann, this divine sovereignty over nations is displayed in this section by the pronouncements of "punishment, suffering, and nullification for the several nation-states that are characteristically seen as opposed to the rule of Yahweh."[71] While the nature of their opposition to YHWH is not always very clear, Brueggemann groups them under three larger categories of autonomy, self-sufficiency, and hubris.[72] Thus, whatever particular historical realities gave rise to each of these oracles, Brueggemann argues, that they have been recontextualized to fit their present canonical setting, "It is evident that in the canonical shaping of the book of Isaiah, these oracles now function *in the book of Isaiah* in order to advance the general theme of Yahweh's sovereignty."[73]

In Brueggemann's mind, the sustained emphasis on the global role of YHWH cuts across Isaiah 1–12 and Isaiah 13–23. This emphasis could explain Brueggemann's lack of focused attention to the shift from Assyria to Babylon between these two sections of Isaiah. Only an intentional search for the explanation across the whole section of this commentary yields a complete picture. Brueggemann's comments on Isaiah 13–23 merely mention the oracle against Babylon in the list of other oracles in the collection. The rationale for the inclusion of the oracle against Babylon is that Babylon is seen as "the leading superpower on the horizon of the book of Isaiah (13:1—14:23)"[74] while Assyria is envisioned as "the older and representa-

---

68. Bruggemann, *Isaiah*, 112.
69. Ibid.
70. Ibid.
71. Ibid.
72. Ibid.
73. Ibid., 113. The emphasis is original to Brueggemann.
74. Ibid.

tive superpower (14:24–27)."⁷⁵ Once we turn to Brueggemann's opening comments on Isaiah 13:1–22, we find a further rationale for the placement of the Oracle against Babylon at the head of the collection as the key geopolitical threat to Judah in the sixth century, "It is no doubt crucial that among these threats the first to be singled out is Babylon, the dominant superpower in the sixth century and surely the pivotal feature in the geopolitical landscape of the book of Isaiah."⁷⁶ Finally, buried in the middle of Brueggemann's discussion on Isaiah 13:17–22a is his understanding of Babylon's paradigmatic function,

> Babylon is not to be taken too literally but functions as a figure for any and every geopolitical power that runs against the intention of Yahweh. Whatever may have been the historical locus and interest of the poem in its primary utterance, there is no doubt that the poem in its canonical place can function in this . . . way, as a model concerning every challenge to the power of Yahweh. Thus again we attend to the historical realism of the book of Isaiah but then accept a rereading as a legitimate reading of a canonical text.⁷⁷

E. Brueggemann's Reading of the מָשָׁל of Isaiah 14:3–23

Brueggemann titles the section of his commentary that deals with Isaiah 14:3–23, "Welcome to Death!"⁷⁸ The wording is not accidental. It seeks to capture the extreme language of the text that paints a picture of the downfall of the cosmic tyrant in a way that makes YHWH's verdict on Babylon "emotively available to the listening community of staggered, hope-filled Jews."⁷⁹

Verses 3–4a frame the anti-Babylonian poem as a mocking poem that according to Brueggemann "may be simply an emotional catharsis of pent-up feelings and an act of vengeance,"⁸⁰ yet there might be much more. That more, Brueggemann postulates, would be Israel's "vocal way of claiming God-given freedom."⁸¹ The language of "hard labor" and "rest" prompts Brueggemann to flag echoes of traditional Old Testament themes. God's people will one day experience the release from the oppressive regime that

75. Ibid.
76. Ibid., 115.
77. Ibid., 121.
78. Ibid., 125.
79. Ibid.
80. Ibid.
81. Ibid.

will echo the Exodus narrative and there may also be a "slight reference" to the Flood narrative (cf. Gen 5:29).[82]

The announcement of the tyrant's downfall in verses 4b–7a is presented, according to Brueggemann, in a way that makes it resonant with the Hebrew notion of the Sabbath rest,

> The double use of the word "cease" in verse 4b is *shabbat* (=sabbath). There is now a complete "cessation" of tyrannical power, a cessation like Israel stopping work on the sabbath. The Babylonian way of power in the world is now completely nullified and eliminated. The "sabbath" of such abuse is caused by the Lord of the sabbath, who is powerful, relentless, and determined to prevail. This Yahweh is angry at the unspeakable violation of Yahweh's own purpose; and so "with blows," that is, assault that will not stop, the empire is terminated.[83]

In linking the downfall of the tyrant with the Sabbath rest Brueggemann makes an interesting interpretive move that is worth pausing to ponder. The text itself does not carry the noun שַׁבָּת (Sabbath), but rather a verb שָׁבַת (to cease, rest), even though Brueggemann writes as though it were a noun. While linguistically there still remains some ambiguity whether the noun is primary or derivative of the verb, it is worth pointing out that of the seventy one uses of the verb שָׁבַת, the Sabbath context is only limited to a portion of its use in the Qal stem, appearing only in thirteen of twenty-seven cases.[84] Thus, the Sabbath resonance might be possible, but it is certainly not required in the Isaiah 14 context. Brueggemann, who comes to the text open to deeper theological resonances, encounters the root שבת and develops it in a way that while less than straightforward is theologically evocative. According to him, this is not just a repose for God's people but rather a cosmic rest that the entire creation gets to participate in and enjoy. In a statement reflective of his characteristic social-critical awareness, Brueggemann asserts YHWH's sovereign control in bringing this global denouement about, "In a world governed by Yahweh, nobody is free to practice exploitative brutality, but the tyrant always learns that too late."[85]

Brueggemann describes what goes on in these opening verses as a "rhetorical trick."[86] While the text looks like a lament over the dead tyrant, it is in reality something else. "What purports to be a statement of grief is

82. Ibid.
83. Ibid., 126.
84. "שָׁבַת," n.p. *TWOT*.
85. Brueggemann, *Isaiah*, 126.
86. Ibid.

in fact an utterance of celebrative gloating."⁸⁷ Brueggemann's definition of the משל as a "rhetorical trick" which amounts to "celebrative gloating" is, as discussed above in chapter 1, not the only way of understanding the משל and it emphasizes only one of the possible dimensions of this multifaceted and complex term which in our analysis is more than an ancient script for jeering over a dead enemy but rather an imaginative scenario that invites its readers into thoughtful and creative engagement in life before God.

The dismantling of the regime renders the tyrant irrelevant. His spiraling down into powerlessness is documented in verses 7b–11. Two things are noteworthy. First, Brueggemann reads the language of the lush forests of Lebanon joining Israel's delight as the reversal of the destructive impact of the oppressive regime on the ecological systems. "As Israel is free, so the trees are safe!"⁸⁸ While one might suspect a degree of anachronistic over-reading of the environmental sensitivities of our own age cropping up here, it is still worth taking note of it as an example of what a contemporary Christian interpreter notices in the ancient Hebrew text. Second, it is interesting to note that when Brueggemann's rhetoric matches the text's own rhetoric, his comments are both instructive and evocative. This is clear in his description of the arrival of the toppled-down tyrant in Sheol. Brueggemann colorfully describes Sheol as "the dark netherworld where discarded people are housed who no longer have power for life."⁸⁹ It is not a place of punishment but rather a storehouse "where the dead are kept in their impotence."⁹⁰ The tyrant is presented as "completely broken and irrelevant, warranting no attention at all."⁹¹ The certain finality of the downfall is captured memorably by Brueggemann, "Everything treasured by the oppressor is now lost; his fate is mean, messy, and humiliating."⁹²

Verses 12–20a reflect on the stunning reversal of fortunes that takes place in the case of this tyrant. Brueggemann offers a sustained reflection on the "inscrutable turns in public power."⁹³ He pays close attention to what he refers to as the "exotic rhetoric" of this section.⁹⁴ He points out that the section opens in verse 12 with the phrase "how," which he identifies as a term for a lament. Brueggemann then goes on to highlight the

87. Ibid.
88. Ibid., 127.
89. Ibid., 128.
90. Ibid.
91. Ibid.
92. Ibid.
93. Ibid., 131.
94. Ibid., 129.

rhetorical function of this framing of verses as a lament, "It is as though one is invited to grief."[95] He acknowledges that there could be a reason for genuine lament, "One can grieve, imagining the illusion that produced such self-deception and disappointment."[96] Yet, he goes on to highlight that the rhetoric of this text intends for the grief to be "only a staged ploy."[97] Instead of true mourning the introductory note of lament "turns to exuberance. In the world of the poet, the rule of good has withstood the threat. The world is safe, and we are delivered!"[98]

Conventional approaches to discussing verses 12–15 focus on the ancient Near Eastern background and mythopoetic parallels. The extent of Brueggemann's flagging of this time-honored way of entering into these verses, is limited to the phrase "Day Star, son of Dawn," which Brueggemann argues, "surely appeals to older elemental myths about primordial ambition and pride."[99] The alternative to the appeal to the "old myths," Brueggemann insists, would be to consider "the imagery of the movie *Star Wars* and the imaginative tale of cosmic, intergalactic conflict between the powers of good and evil."[100] Brueggemann's appeal to the imagery and ethos of a *Star Wars* movie seeks to highlight a paradigmatic picture of the oppressive use of power. "Here is the quintessential evil one, the cosmic brutalizer of the innocent who wants to usurp the throne room of the good."[101]

Brueggemann carefully guides his readers through the text's portrayal of the tyrant's internal world stressing the details of "self-promoting imagination" expressed in five shameless "I" statements in verse 14.[102] In a move reflective of his sensitivity to the sociopolitical realities, Brueggemann links the tyrant's internal world with his exercise of power,

> All these assertions have to do with self-exaltation and self-elevation, all engineered by the "I." Of course, the oppressor (perhaps) does not say such things out loud, but only by acts of policy. The "I" of arrogance asserts autonomy, drives out Yahweh, and denies submission to Yahweh. That is what oppressive power in public policy is about.[103]

95. Ibid.
96. Ibid.
97. Ibid.
98. Ibid.
99. Ibid.
100. Ibid.
101. Ibid.
102. Ibid., 130.
103. Ibid.

In an interesting interpretive move Brueggemann reads verses 15–20a as a part of YHWH's verdict, "The arrogant speech of elevation (vv. 13–14) is countered by a disjunctive 'But you.' Now the 'you' of the oppressor is drawn into the world of Yahweh's magisterial utterance and is therefore no longer autonomous."[104] It is a way to underscore that "such arrogant agents are not in fact autonomous, are not free for exploitative policy, and cannot in the end occupy the throne room of heaven, for Yahweh is already there and takes up all the space."[105] The inscrutable character of YHWH finds its expression in this mind-boggling fact. The uttered verdict of YHWH is sufficient to curb the tyrant's autonomy and curtail his abusive use of power. Brueggemann rounds out his discussion by drawing a parallel with a similar fate dealt out to the failed king Jehoiachim by Jeremiah (22:18–19). All this points to one overarching thought affirmed across the biblical corpus, "The Bible knows that brutal power cannot last and regularly ends in humiliation."[106]

With verses 20b–21, Brueggemann's camera shifts. Readers are invited to see beyond the humiliated ruler to the distant future. Verses 20b–21 assure the reader that there is no room for the resurgence of this cosmic violence. Brueggemann asserts, "For every Nebuchadrezzar, there is a neo-Nebuchadrezzar."[107] The order to prepare for the slaughter of the tyrant's sons is seen by Brueggemann as a necessary preventive measure against the future brutality. The sweep must be complete if the peace is going to be lasting.

The section closes with the final words of YHWH. In verses 22–23 YHWH's utterance of judgment underscores the true ultimate agency of the tyrant's downfall. Like a chess player free to move around the board, YHWH replaces Babylon with a hedgehog with no remnant left behind. "It is Yahweh, not a human agent, who finally acts to eliminate oppression for the world of Judaism."[108] Once again Brueggemann highlights YHWH's supremacy in the chaotic realm of political unpredictability. YHWH reigns. That is bad news for tyrants, but good news for the oppressed.

---

104. Ibid.
105. Ibid.
106. Ibid., 132.
107. Ibid.
108. Ibid., 133.

F. *Evaluation of Brueggemann's Reading of the* משל *of Isaiah 14:3-23*

Christian readers can readily and appreciatively follow Brueggemann's lead in reading Isaiah 14:3-23 as a portrayal of YHWH's victory over a cosmic tyrant. The picture of God who reigns supreme in the midst of the chaotic and at times maddening realities of the cosmos has deep resonances in Christian faith (e.g., Matt 28:18-20; Luke 17:20-21; Rev 21:1-4). Brueggemann's reading of the משל of Isaiah 14:3-23 displays the strength of his characteristic emphases that are worth highlighting here.

First, Brueggemann's insistence on taking biblical texts with imaginative seriousness enables him to navigate the complex poetic terrain laden with mythopoetic elements in such a way that makes it fully available for reader's existential engagement. One prime example of that would be the way he handles Isaiah 14:12-20,

> The reversal happens in the historical process, and one can, of course, identify "historical" reasons and agents for the fall of an abusive superpower. In the horizon of the biblical text, however, the reversal is not sociopolitical; it is rhetorical. The poem is something of a "performative utterance" whereby each time the poem is recited, the oppressed community of the faithful can witness again to the fall and can again celebrate and claim its new God-given freedom. Or in the hearing of the poem, the presently oppressed can engage in anticipation of a reversal, even if it has not yet begun in visible, sociopolitical terms.[109]

While throughout his commentary Brueggemann displays a keen awareness of pertinent historical-critical issues, his reading the text with imaginative seriousness enables him to keep it from a mere exercise in digging up ancient literary artifacts. Though the text itself addresses Judah in the wake of the downfall of a Babylonian tyrant, Brueggemann's imaginative reading seeks to make this text available for those who are far from experiencing such joyful repose from the oppressive reign—the move that gives his reading such enduring worth that positions his commentary as a valuable resource for the church worldwide.

Furthermore, Brueggemann's sensitivity to the issues of power and social dimensions related to its appropriation and distribution makes his reading especially resonant in our own world. His reflection on the arrival of the dead tyrant to Sheol (14:7b-11) is very characteristic of Brueggemann's reading of the text with deep sociopolitical awareness,

---

109. Ibid., 129.

> Whereas the rhetorical dismantling in all its harshness may have been aimed at Babylon, in canonical form the onslaught means to school the imagination of the community of faith. It intends to provide a world in which abusive power is seen to be flimsy and precarious, and sure to pass. So Judah relishes the poetry in its endless counter power and continues to cling to this horizon of Yahweh's governance, especially in the face of oppressors who always seem strong to perpetuity. They are not to perpetuity! They are fated to Sheol. The reception committee of impotence is already gathering to greet the next oppressor.[110]

In Brueggemann's reading, the world is not a random collection of circumstances where anyone is free to grab power and use it at will, rather one is presented with the world shot through with evidence of YHWH's governance even if at times such evidence is rather slim. Brueggemann's reading invites all those who are currently facing such unjust exercise of power by both validating their feelings that such abuse is evil and holding out a promise that the oppressive regime no matter how long or brutal does not have a final word.

As evocative and imaginatively engaging as Brueggemann's reading is, it is this characteristic emphasis on the Jewishness of God that makes it somewhat unclear as to how to enter into this text as Christian scripture. Those who come to this text as Christian scripture might wonder what difference does it make to hear Isaiah 14 in the light of traditional Christian understanding of God, not simply as YHWH, but as primarily "the God and Father of our Lord Jesus Christ" (2 Cor 1:3). This bracketing of Jesus, while respectful of Jewish readings of this text, leaves the Christian reader perhaps a little puzzled.

Finally, Brueggemann's discussion of verses 12–20a draws an interesting contemporary parallel. Brueggemann's appeal to *Star Wars* in his description of the downfall of the tyrant is indicative of his sharp imagination that wonderfully relates the world of the text to the world in front of the text. And he recognizes that ancient mythic imagery may best be understood via modern mythic imagery—the recognition that makes Brueggemann such a powerful voice in a contemporary church setting. As evocative as it is, the appeal to *Star Wars* has its limitations. While the conflict theme is indeed there and Emperor Palpatine, also known as Darth Sidious, does represent someone desiring to climb the heights of power and is later thrown down, he does not figure large in the imaginative foreground. *Star Wars* features more prominently Anakin Skywalker, who is

---

110. Ibid., 128.

corrupted and turned into a ruthless cyborg, Darth Vader, who serves the Galactic Empire. The sight of his son's agony breaks the dark side's hold on Darth Vader and he throws his evil master, Emperor Palpatine, down the Death Star's reactor shaft. In the process, he is mortally wounded and dies well in the arms of his son, Luke Skywalker. Thus the overall larger narrative of *Star Wars*, especially its portrayal of the redemptive death of Anakin Skywalker, seems to have limited thematic resonance with Isaiah 14 with its focus on the massive human ambition which is cast down. Later on we will consider a possibly more resonant modern parallel in J. R. R. Tolkien's depiction of the rise and downfall of Morgoth and Sauron in *The Silmarillion* and *The Lord of the Rings*.

Christopher Seitz

In his endorsement on the back of Seitz' book *Prophecy and Hermeneutics*, Gary Anderson wrote, "Chris Seitz is one of the most insightful and creative biblical theologians working in the field today."[111] Though suspect of possibly being a marketing ploy, this endorsement from a seasoned scholar like Anderson reflects Seitz's weighty contribution to the field of biblical studies in general and the Old Testament in particular. While unlike Brueggemann, Seitz has not produced writings where he has had a chance to critically reflect on his own formative influences, it is still necessary at least briefly to situate him on the theological and ecclesial maps before delving into his reading of Isaiah 14.

As his academic location, Seitz currently holds a position of senior research professor of biblical interpretation at Toronto School of Theology, Wycliffe College having previously taught at Yale and St. Andrews universities. As far as his ecclesial setting, he is an ordained priest in the Episcopal church. Seitz has served parishes both in the US (Texas, Connecticut, Pennsylvania) as well as in Europe (Germany, France, and Scotland). Furthermore, a stout advocate of the global Anglican communion, he is an executive director of the Anglican Communion Institute. Thus, in a way analogous to Brueggemann, Seitz stands firmly on the border of the scholarly and ecclesial worlds seeking to bring the benefits of the academic study to the benefit of a person in the pew.

111. Seitz, *Prophecy and Hermeneutics*.

A. Context of Seitz's Work

Despite the similarities of the background, Seitz carries out his theological interpretation in ways different from that of Brueggemann's work. Brueggemann's sociopolitical concerns do not feature prominently in Seitz' writings. Neither does Seitz utilize Ricoeur's line of thinking, though he does appeal to the robust use of imagination in reading of biblical texts. All this amounts to the simple realization that two prominent proponents of theological interpretation go about their task in somewhat different ways.

A helpful entry point in exploring Seitz's context would be to consider his rationale for stressing the importance of theological interpretation in the first place. The current crisis in biblical studies, Seitz argues, is as much about the role of historical-critical approaches as it is about the way scholarship handles the theological questions raised by the biblical texts. He insists that theological questions were at the forefront of biblical scholarship during the rise of historical-critical study in the nineteenth century. Seitz observes,

> In the middle of the previous century and for many decades into our own, these questions did not just hover near the fray but were first-order questions demanding first-order answers if the discipline was to have any integrity as a historically oriented one still tuned to the life of the church and an earlier history of interpretation.[112]

Yet, according to Seitz, what began as a helpful inquiry into historically bound questions, has taken a problematic turn,

> What may have happened in recent years is that the central theological questions receded as the discipline, historically oriented as it has been, simply never ceased to find new historical questions to occupy itself with and chose to focus on them as though the theological matters would somehow fall into place when all was said and done.[113]

The result of overlooking the central theological questions was that "historical questions began to take on a life of their own, and run today virtually on autopilot."[114] Yet what is missed in the midst of this historical-critical inquiry is of fundamental significance. Seitz writes,

---

112. Seitz, *Figured Out*, 14.
113. Ibid.
114. Seitz, *Word Without End*, 10.

What is at stake is retention of the actual form of the witness. The final form of scripture has theological significance. To refer to Moses as "author" of the Torah, David as the voice of the Psalms, Solomon as collector of Proverbs, or the Paul or James or John of the New Testament with the literatures associated with them need not carry with it the burden of historicism. Rather, such reference coheres with the plain sense of scripture's presentation and must be considered a piece of historical datum not to be cast off by historicist quests for this or that datum behind the witness.[115]

One major area of concern for Seitz is that historical criticism "had failed to do constructive theological work involving the identity of God in the most basic sense."[116] What does Seitz have in mind here? "By focusing on how Israel thought about God; how Israel's religion issued forth into New Testament religion (or how, with Bultmann, it did not); how traditions changed and shifted over time, redactors then getting the final word; or what Jesus said about the kingdom or who he thought he was (the stock-in-trade of historical-critical theologizing), how might it then be possible to speak of God as one, as three and as disclosed in a unique way in Israel's testimony from the Old Testament?"[117] While appreciative of historical criticism bringing the focus on history, tradition, and religion, Seitz is left wondering, "Could it be said that God could speak, in time and space or through the canonical deposit of prophets and apostles, as had been assumed throughout the history of interpretation before the rise of 'history' (historicism) as a non-negotiable category of significance?"[118] Hence, Seitz is led to assert that it has come about that "historical criticism plays no positive theological role whatsoever."[119]

Having denied enduring theological value of historical criticism, Seitz is prepared to grant it a "preparatory function" for someone seeking to read the Bible as Christian scripture.[120] The following is Seitz' summary of this preparatory function,

> First, it is to exercise its explanatory function in helping us to appreciate the letter of the biblical text in all its foreignness and complexity. It is to teach us to be close readers, straining

115. Seitz, *Figured Out*, 8.
116. Ibid., 4.
117. Ibid.
118. Ibid.
119. Seitz, *Word Without End*, 97.
120. Ibid.

to hear something other than our own voices. Second, it is not to confuse its explanatory function with matters of exposition, ethical and theological application, or simple rhetorical persuasion. Explanation is not the same thing as *kerygma*, exposition, synthesis. Third, it is to restrict itself to the task of spotting repugnance, of showing how it is that the Bible is not a simple, single-authored document, free of seams and tensions, literary, theological and logical.[121]

Ultimately, Seitz insists, the goal is not to be sidetracked by these preliminary considerations, but rather, as he puts it, "the true goal of biblical interpretation for the church is not ignoring or denying, but moving beyond 'repugnance.'"[122] In his mind, that "moving beyond" could be fruitfully facilitated by the canonical approach proposed by his mentor and colleague, Brevard Childs. The strength of the canonical approach, according to Seitz, lies in the fact that it "does not minimize the historical dimension; neither does it seek to do away with approaches that take it seriously enough to spot problems and tension in the literary presentation."[123] Rather, the canonical approach seeks to give "proper proportion and care to return to the final form of the text as its own piece of historical reality and witness to God's ordering of the world."[124]

Seitz argues that the basic challenge of reading the Old Testament in the church is not its historical distance, though "historical criticism offered for generations of readers of the Old Testament something to do: entire careers have been built fine-tuning the documentary hypothesis or wrestling with whether the early Israelites were donkey or camel nomads."[125] Rather, it has to do with coming to grips with the fact that "the Old Testament tells a particular story about a particular people and their particular God, who in Christ we confess as our God, his Father and our own, the Holy One of Israel."[126] Those who come to read the Old Testament as Christian scripture are urged to grasp that "we have been read into a will, a first will and testament, by Christ."[127] Seitz insists,

> If we do not approach the literature with this basic stance—of estrangement overcome, of an inclusion properly called

---

121. Ibid.
122. Ibid.
123. Seitz, *The Character of Christian Scripture*, 39.
124. Ibid.
125. Seitz, *Word Without End*, 12.
126. Ibid., 11.
127. Ibid.

"adoption"—historical-critical methods or a hermeneutic of assent will still stand outside and fail to grasp that God is reading us, not we him. "Second naiveté" was fine as an antidote to liberalism's deconstructive acids; but at some point we are talking about a prior claim, made by the literature itself, within a rule of faith, by which God is believed to speak directly.[128]

Seitz stresses that the church "reads the final form of Christian scripture as canon, the parts informing the whole, the whole informing the parts, according to a rule of faith."[129] Seitz claims that "the rule of faith in the early church fathers is a correlating of the gospel with the stable and authoritative claims of the Scriptures of Israel, seen now as a first testament and crucial foundational witness."[130] Thus, the Rule of Faith, when understood properly, relates the confession of Jesus as Lord with the Old Testament, in such a way as to position him as the central focus of the two-testament canon. Seitz observes:

> The rule of faith is the scripturally grounded articulation, based upon a proper perception of the hypothesis of Scripture, that Jesus Christ is one with the God who sent him and who is active in the Scriptures inherited, the Holy Spirit being the means of testifying to his active, if hidden, life in the "Old Testament" and our apprehension of that. Testimony to who Jesus is, in the period of his earthly life and the apostolic testimony to that, "accorded testimony" is in the very nature of the claim to speak rightly of him. It is this claim that the rule of faith seeks to guard, ruling out alternatives that have failed to see the order and coherence of the Scriptures, in their totality, as speaking of Christ.[131]

This placing of Jesus at the center of the two-testament canon explains why Seitz is so insistent on the use of terms "Old Testament" and "New Testament." The current wave of change has favored the term "Hebrew Bible" in reference to the Old Testament out of respect for the Jewish readers. It has become a common trend to compare the church's reading of the Old Testament with "reading someone else's mail."[132] Seitz argues that the phraseology of Old/New Testament is not intended to communicate Christian supersessionism, but rather makes a profound theological point. He writes, "These two terms are alone capable of making clear why it is that

128. Ibid.
129. Seitz, *Figured Out*, 81.
130. Seitz, *The Goodly Fellowship of the Prophets*, 97.
131. Seitz, *The Character of Christian Scripture*, 198.
132. Van Buren, "Reading Someone Else's Mail," 595–606.

Christians, as against the simply curious, read the Old Testament to begin with—something that 'Hebrew Bible' cannot do."[133] Seitz's rationale for that bold statement is worth quoting at length,

> The term "New Testament" makes it clear that Israel's covenant with God is the sole rationale for the existence of sacred texts to begin with, whatever we might call them. God covenanted with Israel, and not just with humanity in general. The only means by which others have access to that relationship is by the blood of Christ, which is itself described as a covenant "poured out for many for the forgiveness of sins" (Matt. 26:28). The first covenant was ratified by blood, as the New Testament understands it, based upon the Old (Exod. 24:6–8), and in like manner so too the second (Heb. 9:15–22). In this way, those far off—"without God in the world" (Eph. 2:13)—were brought near. In this process the "oracles of God" (Rom. 3:2) received a new title that explained how what had been entrusted to the Jews was now a scriptural witness with wider significance and wider readership.[134]

Hence, Seitz argues, the decision to refer to the Jewish sacred texts as the Old Testament was not a pejorative move on the part of the early church, but rather intended "to clarify how and on what terms these scriptures of Israel remained scriptures for the church, and by what manner of inclusion they could be read in the first place."[135] To put it another way, "as terms which work in conjunction with one another "Old Testament' and 'New Testament' present a theological argument for how someone else's mail is not 'Hebrew Bible' or 'Jewish Scripture' but the permanent, accessible witness to the One with whom we have to do, who has been fully revealed in Jesus Christ."[136]

Seitz is convinced that what the church needs is "to let the OT speak in its own idiom as Christian Scripture."[137] On the one hand, this means going beyond the time-honored strategy of seeing the Old Testament through a Pauline lens or, more broadly, being limited to the use of the Old Testament in the New. On the other hand, Seitz rejects the idea of the Old Testament as something "sympathetically Jewish"—an entity with fragile linkage to Jesus. He memorably quips, "The Old Testament is not a relative with a gas

---

133. Seitz, *Word Without End*, 71.
134. Ibid.
135. Ibid.
136. Ibid., 73.
137. Seitz, *The Character of Christian Scripture*, 203.

problem, as a former colleague once said, that we must accept and try politely to work around."[138] Rather, Seitz insists,

> The Old Testament is the witness of the One God with whom we have to do, who has sent his Son for the salvation of the world, breaking down a dividing wall and bringing those who are far off near by the blood of Jesus Christ. The Old Testament has a horizon that is not exhausted in what we can say about Jesus, for its language and its divine promises lie not behind the New, but show the way ahead of the New that fulfillment may be a promise made good on, to the glory of the Father, who with the Son and Holy Spirit is One God, unto the ages of ages.[139]

In the end, Seitz insists, "A christological interpretation of the Old Testament—or of the New Testament—warrants our attention only to the degree to which it conforms with trinitarian truth about God, and conveys exegetical and interpretive guidelines commensurate with that truth."[140] It is his more explicit christological approach that makes Seitz distinctive from Brueggemann, thus demonstrating that contemporary concerns with renewed theological interpretation represent a spectrum of approaches.

B. Seitz's Approach to Reading the Book of Isaiah

The canonical approach advocated by Seitz envisions the unity of the book of Isaiah as a whole. He utilizes an imagery of an old single-story farmhouse, which upon close examination reveals that several smaller buildings have been over time combined to make it. An interior wall covered with exterior shingles, hallways that do not connect, and an oddly placed window all reveal signs of previous intentionality that has been transformed to make this farmhouse. Similar things could be noted about the final form the book of Isaiah. Seitz writes,

> Critics were right to spot a certain unwieldiness in form in the Book of Isaiah—more so perhaps than in my farmhouse. This is why three divisions were made. Internally, it is difficult to get from room to room in Isaiah. This must be admitted. But this difficulty may not be so overwhelming as the present critical theory suggests—that, standing in one section of the house, we

---

138. Seitz, "Christological Interpretation of Texts," 226.
139. Ibid.
140. Ibid.

cannot move to another room without exiting altogether and then entering the new section by its own external door.[141]

Seitz is careful to point out that such unified reading the book of Isaiah is not an easy undertaking,

> Now, with an interest in unitary readings or canonical approaches, questions of a theological character have once again resurfaced. But we should stop and ask: why a focus on the book as a unitary whole? For theological reasons or for aesthetic reasons? Because older fragmentation has tired us out? Or because meaning is regarded as the imposition of a reader's concerns on a text, and we now have readers interested in unity? This is clearly problematical. If readers are the ones finding unity, how would this shift be any more theological than what obtained in an older model? Questions such as these point to a considerable degree of confusion among Isaiah interpreters at present.[142]

At the same time, Seitz insists that while the seams and previous logic could be detected, it does not mean that these three buildings could still function on their own. "The finished house was more one than three."[143] Seitz insists that the unity and coherence of the Isaiah material is to be sought, to borrow Rendtorff's phrase, in the "reciprocal relationships" between the literary blocks of First, Second, and Third Isaiah.[144] In other words, while hard, the coherence of the canonical book of Isaiah is possible to discern. For Seitz the unified coherence of the final form of the book of Isaiah is not tied with the theory of inspiration that is linked with an inspired individual and his message. Rather, "concern for the book of Isaiah *in its entirety* involves the expectation that a single perspective—that of God or that of Isaiah as God's spokesman—pervades all sixty-six chapters."[145]

What holds the book of Isaiah together is its main character—God. The book of Isaiah is different from other prophetic books such as Jeremiah or Ezekiel, argues Seitz. The difference is in the degree to which the figure of YHWH dominates its center stage. Seitz writes, "God's dialogue in Isaiah is not primarily with a prophetic figure (Isaiah) or with prophetic successors (the servant; servants), though these take up very important roles. God's

---

141. Seitz, "Isaiah 1–66," 109.

142. Seitz, *Word Without End*, 113–14.

143. Seitz, "Isaiah 1–66," 109.

144. Seitz, "The One Isaiah//The Three Isaiahs," 17. The phrase "reciprocal relationships" is from the English translation of Rendtorff, *The Old Testament: An Introduction*, 190–200.

145. Seitz, *Word Without End*, 127.

dialogue is with Israel and the cosmos, God's entire created order."[146] If there is a supporting character, it is not the prophetic figure, but Zion. According to Seitz, "Zion functions as the concrete expression of God's dwelling with his creation."[147] Seitz goes as far as to suggest that the Book of Isaiah could be rightly called "The Drama of God and Zion."[148]

c. Seitz's Framing Comments Regarding the Oracle Against Babylon in Isaiah 13–14

In our discussion of Seitz's framing comments regarding Isaiah 13–14 we will highlight three particular issues that are important in grasping Seitz's reading of the משל of Isaiah 14.

First, it is worth briefly noting that according to Seitz the collection of Oracles Against the Nations contains Isaiah 13–27 as opposed to splitting that block into two units, Isaiah 13–23 and Isaiah 24–27, with that later block being designated as a later collection of apocalyptic oracles.[149] Seitz points out that even if one grants that Isaiah 24–27 could be properly designated as "apocalyptic," the recent shifts in scholarly understanding of Jewish apocalyptic thought shed doubt on the need to place such literature in a much later historical period than Isaiah 13–23. Furthermore, he is unsure if one can distinguish these two blocks in regards to their subject matter,

> Chapters 13–23 and 24–27 are united in their depiction of God's widespread judgment over all human pride and national military pretension. In contrast to human arrogance and folly, God has in mind a pleasant vineyard and a scene of national reunion and the obedient worship of diverse peoples. From both a literary and historical perspective, chapters 13–27 are framed by a concern with the destiny of Babylon, both as agent of judgment

---

146. Seitz, "Isaiah 1–66," 122.

147. Ibid.

148. Ibid.

149. Duhm's groundbreaking commentary suggested that several independent "booklets" (*Büchlein*) were brought together to produce the book of Isaiah. Based on that hypothesis, Duhm suggested that the material of Isaiah 13–23 was independent of Isaiah 24–27. He argued that the material of Isaiah 24–27 alongside of Isaiah 34–35 was strongly influenced by late apocalyptic thought. Hence, he argued that the Oracles Against the Nations should be properly bracketed as Isaiah 13–23 (See Duhm, *Das Buch*, 12–3). This suggestion has over time found a wide scholarly acceptance (Among many others see Childs, *Isaiah*, 113–16, 171–74; Driver, *Introduction*, 211, 219–23; Gray, *Isaiah I–XXVII*, 232, 397–404).

and as final symbol of national arrogance and blind disregard for the ways of Israel's God and his chosen people Israel.[150]

Furthermore, Seitz argues that the search for the origins of the collection of the Oracles Against the Nations needs careful attention to the theological rationale behind bringing this collection of oracles together and the way they are intended to function in their current canonical setting. First, this collection of Oracles Against the Nations reveals a certain pattern of God's involvement in human affairs which is true during the time of Assyria and Babylon, namely that "God may will the destruction of his own people in order to remove all vestiges of human pride and idolatrous schemes. But what holds true for the judged holds true for the judge as well, and for all nations on earth."[151]

Second, the scene of God's worldwide judgment in these chapters prepares the reader for the description of Jerusalem's deliverance in 701 BC depicted in Isaiah 36–38. It shows that "God can save a city and its people on the strength of the king's trust."[152] The faithful king could at least slow down the hand of divine judgment even if he is not able to fully avert it.

Third, Seitz argues that the primary concern of Isaiah 13–27 is to establish the God of Israel as "God of all peoples and as judge over all forms of human pride and idolatry."[153] It is the hand of YHWH rather than shrewd foreign diplomacy that accomplished things in this world. "The nations section reveals the folly of all political scheming when it takes place independently of trust in the one God of all nations."[154] YHWH establishes the nations and he is the one who tears them down—this is the basic yet profound theological motif of Isaiah 13–27. Seitz argues that the canonical text of the book of Isaiah is not at pains to prove that YHWH is superior to the gods of other nations, rather it seeks to underscore that YHWH is the rightful God of the nations. "Isaiah reveals that trust in foreign allegiances very quickly turns into a form of idolatry, a belief that some force in the human realm of activity can be better trusted than the God who sets up nations and brings them down."[155]

Fourth, the collection of Oracles Against the Nations is the good news for Israel. Seitz perceives that in this picture of cosmic judgment God's people can find notes of hope as God always remains a refuge for those who are

150. Seitz, *Isaiah*, 118.
151. Ibid., 124.
152. Ibid., 124–25.
153. Ibid., 126.
154. Ibid., 125.
155. Ibid.

poor and needy. They wait in anticipation for Jerusalem to emerge as a new center (26:1). They rest in God's attentive presence in the midst during this period (26:20). And, ultimately, they trust that "the time will come to sing of a new pleasant vineyard (27:2), as Jacob takes root and Israel blossoms and puts forth shoots (27:6)."[156]

The last of Seitz's overall points about Isaiah 13-27 is that the key to understanding the existence of the Oracles Against the Nations at this juncture of the book of Isaiah, according to Seitz, lies with the framing role of Babylon in this material. Seitz argues that Babylon plays the decisive role both at the opening of this collection (13:1—14:23) and at its closing (chapters 21-27). On the one hand, Seitz insists, "Babylon is depicted on analogy to Assyria."[157] Babylon functions as the agent of divine judgment. Just as YHWH used Assyria as his rod (10:5), so now he will use Babylon. Seitz points out that this "replacement motif" is made explicit in Isaiah 23:13, "Look at the land of the Chaldeans! This is the people; it was not Assyria."[158] Similarly, the fate of Assyria awaits Babylon. The "agent of judgment judged" sentence awaits Babylon, "Fallen, fallen is Babylon; and all the images of her gods lie shattered on the ground" (21:9).

On the other hand, Seitz argues that the depiction of Babylon in the final form of the Oracles Against the Nations goes well beyond the role envisioned for Assyria. Babylon is cast as a worldwide force. Its destructive exercise of power effects the whole earth (13:5). The entire cosmos experiences the effects of its reign (24:4-5). Seitz writes, "Babylon in its might and military power wreaks a judgment so awesome that all earth's citizens are obliged to recognize a show of strength without real analogy, going well beyond the judgment wreaked by Assyria."[159]

What is of particular interest is the way Seitz understands the function of the Oracle Against Babylon in Isaiah 13:1-14:23. Consistent with his replacement motif, Seitz argues, "Whatever its primary historical origin, the opening material in 13:1—14:23 concerning Babylon now functions to subsume an original depiction of Assyria as 'agent of judgment judged' under the broader perspective of later Babylonian hegemony, a new and more ferocious 'agent of judgment judged.'"[160] He goes on to insist, "this opening material provides a lens through which the series of nations oracles to

---

156. Ibid., 127.
157. Ibid., 123.
158. Ibid., 120.
159. Ibid., 124.
160. Ibid., 120.

follow is to be interpreted."¹⁶¹ Far from being just the first of many thematically linked oracles, this opening material shows both "the final gathering of all earthly power and strength for an assault that goes beyond any prior effort" and its, surely paradigmatic, downfall.¹⁶²

Before looking at the detailed analysis of Seitz's reading of the משל of Isaiah 14:3–23 we will probe further his comment about the material of Isaiah 13–14 serving as a lens to the larger block of material in Isaiah. Seitz insists that the larger governing conceptions are the key to understanding how various sections of the developing book of Isaiah were editorially linked together.¹⁶³ According to Seitz, one of these governing concerns in the book of Isaiah is the theme of an overarching plan of God in history. He writes, "From Assyria, to Babylon, to Persia, chapters 13–14 link the original proclamation of Isaiah, regarding the rod of God's anger, with the coming Babylonian threat and the final destruction of Babylon by Persia—all of this accomplished under the conception of God's 'plan that is planned concerning the whole earth' (14:26)."¹⁶⁴ While cursory reading of Isaiah 13–27 might leave the reader with a sense of YHWH's judgment is nothing more than a perpetuation of a terrible cycle of senseless violence, Seitz argues that Isaiah's emphasis on God's involvement in human history insists that, contrary to what might appear, this is happening in accordance to God's plan, "God stands firm on the conviction that all takes place according to a mysterious plan of old and that in the end justice will be done, as violence and destruction finally eliminate all forms of pride and arrogance of those who themselves wreak the judgment."¹⁶⁵

D. Seitz's Reading of the משל of Isaiah 14:3–23

Seitz opens his discussion with the vision of final justice in Habakkuk 2 which is both vividly portrayed and yet invites patient waiting. He argues that a similar movement is going on in Isaiah 14. Chapter 14 begins with the promise of the return and restoration that God's people will experience as a result of his intervention in human affairs. With the final rest comes a taunt against the oppressor, Babylon.

Seitz understands the oppression of Babylon portrayed in verses 4–8 to be both worldwide and unprecedented. He argues that while the first royal

---

161. Ibid., 127.
162. Ibid., 128.
163. Ibid.
164. Ibid., 131.
165. Ibid., 132.

oracle in Isaiah 9:1-7 described the punishment of Assyria in the day of Midian, what transpires in Isaiah 14 is of a completely different magnitude, "The whole earth was made to feel the oppressive weight of Babylon's rule, and now the whole earth breaks into singing."[166]

Verses 9-15 paint a tragic picture of the reversal of fortunes. Seitz writes,

> Babylon had climbed high into the heavenly reaches, high above the highest cedars of Lebanon, claiming an ascendancy equal to the Most High. There in the assembly of the deities of the nations, in the abode of the Most High God in the far north, Babylon sought identity with God. Instead, its king found himself in Sheol among the graves of kings long dead.[167]

It is clear that Seitz is aware of the ancient mytho-poetic resonances inherent in verses 12-15. Unlike Brueggemann, who turns to a contemporary parallel with *Star Wars*, Seitz makes a different interpretive move. These verses, in Seitz's mind, invite a resonance with Psalm 82 where YHWH is portrayed as standing in the midst of his divine council. YHWH brings charges against the gods of the earth—charges that include injustice and neglect of the poor and the weak (Ps 82:2-4). Seitz points out, "Perhaps in ironic condemnation, Yahweh addresses these unjust gods as divine sons of the Most High: 'Nevertheless, you shall die like mortals, and fall like any prince' (Ps. 82:7). For, as the psalm concludes, all nations stand under the sovereignty of Israel's God."[168] Thus, rather than turning to other ancient Near Eastern texts, Seitz relies on Psalm 82 alone to offer interpretive imagery for understanding Isaiah 14:12-15.

Seitz ends his discussion of this section by wondering "how such a portrayal of Babylon's final destiny could have been generated."[169] He concludes that the answer to this question lies in the actual historical realities which Israel had to face in Babylonian oppression. The weight of Babylon's oppression far superseded even the Assyrian brutality. From their perspective the Babylonian regime had its sights set on world-wide domination. Hence, the משל of Isaiah 14 seeks to capture the flavor of that limited, but very real and vivid experience. Seitz remarks, "From Israel's perspective, this was a nation that sought to rule the world at any cost. And it did so

---

166. Ibid., 134-35.
167. Ibid., 135.
168. Ibid.
169. Ibid.

without regard for most minimal standards of justice, arrogating to itself the status of the divine with a justice that proceeded from themselves."[170]

Seitz closes his analysis where it all began—the parallel with the vision of Habakkuk. If the oppression is worldwide, then the implications of the downfall of the tyrant are equally far reaching, "The Taunt of Isaiah 14 affirms that no nation on earth, however powerful and however terrifying, can finally void the justice that created the earth and all its people."[171] The vision seems grand and hardly possible. Yet it is all in YHWH's hands. What might one do if the vision is slow in being realized? As Habakkuk has suggested one is to wait for it (2:3). Those with an upright heart are wise to persist in hope and not fail (2:4). YHWH's justice will surely come, without delay (2:3).

E. Evaluation of Seitz's Reading of the משל of Isaiah 14:3–23

Seitz has spoken poignantly about the urgency for the church "to let the OT speak in its own idiom as Christian Scripture."[172] His reading of Isaiah 14 is an interesting example of what it might look like to hear the voice of the Old Testament in its own right as Christianly significant. Seitz's suggestive use of Habakkuk 2 and Psalm 82 positions this text to be heard in the paradigmatic light of traditional Christian concerns for the justice and sovereignty of God. This interpretive move on the part of Seitz is worth pondering at length.

As Seitz has pointed out, Habakkuk 2:6–20 contains a taunt against arrogant Babylon in the shape of five woes that underscore the atrocities committed by this nation. There are significant thematic resonances between this taunt and that contained in Isaiah 14 like plundering the nations (2:8), cutting off peoples (2:10), and the violent treatment of Lebanon (2:17). While similar in their taunts that anticipate the downfall of Babylon, Habakkuk's concern for patient waiting in the face of a slow realization of the promised downfall of Babylon, while evocative, does not appear to be paramount in Isaiah 14. Using Habakkuk 2 as the framing device of his reading of Isaiah 14 Seitz runs a risk of allowing Habakkuk to crowd out the Isaiah 14 text. Is this a risk worth taking? The answer is not straightforward. It would depend on the purposes of one's reading. Seitz comes to the text seeking to read it as Christian scripture. Part of that concern is to make this

170. Ibid., 136.
171. Ibid.
172. Seitz, *The Character of Christian Scripture*, 203.

text evocatively available for its contemporary readers' own faith journey with God. The use of Habakkuk 2 allows him to open up this text to be read by those whose own existential realities are more reflective of that of Habakkuk than Isaiah 14. In other words, Habakkuk 2 gives voice for faith communities currently under pressure to read Isaiah 14 in hope-filled waiting. Habakkuk's own question of "How long?" (1:2) becomes resonant in today's context and challenges modern readers to live with the same patient anticipation, "It will surely come; it will not delay" (2:4).

Furthermore, Seitz's emphasis on the portrayal of YHWH as the cosmic sovereign standing in the midst of the council of gods in Psalm 82 risks displacing the poignant imagery of human hubristic assent and violent casting down. Once again, it behooves us to ask whether this risk is justified. Psalm 82, while lacking the emphasis on the hubristic climbing up into the divine realm, gives voice to questions of social concern that traditionally occupy those who approach the Old Testament as Christian scripture,

> 2 "How long will you judge unjustly
>   and show partiality to the wicked? Selah
> 3 Give justice to the weak and the orphan;
>   maintain the right of the lowly and the destitute.
> 4 Rescue the weak and the needy;
>   deliver them from the hand of the wicked."

Those who are faced with oppressive violence are forced to wonder if a just and peaceful world is possible. Psalm 82 affirms that such a world is indeed available under the sovereign auspices of YHWH who dislodges these "divine" powers. They are demoted, being stripped of their powers, and downgraded to encounter death like a fallen human prince (82:6-7). While Isaiah 14 envisions a human ruler exercising violence to climb up to the divine realm, Psalm 82 depicts the movement in the opposite direction. Both affirm the limited nature of oppressive power and terminal judgment on any who rely on it—be it divine or human in its nature.

Thus, while in some ways Seitz's move to utilize the intertextual resonances with Habakkuk 2 and Psalm 82 raises questions whether the voice of Isaiah 14 is genuinely heard, or whether it may be to some extent drowned out by these texts, the result is both suggestive and illuminating. It broadens the text's appeal and makes it imaginatively available to modern day faith praxis, inviting both patient waiting and certain hope in the light of YHWH's benevolent and sovereign rule. In the end, those who come to Seitz's reading with faith-shaped lens might be prompted to pray the prayer that rounds out Psalm 82:

8 Rise up, O God, judge the earth;
    for all the nations belong to you!

Reading on the Way to Emmaus: How Jesus Recalibrates our Reading of the משׁל of Isaiah 14:3–23

"Then beginning with Moses and all the prophets, he interpreted to them the things about himself in all the scriptures."[173] These words of the Gospel of Luke bring us to the heart of the encounter of the early disciples with the risen Jesus. In the aftermath of Jesus' death on the cross in Jerusalem, two of them are making a seven mile journey to the village of Emmaus. Jesus appears in the middle of their journey and engages them with a probing question, "What are you discussing," without being recognized by them (24:17). The conversation with Jesus that follows is permeated with sadness as the disciples disclose that their hopes of Jesus being the one to redeem Israel have been dashed (24:21). That sadness is also mingled with puzzlement at the news of the empty tomb brought by the women who also testified to having encountered an angel assuring them that Jesus was alive (24:24). Jesus rebukes his traveling companions for their failure to believe the message of the prophets. Otherwise, they would have grasped that the Messiah had to suffer these things prior to entering into his glory (24:26). Having addressed the slowness of their grasp on the prophetic message, Jesus opens the scriptures and shows how they make sense of what they had encountered in him.

Reflecting on this Lukan account, Moberly writes, "Presumably the logic of Jesus' expounding the scriptures to his puzzled disciples is that these scriptures provide a context and a content for making sense of Jesus, when all that the disciples already know about him has not 'clicked.'"[174] Moberly argues that Jesus' assumption here is that Israel's scripture makes sense of him. While these Jewish believers know their scriptures well, they are now invited by Jesus to read them "in a new way, in the light of all that has happened to Jesus, so that they can see in these scriptures what they have not seen before."[175] Not only do Israel's scriptures make sense of Jesus, but now Jesus also helps make sense of them. In other words, Moberly insists, "a dialectic between Jesus and Israel's scriptures is envisaged, both necessary for Christian understanding of the crucified and risen Lord."[176]

---

173. Luke 24:27 (NRSV)
174. Moberly, *Theology*, 145.
175. Ibid., 146.
176. Ibid.

We turn to Moberly's reflection on Luke 24 because he provides a succinct way into thinking about distinct ways of recontextualizing Old Testament texts such as Isaiah 14 in such a way that they are heard as Christian scripture today. According to Moberly, "The challenge for Christian interpretation of the book of Isaiah is to have historical respect for the distinctive Isaianic voices in their own right and then combine that with taking seriously a Christian understanding of God in Christ as the frame of reference within which the Isaianic witness is now to be understood and appropriated."[177] The aim of our reflection that follows is to attempt to do just that, namely, to understand and appropriate the משל of Isaiah 14 in the Christian framework of understanding God in light of the revelation of Jesus Christ.

Reading Isaiah 14 *with* Jesus: The Use of the משל of Isaiah 14 in Jesus' Teaching

The Synoptic tradition records Jesus turning to the imagery of the משל of Isaiah 14 in his speech denouncing the Galilean towns that fail to respond to his call to repentance.[178] Two versions of Jesus' speech are found in Matthew 11:20–24 and Luke 10:13–15. The towns of Chorazin, Bethsaida, and Capernaum are singled out as the paradigmatic icons of refusal to repent.

ΚΑΤΑ ΜΑΘΘΑΙΟΝ 11:20–24	ΚΑΤΑ ΛΟΥΚΑΝ 10:13–15
20 Τότε ἤρξατο ὀνειδίζειν τὰς πόλεις ἐν αἷς ἐγένοντο αἱ πλεῖσται δυνάμεις αὐτοῦ, ὅτι οὐ μετενόησαν·	
21 οὐαί σοι, Χοραζίν, οὐαί σοι, Βηθσαϊδά· ὅτι εἰ ἐν Τύρῳ καὶ Σιδῶνι ἐγένοντο αἱ δυνάμεις αἱ γενόμεναι ἐν ὑμῖν, πάλαι ἂν ἐν σάκκῳ καὶ σποδῷ μετενόησαν.	13 Οὐαί σοι, Χοραζίν, οὐαί σοι, Βηθσαϊδά· ὅτι εἰ ἐν Τύρῳ καὶ Σιδῶνι ἐγενήθησαν αἱ δυνάμεις αἱ γενόμεναι ἐν ὑμῖν, πάλαι ἂν ἐν σάκκῳ καὶ σποδῷ καθήμενοι μετενόησαν.
22 πλὴν λέγω ὑμῖν, Τύρῳ καὶ Σιδῶνι ἀνεκτότερον ἔσται ἐν ἡμέρᾳ κρίσεως ἢ ὑμῖν.	14 πλὴν Τύρῳ καὶ Σιδῶνι ἀνεκτότερον ἔσται ἐν τῇ κρίσει ἢ ὑμῖν.

---

177. Ibid., 162.

178. In our discussion here we are not engaging with the issues of the tradition-history or composition of the material, but rather are working with the literary and canonical setting of the material on the lips of Jesus. In so doing our focus in reading the Gospel accounts "with Jesus" is to a certain degree a reading with the evangelists that follows their rendering of Jesus and his ministry.

ΚΑΤΑ ΜΑΘΘΑΙΟΝ 11:20-24	ΚΑΤΑ ΛΟΥΚΑΝ 10:13-15
23 καὶ σύ, Καφαρναούμ, μὴ ἕως οὐρανοῦ ὑψωθήσῃ; ἕως ᾅδου καταβήσῃ· ὅτι εἰ ἐν Σοδόμοις ἐγενήθησαν αἱ δυνάμεις αἱ γενόμεναι ἐν σοί, ἔμεινεν ἂν μέχρι τῆς σήμερον.	15 καὶ σύ, Καφαρναούμ, μὴ ἕως οὐρανοῦ ὑψωθήσῃ; ἕως τοῦ ᾅδου καταβήσῃ.
24 πλὴν λέγω ὑμῖν ὅτι γῇ Σοδόμων ἀνεκτότερον ἔσται ἐν ἡμέρᾳ κρίσεως ἢ σοί.	

The first two towns to be addressed are Chorazin and Bethsaida. Chorazin only appears in the New Testament twice, in these texts (Matt 11:21; Luke 10:13). It has been identified with the ruins of Khirbet Kerazin, located on the northern shore of the Sea of Galilee just an hour's journey north of Capernaum.[179] Bethsaida was the home of Peter, Andrew, and Phillip (John 1:44; 12:21). It was located east of the Jordan river on the northern shore of the Sea of Galilee as well.[180] Archeological excavations have indicated that Chorazin and Bethsaida were populous towns comparable in size and importance with Capernaum.[181] These towns are denounced for their failure to respond to the deeds of power done in their midst during the ministry of Jesus. This is a peculiar charge, at least partially. While Bethsaida is a location of Jesus feeding the five thousand (Luke 9:10-17), Chorazin never figures in any of the Gospels in connection with Jesus' deeds of power. Their attitude is compared with that of Tyre and Sidon, which takes the alert reader back to Isaiah 13-23 to which our text Isaiah 14:3-23 belongs.[182] Oracles concerning Tyre and Sidon close the Oracles Against the Nations. These sea-faring towns reflect a stunning reversal of fortunes. Tyre is addressed as an "exultant city whose origin is from days of old" (Isa 23:7). Its prominent role in the economic realm is expressed in calling it "the merchant of the nations" (23:3). Furthermore Tyre is seen as a "bestower of crowns" (23:8), while its merchants are "the honored of the earth" (23:9). According to Childs, "The lament focuses on the contrast between a proud, ancient city whose merchants prowled the earth in honor and power, to its status of dishonor and shame."[183] Childs has pointed out that the Oracles Against the Nations

---

179. Albright and Mann, *Matthew*, 142.

180. Mounce, *Matthew*, 106.

181. France, *The Gospel of Matthew*, 438.

182. Tyre and Sidon figure prominently in Old Testament prophetic denouncements. See also Jer 25:22; 27:3; 47:4; Ezek 26:1—28:24; Joel 3:4; Amos 1:9-10; Zech 9:2-4.

183. Childs, *Isaiah*, 168.

are bracketed with oracles dealing with two types of super-powers in the Ancient World. They open with oracles against Babylon and the Babylonian king who stand for the greatest power on land. They close with these oracles against Tyre and Sidon which represent the greatest power on sea. This is a literary strategy that highlights YHWH's supremacy over all the nations.[184] Hence Chorazin and Bethsaida in Matthew 11:20-24 and Luke 10:13-15 are rhetorically charged with an unresponsiveness greater than that of these famous ancient political and economic powerhouses. According to Jesus, in Matthew and Luke's presentation, even these highly exalted towns would have responded to Jesus' ministry, but not Chorazin and Bethsaida. Their refusal to repent brings about the denouncement from Jesus that echoes YHWH's intentionality towards Tyre and Sidon in Isaiah 23:9,

> The LORD of hosts has planned it—
> to defile the pride of all glory,
> to shame all the honored of the earth.

From the denunciation of Chorazin and Bethsaida the focus shifts to Capernaum. The issue seems to be the same as in the case of the other two Galilean towns. What was somewhat muffled in the case of Chorazin and Bethsaida, becomes apparent here. Both Matthew 11:23 and Luke 10:15 read,

> And you, Capernaum,
> will you be exalted to heaven?
> No, you will be brought down to Hades.[185]

There is a wide-spread agreement among interpreters that this denouncement echoes the language of Isaiah 14 (LXX), especially verse 13 (I will ascend to heaven) and verse 15 (you will be brought down to Hades).[186]

How does the Isaiah 14 imagery fit in Jesus' stern words against these Galilean towns? Tuckett has argued convincingly that by the first century the language of Isaiah 14 has become a part of an exegetical tradition where it was used to refer to those who stood in opposition to the righteous sufferer.[187]

---

184. Childs, *Isaiah*, 167.

185. Just as in the English translation of Matthew and Luke passages, the Greek here is identical in both texts except the definite article in reference to Hades in the Lucan account.

186. Davies and Allison, *Matthew 8-18*, 267; Evans, *Saint Luke*, 452; Fitzmyer, *Gospel According to Luke X-XXIV*, 854-55; France, *Matthew*, 439; Hagner, *Matthew*, 314; Luz, *Matthew 8-20*, 153; Nolland, *Luke 9:21—18:34*, 557; Nolland, *Gospel of Matthew*, 468.

187. Tuckett, "Isaiah," 58.

He marshals several texts in support of his thesis, such as 1 Enoch 46 and 2 Maccabees 9. The most evocative among them is Wisdom of Solomon 4:18–19. Drawing a contrast between the destinies of the righteous and the wicked, Wisdom 1–5 highlights the ultimate triumph of a righteous life which has the support of YHWH himself who is the one ultimately fighting their battles. Wisdom 4:18–19 warns against mockery of the early death that the righteous often face, insisting that the long life of the unrighteous in the end proves pointless,

> **18** The unrighteous will see, and will have contempt for them,
> but the Lord will laugh them to scorn.
> After this they will become dishonored corpses,
> and an outrage among the dead forever;
> **19** because he will dash them speechless to the ground,
> and shake them from the foundations;
> they will be left utterly dry and barren,
> and they will suffer anguish,
> and the memory of them will perish.

Elsewhere Tuckett suggests a possible allusion to the language of the fourth servant song of Isaiah 52:13 (LXX ὑψωθήσεται) in the Matthean use of the word ὑψωθήσῃ in Matthew 10:15.[188] He claims that the force of harsh denouncement against Capernaum pivots around the emphatic σύ (Do you think that *you* will be exalted?). Behind this emphatic rhetoric lingers an unstated belief that it is not Capernaum but rather someone else, namely Jesus as the figure of the suffering servant who will be exalted.[189] In the end, Tuckett concludes that the use of Isaiah 14 imagery in Jesus' denouncement speech is intended to place Jesus' experience of rejection into the broader context of the experience of the "righteous sufferer" in early Judaism.[190]

Seen in this light, the canonical texts envision the imagery of the משל of Isaiah 14 receiving a broader application in the ministry of Jesus as a reference to those who reject the mission and message of Jesus. There are two interpretive moves that are worth touching on. First, the language of exaltation that described the self-seeking tyrant of Babylon is now applied to ordinary Galilean towns, such as Capernaum, which chose not to respond rightly to Jesus' announcement of the coming kingdom of God. Jesus' emphatic words against Capernaum (Do you think that *you* will be exalted?),

---

188. Tuckett, "Scripture," 209.
189. Ibid., 210.
190. Tuckett, "Isaiah," 58.

have been stripped of negative moral trappings that surround the picture of the tyrant's quest for self-glory and become a powerful statement in the wisdom debate about what makes for flourishing life as the people of God. In other words, Capernaum and the other two Galilean towns could be envisioned not guilty of pride per se but rather of failing to see the wisdom of the path that Jesus offers Israel.

Second, the interpretive move attributed by the canonical texts to Jesus identifies the downfall of the king of Babylon with the fate of Capernaum as it chooses to reject Jesus. The faithful Jews saw themselves as enduring persecution at the hands of pagan oppressors while waiting patiently for YHWH's final intervention into the flow of history to deliver his people. Seen in that light, one could envision a reading of Isaiah 14 by the covenant-keeping community at Capernaum as ones who would pick up the משל when YHWH brings his long awaited rest. Jesus' interpretive move turns the tables around. In rejecting his mission, Capernaum has essentially aligned itself with the likes of the king of Babylon. Jesus, not Capernaum, is the righteous sufferer, who will have the right to pick this משל. Wright is suggestive in his observations regarding our text in Matthew, "The horrifying thing was that Jesus was using, as models for the coming judgment on villages within Israel, images of judgment taken straight from the Old Testament, where they had to do with the divine judgment *on the pagan nations*."[191] Here lies the striking reversal of fortunes. Towns like Capernaum which reject Jesus find themselves facing the judgment long anticipated to fall on the pagan oppressors. Even more, Jesus turns out to be the righteous sufferer who will finally be vindicated and exalted—the fate eloquently described in biblical texts such as Philippians 2:6–11, Hebrews 12:2, and 1 Peter 1:11.

Harsh words of Jesus directed at small Galilean towns are envisioned by such a reading strategy as attempting to wake them up and invite them to ponder afresh the eschatological significance of Jesus' deeds of power. The use of the imagery of the משל of Isaiah 14 on the lips of Jesus states emphatically that the rejection of his mission will not lead to exaltation but rather ought to anticipate a reversal of fortunes—namely finding their destiny linked with some of the most hated pagan oppressors, of whom the king of Babylon was surely one of the most notorious. Thus, the reflective aspect of the משל of Isaiah 14 is retained, even if the imagery is recast in a fresh light, becoming a paradigmatic picture of any human notion of exaltation devoid of reference and association with God in Christ.

---

191. Wright, *Jesus and The Victory of God*, 329–30. Italics in the original.

A. *Excursus: Luke 10:18 and its influence on the reading of Isaiah 14*

Upon the return from the mission of the seventy(-two) of his disciples, the following words have been placed on the lips of Jesus in Luke 10:18, "ἐθεώρουν τὸν σατανᾶν ὡς ἀστραπὴν ἐκ τοῦ οὐρανοῦ πεσόντα." Classically these words of Jesus have been taken as a reference to Isaiah 14:12. As mentioned in chapter 4, Origen already links his reading of Isaiah 14 with Luke 10:18, thus fortifying his reading of Isaiah 14 as a downfall of Satan by appealing to the authority of Jesus' teaching.[192]

While contemporary scholarship has generally acknowledged the time-honored link between Isaiah 14:12-15 and Luke 10:18, the current consensus seems to be that this is not a link inherent to the text, but is rather to be found in the history of reception.[193] It is worth noting that neither Brueggemann nor Seitz choose to interact with this classical reading in their commentaries. Similarly interesting is Childs' silence on this matter. Even if his commentary on Isaiah was limited in its scope and size, one would have expected an interaction with it in his *The Struggle to Understand Isaiah as Christian Scripture*, most notably in chapters on the early reception of the Hebrew Bible in the LXX and the New Testament (chapter 1) and Origen's reading of Isaiah (chapter 5). Other noteworthy theological interpreters of Isaiah, Motyer and Goldingay, have also chosen not to interact with this issue. Finally, Oswalt, while mentioning it briefly, dismisses it saying, "the great expositors of the Reformation were unanimous in arguing that the context here does not support such interpretation."[194]

On historical-critical grounds, it has been argued that this statement has its roots in Jesus' baptismal vision which inaugurated his earthly mission.[195] Gathercole has pointed out that the introductory formula "I saw..." is often used in the Old Testament as a marker of the future events. Thus, he takes this phrase in Luke 10:18 to be a vision of the eschatological events seen by the earthly Jesus.[196] Evans sees it as a reference to a wider tradition of the fall of celestial bodies found in the 1 Enoch material and other Jewish texts.[197] Nolland explicitly denies the connection with Isaiah 14, and argues that the imagery of the fall from heaven is closer to the *Testament*

---

192. See my discussion on page ***.
193. So Fitzmyer, *Luke X–XXXIV*, 862. Though see Marshall, *Luke*, 428-29.
194. Oswalt, *Isaiah 1–39*, 320.
195. Marcus, "Jesus' Baptismal Vision," 512-21.
196. Gathercole, "Jesus' Eschatological Vision," 143-63.
197. Evans, *Luke*, 454.

of Solomon 20:16–17, which reads, "we [demons] ... fall ... like flashes of lightning to the earth."[198] According to him, "In vision [Jesus] has seen the coming triumph of the kingdom of God over the rule of Satan and has identified this triumph as his own task. He sees this as what God intends to achieve through him. This vision is becoming reality in his own ministry of exorcism, healing, and proclaiming of the kingdom of God."[199] In so doing, Nolland argues, Jesus' words function in a way resonant with the Old Testament prophetic visions which both anticipate the course of future events and define the role of the prophet himself. Finally, based on the possibility that the imperfect ἐθεώρουν is a third plural, rather than a first singular, Hill has proposed an alternative translation, "They saw Satan fall." "They" would be taken as a reference to the demons who saw their leader, Satan, be dethroned and thus became subject to Jesus' disciples.[200]

This brief survey of hermeneutical moves made by contemporary scholars indicates that in its current context this phrase on the lips of Jesus seems to be at a distance from the situation in Isaiah 14. Yet, though it is best taken as Jesus' comment on the impact of his disciples' mission, it must be acknowledged that the congruence of the language between Luke 10:18 and Isaiah 14:12 has encouraged the imaginative use of the imagery. Thus, however contextually detached, the philological and thematic similarity of the words of Jesus seem to have been an impetus for the imaginatively serious use of them for reading Isaiah 14:12–15 as a reference to the downfall of Satan. This tradition which lasted for centuries was challenged by the criticism of the Reformers, most notably Calvin. Yet the classical reading still sustained itself beyond the criticism of the Reformers as evident in the writings of Milton and Blake, though contemporary theological interpreters have chosen not to engage with it.

Reflecting on Isaiah 14 *in Light of* Jesus: True Humanity as Being in the Likeness of God

The משל of Isaiah 14 depicts the tyrant of Babylon saying, "I will make myself like the Most High (אֶדַּמֶּה לְעֶלְיוֹן)" (14:14). The human quest for exaltation which culminates in fashioning of one's self in the likeness of God has a rich potentiality for reading in a Christian frame of reference especially if one turns to the greater theological tradition.

198. Nolland, *Luke 9:21—18:34*, 563.
199. Ibid., 564.
200. Hill, "Luke 10:18—Who Saw Satan Fall?" 25–40.

The mythic resonances of the imagery of the king of Babylon discussed in earlier chapters have positioned it to be read paradigmatically in general and in particular, in certain Christian contexts, as a reference to Satan. While our discussion in earlier chapters has traced the trajectory along which such thinking emerged in the church, we do not, alongside of Calvin, find this as a viable construal. Nevertheless, this association affirms that this is a pattern bigger than one figure in history and thus ostensibly represents a typical creaturely desire for greatness. The potentiality for reading the tyrant's quest to be like God in a Christian frame of reference becomes heightened when read alongside of the time-honored Christian understanding of Jesus as representing the true likeness of God seen in such canonical texts as Colossians 1:15–20. Martin has argued that Colossians 1:15–20 "embodies an early Christian tribute, set in hymnic form, to the Church's Lord, which the writer borrows from the liturgical praxis which was familiar both to himself and his readers."[201] The text's comprehensive statements about the preeminence of Jesus Christ are built on the sweeping affirmation that "he is the image (εἰκών) of the invisible God" (1:15). Furthermore, one might compare the kingly role that Jesus plays in the Johannine tradition (John 12:15; 18:37; 19:19–22; Rev 17:14; 19:6). All this makes the paradigmatic portrayal of the King of Babylon in Isaiah 14 a worthy counterpart to Jesus. The contrast between the King of Babylon and Jesus invites existential questions about what constitutes true human greatness. To touch on them we must first take a step back and ponder the notion of humans reflecting the likeness of God. Having done so we will be in a better position to address some specific ways the King of Babylon stands as a negative counterpart to Jesus.

The Isaianic picture of a human quest for greatness, irrevocably linked with its relationship with the divine, invites us to ponder Barth's memorable words,

> God wants man to be His creature. Furthermore, He wants him to be His *partner*. There is a *causa Dei* in the world. God wants light, not darkness. He wants cosmos, not chaos. He wants peace, not disorder. He wants man to administer and to receive justice rather than to inflict and to suffer injustice. He wants man to live according to the Spirit rather than according to the flesh. He wants man bound and pledged to Him rather than to any other authority. He wants man to live and not to die. Because He wills these things God is Lord, Shepherd, and Redeemer of man, who in His holiness and mercy meets His creature; who judges and forgives, rejects and receives, condemns and saves . . . He wants

---

201. Martin, "An Early Christian Hymn," 205.

man, not as a secondary God, to be sure, but as a truly free follower and co-worker, to repeat His divine "Yes" and "No."[202]

This dynamic of Creator-Creature relationship is expressed memorably in Genesis 1:26, where the reader is told of God's decree, "Let us create humankind in our image (צלם), according to our likeness (דמת); and let them have dominion over the fish of the sea, and over the birds of the air, and over the cattle, and over all the wild animals of the earth, and over every creeping thing that creeps upon the earth." While many since Irenaeus have proposed a substantive difference between the words צלם (image) and דמת (likeness) in Genesis 1:26,[203] Westermann, in a way typical of modern scholars, generally has argued that these words carry the same meaning and are often used interchangeably, as in Ezekiel 23:14-15:[204]

> 14 But she carried her whorings further; she saw male figures carved on the wall, images (צלם) of the Chaldeans portrayed in vermilion, 15 with belts around their waists, with flowing turbans on their heads, all of them looking like officers—a picture (דמת) of Babylonians whose native land was Chaldea.

Hence, Westermann insists that "we have not two but one expression."[205] It is an expression that points to what Westermann claims to be the "most striking statement" of the creation narrative—"over and above God being the creator, preserver and sustainer of creation, is that God created human beings in his image."[206] Termed *Imago Dei*, this linking of humans with the divine image has throughout history served as a fruitful way to construct a Christian notion of self and personhood. Westermann has insightfully pointed out both the significance of this concept in Christian theology and its relative textual obscurity:

> Since biblical interpretation came in contact with Greek thought and the modern understanding of humanity, scarcely any passage in the whole of the Old Testament has retained such interest as the verse which says that God created the person according

---

202. Barth, *The Humanity of God*, 80-81.

203. For the history of interpretation, see Barr, "Image of God," 11-26; Clines, "The Image of God in Man," 53-103; De Lacey, "Image and Incarnation," 3-28; Miller, "'Image' and 'Likeness' of God," 289-304; Hamman, *L'homme, image de Dieu*, 106-13; Jónsson, *The Image of God*, 10-22; Köhler, "Die Grundstelle der imago-Dei-Lehre," 16-22; Sawyer, "The Meaning of *betselem elohim*," 418-26; Van Leeuwen, "Form, Image," 643-48; Welker, "Creation and the Image of God," 436-48.

204. Westermann, *Genesis*, 145-46.

205. Ibid., 145.

206. Ibid., 604.

> to his image. The literature is limitless. The main interest has been on what is being said theologically about humankind: what is a human being? What is striking is that one verse about the person, almost unique in the Old Testament, has become the center of attention in modern exegesis, whereas it has no such significance in the rest of the Old Testament and, apart from Ps 8, does not occur again.[207]

In the Old Testament the concept of *Imago Dei* is confined to three texts in Genesis (1:26–27; 5:1–3; 9:5–6). Additionally one finds two clear references to it in the New Testament (1 Cor 11:7 and Jas 3:9). It is no wonder that this concept has opened itself to interpretive debate. Norman Snaith has pointedly observed:

> Many "orthodox" theologians through the centuries have lifted the phrase "the image of God" (*imago Dei*) right out of its context, and, like Humpty-Dumpty, they have made the word mean just what they choose it to mean.[208]

With this caveat in mind, we turn to Douglas John Hall, who has helpfully summed up various historical conceptions of *Imago Dei* under two headings.[209] The first is the substantialistic conceptions that see *Imago Dei* as something imparted into human beings such as immortality, freedom or rationality. Here *Imago Dei* implies that

> human species possesses certain characteristics or qualities that render it similar to the divine being. These characteristics or qualities are built into *anthropos*; they are aspects of human nature as such. They are "capacities," "qualities," "original excellencies," or "endowments" that inhere in our creaturely substance (hence the "substantialistic concept" of the "imago").[210]

Second, the relational category envisions *Imago Dei* as

> an inclination or proclivity occurring within the relationship . . . between Creator and creature. The image of God is something that "happens" as a consequence of this relationship. The human creature images (used as verb) its Creator because and insofar

---

207. Ibid., 148.
208. Snaith, "The Image of God," 24.
209. Hall credits the origin of these two categories to Paul Ramsey. See Ramsey, *Basic Christian Ethics*.
210. Hall, *Imaging God*, 89.

as it is "turned towards" God. To be *imago Dei* does not mean to have something but to be and do something: to image God.[211]

It is in this relational category that Hall finds a fruitful way forward. Hall's analysis displays that the roots of the relational way of thinking regarding *Imago Dei* go back to the sixteenth-century Reformers, especially to Luther and Calvin. According to Hall, Luther's primary reason for rejecting substantialistic conceptions of *Imago Dei*, including those of his favorite Augustine, was that he was "moved in a fundamental way by the relational character of the whole biblical testimony."[212] Luther's articulation of justification by grace alone, through faith alone (*sola gratia, sola fide*) hinged on his coming to grips with the fact that the primary categories of Christian belief were all relational,

> *Grace* was not a substance but a deed, a continuing gift-deed of the living God to living creatures; *faith* was not the assent to objectifiable dogmas or propositions about God, but assent to God's person and presence, an ongoing response of trust (*Vertrauen*) that is the creature's right response to the gift of grace; sin was not a quantitative thing, measurable in misdeeds and wicked thoughts that could be reckoned up, confessed, and balanced off through equally quantifiable acts of penance, but rather the abrogation of relationship, turning away from God; *righteousness*—a word Luther learned to abhor while it was interpreted as a quality that he knew he did not and could not possess—became for him the designation of a new and right relationship with God.[213]

Furthermore, Hall's analysis demonstrates how significant was the relational way of thinking regarding *Imago Dei* for Calvin. This comes through most clearly in Calvin's writings on the ways the creation, as God's masterpiece, reflects his glory. Calvin argues that while all of creation is involved in that process, human beings as the *imago* do so in a peculiar way. Calvin's reasons, Hall insists, are not about

> the distinction between human and nonhuman in terms of superior qualities in the former; rather, it has to do with the specific vocation of the human being. This vocation is: representatively and articulately to mirror the *doxa theou* from a position within the creation. Such a vocation is possible not

---

211. Ibid., 98.
212. Ibid., 99.
213. Ibid.

because of any quality or talent belonging to the human creature as such, but because, so long as it is turned towards its Creator, this creature reflects (images) the Creator within creation as a mirror reflects the sun.[214]

Calvin's metaphor of a mirror is significant for Hall's thinking regarding the relational category of the *Imago Dei*. According to Hall, the function of a mirror is that it reflects what it is turned towards. He quotes approvingly Torrance's thought that "only while the mirror actually reflects an object does it have the image of that object."[215] This brings us to Hall's probing thoughts on what the loss of the image might imply,

> When the "mirror" turns away from God and toward, say, pleasure, or the quest for security in things, or satisfaction in the self, it exchanges the divine image for something else. That is, when the human creature falls away from God, it loses the qualities that pertain to the relationship with God—just as the son in Jesus' famous parable, turning away from his father's house, forfeits certain conditions that pertained because of the relationship with his father. . . . In our state of estrangement from this source and ground we no longer image God, not because we have lost some inherent quality of our creaturehood but because we are literally disoriented. Thus in all of our thoughts, words, and deeds, even the best and bravest of them, we manifest the peculiarities of a broken relationship rather than the qualities accompanying a positive communion with the source of our being.[216]

Consequently, Hall suggests that the key to thinking of *Imago Dei* in relational terms is to take it as a verb rather than a noun. Thus he moves conversation to our "imaging of God" not as possessing some inherent quality or definitive attribute but as a vocation endowed on humanity by God. According to Hall, we image God "if and when and as we stand in a positive (responsive) relationship with God."[217]

Hall's interpretive move seems especially suggestive to those who come to Isaiah 14 as Christian scripture. He writes, "What we have not yet observed—what indeed most Western religious and secular history as a whole seems not to have observed—is how the interpretation of the connection between imaging God and having dominion is altered by the

---

214. Ibid., 104.
215. Ibid. Quote is from Torrance, *Calvin's Doctrine of Man*, 36.
216. Hall, *Imaging God*, 105–6.
217. Ibid., 107.

confession that Jesus is Lord."[218] Hall argues that when one takes Jesus as a paradigmatic model of what imaging God really looks like in this world one comes to embrace dominion *as* stewardship in its fullest sense of self-sacrifice. He writes, "The 'lordship' of the Crucified, if seriously grasped, radically transforms our preconception of dominion, exchanging for the concept of a superior form of being one of exceptional and deliberate solidarity (being-with), and for the notion of mastery a vocation to self-negating and responsible stewardship."[219] Hall goes on to wonder, "How could this christological critique of the human will to power have been so blatantly ignored in Christendom?"[220] In light of Hall's perceptive question, we turn our attention to the comparative analysis of the king of Babylon and Jesus as two distinct pictures of what one makes of the human quest for power and greatness.

A. *King of Babylon vs. Jesus Christ: Two Ways to Imago Dei*

The king of Babylon in Isaiah 14 seeks to become like God. Jesus is the likeness of God. The tyrant exploits others to gain equality with God. Jesus refuses to exploit his equality with God for selfish gain. The king of Babylon is a human being who is trying to transcend his humanity. Being in the form of God, Jesus willingly takes on the form of a human being and even embraces arguably the most challenging variety of it, namely a slave-like death on the cross. The contrast of these colorful images bring us to the heart of the question we set out to answer regarding reading Isaiah 14 as Christian scripture today. Where is true human greatness to be found? In this juxtaposition the notion of human flourishing is linked with the time-honored dynamic of the human-divine relationship. If one were to heuristically use Hall's categories for conceiving *Imago Dei*, then apparently either one makes oneself into a god as the king of Babylon (substantialistic conception) or one stands in faithful, obedient, and responsive relationship to God like Jesus (relational conception). Thus one is faced with the question of what kind of life fruitfully reflects *Imago Dei*. Four contrasting aspects may be brought out when comparing these two figures.

First, one detects divergent overarching directions of life. To use the contemporary language, we are faced with upward and downward

218. Ibid., 185.
219. Ibid., 186.
220. Ibid.

movements.[221] The king of Babylon climbs to the perceived heights. He stands as a paradigmatic picture of those who seek to transcend the life of a mere mortal in the company of gods. Jesus' life moves the opposite direction. He leaves the perceived heights of significance and descends to the lowest depths. George Herbert's memorable words summarize it well,

> Hast thou not heard, that my Lord JESUS di'd?
> Then let me tell thee a strange story.
> The God of power, as he did ride
> In his majestick robes of glorie
> Resolv'd to light; and so one day
> He did descend, undressing all the way.
>
> The stars his tire of light and rings obtain'd,
> The cloud his bow, the fire his spear,
> The sky his azure mantle gain'd.
> And when they ask'd, what he would wear;
> He smil'd and said as he did go,
> He had new clothes amaking here below.[222]

Second, one is invited to ask what motivates each direction of life. The king's god-like aspirations are cast in a condemning light. In self-aggrandizing arrogance he strikes the peoples (14:6), grabs resources (14:8) and hoards power (14:17). The prideful gaze upward energizes him to marshal his resources towards his own gain.

The synoptic tradition paints a picture of Jesus that stands in stark contrast to the king of Babylon. According to the Gospel of Matthew Jesus referred to himself as "gentle and humble in heart" (Matt 11:29). He is depicted saying these words in the context of his invitation for people to come and take his yoke upon them. His humble posture in linked with his mission of revealing the Father to his disciples (Matt 11:27). In Gethsemane he pleads with the Father, "Father, if you are willing, remove this cup from me." Yet with the agonizing painful prospect of death before him, Jesus yields to the Father's will, "Nevertheless, not my will, but yours, be done" (Luke 22:42).

---

221. Henri Nouwen is credited with the creation of a memorable imagery of "downward mobility" as a conscious posture of resistance against the Western corporate notion of "upward mobility." See, especially, Nouwen, *The Selfless Way of Christ*, 17–44.

222. Herbert, *The Country Parson*, 276.

The Johanine tradition paints a similar picture of a life energized by the relationship with the Father. In the Gospel of John, we encounter Jesus saying, "Truly, truly, I say to you, the Son can do nothing of his own accord, but only what he sees the Father doing. For whatever the Father does, that the Son does likewise" (John 5:19). Jesus is motivated by the faithful response to the Father. He does what pleases the Father, "My food is to do the will of him who sent me and to accomplish his work" (John 4:34). In the hour of death Jesus says, "Now is my soul troubled. And what shall I say? 'Father, save me from this hour'? But for this purpose I have come to this hour. Father, glorify your name" (John 12:27–28).

Third, these two different modes of existence bear a radically different fruit. The king's reign was characterized by wrath, anger, and unrelenting persecution (14:6). The earth trembled and kingdoms shook as he exercised his dominion (14:16). Cities were sacked, people were abused, and the world turned into a desert (14:17). At the height of his depravity he turned against his own, killing his people and devastating his own land (14:20). In many ways the king of Babylon suggests that Nietzsche's suspicion might be correct that "man is the cruelest animal."[223]

The life of Jesus bears a different fruit. The essence of what Jesus anticipates becomes evident when John the Baptist sends his two disciples with a simple question, "Are you the one who is to come, or shall we look for another?" (Matt 11:3). Having been imprisoned, John was evidently following Jesus' ministry from a distance and, for whatever reason, what he saw did not meet his expectations of what the Messiah would do. The answer he receives highlights the heartbeat of Jesus' understanding of his own mission. Jesus sends John's disciples back with these words, "Go and tell John what you hear and see: the blind receive their sight and the lame walk, lepers are cleansed and the deaf hear, and the dead are raised up, and the poor have good news preached to them. And blessed is the one who is not offended by me" (Matt 11:4–6). At one point, in the Johanine tradition, Jesus sums up his mission the following way, "I came that they may have life and have it abundantly" (John 10:10).

Fourth, these two lives have radically different outcomes. On the face of it both lives suffer a similar fate of humiliating death. For the tyrant it is a death that lacks a proper burial while being thrown out as a useless piece of wood (Isa 14:19). His body is exposed to decay with maggots fashioning his bed and worms serving as his cover (Isa 14:11). Jesus dies the death of a common criminal. In the way similar to the reception the dead rulers give to the tyrant (Isa 14:10), Jesus is sneered at by the onlooking crowd and

223. Nietzsche, *Thus Spoke Zarathustra*, 175.

mocked by the elders of Israel on his way to death (Matt 27:39–44). The Roman soldiers repeatedly ridicule and brutalize him as they prepare him for the crucifixion (Mark 15:16–20). Finally, he dies being nailed to the cross as an outcast and rejected criminal. It is no wonder that the apostle Paul would speak of the cross as "a stumbling block to Jews and foolishness to gentiles" (1 Cor 1:23).

Yet as similar as their deaths might be, the tyrant and Jesus are accorded two different outcomes. The king of Babylon sinks into oblivion. The ultimate tragedy of life squandered in the unmitigated self-aggrandizement is the name of the tyrant being erased from human memory forever (Isa 14:20–21). It is worth reflecting on the paradox inherent in this Isaianic portrayal of the king of Babylon becoming a part of Israel's canonical scriptures. One might even wonder which is more tragic, being forgotten or being remembered as the paradigmatic picture of wasted life.

Jesus anticipates a different fate. While the crucifixion signals the low point of his abasement, Jesus is exalted in the resurrection. As Athanasius of Alexandria would write in the fourth century, "A marvelous and mighty paradox has thus occurred, for the death which they thought to inflict on Him as dishonor and disgrace has become the glorious monument to death's defeat."[224] These words echo Philippians 2:6–11 which is a significant witness to the early church's understanding of Jesus. Here we find the resurrection described in the language of exaltation, "Therefore, God also highly exalted him" (Phil 2:9). As a part of this divine exaltation Jesus is singled out as a recipient of creation-wide Lordship and praise (Phil 2:10–11). The one who humbles himself in obedient responsiveness to God ultimately finds his life exalted and affirmed on the cosmic scale.

Resonating with Isaiah 14 *After* Jesus: A Memorable Outworking to the Theme of Exaltation and Abasement in J. R. R. Tolkien's Characters of Morgoth and Sauron

One can often find the subject matter of scripture portrayed enduringly in contemporary literary works and popular films. It is not surprising then that the quest for creaturely exaltation has been frequently represented in Disney characters (Hades in *Hercules,* Scar in the *Lion King,* the Evil Queen in *Snow White*), since many Disney films consistently exploit mythically relevant motifs. Having considered the first-century reading of the משל of Isaiah 14 and its resonance in the broader Christian theological tradition,

---

224. St. Athanasius, *On the Incarnation,* 54.

we now turn our attention to the way the perennial quest for creaturely self-exaltation and subsequent abasement is represented in the memorable characters birthed by J. R. R. Tolkien's imagination. Shippey argues persuasively that Tolkien should be considered "Author of the Century."[225] This provocative description reflects the simple fact that despite some critics' attempts to dismiss his importance, Tolkien's writings have enjoyed a widespread popularity for several decades. Tolkien continues to resonate with his audience because he shows how myth depicts reality. He himself lamented the unfortunate neglect of this genre in his contemporary world, "Fairy-stories have in the modern lettered world been relegated to the 'nursery,' as shabby or old-fashioned furniture is relegated to the play-room, primarily because the adults do not want it, and do not mind if it is misused."[226] On the contrary, Tolkien has insisted that "History often resembles 'Myth' because they are both ultimately made of the same stuff."[227] In other words, both history and myth have a capacity to portray the truth of reality. Tolkien's world rings true. We recognize issues like quest for power when they are depicted with full imaginative seriousness. What is true of Tolkien's Middle-Earth is also true of the משל of Isaiah 14. Drawing on ancient mythic imagination, especially in verses 12–15, the משל presents a "glimpse of the underlying reality of truth."[228] Thus, Tolkien's portrayal of Morgoth and Sauron promises to be a worthy literary counterpart to the משל of Isaiah 14.

A. The Theme of Exaltation and Abasement in Tolkien's Portrayal of Morgoth and Sauron

Tolkien has pointed out the hideous nature of creaturely overreach for power when he suggested that while the 'angelic' powers of his mythological world "were capable of many degrees of error and failing," by far the worst was "the absolute Satanic rebellion and evil of Morgoth and his satellite Sauron."[229] To these figures one might also perhaps add a third, Saruman—the notorious leader of The White Council, whose quest for power and ultimate fall plays a significant role in *The Lord of the Rings*. Nevertheless, we will stay with Tolkien's own imaginative emphasis that seems to give more weight to the hubris of the characters of Morgoth and Sauron.

---

225. Shippey, *Author of the Century*.
226. Tolkien, "On Fairy-stories," 58.
227. Ibid., 55.
228. Ibid., 88.
229. Carpenter, *The Letters of J. R. R. Tolkien*, 202.

Morgoth was originally known as Melkor, the most powerful of the angelic Ainur created by Ilúvatar in the Timeless Halls as "the offspring of his thought."[230] Despite being the greatest among the Ainur, Melkor rebelled against his creator.

Ilúvatar endowed each of his Ainur with a portion of his power and knowledge inviting them to sing Eä (the Universe) into existence. He gave them his theme and bid them to bring forth their music,

> Of the theme that I have declared to you, I will now that ye make in harmony together a Great Music. And since I have kindled you with the Flame Imperishable, ye shall show forth your powers in adorning this theme, each with his own thoughts and devices, if he will. But I will sit and harken, and be glad that through you great beauty has been wakened into song.[231]

When the chorus of the Ainur embarked on the fully collaborative Great Music elaborating on Ilúvatar's theme, Melkor participated with all the others, yet chose to "interweave matters of his own imagining that were not in accord with the theme of Ilúvatar."[232] The impetus for this disruptive move was to be found in Melkor's desire "to increase the power and the glory of the part assigned to himself."[233] Impatient with the process of musical learning and collaboration, Melkor often wandered alone into the void that would eventually become Eä through the music of the Ainur. In his wanderings "desire grew hot within him to bring into Being things of his own."[234] It is out of that ill-formed longing that Melkor descended to Arda with numerous Ainur. While other Ainur went to live and rule Arda as Ilúvatar's regents, Melkor's plan slowly became "to subdue to his will both Elves and Men, envying the gifts with which Ilúvatar promised to endow them; and he wished himself to have subjects and servants, and to be called Lord, and to be master over other wills."[235]

Though named by Ilúvatar Melkor (He who arises in might), he forfeited that name as the Noldor, the elves who experience most of his malice, refused to utter that name and instead gave him the name "Morgoth, the Dark Enemy of the World."[236] With resemblance of the imagery of Isaiah 14, Tolkien describes the fate of Morgoth in vivid colors,

230. Tolkien, *The Silmarillion*, 3.
231. Ibid.
232. Ibid., 4.
233. Ibid.
234. Ibid.
235. Ibid., 8.
236. Ibid., 23.

> Great might was given to him by Ilúvatar, and he was coëval with Manwë. In the powers and knowledge of all the other Valar he had part, but he turned them to evil purposes, and squandered his strength in violence and tyranny. For he coveted Arda and all was in it, desiring the kingship of Manwë and dominion over the realms of his peers. From splendor he fell through arrogance to contempt for all things save himself, a spirit wasteful and pitiless. Understanding he turned to subtlety in perverting to his own will all that he would use, until he became a liar without shame. He began with the desire of Light, but when he could not possess it for himself alone, he descended through fire and wrath into a great burning, down into Darkness.[237]

In the end, the Valar intervene and utterly defeat the forces of Morgoth. His abasement, once again, evokes reflective parallels with the final reversal of fortunes experienced by the tyrant of Babylon,

> Then the sun rose, and the host of the Valar prevailed, and wellnigh all the dragons were destroyed; and all the pits of Morgoth were broken and unroofed, and the might of the Valar descended into the deeps of the earth. There Morgoth stood at last at bay, and yet unvaliant. He fled into the deepest of his mines, and sued for peace and pardon; but his feet were hewn from under him, and he was hurled upon his face. Then he was bound with the chain Angainor which he had worn aforetime, and his iron crown they beat into a collar for his neck, and his head was bowed upon his knees.[238]

> Morgoth himself the Valar thrust through the Door of Night beyond the Walls of the World, into the Timeless Void; and a guard is set for ever on those walls, and Eärendil keeps watch upon the ramparts of the sky.[239]

According to Tolkien, Morgoth's evil intention was supremely complemented by his trusted lieutenant, Sauron, who "was only less evil than his master in that for long he served another and not himself."[240] Originally, Sauron was one of the Maiar of Aulë, who "remained mighty in the lore of that people."[241] He was among the Ainur who entered into Eä but was soon seduced by Melkor and thus became "the greatest and most trusted of the

237. Ibid.
238. Ibid., 303.
239. Ibid., 306.
240. Ibid., 23–24.
241. Ibid., 23.

servants of the Enemy, and the most perilous."[242] His wielding of power towards his twisted ends is resonant with the devastating effects of the reign of the king of Babylon, "Sauron was become now a sorcerer of dreadful power, master of shadows and of phantoms, foul in wisdom, cruel in strength, misshaping what he touched, twisting what he ruled, lord of werewolves; his dominion was torment."[243]

After the War of Wrath and the downfall of Morgoth, Sauron emerged as his own master seeking to subdue Middle-Earth by crafting the One Ring to control the Rings of Power,

> Now the Elves made many rings; but secretly Sauron made One Ring to rule all the others, and their power was bound up with it, to be subject wholly to it and to last only so long as it too should last. And much of the strength and will of Sauron passed into that One Ring; for the power of the Elven-rings was very great, and that which should govern them must be a thing of surpassing potency; and Sauron forged it in the Mountain of Fire in the Land of Shadow. And while he wore the One Ring he could perceive all the things that were done by means of the lesser rings, and he could see and govern the very thoughts of those that wore them.[244]

Sauron audaciously claims the title of "King of Kings and Lord of the World."[245] His quest for self-exaltation is well summed up by Tolkien in one of his letters, "Sauron desired to be a God-King, and was held to be this by his servants; if he had been victorious he would have demanded divine honor from all rational creatures and absolute temporal power over the whole world."[246]

Once again, we are struck by the resonance of the ultimate fate of Sauron with that of the king of Babylon. When Gollum fell into the Cracks of Doom carrying the One Ring, thus causing the Ring to be unmade, the foundations of Barad-dûr came undone and the great fortress of Sauron crumbled. "Towers fell and mountains slid; walls crumbled and melted, crashing down; vast spires of smoke spouting steams went billowing up, up, until they toppled like an overwhelming wave, and its crest curled and came foaming down upon the land."[247]

242. Ibid., 341.
243. Ibid., 182.
244. Ibid., 344.
245. Carpenter, *Letters*, 155.
246. Ibid., 243–44.
247. Tolkien, *The Return of the King*, 925–26.

With the One Ring destroyed, Sauron was stripped of his power. His armies, powerless and demoralized, were utterly vanquished. Tolkien's vivid imagination portrays Sauron's final destiny as that of an impotent spirit hovering over the ashes of Mordor not unlike the dead tyrant of Babylon in the company of the shades of Sheol,

> "The realm of Sauron is ended!" said Gandalf. "The Ring-bearer has fulfilled his Quest." And as the Captains gazed to the Land of Mordor, it seems to them that, black against the pall of cloud, there rose a huge shape of shadow, impenetrable, lighting-crowned, filled all the sky. Enormous it reared above the world, and stretched out towards them a vast threatening hand, terrible but impotent: for even as it leaned over them, a great wind took it, and it was all blown away, and passed; and then a hush fell.[248]

B. Thinking Christianly about the Theme of Creaturely Exaltation and Abasement with J. R. R. Tolkien

While Tolkien rejected any notion of allegory as applied to his epic, it has been pointed out that deep parallels can be detected between Tolkien's narrative and the Christian story.[249] Shippey compares Tolkien's myth of Creation with a "summary list of doctrines of the Fall of Man common to Milton, to St. Augustine, and to the Church as a whole" that C. S. Lewis presented in his *A Preface to Paradise Lost*.[250] Shippey writes,

> Significantly he left a gap in *the Silmarillion*, or designed a dovetail, for the Fall of Man as described in the Old Testament. In his work the human race does not originate "on stage" in Beleriand, but drifts into it, already sundered in speech, from the East. There something terrible has happened to them of which they will not speak: "A darkness lies behind us . . . and we have turned our backs on it." Furthermore they have met "the Lord of the Dark" before they meet the Elves; Morgoth went to them as soon as they were created, to "corrupt or destroy." Clearly one

---

248. Ibid., 928.

249. Tolkien's dislike for allegory is clearly expressed in his foreword to the second edition of *The Fellowship of the Ring*, "I cordially dislike allegory in all its manifestations, and always have done so since I grew old and wary enough to detect its presence. I much prefer history—true or feigned—with its varied applicability to the thought and experience of readers. I think that many confuse applicability with allegory, but the one resides in the freedom of the reader, and the other in the purposed domination of the author." See Tolkien, *The Fellowship of the Ring*, xix.

250. Shippey, *The Road to Middle-Earth*, 235.

can, if one wishes, assume that the exploit of Morgoth of which the Eldar never learnt was the traditional seduction of Adam and Eve by the serpent, while the incoming Edain and Easterlings are all descendants of Adam flying from Eden and subject to the curse of Babel.[251]

In the end, Shippey concludes that in Tolkien we encounter "a calque on Christian story."[252]

Shippey's observations could be meaningfully nuanced by turning to Tolkien's own thoughts found in his letters. In a letter to a close family friend, Father Robert Murray, Tolkien wrote,

> *The Lord of the Rings* is of course a fundamentally religious and Catholic work; unconsciously so at first, but consciously in the revision. That is why I have not put in, or have cut out, practically all references to anything like "religion," to cults or practices, in the imaginary world. For the religious element is absorbed into the story and the symbolism.[253]

Tolkien admitted that this was not so much a result of carefully planned strategy but rather is reflective of the faith that "has nourished me and taught me all the little that I know."[254] Furthermore, it is interesting to consider Tolkien's response to W. H. Auden's review of *The Return of the King*. While being appreciative of Auden's largely sympathetic review, Tolkien denied the charges that his was an attempt to "objectify" his own personal experience for readers' pleasure, presenting them with an imaginary epic Quest of the Ring. He wrote, "The story is not about JRRT at all, and it is at no point an attempt to allegorize his experience of life."[255] Tolkien insisted that he was historically minded. He stressed that "Middle-earth is not an imaginary world."[256] Rather, it is "an imaginary historical moment on 'Middle-earth'—which is our habitation."[257] Indeed, Shippey has suggested that the continuing appeal of Tolkien's fantasy is not a "mere freak of popular taste," but rather is due to the fact Tolkien's work is a "deeply serious response to what will be seen in the end as the major issues of his century."[258] At the top of

---

251. Ibid., 236.
252. Ibid.
253. Carpenter, *Letters*, 172.
254. Ibid.
255. Ibid., 239.
256. Ibid.
257. Ibid., 244.
258. Shippey, *Author of the Century*, 18.

these issues Shippey places "the origin and nature of evil (an eternal issue, but one in Tolkien's lifetime terribly re-focused)."[259]

On the one hand, there are indeed touch points with the overarching Christian story where meaningful parallels could be found between Satan and Morgoth. Tolkien writes, "I do not think that any rate any 'rational being' is wholly evil. Satan fell. In my myth Morgoth fell before Creation of the physical world."[260] On the other hand, it is interesting to note how Tolkien envisions Sauron:

> In my story Sauron represents as near an approach to the wholly evil will as is possible. He had gone the way of all tyrants: beginning well, at least on the level that while desiring to order all things according to his own wisdom he still at first considered the (economic) well-being of other inhabitants of the Earth. But he went further than human tyrants in pride and the lust for domination, being in origin an immortal (angelic) spirit. In *The Lord of the Rings* the conflict is not basically about "freedom," though that is naturally involved. It is about God, and His sole right to divine honour.[261]

It is these resonances with "the way of all tyrants" that make Tolkien's story so evocatively parallel with Isaiah 14. Pride and lust for dominion serve as a powerful drive towards creaturely self-exaltation. Yet in the tragic reversal of fortunes that drive carries within itself its own death sentence as God retains his sole right to divine honor. Thus, both stories underscore the perennial truth that malevolent rulers will be defeated, their nefarious schemes will be thwarted, and their kingdoms will crumble.

These stories offer contemporary readers, who have not yet seen the tyrants of our times crumble, an impetus to persevere. We hear in Frodo's words uttered in the midst of the darkness of yet-to-be-resolved narrative tension, "They cannot conquer forever!"[262] the same hope that sustains the readers of Isaiah 14 who long to share in the celebration to follow YHWH's decisive intervention, "How the oppressor has ceased, the insolent fury ceased!" (14:4). Christian readers are fortified in hope that when Samwise Gamgee says, "Above all shadows rides the Sun,"[263] these are not just wishful words of a fanciful tale but the enduring hope evocatively voiced in the turbulent moments of journey echoing and anticipating what we hear in the

---

259. Ibid.
260. Carpenter, *Letters*, 243.
261. Ibid.
262. Tolkien, *The Two Towers*, 311.
263. Tolkien, *The Return of the King*, 195.

משל of Isaiah 14, "The LORD has broken the staff of the wicked, the scepter of rulers" (14:5)—words that find their ultimate expression in the words of Jesus on the cross, "It is finished" (John 19:30), signaling that evil, however prevalent and daunting, will be vanquished forever in him.

Tolkien himself spoke to this, however dimly seen, hope in his letter to Amy Ronald, "Actually I am a Christian, and indeed a Roman Catholic, so that I do not expect 'history' to be anything but a 'long defeat'—though it contains (and in a legend may contain more clearly and movingly) some samples or glimpses of final victory."[264] It is these samples and glimpses of the final victory that radiate through Tolkien's vividly construed imaginary world of Middle Earth and evocatively amplified downfalls of Morgoth and Sauron giving his readers something more than "just a fool's hope."[265]

---

264. Carpenter, *Letters*, 255.
265. Tolkien, *The Return of the King*, 83.

8

Conclusion

MY AIM IN THIS book has been to explore in practice what reading the Old Testament as Christian scripture today could look like. Chapter 1 explored the key philological issues often discussed in scholarship. These issues range from the use of *hapax legomemon* words such as מדהבה in verse 4 to the range of meaning inherent in the use of the word ארץ (earth) in verse 7. All this amounted to highlighting the challenges inherent in translating a text from one language to another. The process involves more than translating words but also transcribing worlds. Chapter 2 discussed the meaning and function of the word משל at the opening of this poem. Following Polk's lead, I find the genre of משל to be a powerful tool for drawing a paradigmatic comparison seeking to shape the audience's response. As Alter aptly states it, this is a poem with "archetypifying force,"[1] which takes a conventional form of a funeral dirge and uses it for its own purposes, namely to portray in vivid colors the folly of a human quest for self-exaltation. Chapter 3 sought to enter the imaginative world of the משל of Isaiah 14:3–23 in order to give a sense of the poem as a whole. Chapter 4 addressed three significant issues that are commonly brought up in scholarly discussions regarding this text. The goal was not merely to rehearse old arguments but to show that the issues of myth and history are very closely intertwined and any serious reading of this text must take seriously the mythological background and function of the הֵילֵל בֶּן־שָׁחַר image in Isaiah 14:12–15, the historical referent of the unnamed king of Babylon, and the formation of the Oracles Against the Nations in Isaiah 13–23, which is the canonical home of Isaiah 14:3–23. Chapter 5 examined how this text has been read as Christian scripture through the centuries by focusing on two significant historical figures, Origen and Calvin. Rather than a comprehensive survey, it was an attempt to shed light on a particular issue, i.e. the reading of Isaiah 14:12–15 as a portrayal of the downfall of Satan. Exploring the contexts of each of these expositors and their range of exegetical emphases, it became clear that theological presuppositions and existential interests play a significant role in their

1. Alter, *Art*, 146.

varied readings of the text as Christian scripture. Chapter 6 explored the issue of reading Isaiah 14:3–23 as Christian scripture today. Having drawn a contrast between two premier Christian interpreters, Brueggemann and Seitz, I ventured to offer a few thoughts on how one can read this text fruitfully today in relation to Jesus Christ. I offered a reading of this text *with* Jesus focusing on key texts where references to Isaiah 14 have been placed on the lips of Jesus by the New Testament texts. Furthermore, I suggested reading this text *in the light of* Jesus through exploring the contrasting portrayals of the King of Babylon and Jesus as *Imago Dei*. Finally, I explored the reading of this text *after* Jesus by examining Tolkien's portrayal of Morgoth and Sauron as a contemporary attempt to think Christianly about the theme of creaturely exaltation and abasement.

It is appropriate to conclude this book by briefly commenting on the logic that holds it all together. What makes reading the OT as Christian Scripture different from other approaches to the OT? The words of Levenson addressing the strengths and limitations of historical-critical inquiry could be heuristically helpful in illuminating what is at stake here, "The challenge to historical critics of the Old Testament who wish to be Christian and their work to be Christian has been to find a way to read the Old Testament that is historically sound but also lends credibility to its literary context, its juxtaposition to the New Testament to form a coherent book."[2]

The underlying presupposition of my book has been that the reading of Isaiah 14:3–23 as Christian Scripture ought to seek the reciprocal relationship between historical and theological inquiry. Levenson has articulated well the concerns of the historical-critical analysis, "No intellectually responsible exposition ... can take place without locating the text unshakably within the historical circumstances of its composition."[3] While there are limitations to historical inquiry and its ability to locate texts in their historical contexts with precision, it has served scholarship well. Hence, one does not set aside the accumulated wisdom of biblical scholarship but rather seeks to carefully utilize and integrate its best findings for theological purposes. Exploring the philological nuances and probing questions of myth and history in Isaiah 14 sharpen our understanding of the text at hand. However problematic the historical-critical inquiry might be, one does not dispense with the familiar philological and historical discussions but orients them towards reading the biblical text in relation to continuing Christian faith.

Furthermore, Origen and Calvin display different aspects of the hermeneutical challenges that arise when the Isaiah text is read in relation to

---

2. Levenson, *The Hebrew Bible*, 10.
3. Ibid., 5.

continuing Christian faith, as do Brueggemann and Seitz and my own reading in a contemporary context. It is instructive to note that all five of these readings seek to offer a careful exegesis of the text while bringing to the forefront larger theological issues. As Levenson has pointed out, the goal of traditional theological interpretation is "examination of how the vitality of yesteryear can energize the present."[4] The veracity of that statement is seen when one recognizes that while Origen comes to Isaiah 14 shaped by his interest in exploring the issue of creaturely free will as it relates to the origins of evil, Calvin is focused on the complexities surrounding divine sovereignty as it relates to taking one's faith seriously in the turbulent times of Europe in the Reformation era. It is these bigger perennial theological issues that guide their careful reading of the text. In similar fashion, both Brueggemann and Seitz seek to orient their reading to the larger issues of Christian faith and praxis, albeit without such singular focus as that found in the readings of Origen and Calvin. It is worth noting that neither Brueggemann nor Seitz seek to interact with the classical readings of this text. Especially interesting is their silence regarding the reading of Isaiah 14:12–15 as the downfall of Satan. Coming from such a prolific advocate of reengaging with the long history of the theological reading throughout the history of the church as Seitz, the lack of interaction with it especially peculiar. It is in this vein that my own modest contribution attempts to stand closer to the classical readings even if not following Origen's reading of Isaiah 14:12–15 as the downfall of Satan or Calvin's interest in divine sovereignty. Particularly, my engagement with Tolkien's portrayal of the creaturely quest for self-exaltation seeks to capture some of the classical concerns regarding larger existential issues. All of this signals the fact that theological interpretation is not "one thing" done in "this one way." While not an endorsement of unrestrained plurality of meanings of the text, such variety of emphases in readings of Isaiah 14 shows that in many ways one's reading of Isaiah as Christian scripture seems to be always "contemporary," i.e. closely tied with one's context, theological presuppositions, and existential interests.

In the end, I am led to quote from Moberly, "Theological interpretation is reading the Bible with a concern for the enduring truth of its witness to the nature of God and humanity, with a view to enabling the transformation of humanity into the likeness of God."[5] It is my hope that this book could make a, however small, contribution to this enduring task by demonstrating what it looks like when applied to such a complex yet memorable text as Isaiah 14:3–23.

4. Ibid.
5. Moberly, "Theological Interpretation," 163.

Bibliography

Abusch, T. "Ghost and God: Some Observations on a Babylonian Understanding of Human Nature." In *Self, Soul and Body in Religious Experience,* edited by Albert I. Baumgarten with Jan Assmann and Guy G. Stroumsa, 327–78. Studies in the History of Religion. vol. 78. Leiden: Brill, 1998.

Albani, M. "The Downfall of Helel, the Son of Dawn: Aspects of Royal Ideology in Isa 14:12–13." In *The Fall of the Angels,* edited by Christoph Auffarth and Loren T. Stuckenbruck, 62–86. Leiden: Brill, 2004.

Albrektson, B. "Difficilior Lectio Probabilior: A Rule of Textual Criticism and Its Use in Old Testament Studies." *OtSt* 21 (1981) 3–18.

———. *Text, Translation, Theology: Selected Essays on the Hebrew Bible.* Burlington, VT: Ashgate, 2010.

Albright, W. F. *Archeology and the Religion of Israel.* OTL. 1942. Reprint. Louisville, KY: Westminster John Knox, 2006.

———. *Yahweh and the Gods of Canaan: A Historical Analysis of Two Contrasting Faiths.* Garden City, NY: Doubleday, 1968.

Albright, W. F., and C. S. Mann. *Matthew.* AB. Garden City, NY: Doubleyday, 1971.

Allen, M., and J. Fisher, eds. *The Complete Poetry and Prose of Geoffrey Chaucer.* Boston: Wadsworth, 2010.

Alter, R. *The Art of Biblical Poetry.* New York: Basic, 1985.

Arnold, B. T. *Who Were the Babylonians?* SBLABS 10. Atlanta: Society of Biblical Literature, 2004.

Astour, M. C. *Hellenosemitica: An Ethnic and Cultural Study in West Semitic Impact on Mycenaean Greece.* Leiden: Brill, 1967.

Athanasius, St. *On the Incarnation.* Crestwood, NY: St. Vladimir's Seminary Press, 1993.

Augustine. *The City of God Against the Pagans.* Edited by R. W. Dyson. Cambridge: Cambridge University Press, 1998.

———. *The Confessions of Saint Augustine.* Translated by John K. Ryan. New York: Doubleday, 1960.

———. "Exposition on the Psalms." *NPNF1* vol. 8.

———. "Homilies on the Gospel of St. John." *NPNF1* vol. 7.

———. "On the Morals of the Manichaeans." *NPNF1* 4:69–89.

Bailey, L. R. *Biblical Perspectives on Death.* Philadelphia: Fortress, 1979.

Balthasar, H. U. von. "Preface." In *Origen: An Exhortation to Martyrdom, On Prayer, First Principles: Book IV, Prologue to the Commentary on the Song of Songs, Homily XXVII on Numbers.* Translated by Rowan A. Greer. New York: Paulist, 1979.

Bamberger, B. J. *Fallen Angels: Soldiers of Satan's Realm.* Philadelphia: Jewish Publication Society, 1952.

Barr, J. *Comparative Philology and the Text of the Old Testament: With Additions and Corrections.* Winona Lake, IN: Eisenbrauns, 1987.
———. *The Concept of Biblical Theology: An Old Testament Perspective.* London: SCM, 1999.
———. *The Garden of Eden and the Hope of Immortality.* London: SCM, 1992.
———. "The Image of God in the Book of Genesis: A Study of Terminology." *BJRL* 51 (1968) 11–26.
Barth, C. *Die Errettung vom Tode in den individuellen Klage- und Dankliedern des Alten Testaments.* Zürich: Zollikon, 1947.
Barth, H. *Die Jesaja-Worte in der Josiazeit: Israel und Assur als Thema einer produktiven Neuinterpretation der Jesajaüberlieferung.* WMANT 48. Neukirchen-Vluyn: Neukirchener, 1977.
Barth, K. *The Humanity of God.* Louisville, KY: Westminster John Knox, 1996.
Barton, J. *The Nature of Biblical Criticism.* Louisville, KY: Westminster John Knox, 2007.
Bauckham, R. *The Fate of the Dead: Studies on the Jewish and Christian Apocalypses.* Leiden: Brill, 1998.
Baumgartner, W. *Zum Alten Testament und seiner Umwelt: ausgewählte Aufsätze.* Leiden: Brill, 1959.
Begg, C. T. "Babylon in the Book of Isaiah." In *The Book of Isaiah/ Le livre d'Isaïe*, edited by J. Vermeylen, 121–25. Leuven: Leuven University Press, 1989.
Bentley, R., ed. *A Selection of Most Celebrated Sermons of M. Luther and J. Calvin.* New York: Carvill, 1829.
Berlin, A. *Poetics and Interpretation of Biblical Narrative.* Winona Lake, IN: Eisenbrauns, 1994.
Blenkinsopp, J. *Isaiah 1–39.* AB. New Haven: Yale, 2000.
Bloch-Smith, E. *Judahite Burial Practices and Beliefs about the Dead.* JSOTSS 123. Sheffield, UK: Sheffield Academic Press, 1992.
Boadt, L. "Understanding the Mashal and Its Value for Jewish-Christian Dialogue in a Narrative Theology." In *Parable and Story in Judaism and Christianity*, edited by Clemens Thoma and Michael Wyschogrod, 172–76. New York: Paulist, 1989.
Bonkamp, B. *Die Bibel im Lichte der Keilschriftforschung.* Recklinghausen: Visarius, 1939.
Booth, W. C. *A Rhetoric of Irony.* Chicago: University of Chicago Press, 1974.
Bottéro, J. "La mythologie de la mort en Mésopotamie ancienne." In *Death in Mesopotamia: Papers Read at the XXVIe Rencontre Assyriologique Internationale*, edited by Bendt Alster, 25–52. Copenhagen: Akademisk Forlag, 1980.
Bouwsma, W. J. "Calvinism as Renaissance Artifact." In *John Calvin & the Church*, edited by Timothy George, 28–41. Louisville, KY: Westminster John Knox, 1990.
———. *John Calvin: A Sixteenth-Century Portrait.* New York: Oxford University Press, 1988.
Breasted, J. H. *Ancient Records of Egypt: Historical Documents.* Vol. 1. Chicago: University of Chicago Press, 1906.
Bremmer, J. N. "Remember the Titans!" In *The Fall of the Angels*, edited by C. Auffarth and L. T. Stuckenbruck, 35–61. Leiden: Brill, 2004.
Briant, P. *From Cyrus to Alexander: A History of Persian Empire.* Translated by Peter T. Daniels. Winona Lake, IN: Eisenbrauns, 2002.
Brichto, H. C. "Kin, Cult, Land and Afterlife—A Biblical Complex." *HUCA* 44 (1973) 1–54.

Brinkman, J. A. *A Political History of Post-Kassite Babylonia: 1158-722 B.C.* Rome: Pontifical Biblical Institute, 1968.
Brueggemann, W. *Interpretation and Obedience: From Faithful Reading to Faithful Living.* Minneapolis: Fortress, 1991.
———. *An Introduction to the Old Testament: The Canon and Christian Imagination.* Louisville, KY: Westminster John Knox, 2003.
———. *Isaiah 1-39.* WBC. Louisville, KY: Westminster John Knox, 1998.
———. *Old Testament Theology: An Introduction.* Nashville: Abingdon, 2008.
———. *Old Testament Theology: Essays on Structure, Theme, and Text,* edited by Patrick D. Miller. Minneapolis: Fortress, 1992.
———. *Out of Babylon.* Nashville: Abingdon, 2010.
———. *A Pathway of Interpretation.* Eugene, OR: Cascade, 2008.
———. *Peace.* St. Louis, MO: Chalice, 2001.
———. *Testimony to Otherwise: Witness of Elijah and Elisha.* St. Louis, MO: Chalice, 2001.
———. *The Creative Word: Canon as a Model for Biblical Education.* Philadelphia: Fortress, 1982.
———. *Theology of the Old Testament.* Minneapolis: Fortress, 1997.
———. *Theology of the Old Testament: Testimony, Dispute, Advocacy.* Minneapolis: Fortress, 1997.
———. "The Re-emergence of Scripture: Post-liberalism." In *The Bible in Pastoral Practice,* edited by Paul Ballard and Stephen R. Holmes, 153-73. Grand Rapids: Eerdmans, 2005.
Brueggemann, W., and C. J. Sharp. *Living Countertestimony: Conversations with Walter Brueggemann.* Louisville, KY: Westminster John Knox, 2012.
Bückers, H. *Die Unsterblichkeitslehre des Weisheitsbuches.* Münster: Aschendorff, 1938.
Budde, K. "Das hebräische Klagelied." *ZAW* 2 (1882) 1-52.
Bunson, M. *Encyclopedia of Ancient Egypt.* Rev. ed. New York: Facts on File, 2012.
Calvin, J. *Calvin's New Testament Commentaries: 2 Corinthians and Timothy, Titus & Philemon.* Vol. 10. Translated by T. A. Smail. Grand Rapids: Eerdmans, 1964.
———. *Calvin's New Testament Commentaries: Galatians, Ephesians, Philippians and Colossians.* Vol. 11. Translated by T. H. L Parker. Grand Rapids: Eerdmans, 1965.
———. *Calvin's New Testament Commentaries: Romans and the Thessalonians.* Vol. 8. Translated by Ross MacKenzie. Grand Rapids: Eerdmans, 1960.
———. *Commentary on the Book of the Prophet Isaiah.* 4 vols. Translated by William Pringle. Grand Rapids: Eerdmans, 1953.
———. *Commentary on the Book of Psalms.* 5 vols. Translated by James Anderson. 1845. Reprint. Grand Rapids: Baker, 1979.
———. *Commentary upon the Acts of the Apostles.* 2 vols. Translated by Henry Beverage. Grand Rapids: Eerdmans, 1949.
———. *Concerning the Eternal Predestination of God.* Translated by J. K. S. Reid. Cambridge: James Clarke & Co, 1961.
———. *Institutes of the Christian Religion.* Translated by Henry Beverage. Grand Rapids: Eerdmans, 1995.
Caquot, A. "Les Rephaim ougaritiques." *Syria* 37 (1960) 75-93.
Carmignac, J. "Six passages d'Isaïe éclairés par Qumran." In *Bibel und Qumran: Beiträge zur Erforschung der Beziehungen zwischen Bibel- und Qumranwissenschaft,* edited by Siegfried Wagner, 37-46. Berlin: Evangelische Haupt-Bibelgesellschaft, 1968.

Carpenter, H. ed. *The Letters of J. R. R. Tolkien.* Boston: Houghton Mifflin, 1981.
Cassuto, U. *The Goddess Anath.* Jerusalem: Magnes, 1971.
Cheyne, T. K. *Introduction to the Book of Isaiah.* London: A. & C. Black, 1895.
———. *The Prophecies of Isaiah: A New Translation with Commentary and Appendices.* 2 vols. London: Kegan Paul, Trench, 1882.
Childs, B. *Biblical Theology in Crisis.* Philadelphia: Fortress, 1970.
———. *Biblical Theology of the Old and New Testaments: Theological Reflection on the Christian Bible.* Minneapolis: Fortress, 1992.
———. "Interpreting the Bible Amid Cultural Change." *Theology Today* 54 (1997) 200–11.
———. *Introduction to the Old Testament as Scripture.* Philadelphia: Fortress, 1979.
———. *Isaiah.* OTL. Louisville, KY: Westminster John Knox, 2001.
———. *The Struggle to Read Isaiah as Christian Scripture.* Grand Rapids: Eerdmans, 2004.
Clemens, D. M. "Review of *Of Dead Kings and Dirges: Myth and Meaning in Isaiah 14:4b–2.*" *JNES* 66.3 (2007) 213–16.
Clements, R. E. *Isaiah 1–39.* NCB. Grand Rapids: Eerdmans, 1980.
Clines, D. J. A. "The Image of God in Man." *TB* 19 (1968) 53–103.
Cobb, W. H. "The Ode in Isaiah xiv." *JBL* 15.1/2 (1896) 18–35.
Cohen, A. C. *Death, Rituals, Ideology, and the Development of Early Mesopotamian Kingship: Towards a New Understanding of Iraq's Royal Cemetery of Ur.* Leiden: Brill, 2005.
Collins, J. "Introduction: Toward the Morphology of a Genre." In *Apocalypse: The Morphology of a Genre,* edited by John J. Collins, 1–20. Semeia 14. Atlanta: Society of Biblical Literature, 1979.
Coogan, M. D., and M. S. Smith. *Stories from Ancient Canaan.* 2nd ed. Louisville, KY: Westminster John Knox, 2012.
Cook, P. M. *A Sign and a Wonder: The Redactional Formation of Isaiah 18–20.* Leiden: Brill, 2011.
Cooper, J. S. "The Fate of Mankind: Death and Afterlife in Ancient Mesopotamia." In *Death and Afterlife: Perspectives of World Religions,* edited by Hiroshi Obayashi, 19–33. New York: Greenwood, 1992.
Cordova, C. E. *Millennial Landscape Change in Jordan: Gaearcheology and Cultural Ecology.* Phoenix: The University of Arizona Press, 2007.
Craigie, P. C. "Helel, Athtar, and Phaethon. (Jes 14:12–15)." *ZAW* 85 (1973) 223–25.
Cross, F. M. *Canaanite Myth and Hebrew Epic: Essays in the History of the Religion of Israel.* Harvard: Harvard University Press, 1973.
Crouzel, H. *Origen: The Life and Thought of the First Great Theologian.* Translated by A. S. Worrall. San Francisco: Harper & Row, 1989.
Curkpatrick, S. "Between *Mashal* and Parable: 'Likeness' as a Metonymic Enigma." *HBT* 24 (2002) 58–71.
Dandamaev, M. A. *A Political History of the Achaemenid Empire.* Leiden: Brill, 1989.
Daniélou, J. *Origen.* Translated by Walter Mitchell. New York: Sheed and Ward, 1955.
Darr, K. P. *Isaiah's Vision and the Family of God.* Louisville, KY: Westminster John Knox, 1994.
Davies, W. D., and D. C. Allison. *Matthew 8–18.* ICC. London: T. & T. Clark, 2004.
Davis, E. F., and R. B. Hays, eds. *The Art of Reading Scripture.* Grand Rapids: Eerdmans, 2003.

Day, J. "The Development of Belief in Life after Death in Ancient Israel." In *After the Exile: Essays in Honour of Rex Mason*, edited by John Barton and David J. Reimer, 231–57. Macon, GA: Mercer University Press, 1996.

———. *Yahweh and the Gods and Goddesses of Canaan*. Sheffield, UK: Sheffield Academic, 2000.

Deal, K. H. *Wildlife and Natural Resource Management*. Clifton Park, NY: Delmer, 2011.

Delitzsch, F. *Biblical Commentary on the Prophecies of Isaiah*. Edinburgh: T. & T. Clark, 1894.

Dempsey, C. J. *Isaiah: God's Poet of Light*. Atlanta: Chalice, 2010.

Derrida, J. "The Law of Genre." In *Modern Genre Theory*, edited by David Duff, 219–31. Harlow, UK: Longman, 2000.

Diggle, J. *Euripides: Phaethon*. Cambridge: Cambridge University Press, 2004.

Dille, S. J. *Mixing Metaphors: God as Mother and Father in Deutero-Isaiah*. London: T. & T. Clark, 2004.

Dillmann, A. *Der Prophet Jesaja*. 6th ed. Kurzgefasstes exegetisches Handbuch zum Alten Testament 5. Leipzig: Hirzel, 1898.

Driver, G. R. *Canaanite Myths and Legends*. Edinburgh: T. & T. Clark, 1956.

———. "Review of M. Dahood, *Proverbs and Northwest Semitic Philology*." *JSS* 10 (1965) 112–17.

Driver, S. R. *An Introduction to the Literature of the Old Testament*. Rev. ed. New York: Scribner's Sons, 1912.

Duhm, B. *Das Buch Jesaia*. Göttingen: Vandenhoeck & Ruprecht, 1892.

Durham, C. W., and K.A. Pruitt eds. *Uncircumscribed Mind: Reading Milton Deeply*. Cranbury, NJ: Associated University Presses, 2007.

Eco, U. "Between Author and Text." In *Interpretation and Overinterpretation*, edited by Stefan Collini, 67–88. Cambridge: Cambridge University Press, 1992.

Eichrodt, W. *Der Herr der Geschichte: Jesaja 13–23 und 28–39*. Stuttgart: Calwer, 1967.

Eissfeldt, O. *Der Maschal im Alten Testament*. BZAW 24. Gießen: Töpelmann, 1913.

———. *The Old Testament: An Introduction*. Translated by Peter R. Ackroyd. New York: Harper and Row, 1965.

Emerton, J. A. "Are there Examples of Enclitic *mem* in the Hebrew Bible?" In *Texts, Temples and Traditions: A Tribute to Menahem Haran*, edited by Michael V. Fox et al., 321–38. Winona Lake, IN: Eisenbrauns, 1996.

Erlandsson, S. *The Burden of Babylon: A Study of Isaiah 13:2—14:23*. Lund: Gleerup, 1970.

Eusebius of Caesarea. *Commentary on Isaiah*. Ancient Christian Texts. Translated by Jonathan J. Armstrong. Dower Grove, IL: IVP Academic, 2013.

———. *Preparation for the Gospel*. Reprint. Eugene, OR: Wipf and Stock, 2002.

Evans, C. F. *Saint Luke*. 2nd ed. London: SCM, 2008.

Ferris, P. W., Jr. *The Genre of Communal Lament in the Bible and the Ancient Near East*. SBLDS 127. Atlanta: Scholars, 1992.

Fisher, H. G. "Notes on Sticks and Staves in Ancient Egypt." *MMJ* 13 (1978) 5–32.

Fitzmyer, J. A. *Scripture, the Soul of Theology*. New York: Paulist, 1994.

———. *The Gospel according to Luke X–XXIV*. The Anchor Bible 28A. Garden City, NY: Doubleday, 1985.

Fohrer, G. *Das Buch Jesaja*. Vol.1. ZBK. Zurich: Zwingli, 1960.

Forsyth, N. *The Old Enemy: Satan and the Combat Myth*. Princeton: Princeton University Press, 1987.

———. *The Satanic Epic*. Princeton: Princeton University, 2003.
Fowl, S. E. *Theological Interpretation of Scripture*. Eugene, OR: Cascade, 2009.
Fowler, A. *Kinds of Literature: An Introduction to the Theory of Genres and Modes*. Cambridge: Harvard University Press, 1982.
France, R. T. *The Gospel of Matthew*. NICOT. Grand Rapids: Eerdmans, 2007.
Freeman, P. *Alexander the Great*. New York: Simon & Schuster, 2011.
Gallagher, W. R. "On the Identity of Helel ben Sahar of Isa. 14:12–15." *UF* 26 (1995) 131–46.
———. *Sennacherib's Campaign to Judah: New Studies*. Leiden: Brill, 1999.
Gaster, T. H. *Thespis: Ritual, Myth and Drama in the Ancient Near East*. New York: Harper and Row, 1950.
Gathercole, S. J. "Jesus' Eschatological Vision of the Fall of Satan: Luke 10.18 Reconsidered." *ZNW* 94 (2003) 143–63.
George, T. "Introduction." In *John Calvin & the Church*, edited by Timothy George, 15–27. Louisville, KY: Westminster John Knox, 1990.
Geuss, R. *The Idea of a Critical Theory: Habermas and the Frankfurt School*. New York: Cambridge University Press, 1981.
Gibbon, E. *The History of the Decline and Fall of the Roman Empire*. Vol. 1. New York: Harper, 1831.
Gibson, J. C. L. *Canaanite Myths and Legends*. Edinburgh: T. & T. Clark, 1978.
Ginsberg, H. L. "Reflexes of Sargon in Isaiah After 715 B.C.E." *JAOS* 88.1 (1968) 49–53.
Glassner, J. *Mesopotamian Chronicles*. Leiden: Brill, 2004.
Godbey, A. H. "The Hebrew Mashal." *AJSL* 39 (1922–23) 89–108.
Goldingay, J. *Isaiah*. NIBC. Peabody, MA: Hendrickson, 2001.
———. *The Theology of the Book of Isaiah*. Downers Grove, IL: InterVarsity, 2014.
Goldingay, J., and D. Payne. *A Critical and Exegetical Commentary on the Book of Isaiah 40–55*. 2 vols. London: T. & T. Clark, 2006.
Good, E. M. *Irony in the Old Testament*. Sheffield, UK: Almond, 1981.
Gosse, B. *Isaïe 13, 1–14, 23 dans les traditions littéraires du livre d'Isaïe et dans la tradition des oracles contre les nations*. Göttingen: Vandenhoeck & Ruprecht, 1988.
Gottwald, N. K. *All the Kingdoms of the Earth*. New York: Harper, 1964.
Gowan, D. E. *When Man Becomes God: Humanism and Hybris in the Old Testament*. Pittsburgh: Pickwick, 1975.
Gowler. D. B. *What Are They Saying About the Parables?* New York: Paulist, 2000.
Grassi, J. A. "CHILD, CHILDREN." *ABD* 1:904–7.
Gray, G. B. *A Critical and Exegetical Commentary on the Book of Isaiah I–XXXIX*. ICC. Edinburgh: T. & T. Clark, 1912.
———. "DTN and RPUM in Ancient Ugarit." *PEQ* 84 (1952) 39–41.
———. "The Rephaim." *PEQ* 81 (1949) 127–39.
Gray, J. *The Legacy of Canaan: the Ras Sharma Texts and Their Relevance to the Old Testament*. Sup. *VT* 5. Leiden: Brill, 1957.
Grayson, A. K. *Assyrian Royal Inscriptions, Part 2: From Tiglath-pileser I to Ashur-nasir-apli II*. Wiesbaden, Germany: Harrassowitz, 1976.
Greene-McCreight, K. E. *Ad Litteram: How Augustine, Calvin, and Barth Read the "Plain Sense" of Genesis 1–3*. New York: Lang, 1999.
Greer, R. A. *Theodore of Mopsuestia: Exegete and Theologian*. Westminster: Faith, 1961.
Gregory the Great. "The Book of Pastoral Rule and Selected Epistles." In *NPNF2* 12:1–72.

———. "Epistle XVIII: To John, Bishop." In *NPNF2* 12:166–69.
———. "Epistle XXI: To Constantina Augusta." In *NPNF2* 12:171–73.
———. *Homiliae in Hiezechihelem*. In *CCSL* 142:326–27.
Grelot, P. "Isaïe 14, 12–15 et son arrière-plan mythologique." *Revue de l'histoire des religions*, 149.1 (1956) 18–48.
———. "Sur la vocalización de הילל (Is. XIV, 12)." *VT* 6 (1956) 303–4.
Gunkel, H. *Creation and Chaos in the Primeval Era and the Eschaton: A Religio-historical Study of Genesis 1 and Revelation 12*. Translation of *Schöpfung und Chaos in Urzeit und Endzeit: eine religionsgeschichtliche Untersuchung über Gen 1 und Ap Joh 12*. Göttingen: Vandenhoeck and Ruprecht, 1895. Grand Rapids: Eerdmans, 2006.
Guthe, H. *Das Zukunftsbild des Jesaia*. Leipzig: Breitkopt & Härtel, 1885.
Hageneder, F. *The Meaning of Trees: Botany–History–Healing–Love*. San Francisco: Chronicle, 2005.
Hagner, D. *Matthew 1–13*. WBC 33A. Dallas: Word, 1993.
Hall, D. J. *Imaging God: Dominion as Stewardship*. Grand Rapids: Eerdmans, 1986.
Hallote, R. S. *Death, Burial, and Afterlife in the Biblical World: How the Israelites and Their Neighbors Treated the Dead*. Chicago: Dee, 201.
Hamblin, W. J. *Warfare in the Ancient Near East: Holy Warriors at the Dawn of History*. New York: Routledge, 2006.
Hamman, A. G. *L'homme, image de Dieu: essai d'une anthropologie chrétienne dans l'Église des cinq premiers siècles*. Relais-études 2. Paris: Desclée, 1987.
Hansmann, J. "Gilgamesh, Humbaba and the Land of the *Erin* Trees." *Iraq* 38 (1976) 23–35.
Hanson, R. P. C. *Allegory and Event: A Study of the Sources and Significance of Origen's Interpretation of Scripture*. Richmond, VA: John Knox, 1959.
Harris, R. L. "The Meaning of the Word Sheol as Shown by Parallels in Poetic Texts." *JETS* 4 (1961) 129–35.
Harrison, R. P. *Forests: The Shadow of Civilization*. Chicago: University of Chicago Press, 1992.
Hausig, H. W., ed. *Wörterbuch der Mythologie: Götter und Mythen im Vorderen Orient*. Vol. 1. Stuttgart: Klett, 1965.
Hayes, J. H., and S. A. Irvine. *Isaiah: The Eighth Century Prophet: His Times and His Preaching*. Louisville, KY: Abingdon, 1987.
Hays, C. B. *Death in the Iron Age II and in First Isaiah*. Forschungen zum Alten Testament 79. Tübingen: Mohr Siebeck, 2011.
Hays, R. B. "Reading the Bible with Eyes of Faith: The Practice of Theological Exegesis." *JTI* 1.1 (2007) 5–21.
Healey, J. F. "Mot." In *DDD*, 1122–32.
Heidel, A. *The Gilgamesh Epic and Old Testament Parallels*. Chicago: University of Chicago Press, 1946.
Heidl, G. *Origen's Influence on the Young Augustine: A Chapter of the History of Origenism*. Piscataway, NJ: Gorgias, 2003.
Heilmeyer, M. *Ancient Herbs*. Los Angeles: Getty, 2007.
Heine, R. E. *Origen: Scholarship in the Service of the Church*. Oxford: Oxford University Press, 2010.
Heiser, M. S. "The Mythological Provenance of Isa. XIV 12–15: A Reconsideration of the Ugaritic Material." *VT* 51, Fasc. 3 (2001) 354–69.
Herbert, A. S. "The 'Parable' (*Māšāl*) in the Old Testament." *SJT* 7 (1954) 180–96.

Herbert, G. *The Country Parson. The Temple.* Mahwah, NJ: Paulist, 1981.
Hesiod. *Theogony, Works and Days, Testimonia.* Translated by Glenn W. Most. LCL 57. Harvard: Harvard University Press, 2007.
Hill, J. V. "Luke 10.18—Who Saw Satan Fall?" *JSNT* 46 (1992) 25–40.
Hippolytus. "Treatise on Christ and Antichrist." In *ANF* 5:204–19.
Hitzig, F. *Der Prophet Jesaja.* Heidelberg: Winter, 1833.
Holladay, W. L. "Text, Structure, and Irony in the Poem on the Fall of the Tyrant, Isaiah 14." *CBQ* 61 (1999) 633–45.
Homer. *The Odyssey.* Translated by Robert Fitzgerald. New York: Farrar, Straus and Giroux, 1998.
Horwitz, W. J. "The Significance of the Rephaim." *JNSL* 7 (1979) 37–43.
Huffmon, H. B. "Shalim." In *DDD*, 755–57.
Hummel, H. D. "Enclitic *Mem* in Early Northwest Semitic, Especially Hebrew." *JBL* 76 (1957) 85–106.
Hurtado, L. "GOD." *DJG*, 270–76.
Iannucci, A. A., ed. *Dante, Cinema and Television.* Toronto: University of Toronto, 2004.
Jacobsen, T. *The Sumerian King List.* Chicago: University of Chicago Press, 1939.
Jahnow, H. *Das hebräische Leichenlied im Rahmen der Völker-dichtung.* BZAW 36. Gießen: Töpelmann, 1923.
Jerome. "Against Jovinianus." In *NPNF2* 6:346–416.
———. "Dialogue against Pelagians." In *NPNF2* 6:447–82.
———. *Commentariorum in Isaiam Prophetam.* In *CCSL* 73.
———. "Letter XXII: To Eustochium." In *NPNF2* 6:22–40.
———. "Letter CXXXIII: To Ctesiphon." In *NPNF2* 6:272–79.
Jirku, A. "Rapa'u, der Fürst der Rapa'uma-Rephaim." *ZAW* 77 (1965) 82–83.
Johnston, P. S. *Shades of Sheol: Death and Afterlife in the Old Testament,* 128–42. Downers Grove, IL: IVP Academic, 2002.
Jong, M. J. de. *Isaiah Among the Ancient Near Eastern Prophets: A Comparative Study of the Earliest Stages of the Isaiah Tradition.* Leiden: Brill, 2007.
Jónsson, G. A. *The Image of God: Genesis 1:26–28 in a Century of Old Testament Research.* Translated by Lorraine Svendsen, 10–22. Lund: Almqvist and Wiksell, 1988.
Josephus. *The Life. Against Apion.* LCL 186. Translated by H. St. J. Thackeray. Cambridge: Harvard University Press, 1997.
Kaiser, O. *Isaiah 13–39.* OTL. Philadelphia: Westminster, 1974.
Kaminsky, J. S. "Review of *Theology of the Old Testament: Testimony, Dispute, Advocacy.*" *RBL.* 8 Nov 1999. Online: https://www.bookreviews.org/bookdetail.asp?TitleId=76&CodePage=76,4878.
Keel, O. *The Song of Songs: A Continental Commentary.* Minneapolis: Fortress, 1994.
———. *The Symbolism of the Biblical World: Ancient Near Eastern Iconography and the Book of Psalms.* Translated by Timothy J. Hallett. Winona Lake, IN: Eisenbrauns, 1997.
Keil, C. F., and F. Delitzsch. *Isaiah.* Vol.7. Grand Rapids: Eerdmans, 1969.
Kelle, B. E. "Wartime Rhetoric: Prophetic Metaphorization of Cities as Females." In *Writing and Reading War: Rhetoric, Gender, and Ethics in Biblical and Modern Contexts,* edited by Brad E. Kelle and Frank Ritchel Ames, 95–112. Atlanta: Society of Biblical Literature, 2008.
Keown, G. L. "A History of the Interpretation of Isaiah 14:12–15." PhD diss., Southern Baptist Theological Seminary, 1979.

Kilian, R. *Jesaja*. Vol. 1. BKAT 10. Neukirchen-Vluyn: Neukirchener Verlag, 1965.
Kilpatrick, G. G. D. "Exposition of Chapters 1–39." In *The Interpreter's Bible*, edited by George Arthur Buttrick et al. Vol. 5. New York: Abingdon, 1956.
King, P. J., and L. E. Stager. *Life in Biblical Israel*. Louisville, KY: Westminster John Knox, 2001.
Kissane, E. J. *The Book of Isaiah: Translated from a Critically Revised Hebrew Text with Commentary*, vol. 1 *(I–XXXIX)*. Dublin: Richview, 1941.
Kitto, J. ed. *The Cyclopedia of Biblical Literature*. Vol. 1. New York: American Book Exchange, 1881.
Klein, R. W. *Textual Criticism of the Old Testament From the Septuagint to Qumran*. Philadelphia: Fortress, 1974.
Knibb, M. A. "Life and Death in the Old Testament." In *The World of Ancient Israel: Sociological, Anthropological and Political Perspectives*, edited by R. E. Clements, 395–415. Cambridge: Cambridge University Press, 1989.
Knobel, A. *Der Prophet Jesaja*. 4th ed. Kurzgefasstes exegetisches Handbuch zum Alten Testament 5. Leipzig: Weidmann, 1843.
Koenig, N. A. "Lucifer." *ET* 18 (October 1906–September 1907) 479.
Köhler, L. "Die Grundstelle der imago-Dei-Lehre, Gen. 1:26." *Theologische Zeitschrift* 4 (1948) 16–22.
König, E. *Das Buch Jesaja: Eingeleitet, übersetzt und erklärt*. Gütersloh: Bertelsmann, 1926.
———. *Historisch-Kritisches Lehrgebäude der Hebräischen Sprache*. Vol. 2.1. Leipzig: Hinrichs, 1895.
Korpel, M. C. A. *A Rift in the Clouds: Ugaritic and Hebrew Descriptions of the Divine*. UBL 8. Münster: Ugarit-Verlag, 1990.
Kraus, H. J. "Calvin's Exegetical Principles." *Interpretation* 31 (1997) 8–18.
Lacey, D. R. de. "Image and Incarnation in Pauline Christology: A Search for Origins." *Tyndale Bulletin* 30 (1979) 3–28.
Landes, G. E. "Jonah: A *Māšāl*?" In *Israelite Wisdom: Theological and Literary Essays in Honor of Samuel Terrien*, edited by John G. Gammie et al., 137–46. Missoula: Scholars, 1978.
Langdon, S. H. "The Star Hêlel, Jupiter?" *Expository Times* 42 (1931) 172–74.
Leeuwen, R. C. van. "Isa 14:12, *Hôlēš ʾal GWYM* and Gilgamesh XI, 6." *JBL* 99 (1980) 173–84.
Leick, G. *A Dictionary of Ancient Near Eastern Mythology*. New York: Routledge, 1991.
Leith, J. H. "Calvin's Doctrine of the Proclamation of the Word and Its Significance for Today." In *John Calvin & the Church*, edited by Timothy George, 206–29. Louisville, KY: Westminster John Knox, 1990.
Levenson, J. *The Hebrew Bible, The Old Testament, and Historical Criticism*. Louisville, KY: Westminster/ John Knox, 1993.
———. "Is Brueggemann Really a Pluralist?" *HTR* 93.3 (2000) 265–94.
———. *Resurrection and the Restoration of Israel: The Ultimate Victory of the God of Life*. New Haven: Yale University Press, 2006.
Levering, M. *Participatory Biblical Exegesis: A Theology of Biblical Interpretation*. Notre Dame, IN: University of Notre Dame Press, 2008.
Levine, B. A., and J. de Tarragon. "Dead Kings and Rephaim: The Patrons of the Ugaritic Dynasty." *JAOS* 104 (1984) 649–59.
Lewis, C. S. *A Preface to Paradise Lost*. Oxford: Oxford University Press, 1961.

Lewis, T. J. "Dead, The Abode of." *ABD* 2:101–5.
L'Heureux, C. E. "The *yelîdê hārāpā*'—A Cultic Association of Warriors." *BASOR* 221 (1976) 83–85.
Liebreich, L. J. "The Compilation of the Book of Isaiah 1." *JQR* 46 (1955–56) 259–77.
———. "The Compilation of the Book of Isaiah 2." *JQR* 47 (1956–57) 114–38.
Lie, A. G., ed. *The Inscriptions of Sargon II King of Assyria—Part I: The Annals*. Paris: Geuthner, 1929.
Lindenlauf, A. "Thrown Away Like Rubbish—Disposal of the Dead in Ancient Greece." *Papers from the Institute of Archeology* 12 (2001) 86–99. Online: http://repository.brynmawr.edu/cgi/viewcontent.cgi?article=1156&context=arch_pubs.
Liphscitz, N. *Timber in Ancient Israel: Dendroarcharology and Dendrochronology*. Tel Aviv: Tel Aviv University Press, 2007.
Lohmann, P. *Die anonymen Prophetien gegen Babel aus der Zeit des Exils*. Berlin: Blanke, 1910.
Louden, B. *The Iliad: Structure, Myth, and Meaning*. Baltimore: John Hopkins University Press, 2006.
Louth, A. *Discerning the Mystery*. Oxford: Clarendon, 1983.
Lubac, H. de. *History and Spirit: The Understanding of Scripture according to Origen* [Translated from *Histoire et esprit: L'Intelligence de l'Écriture d'après Origène*. Paris: Montaigne, 1950.] Translated by Anne Englund Nash and Juvenal Merriell. San Francisco: Ignatius, 2007.

———. *Medieval Exegesis Volume I: The Four Senses of Scripture*. [Translated from *Exégèse mèdiévale, 1: Les quatre sens de l'écriture*. Paris: Montaigne, 1958.] Translated by Mark Sebanc. Grand Rapids: Eerdmans, 1998.
Luke, H. M. *Dark Wood to White Rose: Journey and Transformation in Dante's Divine Comedy*. New York: Parabola, 1989.
Luther, M. *Luther's Works*. St. Louis: Concordia/Philadelphia: Fortress, 1955–86.
Luz, U. *Matthew 8–20*. Hermeneia. Minneapolis: Fortress, 2001.
Maag, V. "Tod und Jenseits nach dem Alten Testament." In *Schweizerische Theologische Umschau* 34 (1964) 17–37.
Machinist, P. "Assyria and Its Image in the First Isaiah." *JAOS* 103.4 (1983) 719–37.
Macholz, C. "Das 'Passivum Divinum,' seine Anfänge im Alten Testament und der 'Hofstil,'" *ZNW* 81 (1990) 247–53.
Mann, W. E. "Augustine on Evil and Original Sin." In *The Cambridge Companion to Augustine*, edited by Eleonore Stump and Norman Kretzmann, 40–48. Cambridge: Cambridge University Press, 2001.
Margulis, B. "Weltbaum and Weltberg in Ugaritic Literature: Notes and Observations on RŠ 24. 245." *ZAW* 86 (1974) 1–23.
Markos, L. *Heaven and Hell: Visions of the Afterlife in the Western Poetic Tradition*. Eugene, OR: Cascade, 2013.
Marcus, J. "Jesus' Baptismal Vision." *NTS* 41 (1995) 512–21.
Martens, P. W. *Origen and Scripture: The Contours of the Exegetical Life*. New York: Oxford University Press, 2012.
Marti, K. *Das Buch Jesaja*. Tübingen: Mohr, 1900.
Martin, R. P. "An Early Christian Hymn—(Col. 1:15–20)." *The Evangelical Quarterly* 36 (1964) 195–205.

McGrath, A. E. "Reclaiming Our Roots and Vision: Scripture and the Stability of the Christian Church." In *Reclaiming the Bible for the Church*, edited by Carl E. Braaten and Robert W. Jensen, 63–68. Grand Rapids: Eerdmans, 1995.

———. "Shapers of Protestantism: John Calvin." In *The Blackwell Companion to Protestantism*, edited by A. E. McGrath and D. C. Marks, 53–65. Oxford: Blackwell, 2004.

McKane, W. *Proverbs: A New Approach*. OTL. Philadelphia: Westminster, 1970.

McKay, J. W. "Helel and Dawn-Goddess: A Re-Examination of the Myth in Isaiah XIV 12–15." *VT* 20 (1970) 451–64.

Meier, S. A. *Speaking of Speaking: Marking Direct Discourse in Hebrew Bible*. New York: Brill, 1992.

Miller, J. M. "In the 'Image' and 'Likeness' of God." *JBL* 91 (1972) 289–304.

Milton, J. *Paradise Lost*. Edited by Alastair Fowler. London: Routledge, 2013.

Mizrahi, N. "The Textual History and Literary Background of Isa 14,4." *ZAW* 125.3 (2013) 433–47.

Moberly, R. W. L. "Biblical Criticism and Religious Belief." *JTI* 2.1 (2008) 71–100.

———. *Old Testament Theology: Reading the Hebrew Bible as Christian Scripture*. Grand Rapids: Baker Academic, 2013.

———. *Prophecy and Discernment*. Cambridge: Cambridge University Press, 2006.

———. "Theology of the Old Testament." In *The Face of Old Testament Studies: A Survey of Contemporary Approaches*, edited by David W. Baker and Bill T. Arnold, 452–78. Grand Rapids: Baker, 1999.

———. "What Is Theological Interpretation of Scripture?" *JTI* 3.2 (2009) 161–78.

Moor, J. C. de. *An Anthology of Religious Texts from Ugarit*. Leiden: Brill, 1987.

———. "Rapi'uma—Rephaim." *ZAW* 88 (1976) 325–45.

Moran, W. L. "The Hebrew Language in Its Northwest Semitic Background." *The Bible and the Ancient Near East: Essays in Honor of William Foxwell Albright*, edited by G. E. Wright, 59–84. London: Routledge & Kegan Paul, 1961.

Morgenstern, J. "The Mythological Background of Psalm 82." *HUCA* 14 (1939) 29–126.

Motyer, J. A. *The Prophecy of Isaiah*. Downers Grove, IL: InterVarsity, 1993.

Mounce, R. H. *Matthew*. NIBC. Peabody, MA: Hendrickson, 1991.

Muecke, D. C. *Irony and the Ironic*. London: Methuen, 1970.

Muller, R. A. *The Unaccommodated Calvin: Studies in the Foundation of a Theological Tradition*. New York: Oxford University Press, 2000.

Newsom, C. A. "Spying Out the Land: A Report from Genology." In *Bakhtin and Genre Theory in Biblical Studies*, edited by Roland Boer, 19–31. Atlanta: Society of Biblical Literature, 2007.

Nichols, J., ed. *The Works of James Arminius*. 3 vols. London: Longman, Hurst, Rees, Orme, Brown and Green, 1825.

Nickelsburg, G. W. E. *1 Enoch: A Commentary on the Book of 1 Enoch, Chapters 1–36*. Hermeneia. Minneapolis: Fortress, 2001.

Niditch, S. *Folklore and the Hebrew Bible*. Minneapolis: Fortress, 1993.

Niehoff, M. R. *Jewish Exegesis and Homeric Scholarship in Alexandria*. New York: Cambridge University Press, 2011.

Nielsen, K. "Old Testament Metaphors in the New Testament." In *New Directions in Biblical Theology: Papers of Aarus Conference 16–19 September 1992*, edited by Sigfred Pederson, 126–42. Supplements to Novum Testamentum 76. Leiden: Brill, 1994.

———. *There is Hope for a Tree: The Tree as Metaphor in Isaiah*. Sheffield, UK: Sheffield Academic Press, 1989.
Nietzsche, F. *Thus Spoke Zarathustra*. Cambridge Texts in the History of Philosophy. Cambridge: Cambridge University Press, 2006.
Nissen, H. J., and P. Heine. *From Mesopotamia to Iraq: A Concise History*. Chicago: University of Chicago Press, 2009.
Nolland J. *The Gospel of Matthew*. NIGTC. Grand Rapids: Eerdmans, 2005.
———. *Luke 9:21—18:34*. WBC 35B. Dallas: Word, 1993.
Nouwen, H. *The Selfless Way of Christ: Downward Mobility and the Spiritual Life*. Maryknoll, NY: Orbis, 2007.
O'Brien, J. M. *Challenging Prophetic Metaphor: Theology and Ideology in the Prophets*. Louisville, KY: Westminster John Knox, 2008.
O'Connell, R. H. "Isaiah XIV 4B–23: Ironic Reversal through Concentric Structure and Mythic Allusions." *VT* 38.4 (1998) 406–18.
O'Connor, F. *Mystery and Manners: Occasional Prose*. New York: Farrar, Straus and Giroux, 1970.
O'Connor, K. M. "Speak Tenderly to Jerusalem: Second Isaiah's Reception and Use of Daughter Zion." *PSB* 20 (1999) 281–94.
Oldenburg, U. "Above the Stars of El: El in Ancient South Arabic Religion." *ZAW* 82.2 (1970) 187–208.
———. *The Conflict between El and Ba'al in Canaanite Religion*. Leiden: Brill, 1969.
Olyan, S. M. *Social Inequality in the World of the Text: The Significance of Ritual and Social Distinctions in the Hebrew Bible*. Göttingen: Vandenhoeck & Ruprecht, 2011.
———. "Was the 'King of Babylon' Buried before His Corpse Was Exposed? Some Thoughts on Isa. 14:19." *ZAW* 118 (2006) 423–26.
Orelli, C. *The Prophecies of Isaiah*. Edinburgh: T. & T. Clark, 1889.
Origen. *Contra Celsum*. Translated by Henry Chadwick. Cambridge: Cambridge University Press, 1953.
———. *An Exhortation to Martyrdom, Prayer, and Selected Works*. Classics of Western Spirituality. New York: Paulist, 1979.
———. *Homilies on Genesis and Exodus*. Translated by R. E. Heine. Washington: Catholic University of America, 1982.
———. *Homilies on Luke: Fragments on Luke*. Translated by Joseph Lienhard, S.J. Washington, DC: The Catholic University of America, 1996.
———. *On First Principles*. Translated by G. W. Butterworth. New York: Harper & Row, 1966.
Orlinsky, H. M. "*MADHEBAH* in Isaiah XIV 4." *VT* 7 (1957) 202–3.
———. "Studies in the St. Mark's Isaiah Scroll, IV." *JQR* 43 (1953) 329–40.
Oswalt, J. N. *The Book of Isaiah: Chapters 1–39*. NICOT. Grand Rapids: Eerdmans, 1986.
Page, H. R., Jr. *The Myth of Cosmic Rebellion: A Study of Its Reflexes in Ugaritic and Biblical Literature*. Leiden: Brill, 1996.
Parker, S. B. "Shahar." In *DDD*, 754–55.
———. "The Ugaritic Deity Rap'iu." *UF* 4 (1972) 103.
Parker, T. H. L. *Calvin's Old Testament Commentaries*. Louisville, KY: Westminster John Knox, 1986.
———. *John Calvin: A Biography*. Oxford: Lion Hudson, 1975.

Parpola, S. "National and Ethnic Identity in the Neo-Assyrian Empire and Assyrian Identity in Post-Empire Times." *JAAS* 18.2 (2004) 5–22.

Phillips, G. *Alexander the Great: Murder in Babylon*. London: Virgin, 2012.

Poirier, J. C. "An Illuminating Parallel to Isaiah XIV 12." *VT* 49, Fasc. 3 (1999) 371–89.

Polk, T. "Paradigms, Parables and Mĕšālîm: on Reading the Māšāl in Scripture." *CBQ* 45.4 (1983) 564–83.

Pope, M. *El in the Ugaritic Texts*. Leiden: Brill, 1955.

———. "Notes on the Rephaim Texts from Ugarit." In *Essays on the Ancient Near East in Memory of Jacob Joel Finkelstein*, edited by Maria de Jong Ellis, 163–81. Hamden: Archon, 1977.

Potworowski, C. "Origen's Hermeneutics in Light of Paul Ricoeur." In *Origeniana Quinta*, edited by Robert Daily, 161–66. Leuven: Leuven University Press, 1992.

Prestige, G. L. *Fathers and Heretics*. London: SPCK, 1968.

Prinsloo, W. S. "Isaiah 14:12–15—Humiliation, Hubris, Humiliation." *ZAW* 93 (1981) 432–38.

Puckett, D. L. *John Calvin's Exegesis of the Old Testament*. Louisville, KY: Westminster John Knox, 1995.

Quell, G. "Jesaja 14:1–23." In *Festschrift für Friedrich Baumgärtel zum 70. Geburtstag, 14 Januar 1958*, edited by Johannes Herman, 156–57. Erlanger Forschungen 10. Erlangen, Bavaria: University of Erlangen Press, 1959.

Raine, P. *Who Guards the Guardians? Intercultural Dialogue on Environmental Guardianship*. Lanham, MD: University of America Press, 2003.

Ramsey, P. *Basic Christian Ethics*. New York: Scribner's Sons, 1950.

Reade, J. H. *Sacred Poems from Subjects in the Old Testament*. London: Saunders and Otley, 1843.

Reimer, D. J. "Overwhelmed by Theology? Brevard Childs' Commentary on Isaiah." *Expository Times* 113.2 (2001) 51–54.

Rendtorff, R. "The Paradigm is Changing: Hopes—and Fears." *Biblical Interpretation* 1.1 (1993) 34–53.

Retso, J. *The Arabs in Antiquity: Their History from the Assyrians to the Umayyads*. New York: Routledge, 2003.

Ricoeur, P. *Freud and Philosophy: An Essay on Interpretation*. New Haven: Yale University Press, 1970.

———. *Hermeneutics and the Human Science*. Edited by J. B. Thompson. Cambridge: Cambridge University Press, 1981.

Roberts B. J. *The Old Testament Text and Versions*. Cardiff: University of Wales Press, 1951.

Rosenberg R. "The Concept of Biblical Sheol within the context of Ancient near Eastern Beliefs: A Thesis." PhD diss., Harvard University, 1981.

Roux G. *Ancient Iraq*. 3rd ed. New York: Penguin, 1992.

Rufus, Q. C., *The History of Alexander the Great*. New York: Penguin, 2004.

Ryckmans, J. "South Arabia, Religion of." In *ABD* 6:171–76.

Saggs, H. W. F. *The Greatness That Was Babylon: A Survey of the Ancient Civilization of the Tigris Euphrates Valley*. Rev. ed. London: Sidgwick and Jackson, 1988.

Sawyer, J. F. A. *Isaiah Volume 1*. The Daily Study Bible. Philadelphia: Westminster, 1984.

———. "The Meaning of *betselem elohim* ('in the image of God') in Genesis I–XI." *JTS* 25.2 (1974) 418–26.

Schipper, J. *Parables and Conflict in the Hebrew Bible*. Cambridge: Cambridge University Press, 2009.

Schmidt, B. S. "Memory as Immortality: Countering the Dreaded 'Death after Death' in Ancient Israelite Society." In *Judaism in Late Antiquity, Vol. 3*, edited by Jacob Neusner et al., 87–100. Leiden: Brill, 2000.

Schmidt, K. L. "Lucifer als gefallene Engelmacht." *TZ* 7 (1951) 161–79.

Schöpflin, K. "Ein Blick in die Unterwelt (Jesaja 14)." *ThZ* 58 (2002) 299–314.

Schwally, F. "Ueber einige palästinische Völkernamen." *ZATW* 11 (1898) 126–48.

Scurlock, J. A. "Death and the Afterlife in Ancient Mesopotamian Thought." In *Civilizations of the Ancient Near East, Vol. 3*, edited by Jack M. Sasson, 1883–93. New York: Scribner, 1995.

Seitz, C. R. *The Character of Christian Scripture: The Significance of a Two-Testament Bible*. Grand Rapids: Baker Academic, 2011.

———. "Christological Interpretation of Texts and Trinitarian Claims to Truth: An Engagement with Francis Watson's *Text and Truth*." *SJT* 52.2 (1999) 209–26.

———. *Figured Out: Typology and Providence in Christian Scripture*. Louisville, KY: Westminster John Knox, 2001.

———. *The Goodly Fellowship of the Prophets: The Achievement of Association in Canon Formation*. Grand Rapids: Baker Academic, 2009.

———. "History, Figural History, and Providence in the Dual Witness of Prophet and Apostle." In *Go Figure! Figuration in Biblical Interpretation*, edited by S. D. Walters, 1–6. Reprint. Eugene, OR: Pickwick, 2008.

———. "Introduction: The One Isaiah//The Three Isaiahs." In *Reading and Preaching the Book of Isaiah*, edited by Christopher R. Seitz, 13–22. Philadelphia: Fortress, 1988.

———. *Isaiah 1–39*. Interpretation. Atlanta: Westminster John Knox, 1993.

———. "Isaiah 1–66: Making Sense of the Whole." In *Reading and Preaching the Book of Isaiah*, edited by Christopher R. Seitz, 105–26. Philadelphia: Fortress, 1988.

———. *Prophecy and Hermeneutics: Toward a New Introduction to the Prophets*. Grand Rapids: Baker, 2007.

———. *Word Without End: The Old Testament as Abiding Theological Witness*. Grand Rapids: Eerdmans, 1998.

Shipp, M. R. *Of Dead Kings and Dirges: Myth and Meaning in Isaiah 14:4b–21*. Boston: Brill, 2002.

Shippey, T. *J. R. R. Tolkien: Author of the Century*. Boston: Houghton and Mifflin, 2002.

———. *The Road to Middle-Earth: How J. R. R. Tolkien Created a New Mythology*. New York: Houghton Mifflin, 2003.

Skinner, J. *Isaiah I–XXXIX*. CBSC. Cambridge: Cambridge University Press, 1909.

Smith, G. A. *The Book of Isaiah*. Vol. 1. Rev. ed. New York: Harper, 1927.

Smith, M. S. "The God Athtar in the Ancient Near East and His Place in KTU 1.61." In *Solving Riddles and Untying Knots: Biblical, Epigraphic, and Semitic Studies in Honor of Jonas C. Greenfield*, edited by Ziony Zevit, Seymour Gitin, Michael Sokoloff, 627–40. Winona Lake, IN: Eisenbrauns, 1995.

———. *The Origins of Biblical Monotheism: Israel's Polytheistic Background and the Ugaritic Texts*. New York: Oxford University Press, 2001.

Snaith, N. "The Image of God." *ExpT* 86 (October 1974–September 1975) 24.

Snodgrass, K. *Stories with Intent: A Comprehensive Guide to the Parables of Jesus*. Grand Rapids: Eerdmans, 2008.

Soggin, J. A. *Introduction to the Old Testament*. OTL. Translation of the 4th ed. of *Introduzione all'Antico Testamento*. Louisville, KY: Westminster John Knox,1989.
Spronk, K. *Beatific Afterlife in Ancient Israel and in the Ancient Near East*. Neukirchen-Vluyn: Neukirchener Verlag, 1986.
———. "Down with Helel! Assumed Mythological Background of Isa. 14:12." In *"Und Mose schrieb dieses Lied auf": Studien zum Alten Testament und zum Alten Orient. Fs. O. Loretz*, edited by M. Dietrich and I. Kottsieper, with H. Schaudig, 717–26. AOAT 250. Münster: Ugarit-Verlag, 1998.
Staerk, W. *Das assyrische Weltreich im Urteil der Propheten*. Göttingen: Vandenhoeck und Ruprecht, 1908.
Steinmetz, D. "Calvin and the Irrepressible Spirit." *Ex Auditu* 12 (1996) 94–107.
———. "John Calvin on Isaiah 6 a Problem in the History of Exegesis." *Interpretation* 36.2 (1982) 156–70.
———. *Luther and Staupitz: An Essay in the Intellectual Origins of the Protestant Reformation*. Durham, NC: Duke University Press, 1980.
Stern, D. *Parables in Midrash: Narrative and Exegesis in Rabbinic Literature*. Harvard: Harvard University Press, 1991.
Stolz, F. "Die Baume der Gottesgartens auf dem Libanon." *ZAW* 84 (1972) 141–56.
———. *Religion und Rekonstruktion: Ausgewählte Aufsätze herausgegeben von Daria Pezzoli-Olgiati*. Göttingen: Vandenhoeck & Ruprecht, 2004.
———. *Strukturen und Figuren im Kult von Jerusalem*. BZAW 118. Berlin: de Gruyter, 1970.
Suriano, M. J. *The Politics of Dead Kings: Dynastic Ancestors in the Book of Kings and Ancient Israel*. Tübingen: Mohr Siebeck, 2010.
Suter, D. "*Māšāl* in the Similitudes of Enoch." *JBL* 100 (1981) 193–212.
Sweeney, M. A. *Isaiah 1–39*. FOTL. Grand Rapids: Eerdmans, 1996.
———. "On the Way to Duhm: Isaiah in Nineteenth-century Critical Scholarship." In *"AS THOSE WHO ARE TAUGHT": The Interpretation of Isaiah from the LXX to the SBL*, edited by Claire Mathews McGinnis and Patricia K. Tull, 243–63. Atlanta: Society of Biblical Studies, 2006.
Talmon, S. "Biblical *repā'îm* and Ugaritic *rpu/i(m)*," *HAR* 7 (1983) 235–49.
Tertullian, "Against Marcion." In *ANF* 3:269–476.
Thiselton, A. *New Horizons in Hermeneutics*. Grand Rapids: Zondervan, 1992.
Thomas, D. W. "A Consideration of Some Unusual Ways of Expressing the Superlative in Hebrew." *VT* 3 (1953) 209–24.
———. "The Language of the Old Testament." In *Record and Revelation: Essays on the Old Testament by Members of the Society for Old Testament Study*, edited by H. Wheeler Robinson, 374–402. Oxford: Clarendon, 1938.
Tillyard, E. M. W. *The Elizabethan World Picture*. New York: Vintage, 1959.
Tolkien, J. R. R. *The Fellowship of the Ring*. Boston: Houghton Mifflin, 1994.
———. "On Fairy-stories." In *The Tolkien Reader*, 3–84. New York: Ballantine, 1966.
———. *The Return of the King*. New York: Houghton Mifflin, 1994.
———. *The Silmarillion*. Edited by Christopher Tolkien. New York: Ballantine, 2001.
———. *The Two Towers*. Boston: Houghton Mifflin, 1987.
Torjesen, K. J. "'Body,' 'Soul,' and 'Spirit' in Origen's Theory of Exegesis." *ATR* 67 (1985) 17–30.
———. *Hermeneutical Procedure and Theological Method in Origen's Exegesis*. Berlin: de Gruyter, 1986.

Torrance, T. F. *Calvin's Doctrine of Man*. Grand Rapids: Eerdmans, 1957.
Torrey, C. C. "Some Important Editorial Operations in the Book of Isaiah." *JBL* 57.2 (1938) 109–39.
Trigg, J. W. *Origen*. New York: Routledge, 1998.
Tromp, N. J. *Primitive Conceptions of Death and the Netherworld in the Old Testament*. Rome: Pontifical Biblical Institute, 1969.
Tucker, G. M. *The Book of Isaiah 1–39*. NIB VI. Nashville: Abingdon, 1994.
Tuckett, C. "Isaiah in Q." In *Isaiah in the New Testament: The New Testament and the Scriptures of Israel*, edited by S. Moyise and M. J. J. Menken, 51–61. London: T. & T. Clark, 2005.
———. "Scripture and Q." In *From the Sayings to the Gospel*, 3–26. Tübingen: Mohr Siebeck, 2014.
Tull, P. K. *Isaiah 1–39*. SHBC. Macon, GA: Smyth & Helwys, 2010.
Van Buren, P. "On Reading Someone Else's Mail: The Church and Israel's Scriptures." In *Die Hebräische und ihre zweifache Nachgeschichte*, edited by Erhard Bum et al., 595–606. Neukirchen-Vluyn: Neukircher, 1990.
Vanderburgh, F. A. "The Ode on the King of Babylon, Isaiah XIV 4b–21." *AJSL* col. 29.2 (1913) 111–25.
Vanderhooft, D. S. *The Neo-Babylonian Empire and Babylon in the Latter Prophets*. Atlanta: Scholars, 1999.
Van der Toorn, K., and P. W. van der Horst. "Nimrod before and after the Bible." *HTR* 83 (1990) 1–29.
Van Leeuwen, R. C. "Form, Image." In *NIDOTTE*, edited by W. A. Van Gemeren, 4:643–48. Grand Rapids: Zondervan, 1997.
———. "Isa 14:12, *Hôlēš 'Al Gwym* and Gilgamesh XI, 6." *JBL* 99 (1980) 173–84.
Vermeylen, J. *Du Prophète Isaïe à l'Apocalyptique: Isaïe, I–XXXV, miroir d'un demi-millénaire d'expérience religieuse en Israël*. 2 vols. Paris: Gabalda, 1977.
Virgil. *Aeneid*. Translated by Allen Mandelbaum. Berkeley: University of California Press, 2007.
Virolleaud, C. "Les Rephaîm: Fragmentes de Poèmes de Ras-Sharma." *Syria* 22 (1941) 1–30.
Volf, M. *The End of Memory: Remembering Rightly in Violent World*. Grand Rapids: Eerdmans, 2006.
Walton, J. *Ancient Near Eastern Thought and the Old Testament*. Grand Rapids: Baker, 2006.
Watson, W. G. E. *Classical Hebrew Poetry: A Guide to Its Techniques*. Sheffield, UK: JSOT, 1986.
———. "Helel." In *DDD*, 747–48.
Watts, J. W. *Isaiah 1–33*. WORD. Waco, TX: Word, 1985.
Weisman, Z. *Political Satire in the Bible*. Atlanta: Scholars, 1998.
Welker, M. "Creation and the Image of God." *JES* 34.3 (1997) 436–48.
Westermann, C. *Genesis 1–11*. Minneapolis: Fortress, 1994.
Wiesel, E. *From the Kingdom of Memory: Reminiscences*. New York: Doubleday, 1995.
Wildberger, H. *Isaiah 13–27*. Minneapolis: Fortress, 1997.
Wilder, A. N. *Early Christian Rhetoric: The Language of the Gospel*. Cambridge: Harvard University Press, 1971.
Wilke, F. *Jesaja und Assur. Eine exegetisch-historische Untersuchung zur Politik des Propheten Jesaja*. Leipzig: Dieterich, 1905.

Williamson, H. G. M. *The Book Called Isaiah: Deutero-Isaiah's Role in Composition and Redaction*. Oxford: Oxford University Press, 1994.

———. "Review of *Isaiah: A Commentary*." *Theology Today* 59 (2002) 121–24.

Winkler, H. *Altorientalische Forschungen: Erste Reihe (I-VI. 1893-1897)*. Leipzig: Pfeiffer, 1897.

———. *Geschichte Israels in Einzeldarstellungen* II. Leipzig: Pfeiffer, 1900.

———. *Die Keilinschriften und das Alte Testament*. 3rd ed. Berlin: Reuther and Reichard, 1902.

Wright, J. E. *The Early History of Heaven*. Oxford: Oxford University Press, 2000.

Wright, N. T. *Jesus and the Victory of God*. London: SPCK, 1996.

Würthwein, E. *The Text of the Old Testament*. 2nd ed. (Translated from *Der Text des Alten Testaments*). Grand Rapids: Eerdmans, 1995.

Wyatt, N. "The Theogeny Motif in Ugarit and the Bible." In *Ugarit and the Bible: Proceedings of the International Symposium on Ugarit and the Bible. Manchester, September 1992*, edited by G. J. Brooke, A. H. W. Curtis, and J. F. Healey, 395–419. UBL 11. Münster: Ugarit-Verlag, 1994.

Xella, P. "Death and the Afterlife in Canaanite and Hebrew Thought." In *Civilizations of the Ancient Near East, Vol. 3*, edited by Jack M. Sasson, 2059–70. New York: Scribner, 1995.

Yamauchi, E. "Additional Notes on Tammuz." *JSS* 11 (1966) 10–15.

———. "Life, Death, and the Afterlife in the Ancient Near East." In *Life in the Face of Death: The Resurrection Message of the New Testament*, edited by Richard N. Longenecker, 21–50. Grand Rapids: Eerdmans, 1998.

———. "Tammuz and the Bible." *JBL* 81 (1965) 283–90.

Yee, G. A. "The Anatomy of Biblical Parody: The Dirge Form in 2 Samuel 1 and Isaiah 14." *CBQ* 50 (1988) 565–86.

Young, E. J. *The Book of Isaiah: Volume 1 Chapters 1-18*. NICOT. Grand Rapids: Eerdmans, 1965.

Young, F. M. *Biblical Exegesis and the Formation of Christian Culture*. Peabody, MA: Hendrickson, 2002.

Younger, K. L. "Recent Study on Sargon II, King of Assyria." In *Mesopotamia and the Bible*, edited by M. W. Chavalas and K. L. Younger, 288–329. Grand Rapids: Baker, 2002.

Zachman, R. C. "Gathering Meaning from the Context: Calvin's Exegetical Method." *JR* 82.1 (2002) 1–26.

Ziegler, J. *Untersuchungen zur Septuaginta des Buches Isaias*. Münster: Aschendorff, 1934.

Index

Abasement, 75, 241-45
Abraham, 170
Abusch, T., 82
Aeneid (Virgil), 71-72
Aeschylus, 101n27
Against Marcion (Tertullian), 133, 135
Ahaz, 113
Albani, M., 108
Albrektson, B., 16
Alexander the Great (Macedon), 120, 122
Allegory, 245-48, 245n249
Alter, R., 6, 46-48, 249
Amel-Mordach (Babylon), 117
Anderson, G., 209
Antigonus Monophthalmus (Macedonia), 57
Anu (Mesopotamian deity), 98
Aquila, 23-24, 33
Ashurbanipal (Assyria), 85, 87-88
Ashurnasirpal II (Assyria), 57n23, 86-87, 89
Ashur-uballit II (Assyria), 113n81, 122
Assyria. *See also specific ruler or deity*
   Babylon versus, 108-9
   Calvin on, 108-9
   Oracles Against the Nations and, 201-2, 217-20
Astabi (Hurrian deity), 104
Astour, M.C., 21
Athanasius of Alexandria, 240
Athirat (Canaanite deity), 102
Athtar (Canaanite deity), 102, 104-6
Auden, W.H., 246
Augustine, 130, 132, 148-51, 235
Aurivillius, C., 13
"Away from your grave" (v 19a), 31-32

Baal (Canaanite deity), 65, 102, 105-6
Baasha, 88
Babylon. *See also specific ruler or deity*
   Assyria versus, 108-9
   Calvin on, 108-9
   historical referent of "King of Babylon," 108-24 (*See also* "King of Babylon")
   intervention of God against, 53-57
   Oracles Against the Nations and, 127-29, 201-2, 217-20
   tyrannical nature of, 51-55
Bailey, L.R., 65n45
Balthasar, H.U. von, 132
Barr, J., 22, 65n45, 195-96
Barth, K., 197, 232-33
Barthélemy, D., 28
Barton, J., 4
Barzillai, 82
Begg, C.T., 127-28n155
Belshazzar (Babylon), 116n102
Berossus, 118
Bethsaida, condemnation of, 225-27
Biblical hermeneutics, 4
Blake, W., 231
Blenkinsopp, J., 23, 38, 117, 125n141
Bloch-Smith, E., 80n91
Book of Dead, 93
Booth, W.C., 46-47
Bouwsma, W.J., 152-53, 184
"Branch" (v 19b), 32-33
Brueggemann, Walter
   generally, 7-8, 55, 70, 77, 250-51
   overview, 187-89
   approach to Isaiah 14:3-23, 199-200
   context of, 189-98
   on "Day Star, Son of Dawn," 205

Brueggemann, Walter *(continued)*
    on downfall of tyrant in Isaiah
        14:3–23, 202–9
    evaluation of, 207–9
    hermeneutics of suspicion, 194–95
    historical-critical inquiry and, 189,
        207
    intentional advocacy, 193–95
    on Jesus, 189, 199, 208
    on Jewishness of God, 195–97, 208
    on Luke 10:18, 230
    on Oracles Against the Nations,
        201–2
    on parable, 202–6
    postmodernism and, 197–98
    on Sabbath, 203
    survey of treatment of Isaiah 14:3–
        23, 200
Budde, K., 13, 16n23, 25, 39–40, 43–45
Burden Against Babylon, 162–67

Callimachus, 102n30
Calvin, John
    generally, 7–8, 249–51
    overview, 152–54, 181–82
    on Babylon and Assyria, 108–9
    on Burden Against Babylon, 162–67
    on downfall of tyrant in Isaiah
        14:3–23, 170–71, 175–76
    on exaltation, 232, 235–36
    hermeneutical approach, 154–61,
        176–81
    on history, 157–59
    on Holy Spirit, 156–57
    on homilies, 160–61
    on human pride, 172–81
    on Jesus, 156
    on Luke 10:18, 231
    on Old Testament versus New
        Testament, 159–60
    Origen compared, 158–59, 166,
        170–73, 178–79, 182–86
    on Origen's interpretation, 131
    paradigmatic approach to parable,
        167–71
    on philological issues, 13, 33, 36–37
    on predetermination, 185–86
    reading of Isaiah 14:12–15, 171–76
    Renaissance humanism and, 152–54
    on Rule of Faith, 156
    on Sheol, 169–71
    theological presuppositions of,
        185–86
Capernaum, condemnation of, 225–29
Carmignac, J., 23
Cedars of Lebanon. *See* Junipers and
    cedars of Lebanon
Celsus, 137–38
Cephalus (Greek mythological
    character), 101
Chaucer, G., 130
Cheyne, T.K., 31, 126–27
Childs, B., 96, 103, 116, 128–29, 139,
    144, 155–60, 187–88, 188n2,
    212, 226–27, 230
Chorazin, condemnation of, 225–27
Christian Scripture, reading Isaiah
    14:3–23 as
    overview, 7–8, 187, 250
    Brueggemann (*See* Brueggemann,
        Walter)
    Seitz (*See* Seitz, Christopher R.)
Cicero, 101n27
"Cities" (v 21c), 36–37
The City of God (Augustine), 151
Clements, R.E., 90–91, 118
Cobb, W.H., 115–16
Code of Hammurabi, 54–55
The Confessions (Augustine), 151
Contra Celsum (Origen), 132–33, 137
Cook, P.M., 126–27, 126n147
Criagie, P.C., 104
Critical Theory, 191–94, 198
Crouzel, H., 185
Curkpatrick, S., 40
Cush, 14n12
"Cypress" (v 8), 19–20
Cyrus (Persia), 109, 118, 127–28n155

Daniélou, J., 132
Dante, 64, 70
David, 44, 57n22, 82, 159
Day, J., 28–29, 65n45, 99, 102, 107, 117
"Day Star, Son of Dawn" (v 12a)

generally, 74–75, 171
Brueggemann on, 205
mythology of, 97
philological issues regarding, 23–25
De genesi contra manichaeos
  (Augustine), 149
Delitzsch, F., 83, 91–92
Derrida, J., 41
Didymus the Blind, 132
Diggle, J., 101n27
Dillmann, A., 19
Diodorus Siculus, 101n27
Dirges, 43–46
Disney, 240
Döderlein, J.C., 18
Downfall of tyrant in Isaiah 14:3–23
  Brueggemann on, 202–9
  Calvin on, 170–71, 175–76
  fall of Satan equated with, 132–38, 143–47
  underworld journeys and, 78–79
Driver, S.R., 27–28
Duhm, B., 26, 31, 33, 36, 83n101, 109, 118, 125n142, 217n149

Eco, U., 40
Eichrodt, W., 76
Eissfeldt, O., 12, 43–45, 109n70
El (Canaanite deity), 29, 65, 103–7
Elah, 88
Elizabeth I (England), 177
Elyon (Jebusite deity), 107
Emmaus, Jesus on road to, 224–25
Enenkhet (Egyptian naval commander), 81
Enkidu (Mesopotamian mythological character), 62–63
Enlil (Mesopotamian deity), 98–99
Enuma Elish (Mesopotamian creation myth), 52
Eos (Greek deity), 101–3
Epaphus (Greek mythological character), 101
Ephraim, 92
The Epic of Gilgamesh, 61–63, 99
Ereshkigal (Mesopotamian deity), 67–68

Erlandsson, S., 5, 14, 18, 31, 33, 74, 109, 110–11, 168
Esarhaddon (Assyria), 57
Eshmnunazor (Assyria), 85
Etana (Kish), 92
Euripides, 101n27
Eusebius, 89, 118
Evans, C.F., 230
"Evildoers" (v 20–21a), 34–36
Exaltation
  Calvin on, 232, 235–36
  Imago Dei, 233–40
  Jesus versus "King of Babylon," 237–40
  likeness of God and, 231–37
  self-exaltation of tyrant, 74–77, 231–32
  in Tolkien, 241–48
Exhumation, 82–86
Exile, 88–90

Fall of Satan
  downfall of tyrant in Isaiah 14:3–23 equated with, 132–38, 143–47
  Jesus and, 144
  in Luke 10:18, 230–31
  Origen on, 132–38, 143–47
Families, slaughter of, 86–88
"Their fathers" (v 20–21a), 34–36
The Fellowship of the Ring (Tolkein), 245n249
Fifth Ecumenical Council, 148
Fitzmyer, J.A., 5–6
Forsyth, N., 133
Fowl, S.E., 3
Fowler, A., 41
Frankfurt School, 191–92, 198
Free will, 142–43, 185
Freud and Philosophy (Ricoeur), 192–93

Gallagher, W.R., 98–99
Gaster, T.H., 105
Gathercole, S.J., 230
Genesis Homily XIII (Origen), 140
George, T., 153
Gesenius, W., 33, 36

274   INDEX

Geuss, R., 192
Gibbon, E., 77
Gibson, J.C.L., 105
Gideon, 56
Gilgamesh (mythological
　　Mesopotamian character), 26,
　　61–63, 99–100
Ginsberg, H.L., 27, 114
Gnosticism, 132n12
God (YHWH)
　　abasement and, 75
　　anger against tyrant in Isaiah 14:3–
　　　23, 33, 63, 78, 91–94
　　Brueggemann on, 199–203, 206–8
　　intervention by, 53–57, 229
　　non-burial and, 83
　　Oracles Against the Nations and,
　　　128
　　Qina meter and, 17
　　Seitz on, 216, 218–23
　　"trembling" and, 68
Goldingay, J., 118–19, 119n117, 230
Good, E.M., 46
Gosse, B., 5, 127–28n155
Gottwald, N.K., 192
Gowan, D.E., 106
Grassi, J.A., 92
Gray, G.B., 18, 31, 34, 36–37, 92n130
Greene-McCreight, K.E., 156
Greer, R.A., 131–32n7
Gregory the Great, 130–31
Grelot, P., 24, 101, 101n24
Gunkel, H., 26
Guthe, H., 16

Habakkuk, 222–23
Hades, 70–73
Hagar, 182
Hall, D.J., 234–37, 234n209
Hamblin, W.J., 81
Hansmann, J., 63
Hanson, R.P.C., 132
Harris, R.L., 80n89
Hayes, J.H., 113–14
Hays, C.B., 15n14, 36, 58n25, 103, 114
Hays, R.B., 3
Hebrew Syntax (Williams), 30

"Hedgehog" (v 23), 37–38, 94
Heidel, A., 65n45
Heidl, G., 148–49
Heine, R.E., 141–42
Heiser, M.S., 105–6
Helel (Lucifer), 104, 106, 108
Helios (Greek deity), 101, 103
Heracleon, 142
Heraclitus, 137
Herbert, G., 238
Hermeneutics
　　Biblical hermeneutics, 4
　　Brueggemann and, 194–95
　　Calvin and, 154–61, 176–81
　　hermeneutical difficulties in Isaiah
　　　14:3–23, 57–70
　　Origen and, 138–41
　　of suspicion, 194–95
Herod Agrippa, 176
Hesiod, 101–2
Hesperus (Greek mythological
　　character), 102n30
Hezekiah, 111
Hilalu (Ugaritic deity), 103
Hill, J.V., 231
Hippolytus, 136
Hiram (Tyre), 57n22
Historical-critical inquiry
　　generally, 2, 5–6, 250
　　Brueggemann and, 189
　　mythology of Isaiah 14:3–23 and, 96
　　Oracles Against the Nations and,
　　　125
　　Seitz and, 210–12
Hitzig, F., 29, 33
Holladay, W.L., 85n112
Holy Spirit, 156–57
Homer, 70, 73, 137
Homilies, 160–61
Homily XXVII on Numbers (Origen),
　　147
"How" (v 12b), 25
Human pride, 57–59, 172–81
Humbaba (Mesopotamian mythological
　　character), 62–63
Hummel, H.D., 27–28
Hurtado, L., 75

Illil (Mesopotamian deity), 98–99
Imaginative world of Isaiah 14:3–23, 50–95
  overview, 6, 50, 249
  hermeneutical difficulties, 57–70
  junipers and cedars of Lebanon, 57–70 (*See also* Junipers and cedars of Lebanon)
  proper burial, 80–95 (*See also* Proper burial)
  textual reading, 50–57
  underworld journeys, 70–79 (*See also* Underworld journeys)
Imago Dei, 233–40
Inferno (Dante), 70
"Insolence" (v 4b), 13–16
Institutes (Calvin), 154, 156, 162–67, 169, 183–84
Intentional advocacy, 193–95
Introduction to the Old Testament (Brueggemann), 190
Irenaeus, 233
Irony, 46–48
Irvine, S.A., 113–14
Ishtar (Mesopotamian deity), 63, 66–67

Jacob, 92
Jacobus Arminius, 161
Jahnow, H., 39–40
Jehoiakim, 85–86
Jehoshaphat, 56
Jeremiah, 83, 85
Jeroboam, 88
Jerome, 23–24, 130
Jesus
  Bethsaida, condemnation of, 225–27
  Brueggemann on, 189, 199, 208
  Calvin on, 156
  Capernaum, condemnation of, 225–29
  Chorazin, condemnation of, 225–27
  Emmaus, on road to, 224–25
  fall of Satan and, 144
  "King of Babylon" versus, 237–40
  likeness of God in, 231–37
  Origen on, 137, 144, 147
  parables of, 50

  Seitz on, 211, 213–15
Jewishness of God, 195–97, 208
Job, 138
Johnston, P.S., 82–83
John the Baptist, 239
Jonathan, 44
Jong, M.J. de, 85n112
Josephus, 118
Joshua, 30, 55–56, 83
Journal of Theological Interpretation, 4
Junipers and cedars of Lebanon, 57–70
  as metaphor for human pride, 57–59
  mythological context of, 59–64
  Sheol and, 64–70

Kaiser, O., 34, 69, 108, 121, 124, 126–27
Kalland, E.S., 20
Kaminsky, J.S., 195–97
Keel, O., 34, 93
Keil, C.F., 83, 91–92
Keown, G.L., 5
Kilpatrick, G.G.D., 76
Kimhi, D., 13
"King of Babylon"
  Alexander the Great as "King of Babylon," 120
  ancient cognates, 98–108
  Canaanite cognates, 107
  Greek cognates, 100–103
  historical referent of, 108–24
  Jesus versus, 237–40
  Marodach-baladan as "King of Babylon," 111
  Mesopotamian cognates, 98–100
  Nabonidus as "King of Babylon," 118
  Nebuchadnezzar as "King of Babylon," 117
  Sargon II as "King of Babylon," 114–15
  Sennacherib as "King of Babylon," 115–16
  Tiglath-pileser III as "King of Babylon," 110–11, 113–14
  Tolkein and, 243–45
  Ugaritic cognates, 103–6
Kissane, E.J., 84, 121

Klein, R.W., 15
Koenig, N.A., 24
König, E., 24

Laments, 43–46
Landes, G.E., 42
Langdon, S.H., 100n19
Lebanon, junipers and cedars of. See Junipers and cedars of Lebanon
Leith, J.H., 155
Levenson, J., 65n45, 197–98, 250–51
Levering, M., 3
Lewis, C.S., 245
Lindenlauf, A., 82
Lohmann, P., 39–40
Longinus, 101n27
The Lord of the Rings (Tolkien), 209, 241
Lubac, H. de, 139–41
Lucretius, 101n27
Lustful Watchers theory, 133, 137–38
Luther, M., 13–14, 182, 190–91, 235

Machinist, P., 112
Macholz, C., 75
Manasseh, 92
Manichaean dualism, 149–51
Mann, W.E., 149
Marcion, 135–36
Marduk (Babylonian deity), 52–53, 98, 100n19, 110
Margulis, B., 97
Markos, L., 1–2, 71, 73n70
Marodach-baladan (Babylon), 109, 111
Martens, P.W., 132
Marti, K., 35–36, 126
Martin, R.P., 232
Marxism, 191
McGrath, A.E., 3, 152
McKane, W., 12, 42
McKay, J.W., 24–25, 101–2, 101n24
Meier, S.A., 91n127
Melchizedek, 107
Metamorphoses (Ovid), 101n27
Michaelis, J.D., 14–15
Midian, 221
Milton, J., 1–2, 70, 231

Mizrahi, N., 14, 14n12, 16
Moberly, R.W.L., 4, 86, 188n2, 194, 224–25, 251
"Monk's Tale" (Chaucer), 130
Moor, J.C. de, 105
Moran, W.L., 27
Morgoth (Tolkein character), 8, 209, 241–44, 247–48, 250
Moses, 51, 53, 138
Mot (Ugaritic deity), 65–66
Motyer, J.A., 230
Muecke, D.C., 48
Muller, R.A., 154
Murray, R., 246
Myth of Etana, 92
Mythology of Isaiah 14:3–23
    overview, 6–7, 96, 249
    ancient cognates, 98–108
    Canaanite cognates, 107
    "Day Star, Son of Dawn" and, 97
    Greek cognates, 100–103
    historical-critical inquiry and, 96
    historical referent of "King of Babylon," 108–24 (See also "King of Babylon")
    Mesopotamian cognates, 98–100
    Oracles Against the Nations, 125–29 (See also Oracles Against the Nations)
    Ugaritic cognates, 103–6

Nabonidus (Babylon), 58n25, 116–18, 122
Nabopolassar (Babylon), 53
Nadab, 88
Namtar (Mesopotamian deity), 67
Nebuchadnezzar (Babylon), 57n23, 89, 89n123, 116–18, 135, 172–73, 176–78, 206
Negral-Irra (Babylonian deity), 100n19
Newsom, C.A., 41
Niehoff, M.R., 131–32n7
Nielsen, K., 58–59, 58n25
Nietzsche, F., 239
Nimrod, 14n12
Ninurta (Mesopotamian king), 14n12
Nolland, J., 230–31

Non-burial, 82–86
Nouwen, H., 238n221

O'Brien, J.M., 188–89
O'Connell, R., 99–100
O'Connor, F., 49
Odyssey (Homer), 70–73
Oldenburg, U., 104–6
Old Testament Theology (Brueggemann), 195–96
Olyan, S.M., 32, 84–85
Olympus (Mount), 179
On First Principles (Origen), 138, 141–48
On the Morals of the Manichaeans (Augustine), 149
Oracles Against the Nations, 125–29
　generally, 108, 110–11, 119
　Assyria and, 201–2, 217–20
　Babylon and, 127–29, 201–2, 217–20
　Brueggemann on, 201–2
　historical-critical inquiry and, 125
　Persia and, 220
　Seitz on, 217–20
Origen, 131–52
　generally, 5, 7–8, 249–51
　overview, 130–32, 151–52
　Calvin compared, 158–59, 166, 170–73, 178–79, 182–86
　context of, 132–38
　on creation, 141–42
　exegesis of, 147–48
　on fall of Satan, 132–38, 143–47
　on free will, 142–43, 185
　hermeneutical approach, 138–41
　on Jesus, 137, 147
　on Luke 10:18, 230
　reading of Isaiah 14:12–15, 141–48
　theological presuppositions of, 185–86
　Western Church and, 148–51
Orlinsky, H.M., 15
Oswalt, J.N., 37, 93–94, 124, 230
Ovid, 101, 101n27

Page, H.R., Jr., 105–6
Papsukkal (Mesopotamian deity), 67
Parable (משׁל)
　overview, 6, 39–40, 48–49, 249
　Brueggemann on, 202–6
　Calvin, paradigmatic approach of, 167–71
　as dirge, 43–46
　function of in Isaiah 14:3–23, 43–48
　as irony, 46–48
　as lament, 43–46
　literary genre of, 40–42
　as satire, 46–48
　Seitz on, 220–22
　as "taunt," 12–13
Paradise Lost (Milton), 1, 70
Parker, T.H.L., 157, 170
Parpola, S., 89–90
Paul, 182, 240
Pepi II (Egypt), 81
Pepi-nekht (Egyptian official), 81
"Persecute" (v 6b), 18–19
Persia, 109, 118, 220
Peshitta, 13, 15, 18, 23–24, 30, 32–34
Phaeton (Greek mythological character), 100–104, 102n30
Pherecydes, 137
Philological issues, 12–38
　overview, 5–6
　"away from your grave" (v 19a), 31–32
　"branch" (v 19b), 32–33
　Calvin on, 13, 33, 36–37
　"cities" (v 21c), 36–37
　"cypress" (v 8), 19–20
　"Day Star, Son of Dawn" (v 12a), 23–25
　"evildoers" (v 20–21a), 34–36
　"their fathers" (v 20–21a), 34–36
　"hedgehog" (v 23), 37–38
　"how" (v 12b), 25
　"insolence" (v 4b), 13–16
　"persecute" (v 6b), 18–19
　"pomp" (v 11a), 22
　prose versus poetry (v 22–23), 37
　Qina meter (v 5a), 16–17
　"raises" (v 9a), 20–21
　"rouses" (v 9a), 20–21

Philological issues *(continued)*
    "rule" (v 6a), 18
    "shades" (v 9b), 21–22
    "shoot" (v 19b), 32–33
    "slaughter" (v 21b), 36
    "the sounds of your harps" (v 11b), 22–23
    "the stars of God" (v 13), 29
    "strike" (v 6a), 18
    "taunt" (v 4a), 12–13
    tension in gender (v 17a), 29
    "tomb" (v 18), 31
    "who go down to the stones of the pit" (v 19d), 33–34
    "the whole earth" (v 7), 19
    "would not let his prisoners go home" (v 17b), 29–31
    "you who laid the nations low" (v 12c), 25–29
Plato, 101n27
Plutarch, 101n27
Poirier, J.C., 102n30
Polk, T., 6, 12, 42, 249
"Pomp" (v 11a), 22
Postmodernism, 197–98
Post-mortem memory, 92–95
Predetermination, 185–86
A Preface to Paradise Lost (Lewis), 245
Prinsloo, W.S., 102n30
Proper burial, 80–95
    in Egypt, 81
    exhumation versus, 82–86
    exile and, 88–90
    families, slaughter of, 86–88
    in Greece, 82
    in Mesopotamia, 81–82
    non-burial versus, 82–86
    post-mortem memory and, 92–95
Prophecy and Hermeneutics (Seitz), 209
Puckett, D.L., 157

Qina meter (v 5a), 16–17
Qumran scrolls, 14–15, 18, 23, 26, 28, 31–32

"Raises" (v 9a), 20–21
Reception of Isaiah 14:3–23
    overview, 7, 130–31, 186, 249–50

Calvin (*See* Calvin, John)
    Origen (*See* Origen)
Renaissance humanism, 152–54
Rendtorff, R., 2, 187, 216
Retso, J., 89n123
The Return of the King (Tolkein), 246
Ricoeur, P., 6, 139, 191–95, 198, 210
Rinaldi, G., 36
Roland, A., 248
Rosenmüller, E.F.K., 13
"Rouses" (v 9a), 20–21
"Rule" (v 6a), 18
Rule of Faith, 156, 213

Sabbath, 203
Sarah, 182
Sargon II (Assyria), 98, 110, 112, 114–15, 115n98, 122
Satire, 46–48
Saul, 44
Sauron (Tolkein character), 8, 209, 241, 243–45, 247–48, 250
Sawyer, J.F.A., 116n102
Schipper, J., 40–41, 43
Schleiermacher, F., 189
Schmidt, B.S., 92–93
Schwally, F., 21
Seitz, Christopher R.
    generally, 7–8, 54, 108–9, 250–51
    overview, 187–88, 209–10
    approach to Isaiah 14:3–23, 215–17
    canonical approach of, 215–17
    context of, 210–15
    evaluation of, 222–24
    historical-critical inquiry and, 210–12
    on Jesus, 211, 213–15
    on Luke 10:18, 230
    on Old Testament versus New Testament, 212–15
    on Oracles Against the Nations, 217–20
    on parable, 220–22
    on Rule of Faith, 213
Seneca, 101n27
Sennacherib (Assyria), 61, 87, 94, 110–11, 115–16, 122, 180
"Shades" (v 9b), 21–22
Shahar (Ugaritic deity), 103–4, 107–8

Shalim (Ugaritic deity), 103–4, 107
Shalmaneser III (Assyria), 89
Shamash (Mesopotamian deity), 62
Sheol
　Calvin on, 169–71
　junipers and cedars of Lebanon and, 64–70
　philological issues regarding, 19–23, 32, 34
　poetic use of, 80n89
Shipp, M.R., 5, 20, 23, 39, 39n6, 63, 83n103, 99–100
Shippey, T., 241, 245–47
"Shoot" (v 19b), 32–33
Sidon, 226–27, 226n182
Si'gabbar (Assyria), 85
The Silmarillion (Tolkein), 209
Simplicianus, 149
Sin-Shar-ishkun (Assyria), 113n81
"Slaughter" (v 21b), 36
Smith, G.A., 94–95, 111
Smith, M.S., 105
Snaith, N., 234
Solomon, 57n22
"The sounds of your harps" (v 11b), 22–23
Spronk, K., 29, 108
Staerk, W., 16
"The stars of God" (v 13), 29
Star Wars (film), 205, 208–9
Steinmetz, D., 155, 158–59, 177, 190–91
Stoics, 185
Stolz, F., 59–61, 64
Strabo, 101n27
"Strike" (v 6a), 18
The Struggle to Understand Isaiah as Christian Scripture (Childs), 230
Suter, D., 42
Sweeney, M.A., 69, 114–15, 117, 125n142
Symmachus, 32, 34

Tammuz (Mesopotamian deity), 66–67
Targum, 5, 13, 15, 18, 30, 32, 36, 88
"Taunt" (v 4a), 12–13
Tertullian, 133–37, 173, 184
Testimony to Otherwise (Brueggemann), 190

Text of Isaiah 14:3–23, 9–12. *See also* Philological issues
Theodotion, 33
Theological exegesis, 3
Theological interpretation, 2–6, 210, 251
Thomas, D. Winton, 17–18n28, 19
Tiamat (Babylonian deity), 52
Tiglath-pileser III (Assyria), 87, 89, 110–11, 113–14
Tolkein, J.R.R., 240–48
　generally, 8, 209, 250–51
　overview, 240–41
　abasement in, 241–45
　on allegory, 245–48, 245n249
　exaltation in, 241–48
　"King of Babylon" and, 243–45
"Tomb" (v 18), 31
Torjesen, K.J., 139, 141
Torrance, T.F., 236
Torrey, C., 120
Translation of Isaiah 14:3–23. *See* Philological issues
The Tribes of Yahweh (Gottwald), 192
Tromp, N.J., 65–66
Tuckett, C., 227–28
Tull, P.K., 59, 78
Tyre, 133–35, 226–27, 226n182

Underworld journeys, 70–79
　in *Aeneid*, 71–72
　downfall of tyrant in Isaiah 14:3–23 and, 78–79
　in Hades, 70–73
　in *Odyssey*, 70–73
　onlookers and, 77–78
　self-exaltation of tyrant and, 74–77
Utu (Mesopotamian deity), 62

Valentinian determinism, 142
Vanderburgh, F.A., 17
Vanderhooft, D.S., 123
van der Horst, P.W., 14n12
van der Toorn, K., 14n12
Van Leeuwen, R.C., 25–28
Venus, 104–5
Vermeylen, J., 121n127
Virgil, 71–73
Virolleaud, C., 21

A Vision of the Nether World (Assyrian text), 59
Vitringa, C., 13
Vulgate, 13, 18, 23, 30, 32–33, 34

Watts, J.W., 23
Weisman, Z., 45–46
Wellhausen paradigm, 2
Westermann, C., 233–34
"Who go down to the stones of the pit" (v 19d), 33–34
"The whole earth" (v 7), 19
Wildberger, H., 12n5, 17–18, 23, 29–36, 60–61, 64, 78, 83–84, 88–89, 91, 94, 103, 117, 122–24, 125
Williams, R.J., 30–31
Williamson, H.G.M., 125, 127–28, 127–28n155, 188n2

Winkler, H., 114–15, 115n96, 115n98
Wittgenstein, L., 42
"Would not let his prisoners go home" (v 17b), 29–31

Yamauchi, E., 64
Yee, G.A., 6, 44–45, 48, 75
YHWH. *See* God (YHWH)
Young, F.M., 144–45
"You who laid the nations low" (v 12c), 25–29

Zaphon (Mount), 61, 74–76, 98, 104, 179
Zeus (Greek deity), 101
Ziegler, J., 31
Zimri, 88
Zion (Mount), 173–75, 179–80

www.ingramcontent.com/pod-product-compliance
Lightning Source LLC
Chambersburg PA
CBHW071238230426
43668CB00011B/1487